The French Colonial Myth and Constitution-Making in the Fourth Republic

THE FRENCH COLONIAL MYTH AND CONSTITUTION-MAKING IN THE FOURTH REPUBLIC

by D. Bruce Marshall

NEW HAVEN AND LONDON, YALE UNIVERSITY PRESS, 1973

Library of Congress catalog card number: 71-99833
International standard book number: 0-300-01212-8

Designed by Sally Sullivan
and set in Linotype Baskerville type.
Printed in the United States of America by
Vail-Ballou Press, Inc., Binghamton, N.Y.

Published in Great Britain, Europe, and Africa by
Yale University Press, Ltd., London.
Distributed in Canada by McGill-Queen's University
Press, Montreal; in Latin America by Kaiman & Polon,
Inc., New York City; in Australasia and Southeast
Asia by John Wiley & Sons Australasia Pty. Ltd.,
Sydney; in India by UBS Publishers' Distributors Pvt.,
Ltd., Delhi; in Japan by John Weatherhill, Inc., Tokyo.

For my mother and the memory of my father

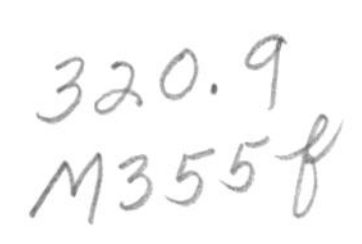

Il n'est pas de présent historique sans
souvenirs et sans pressentiments. L'univers politique,
au milieu du XXe siècle, ne peut être saisi dans
l'instant: chacun y retrouve la marque des événements
que nous avons vécus, de l'avenir qui murit.
Conscience historique, la conscience du présent,
varie avec les continents, les pays, les partis.

Raymond Aron
Dimensions de la conscience historique

CONTENTS

Preface xi
Introduction 1

1 THE LOGIC OF EXPANSION 11
Revolutionary Beginnings 18
Liberal Republicanism 22
The Radical Republicans 29

2 THE REPUBLICAN CONSENSUS 42
The Policy of *Mise en Valeur* 44
The Socialist Opposition 49
The Communist Viewpoint 53
The Resurgence of Nationalism 61
Conflicting Attitudes toward the Colonies 67

3 THE GAULLIST COLONIAL OUTLOOK 75
The Vichy Regime 76
De Gaulle and the Free French 80

4 GAULLISM AND COLONIALISM: DOCTRINE AND PRACTICE 101
The Brazzaville Conference 102
Free France in North Africa 115
Free France in West and Central Africa 125
Free France in the Middle East 128
Free France in Indochina 133
The Paradox of Colonial Reform 138

5 THE POSTWAR POLITICAL MILIEU 144
The New Colonial Elite 152

6 THE INTERNATIONAL CONTEXT 180
France and the United Nations Trusteeship System 181
Reoccupation of Indochina 189

7 TWO PERSPECTIVES ON UNITY 208
The Native Perspective 215
The Metropolitan Perspective 234
The Colonial Myth and Party Rivalries 269

8 THE FORMULA FOR UNITY 273
Revising the Constitutional Draft 273
The Government versus the Constitutional Committee 276
The Price of Unanimity 280
The Native Deputies' Reaction 288
The Formal Institutions 295

9 DECLINE OF THE COLONIAL MYTH 302
The Native Deputies' Resentment 307
The Failure of Unity 312

Notes 317
Bibliography 338
Index 357

PREFACE

French politics hold a special fascination for students of contemporary international relations partly because French leaders often act in unexpected ways. Sometimes their preference for nonconformity has been intentional and has enabled a strong leader like General de Gaulle or Pierre Mendès-France to achieve tactical advantages for the nation. During most of the Fourth Republic, however, French policies appeared more frequently to reflect a concatenation of internal and international factors that induced erratic actions and impotent frustration.

This pattern was particularly evident in French colonial policy, which failed to deal appropriately with the rising force of colonial nationalism that led to a series of colonial wars and finally wrecked the Fourth Republic. A number of questions suggest themselves regarding that policy. Why did the French find the end of empire so difficult to contemplate? Why did they cling so desperately to every overseas position at the end of World War II when France was beset by crushing problems of political, social, and economic reconstruction? Why were her leaders unable to seize the opportunity offered by the relatively fluid state of international relations after the war and the deep, genuine sympathy shared by most colonial and metropolitan groups to begin the transition to a decolonization that many already recognized was inevitable? Most puzzling of all, why were so many Frenchmen willing to sacrifice in order to preserve an imperial political system that was more a memory from the past than a possibility for the future?

These are some of the questions that first led me to undertake this study, an earlier version of which was my dissertation for the Yale Graduate School in 1968. I was attracted to them because they enabled me to unite my long-standing interest in French politics and the affairs of French Africa with my primary concern for the study of national elites and their responses to changing patterns of international power and influence. If I have succeeded in providing at least a partial answer to some of them, the credit must be shared with a number of former teachers and colleagues who generously gave of their time and wisdom. At Yale Harry R. Rudin encouraged my early interest in Africa, and Walter R. Sharp shared with me his knowledge of France; René Rémond, René Henry-Gréard, and the late Inspector-General Georges Gayet kindly assisted my studies in France and in Africa. My colleagues David Kettler, Alvin Rabushka, Stanley Rothman, and Donald E. Weatherbee made valuable comments and suggestions at critical stages in the writing of this book.

My early research in France and French Africa was begun in 1954–55 with the aid of a Fulbright Grant, a Junior Sterling Fellowship from Yale, and a travel grant from the French government. The final revision and preparation of the manuscript was made possible by a grant from the Institute of International Studies at the University of South Carolina and a National Fellowship from the Hoover Institution on War, Revolution and Peace that allowed me to spend a year at the Hoover Institution.

I am happy to recognize the assistance of Peter Duignan, Agnes Peterson, and the staff of the Hoover Library as well as those of the following libraries: Bibliothèque de l'Ecole Nationale de la France d'Outre-mer, Bibliothèque de l'Institut d'Etudes Politiques, Bibliothèque Nationale, Ohio State University Library, and Yale University Library. Thanks also to Judy Yogman, a patient and perceptive editor, and Cloris DeGroot who typed the entire manuscript.

It is my particular pleasure to acknowledge two special obligations. The late Arnold Wolfers, Sterling Professor of International Relations in Yale University, was a source of inspiration and encouragement over many years. It was a privilege to have been his student and an honor to know him as a friend. Above all I thank my wife, Susan, who has shared the occasional joys and frequent frustrations that have marked this work during its long gestation.

INTRODUCTION

Albert Sarraut, the doyen of French colonial officials, once characterized the French Union as "a magnificent tunic of Nessus, which could not be pulled from the shoulders without tearing away the flesh itself. That is France's servitude, but it is also her grandeur." [1] When he wrote those words in 1953 Sarraut intended them to mean that France could not adopt a policy of decolonization without destroying its national unity. He seems, however, to have overlooked the real lesson of the myth of Nessus the centaur. As Sophocles recounts the tale, it was Deianira, the second wife of Heracles, who gave the tunic of Nessus to her husband in hope of holding his love during his many journeys. Heracles had killed Nessus years earlier when he came upon the beast raping Deianira, but the dying Nessus, feigning repentance, promised Deianira that if she would but give her husband a tunic smeared with the centaur's blood, then Heracles would remain faithful to her for the rest of his life. Once donned by the hero, however, the bloody tunic became, instead of the love potion Deianira believed it to be, a deadly poison that drove Heracles to destruction.

This ancient tale of rape, duplicity, and revenge is a revealing allegory of the French approach to decolonization. The constitution of the French Union that was drafted by the Constituent Assemblies in 1945–46, was perceived by most Frenchmen as gift to the native elite, given in the expectation that it would bind the colonial peoples securely to France. The metaphor can easily be overworked, but it is not too fanciful to imagine that the metropolitan leaders, like Deianira, sought only to preserve what they considered their own against the attractions of more seductive rivals. Like the ancient goddess, those modern Frenchmen were also the victims of a mistaken belief and the casualties of their desires. Intent on preserving French grandeur, they failed to recognize the hatred generated by colonial rule and were finally defeated by the mythical beast of nationalism bent on revenge. Moreover, as subsequent events revealed, the colonial settlement of 1946, which they devised, contributed importantly to the death of the Fourth Republic.

The tragic mode of that allegory was also peculiarly appropriate to France, since decolonization was widely perceived in 1946 and for many years thereafter as the ultimate national indignity. Someone once said that the greatest tragedy for a nation is not to be small, but to become so, and the observation applies with special force to France, a nation whose past greatness made the transition to more modest national fortunes extremely painful. Nowhere was that discomfort more evident than in the attempt to come to grips with the rising force of native nationalism after World War II. This book examines that effort in order to explain how accumulated political doctrines, institutions, and experiences can affect the choices that leaders make in a state whose great age gives such factors special importance. It pays particular attention to what has been termed the "colonial myth"—the vision, held by virtually all of the French elite, of an indissoluble link between France and the colonies. That vision dominated the French approach to decolonization in the postwar period, preventing French leaders from realistically assessing the dimensions of native nationalism and predisposing them to respond to nationalist demands in ways that made it impossible to avoid the tragic colonial wars that later destroyed the French Republic.

Focus: The Constituent Assemblies of 1945–46

This is not, however, a history of French decolonization.[2] Rather, it focuses on one relatively brief period of time immediately following World War II, when a number of decisions were reached that were crucial for the future of French relations with the colonial territories. The choice of that historical focus was dictated by the coincidence of a number of conditions, the collective effect of which was to give French decision makers an unprecedented degree of flexibility and an unusually broad range of policy options for the future conduct of relations with the colonies.

French domestic politics during the period of the Provisional Government were in deep turmoil. The Vichy regime had collapsed in disgrace, leaving a temporary void on the right wing of the political party spectrum. The post-Liberation purges had brought new men into leadership positions and displaced many of the old, established guardians of the state and military bureaucracies. The economy was on the verge of collapse. The renewed violence of the occupation and the Liberation had created deep divisions within French society, replacing those maintained by prewar issues, such as clericalism. The most pressing demand was for new political leaders to decide on the host of urgent public concerns.

The constitutional period was also a time of profound changes in France's international relationships. By the end of World War II the locus of power in the international system had shifted decisively away from Europe toward the two superpowers, the United States and the Soviet Union. At the same time a host of smaller states were asserting claims to the attention of the large powers, particularly through the formation of the United Nations Organization. All these changes tended to reflect adversely on French prestige and power. For more than four hundred years France had asserted a leading role in world politics and had often dominated the affairs of her smaller neighbors. Suddenly, in 1945, she found herself reduced to the rank of a modest continental power in a world system dominated by two giant peripheral states. These transformations required a fundamental reassessment of French international ties with former allies as well as enemies and opened up new diplomatic alternatives, though on a sharply reduced scale of grandeur.

The close of World War II also witnessed a powerful upsurge of colonial nationalism in every region of the globe. Indians and Burmese demanded independence from Britain; Indonesian nationalists refused to permit a restoration of Dutch colonial rule; the Philippines became independent of the United States; and even in the most remote areas of Africa, demands for increased autonomy were advanced by the leaders of new nationalist movements. In varying degrees the European colonial powers all resisted the demands for independence, but most ultimately came to terms with the colonial nationalists either through negotiation, as in the case of Britain in India and Burma,[3] or by force, as in the case of the Dutch in Indonesia.[4] France was directly affected by this movement. When Syria and Lebanon denounced the French mandate and declared their independence in 1945, the Provisional Government was obliged to yield. Similarly, the end of the war in Indochina found the French colonial garrisons interned in Japanese prison camps and a Vietnamese nationalist regime in control of the colony. Elsewhere, French authorities confronted insistent demands for greater autonomy by colonial nationalists.

Consequently, by the end of World War II France had reached a major turning point in its domestic political life and in its relationship with the rest of the world, particularly with the colonial peoples. The most imperative need was for effective political leadership. The Constituent Assemblies were responsible for drafting new political institutions to supply such leadership. Part of that effort involved a reconsideration of French colonial relationships, which resulted in the constitution of the French Union. By examining the deliberations of the Constituent Assemblies and the factors that shaped their decisions, it becomes possible to understand the colonial myth and its role in determining the initial outcome of the French encounter with decolonization.

Major Determinants of the French Approach

The French Union was the end product of a complex process of political bargaining. The goals it embodied, the institutions it created, and the policies it established all reflected the interplay of several factors, the most important of which was the colonial myth. The term *colonial myth* is used here in an analytical sense to mean the symbolic language that those politically active groups and individuals who were concerned about colonial issues employed in analyzing colonial problems and rationalizing their policy preferences to a larger public. Hence, the reader should not interpret this term as imputing a false or irrational character to the ideas in question.[5]

The principal characteristic of the colonial myth was that it provided a common universe of discourse to virtually all segments of the political elite, both metropolitan and colonial, who thought of themselves as sharing many goals and expectations. One of its most important effects was to diminish conflict between colonial and metropolitan leaders by focusing their attention on abstract philosophical principles and the formal institutions that could be devised to promote them, rather than on concrete and often conflicting interests. When such conflicts did emerge, the colonial myth also allowed both metropolitan and overseas leaders to justify policies and institutions that promised tangible rewards for themselves and their constituents.

Chapters 1 and 2 trace the development of the colonial myth, which was produced by a fusion of ideas drawn from the traditional doctrines of French republicanism and from various theories of colonialism. An interpretation of republicanism is offered here, based on a reading of French writers, that embodies a complex of political symbols whose meaning has evolved over more than a century of political struggle. Its roots lie in the Revolution of 1789, which transformed the basis of French political authority, destroying the traditional belief in monarchy and imposing a system of government based on popular sovereignty. However, the Revolution produced no agreement on political institutions or procedures. Frenchmen remained deeply divided in their goals and preferences as French political structures were changed to handle the problems of increasing industrialization and modernization that marked the last half of the nineteenth century. The French constitutional consensus was further shaken by the general crisis of European politics that resulted in the two great wars of the twentieth century. Even today the content of the republican myth remains a matter of dispute among many Frenchmen.

The basic themes of the republican myth, as it was formulated under the Third and Fourth republics, are easily identified. The myth depicted France as a nation whose government was based on the principles of justice and reason that the Enlightenment philosophers had associated with human nature. Accordingly, the French republic was viewed as an abstraction representing all French citizens who were bound together into one indivisible state by a formal bond of popular sovereignty. Government was entrusted to a group of elected deputies whose responsibilities included formulating the law and directing an impersonal bureaucracy to enforce it impartially. The general will of the people provided the ultimate sanction behind the acts of Parliament, but since those entrusted could misconstrue or misapply the law, appeals to force through revolutionary action remained possible, indeed at times even obligatory. Thus, the underlying principles of French republicanism—liberty, equality, fraternity—were broad enough to permit divergent interpretations and could be used to justify almost contradictory institutions and policies.

For most of the nineteenth century, republicans opposed the acquisition of colonies because colonial expansion was seen to benefit their domestic enemies—the aristocracy, the military, and the Church hierarchy—or because such acquisitions contradicted their economic doctrines of laissez-faire. As the republicans gained experience in governing France, they discovered that colonial expansion brought increased prestige in relation to the other colonial powers. Expansion also showed the efficacy of republican institutions and confounded the monarchist critics. Moreover, the republicans found that colonies once acquired could not be abandoned without incurring an injury to national pride. Since they needed to be governed, the colonies also served to demonstrate the universal character of republican principles, which were thought to be applicable anywhere, regardless of the social or cultural differences that distinguished the overseas territories from France. Thus, republicans gradually convinced themselves that associating the colonies closely with France would ensure that colonial peoples would share the advantages of modern French political life to their mutual benefit.[6]

This myth of an indivisible republic composed of France and its colonies provided the intellectual gestalt for a variety of reform efforts undertaken during the present century. The most important of these, the policy of *mise en valeur* adopted after World War I and the Blum-Violette reforms of the 1930s, are analyzed in chapter 2.

Both chapters also strive to relate the principal elements of the colonial myth to the several groups of French leaders that were competing for power under the Third Republic. To provide a catalog of the major themes that formed the colonial myth is relatively easy, but to demonstrate the connections between those ideas and the interests and ambitions of the men who held them is much more difficult. The argument offered here must rely on inferences drawn from published statements contained in official records and other personal accounts as well as on the assessments of other historians of French colonialism. Because colonial problems were seldom salient issues for the vast majority of French political leaders, those source materials are quite limited both in scope and quality.

Moreover, writings on questions of colonial policy, by their very nature, are subject to many caveats that apply to all political writing. Official documents and speeches are always self-serving, intended to sway the hearer and only incidentally to inform him. Personal memoirs have the added difficulty of subjecting the reader to the author's faulty memory, lack of information, and personal bias, as well as to distortions of a more calculated sort that reflect his subsequent ambitions.

Interviews with persons directly involved in French colonial affairs during the period under study compensated for some of these weaknesses in the official record. Unfortunately, it was not possible to pursue such interviews in a systematic way. The secondary literature about French colonialism, to which journalists, academic specialists, colonial administrators, and native political leaders have generously contributed, is at least a partial substitute for such direct contacts. In addition to revealing trends in informed thinking on colonial matters, such materials provided direct evidence of the colonial myth in operation.

World War II brought about both a reformulation of the colonial myth and a series of concrete changes in colonial conditions and institutions. First, the military defeat in the metropole split the ruling French elite into Free French and Vichy factions. The followers of both de Gaulle and Pétain had special reasons for paying attention to the colonies, and the rivalry between them created bitter conflicts among Frenchmen overseas. These sometimes led to armed clashes, which seriously undermined French authority in the colonies.

The precarious position of the Free French reinforced General de Gaulle's personal view of French politics, which attributed special importance to the colonies. De Gaulle considered control over the colonies the best means of establishing the political legitimacy of the Free French movement and an essential step in the liberation of the metropole. After the war he was convinced that only by maintaining her presence in the colonies could France regain her rank among the major powers. "For us, in a world like this and with things as they are, to lose the French Union would be a reduction that could cost us our independence," he later argued.[7]

Chapters 3 and 4 outline the importance of the colonies in de Gaulle's vision of France and describe the efforts that were undertaken at his direction, to initiate colonial reforms. Particular attention is given to the Brazzaville Conference of 1944, the ordinance of March 1944 granting voting rights to Algerian muslims, and the declaration of March 1945 proposing the creation of a French Union. In each instance these reforms are shown to have evoked organized resistance from colonial nationalists, which largely negated their intended purposes. Following a pattern that was to become familiar later, institutional reforms inspired by republican principles and aimed at generating popular support for French rule became sources of controversy and channels for challenging French predominance.

A second factor that significantly influenced the working of the Constituent Assemblies was the nature of the metropolitan political milieu. Chapter 5 examines two particularly important aspects of that milieu: the intense rivalries that divided the Communist, Socialist and MRP parties, which formed the Tripartite Government of 1946, and the substantial changes produced by the wartime reforms in the composition of the colonial elite. It also demonstrates that these domestic conditions resulted in the subordination of colonial issues to the tactical considerations of assembly politics and in the encouragement of increasingly divergent interpretations of the colonial myth.

The international political context within which the assemblies worked is discussed in chapter 6. It constituted a third factor that also affected the handling of colonial questions. The formation of the United Nations trusteeship system aroused special concern in France, where it was widely viewed as a scheme to extend American influence over French territories under the guise of anticolonialism. The diplomatic and military conflict that developed during 1946 over Indochina also had a profound effect on the Constituent Assemblies. Together these and other international events intensified domestic political divisions and complicated the problem of reaching a consensus on colonial reforms by making decolonization appear particularly threatening to French interests and prestige.

Principal Results: The Paradox of the French Union

Under the combined pressures of domestic and international crises, the Constituent Assembly set about framing a constitution for the French Union. It soon became apparent, however, that the representatives of native constituencies had quite different views on the nature of the union from those formulated by metropolitan deputies or spokesmen for French settlers overseas. Chapter 7 investigates these differences and explains how the colonial myth was reformulated by the different groups within the Assembly, each of which was intent on shaping the new constitution to benefit itself and its constituents.

The final chapter stresses the tragedy of the French Union, which lay in the inability of French leaders to break out of the intellectual limits imposed by the traditional version of the colonial myth in order to confront the reality of colonial nationalism. Their failure was due primarily to the strategies adopted by the metropolitan parties during the last crucial weeks of the Constituent Assembly. Once their priorities were established, the parties were compelled to bargain with the native deputies in order to reach a constitutional formula that was tolerable to them all. The result was a document filled with apparent contradictions and paradoxes. On one hand it asserted the unity of the metropole and colonies in a single indivisible republic. On the other hand, it recognized the existence of autonomous communities and offered to begin diplomatic negotiations with them to determine the terms for their participation in the French Union. The constitution also recognized the possibility for changes in the status of the various units within the union in the future, but it hedged them with legal restrictions that made such changes quite difficult.

In a more profoundly paradoxical move, it established local representative governments in the various colonies, permitted the organization of political parties, extended rights to free speech and press, and ended the regime of administrative justice for noncitizens. All of these moves tended to promote local self-government and to strengthen the colonial nationalist movements by giving them a means of influencing the local administration and by implicitly recognizing their legitimacy. Simultaneously, however, the constitution tied the colonies to metropolitan institutions in a way that assured continued metropolitan dominance and made changes in colonial policy very difficult, given the existing division of political power within the metropolitan Assembly.

In short, the constitution set the stage for developments that made it highly probable that colonial nationalists would resort to extralegal channels in order to gain their objectives. These actions could only evoke repression by metropolitan authorities dedicated to preserving the unity of the republic and preventing secession. Thus, the failure to comprehend the power of native nationalism in the colonies and to fashion institutions capable of encouraging an orderly process of decolonization in accord with the explicit desires of the native deputies led directly to the tragic colonial wars that dominated

French politics until the 1960s. By understanding that particular failure, it is to be hoped that the reader will also gain a better appreciation of the ways political myths can shape the actions of statesmen in general and thereby affect the lives of us all.

1. THE LOGIC OF EXPANSION

Léopold Senghor, the special *rapporteur* for the French Union articles of the Constitution of 1946, concluded his report to the First Constituent Assembly with the observation that, within the Constitutional Commission, there had developed a complete identity of outlook on the provisions concerning the French Union.

> I want to emphasize once more the unanimity that was reached within the commission on the texts relating to the French Union. . . . I would hope that the same unanimity might be found in the Assembly. This would indeed be in the republican tradition, or more exactly, in the French tradition. [*Applause*] We cannot help recalling the Assembly of 1848 where the cause of antislavery brought together men of all parties, from Victor Schoelcher on the extreme Left to MM. de Broglie and de Montalembert.[1]

Subsequent developments made it clear that the unanimity referred to here concealed very important underlying differences, yet Senghor was certainly correct in detecting a common approach to colonial policy among the political leaders of the time. Furthermore, as the remark indicates, it was an approach closely related to the historic traditions of French republicanism. This close relationship between colonial doctrines and the republican tradition was neither simple nor easily arrived at, however, and since it continued to form a major part of the intellectual equipment of French statesmen throughout the period following World War II, it is important to examine its origins and development.

What distinguished French colonialism during the nineteenth and twentieth centuries from that of other European states was the seriousness with which French leaders embraced the ideal of an ever closer union between France and the colonial territories. This conception of a worldwide community of peoples bound together into a single nation by common ties of economic and political interest, embodied in republican governmental institutions, and sharing a common cultural base, came, by the end of the nineteenth century, to constitute what can be considered the republican colonial myth. The core of the myth was formed by the fusion of two groups of ideas, the first drawn from the political doctrines of French republicanism and the second from a much older tradition of colonial expansion that was rooted in an important segment of the French political elite long before the Revolution of 1789.

To understand how the republican colonial myth came into being and how it functioned it is necessary to review the pattern of French colonial expansion during the nineteenth century from the viewpoint of those republicans who ultimately assumed the responsibility for colonial administration under the Third Republic. Throughout the period in question, the colonial myth provided an intellectual framework within which the ruling elite could seek solutions to two sets of questions. The first concerned the desirability of colonial expansion as a national policy, and the second related to the proper role within the republic for the colonial territories once they had been acquired.

In defending the desirability of colonial expansion, the colonial myth asserted both a principle of justice and a strategy for achieving it. As a question of principle, the idea that France, one of the leading nations of the world and a center of Western civilization—indeed of civilization itself—possessed a special mission to civilize the remote and isolated areas of Africa, the Far East, and the Caribbean, was self-evident to the grandchildren and great-grandchildren of Louis XIV. As a matter of policy, quite apart from its ultimate ends, colonial expansion was the alternative to a foreign policy of continental expansion. Colonial expansion also offered a possible compensation for policies of withdrawal from international affairs during periods of domestic instability. During the first two-thirds of the nineteenth century colonial expansion was a way of seeking to repair the damages done by the British, who were blamed by Frenchmen for the "spoliations" of 1763 and 1814. After 1870 expansion overseas was strongly defended as an alternative to a direct attack against Germany.

In asserting the desirability of colonialism for France the myth tended to portray England as the principal rival, naval power as the best defense, and to identify great power status with French "presence" in many parts of the world. It thus opposed both the conception of France as essentially interested in a policy of continental alliances aimed principally at Germany and the view of France as a status quo power interested mainly in its own internal welfare. The colonial myth advocated an activist foreign policy and justified it on grounds of religion, humanitarianism, and, ultimately, pure nationalism. The image it presented was that of a nation reaching outward in some mighty quest.

Colonies, once acquired, had to be governed, and in this regard the colonial myth drew heavily on the arguments of republican political doctrine to assert that France had a special mission to initiate the colonial peoples into the responsibilities of modern political life. The complex of colonial policies frequently identified by the misleading label of "assimilation" were concerned both with the political organization of the colonies, including their ties to metropolitan France on one hand, and with the policies of social and economic development to be pursued within the colonies. In both instances the republican colonial myth was ambiguous on a number of critical issues, particularly in regard to the level of political activity to be permitted within the colonies. Moreover, because colonial policies were always quite marginal concerns to French governments as well as to the public throughout the period of expansion, the various republican factions that exercised power tended to manipulate the basic themes of the colonial myth in accord with the domestic and international priorities of the time. Rarely were colonial problems treated as matters of national importance in their own right. Nevertheless, over the course of a century from roughly 1830 to 1939, the colonial myth gradually gained both a large measure of internal coherence and a sufficient degree of acceptability so that it provided a common vocabulary and a substantially uniform outlook for the political elites who confronted the problems of drafting a constitution for France and its colonies following World War II.

The character of the colonial myth becomes clearer as one recognizes that its principal themes embraced an amalgam of ideas and institutions devised at different periods by several factions within the political elite who were contending for power during the century when republican institutions were becoming firmly established in France. The colonial myth, like the historical reality that it sought to explain and depict, was not the product of any party or group. It was part of a whole political system that was undergoing changes in its domestic organization and foreign policy in response to pressures both from within and from abroad. The emergence of the colonial myth thus reflected in part the need for increasing participation by various segments of the elite, if not by the public at large, in the conduct of national policy. It also reflected the need to contend with the consequences of colonial expansion in a period of dramatic technological change, which exposed both the ideas of French republicanism and the institutions they had inspired to a series of rude tests. Thus, the emergence of a coherent doctrine, or rather the effort to expound such a doctrine, was not only the product of a century of thought and experience; it was also a signal that the system which generated it was unstable.

In retrospect, it is clear that there was always a paradoxical relationship between republicanism and colonialism. Both the political ideals of republican government and the people who advocated them frequently opposed the acquisition of colonies and criticized the traditional systems of colonial administration. Yet each of the principal republican factions in turn became reconciled to the fact of colonial rule, and some endorsed the principle of expansion. To determine how these changes occurred and what contribution each major faction made to the doctrines and institutions of French colonialism requires a more detailed study of both the men and the institutions than can be undertaken here.[2] It is convenient, however, to identify four basic versions of the colonial myth, which can be seen to reflect the themes of French republicanism in different degrees and with different admixtures of ideas drawn from other traditions. For simplicity, and despite certain criticism to which they may be subject, we will examine the liberal, radical, socialist, and Marxist versions of the colonial myth, which, though sometimes contradictory, were all descended from the same broad tradition of French republicanism.

The terms *republican, republicanism,* and *republican tradition* are used here to describe an assortment of ideas and the people who held them. Although many writers disagree over matters of detail, these people and their doctrines are widely regarded as characteristic of modern French political democracy.[3] For purposes of analysis, we shall consider four elements central to the republican tradition. All have roots extending far back into medieval political and social conflicts, but they received their most dramatic modern expression during the period of the Revolution of 1789.

First, the republican tradition is single-mindedly antifeudal. It is the explicit rejection of all forms of special political privilege, particularly those claimed by the supporters of absolute monarchy, that most firmly unites all republicans regardless of sectarian differences. This conviction has most often taken the form of vigorous opposition to the social and political privileges enjoyed by the hereditary landed aristocracy.

Second, republicanism is animated by an intense spirit of anticlericalism. For historical reasons as well as for reasons of intellectual conviction, republicans have consistently demanded the separation of political and educational affairs from the control of the Church. In their determination to root out of the social and political fabric of French life the far-reaching influence and economic power of the Church of France under the ancien régime, republicans succeeded to a large extent in creating around themselves a secular political and social mythology to replace the traditional concerns of orthodox Christianity.

Third, republicanism takes as the basis for all political life a concept of popular sovereignty derived in large part from an Enlightenment view of the Rights of Man. This concept of a permanent and inalienable sovereignty inherent in the national community, although originally formulated much earlier, was taken to require that the legislative and administrative officers of the state should remain always subordinate to the general will.

Finally, republican thought has consistently concerned itself with the social consequences of political and economic change. While different schools of republicanism have varied widely in their treatment of specific issues, all have displayed a serious awareness of the disruptive forces that have accompanied the continuing development of industrial technology. Social equality as a goal of republican political action was subject to strong restraints because of the unanimity with which the institution of private property was accepted in the eighteenth century. Nevertheless, the assault on feudal property during the Revolution of 1789 encouraged a few republican writers to criticize property in all its forms, and the nineteenth century saw a rapid extension of this social concern.

Taken together, these four themes derived from eighteenth-century political and social thought form the conceptual basis for later republican theories of parliamentary government and social democracy. Along with them, as part of the heritage of the Enlightenment, republicans maintained an increasingly rigid, formalistic regard for political doctrines. Encouraged by the rationalism of an earlier time, they tended to confront the realities of political life in a spirit of optimism qualified only by their inability to reconcile the many conflicts inherent in their doctrines. Particularly where it became necessary to embody doctrines in concrete institutions, compromise proved exceedingly difficult. The progressive application of republican ideas during the nineteenth century also revealed their formalistic approach to matters of doctrine to be perfectly consistent with a long-standing tradition of highly centralized political and administrative institutions.[4]

Beginning with the radical ideals of 1789, expressed in the political institutions of the revolutionary assemblies—especially the Convention of 1792—the political movement of French republicanism has evolved through four major stages.[5] The first stage, which began with the fall of the Bastille and ended with the dispatch of Napoleon to Saint Helena, established the preference for constitutional government over the absolute state in any of its models: the ancien régime, the convention, or the empire.

During the second stage bourgeois liberal groups secured their position against the reaction of the aristocracy, promoted the formal recognition of "the minimum liberties," and stimulated the expansion of capitalism. This stage endured for more than fifty years—from the Bourbon Restoration in 1815 to the fall of the Second Empire in 1870.[6] It was marked by renewed challenges of republicanism, first to the liberal monarchy of Louis Philippe, culminating in the revolution of 1848 and the abortive Second Republic, and finally to Louis Napoleon's Second Empire after the defeat at Sedan, resulting in the establishment of the "Republic of M. Thiers."

The third stage lasted from roughly 1873 to 1905 and saw the gradual establishment of parliamentary institutions and the emergence of political parties. During this heyday of the Third Republic, the principal characteristics of the regime derived from the outlook of the moderate republicans, radicals, and radical socialists who provided its greatest leaders: men such as Jules Ferry, Emile Combes, and Georges Clemenceau. Their policies were nationalistic in foreign affairs, progressive in matters of domestic politics, and conservative on questions of social policy.

By the turn of the century the emergence of a powerful industrial working class and the consolidation of the various socialist movements into a united Socialist party under the leadership of Jean Jaurès in 1905 began a fourth phase in the development of republicanism. This socialist phase, which continued until World War II, was characterized, on the one hand, by a broadening of the scope of traditional democratic political concerns to include the safeguarding of social and economic liberties in addition to the formal equality acquired through the exercise of universal suffrage. On the other hand, it was marked by a continued challenge from antirepublican forces of two sorts.

The traditional conservative opposition of aristocracy, Church, and military was replaced after World War I by a reactionary nationalism with fascist overtones, typified during the interwar period by Action Française and the Croix de Feu, which found its fulfillment and its disgrace in the Vichy regime of Pierre Laval and Henri Pétain. At the same time, a new revolutionary movement arose on the extreme Left as the socialists split, following the Bolshevik Revolution, into a democratic and a communist faction. During the interwar years the Communist party developed deep roots among the industrial working class in northern France and among the peasants in the poor rural areas of the South. By 1946 it had become an important factor in the political life of the French nation and a major element in the crisis of French republicanism.

Roger Soltau has provided a graphic analysis of these stages by which French republicanism passed, during a century of continuing political struggle, from its revolutionary beginnings through a long series of bitter defeats to final victory in the form of a constitutional democratic regime, which, however, soon became increasingly conservative in its outlook as it fell under attack from new revolutionary forces on the extreme Right and Left. Soltau's interpretation of the crisis of French republicanism, although reflecting his concern with the rabid nationalism of the twenties, deserves repeating, for it provides a valuable insight into one aspect of France's colonial crisis.

> To this perpetual strife we see one issue, and one only—such a political transformation as will render meaningless the struggle for

> a central unifying authority. Federalism, Regionalism, Autonomism—call it what you will, as long as it involves the abandoning of the chimera of an unrealizable transcendent unity, conformity to which is to be enforced. If France cannot conceive of diversity within unity, and if unity can only be obtained by a scarcely disguised civil war, then unity, as now understood, must disappear and full expression be given to the diversity which is one of the riches of France. This will be a revolution going deeper than the principles of 1789, or, better, it will be the true expression of those principles. Hence the extraordinary importance of the work of Federalists, Syndicalists, Regionalists, Autonomists, and the like; all in very different ways are threatening the idol of France one and indivisible which is but the perpetuation of the old strifes. Only in the challenging of the political and emotional systems which the conception represents can any internal harmony be envisaged for the future of France.[7]

During the interwar period, however, no French government was able to adjust the republican vision of an indivisible nation sufficiently to encompass more flexible political norms, and the advent of World War II found this problem still unresolved.

As each faction of the republican movement came to power, it had to face the problem of continuing colonial responsibilities under different domestic and international circumstances and hence was led to deal somewhat differently with questions of colonial policy. Consequently, in practice, the republican colonial myth was more than just a collection of abstract principles; it was also a set of policies and institutions that combined the past commitments of several republican factions and reflected their differing hopes and preferences for the future.

Revolutionary Beginnings

The roots of the colonial myth, like those of all French republicanism, lay in the Revolution of 1789. The colonies were present from the beginning, having "placed themselves under the protection of the National Assembly" at the time of the Tennis Court Oath (20 June 1789), when the Third Estate came together and swore to continue meeting until the constitution had been established. Delegates from the West Indian Antilles met and drafted *cahiers de doléances* in which they complained to the Estates General about the lack of local control over public affairs and proposed reforms that would have left the major planters in effective control of the colony.[8] With the aid of some metropolitan deputies, particularly Barnave and Lameth, and supported by the "Club de Massac," which at one point united more than five hundred wealthy planters and traders, the colonists sought to defend their interests in the Constituent Assembly and in the Legislative Assembly.

Among the liberals and more radical republicans, doubts about the value of colonialism and dissatisfaction with the policies of the colonists had become widespread even before the outbreak of the Revolution. Montesquieu and Turgot took up the arguments advanced by Adam Smith in *The Wealth of Nations,* which challenged the principle of the *pacte colonial,* held since the time of Colbert, that the colonies existed for the good of the metropole alone. They strongly rejected its corollary that the monopoly of trade held by the metropole worked to increase its wealth at the expense of all other states. With the advent of free-trade theories, the question of the value of colonies became a matter of showing their economic profitability in an open, competitive market system. This became increasingly difficult to do as the revolutionary assemblies, in response to their philosophical concern for equality, began to show greater concern for the abolition of slavery.

Montesquieu posed the broader philosophical problem when he asked how a democratic state could spread the ideas of liberty and freedom within its own borders and still impose its will on other peoples without undermining its own principles. By attempting to assert its authority over a foreign people, Montesquieu argued, a democratic state would inevitably endanger its own liberty, since it would be compelled to invest too much power in the executive branch of government in order that the officials it sent to the colonies might be able to take the sort of prompt, effective action that the circumstances demanded. Hence, Montesquieu posed a dilemma: Must a democracy either make its officials too strong for its own security or leave them too weak to maintain control over the colonies?

At the same time, Condorcet and the Abbé Raynal, together with other leaders of the revolutionary movement, including Mirabeau, Sieyès, the Abbé Grégoire, Brissot, and Robespierre, many of whom were active in the Société des Amis des Noirs, pressed for the extension of metropolitan legislation to the colonies as the best means of eliminating slavery. Justice, the Rights of Man and of Humanity, Robespierre insisted, required the Constituent Assembly of 1791 to prevent French settlers from depriving the black population of the Antilles of their rights. He repudiated the settlers' threats to declare independence rather than submit to metropolitan laws that made blacks their equals: "Let the colonies perish if they would cost you your honor, your glory, your liberty. I repeat, let the colonies perish if the colonists wish by threats to force us to decree what is most convenient for their interests. . . . We will not sacrifice the nation, nor the colonies, nor the whole of humanity." [9]

This preoccupation with abstract political principles led the Constituent Assembly to adopt a series of laws that gave the colonists the right to determine whether free black persons should be permitted to vote in local elections (8 and 28 March 1790) and later demanded that all black persons be admitted to the future colonial assemblies if they were born of free parents (15 May 1791). When the Constituent Assembly later annulled this action under strong pressure from the colonists, a series of uprisings took place in the Antilles, particularly in Santo Domingo. There the local council, which was dominated by the large planters, constituted itself a sovereign assembly and rejected any authority but that of the king, totally disregarding the actions of the metropolitan assembly.

Faced with such challenges to its sovereignty from several colonies, the Assembly moved to enforce the laws of the metropole, including the law of 4 April 1792, which established the legal equality of all persons, black or white. The convention, by a decree of 16 Pluviôse, Year II (4 February 1794), completed the legal emancipation of the slaves, declaring that "all men, without distinction as to color, who are residents of the colonies, are French citizens and enjoy all the rights assured by the constitution." Finally, the Constitution of the Year III (1795) declared that the colonies were "integral parts of the republic . . . subject to the same constitutional laws." The application of these provisions varied considerably from one colony to another, however, and all were annulled by Napoleon in the decree of 12 May 1802, which reestablished the regime existing before 1789.

The economic consequences of these changes, together with the elimination of the royal charter companies in 1791, were seriously damaging to the colonies, particularly to Senegal and the Antilles, which depended heavily on the slave trade. Furthermore, the colonies suffered severely from the repercussions of the civil war in France and the foreign struggles that accompanied the Revolution. In particular, the long war with England, only temporarily interrupted by the Treaty of Amiens in 1802, left the commerce and administration of the French colonies in ruins.

The colonial policy of the Napoleonic regimes clearly reflected a tactical shift in the focus of French foreign policy away from the Atlantic and toward expansion into the Mediterranean and the Levant. Napoleon later intended to mount a massive, Franco-Russian land invasion of India, in conjunction with an assault on England, to bring down the British Empire. This ambitious scheme ended in failure, although it brought temporary gains in the form of the retrocession of Louisiana in the Treaty of San Ildefonso (1 October 1800) and the restoration of the territories conquered by Britain in the Treaty of Amiens (27 March 1802). As part of the anti-British strategy, Louisiana was sold to the United States a few weeks after its retrocession by Spain, and with the gradual absorption of French military efforts on the Continent, England was able to seize control of many of the remaining French colonies. The Treaty of Paris, which ended the Napoleonic wars (30 May 1814), and the final Act of Vienna (9 June 1815) returned to French control most of the islands and territories France had held in 1792.

During the period of its greatest overseas activity, the Napoleonic Empire was governed by special laws and decrees as provided for in the Constitution of the Year VIII (1800) whose Article 91 stipulated: "The regime of the French colonies is determined by special laws." Further clarification was introduced by the law of 30 Floréal, Year X (20 May 1802), which restored slavery in all the colonies returned to France by the Treaty of Amiens and in all the other colonies beyond the Cape of Good Hope.

Looking at the colonial policies of the revolutionary assemblies and the Napoleonic Empire, it is clear that, where it was attempted, colonial expansion was dictated primarily by foreign policy concerns, especially the desire to overcome the superior economic and military position of England, and that colonial administration and politics remained secondary or even tertiary problems. Given the overarching concern of the liberals and radicals with the establishment of the legitimacy of republican government in the face of an unlimited claim to political authority from the monarchists and the evident dangers of a Bonapartist coup d'etat, it is understandable that they tended to resolve colonial problems by asserting the validity of abstract propositions. Furthermore, the deputies in the assemblies had little knowledge of colonial affairs, apart from a few of the representatives from the maritime towns who had had remote ties with the colonies under the ancien régime. The colonial theories and institutions of that period, consequently, had primarily a symbolic value for later generations of republicans who could trace their ideas back to the source of republican legitimacy in the Revolution of 1789. For nearly sixty years after the defeat of Napoleon, while the republicans struggled to regain power, their attitudes toward colonial problems evolved as they were forced to confront new international pressures and to deal with the consequences of the colonial expansion undertaken largely by their domestic opponents.

Liberal Republicanism

The first major faction of the republican movement whose colonial activities will be examined was composed of what may loosely be called "liberals," using the French sense of the term. These were men who, while preferring an explicitly republican political system, were nevertheless prepared to make compromises with the monarchists, provided sufficient assurances could be given regarding basic rights and guarantees of individual freedom. They represented not only the wealthy bourgeoisie of the countryside and the larger towns, but also a considerable portion of the lesser nobility and the new aristocracy formed during the Napoleonic period, for whom a simple return to the ancien régime was unthinkable. Their political outlook tended to stress formal guarantees of political and civil rights, a minimal system of representation for those with an appropriate stake in society, and the preservation of a strong executive. They never succeeded in resolving the contradictions between those principles of representation and generally alternated between them, with the result that the predominantly liberal regimes of the 1830s and 1850s were upset by a radical revolution in 1848, and then, after a period of more authoritarian rule under the Second Empire, finally gave way to the Third Republic after the defeat at Sedan in 1870.

Free trade was the economic counterpart of political liberalism in nineteenth-century France. From its origins in the political economy of the eighteenth-century philosophies, the policy grew during the nineteenth century into a broad ideology promising not only prosperity for all but peace and a general flowering of civilization as the result of nonviolent, commercial competition replacing the more brutal forms of national egotism. At the start, as suggested earlier, the theory of free trade was held to demonstrate the worthlessness of colonies and the dysfunctional character of overseas expansion for predominantly agricultural societies. Gradually, as the French economy became more industrialized, the same theories took on a new significance, and many of their arguments were reversed to show that, far from being useless, colonies were necessary in order to draw the fullest benefit from free trade, the products of the more industrialized metropole complementing the primary produce of the colonies.

In foreign affairs the liberal regimes of the nineteenth century faced a series of pressing diplomatic and military problems bequeathed to them by the European distrust of France that persisted long after the end of the Revolutionary and Napoleonic wars. Even Britain, which had less reason to fear the example of the French Revolution on its domestic politics, was wary of France's desire for revenge for the humiliation of 1814 as well as for the defeat of 1763. Moreover, quite apart from the particular uneasiness that characterized France's role as a participant in the European concert system of the mid-nineteenth century, there were important changes taking place within the system itself as a result of the efforts toward German and Italian unification, which largely transformed France's position on the Continent between 1815 and 1870.

The liberal version of the republican colonial myth seems to have been the product of the interweaving of three sets of ideas and circumstances. (1) The principles of political liberalism that inspired the reform of French domestic institutions left the role of the colonies in doubt; the wealthy colonists and planters were able to secure their interests in part through political action in the metropolitan legislatures, but equivocation on the issue of slavery left them in difficulty most of the time. (2) Free trade seriously undermined the economic position of the old colonies but provided a justification for seeking some new ones, especially where the promise of commercial advantages seemed certain to be rewarded. (3) The tendency of the liberal governments to treat England with special care also discouraged colonial expansion of any sort, yet the difficulty of pursuing an active foreign policy on the Continent was such that overseas involvements ultimately came to be regarded as less dangerous to France and preferable to a policy of resignation.

To understand how the republicans gradually moved from a position of general opposition to colonial enterprises to one that heartily supported at least certain types of colonial ventures, it is necessary to examine the policies of the July Monarchy, the Second Empire, and the Third Republic, as well as the conceptions that underlay them, in more detail.

The Bourbon Restoration Monarchy presided over fifteen years of reconstruction and recovery following the national humiliation of 1814. The determination to avoid foreign policy commitments that might antagonize England, coupled with the necessity of reviving a society that had been fragmented by religious and social strife as well as by political rivalry, discouraged the Restoration Monarchy from attempting any further colonial expansion, although it presided over the gradual restitution of the old colonies by Britain as the terms of the Treaty of Paris were fulfilled. The predominant interests in the Assembly were agricultural, and most of the deputies therefore looked upon the colonies as potential competitors; hence they refused to listen to the relatively few voices that were raised on behalf of a revived interest in the colonies.

Those who supported colonial expansion advanced two main arguments: first, that colonies were necessary for the restoration of the fleet and the recovery of French maritime commerce; and second, that, since war had become unthinkable, commerce and industry were going to become the new fields of international competition, and colonies were essential to success. For example, Count Louis Molé, minister of the navy in 1818, argued that armaments were necessary only to protect French shipping from pirates and to show the flag in foreign waters so as to safeguard French influence. He also viewed the colonies as an outlet for surplus population which, "left to react upon itself would menace society with too certain dangers." The secretary of state for the navy, Lainé, emphasized to the Assembly in 1821 the interdependency of colonies and the commercial fleet.

> All these things are interrelated in a great state. . . . To renounce colonies is to wish to forswear for the future a maritime commerce; it would be to exile the Frenchmen from the seas, to forbid them to engage in navigation and to make them, so to speak, the Chinese of Europe.[10]

The most lasting results of this slowly reviving interest in colonial expansion were the surprisingly successful role played by the French fleet at the battle of Navarin during the Greek war of independence and the swift conquest of Algiers undertaken with much hesitation by the Polignac government during the last days of the Bourbon Monarchy.

The Orleanist regime of Louis Philippe was at first embarrassed by its colonial inheritance. Many of its supporters shared the views of those liberals who had condemned the colonial policies of the ancien régime in Canada. Moreover, the economists of that period, apart from Sismondi, all agreed that colonialism was not profitable; and only among some of the deputies from the industrializing regions of the Midi who were anxious for commercial expansion was there any support for colonization.[11]

While the political spokesmen of the July Monarchy were inclined to ignore colonial affairs, the leaders of the army and navy were not. Soldiers and sailors, often acting on their own initiative, explored, claimed, subdued, and gradually administered a scattered array of overseas areas, and in so doing set a pattern that came to typify French colonization until the last quarter of the nineteenth century. The army under Bugeaud subdued and administered Algeria, while the navy installed bases along the coasts of Africa and Madagascar and among the islands of the Pacific. Order having been established, commercial and missionary enterprises soon followed. None of these developments, however, produced any serious concern with doctrines of colonization or with the special problems encountered in the colonies. The governments of the day were not overly concerned with such matters.

> On the whole, the liberal [July] Monarchy, although marked by great shifts of opinion, was a regime of moderation and innovation, more empirical than vigorous, lacking either doctrines or goals. The colonies remained external to France, regulated by special laws and decrees and controlled sometimes by the local legislature,

> sometimes by the governor. . . . They were the products of specialists: military men, sailors, and colonists. . . . Barely did they receive attention from Parliament except in case of a defeat or a scandal; a subsidy or a conflict among sugar planters; or more rarely, in regard to the abolition of slavery, which was being reduced bit by bit.[12]

The enlargement of the colonial domain carried out by the July Monarchy did introduce two new elements not characteristic of the old colonial system. First, the newly acquired islands and territories of Africa and the Pacific contained sizable native populations who could not readily be assimilated; and second, they produced goods and required supplies that were very different from those needed or supplied by the plantation colonies of the Antilles or the trading posts of Senegal. "That is, the new acquisitions worked a diversification in the population and economic set-up of the colonial empire. These new qualities broadened the conception of colonial trade and government." [13]

The more authoritarian regime of Louis Napoleon Bonaparte came into being in 1851 by a coup d'etat that ended the Second Republic after a brief but stormy four-year interval. Napoleon III paid only intermittent attention to colonial questions. Preoccupied with strengthening his rule within France and promoting French influence in relation to the other states of Europe, he often seemed uncertain about the value of colonies and tended to treat them as strategic factors in his domestic and international policy. Thus, in Algeria Napoleon experimented with the creation of penal colonies for the settlement of disturbing elements of society. In the Far East he lent support to the efforts of Catholic missionaries who had been more or less successful in ingratiating themselves with the local sovereigns in Vietnam over the preceding century, but who were then being threatened with eviction by the Annamite emperor Tu Duc.

Both these expansionist schemes reflected the shift that had already occurred in French colonial interest away from the old colonies of the West Indies to the new centers of European expansion in the Levant and along the route to China. The reasons for the change were partly economic; the abolition of slavery had by the 1850s largely ended the prosperity of the so-called old colonies of Guadeloupe, Martinique, Guyane, and Réunion, which were allowed to drift along with a regime that left one metropolitan government in direct control of all major political and economic matters.

The Constitution of 14 January 1852 stipulated merely that "the Senate regulates by *senatus-consulte* the constitution of the colonies and Algeria." The senatus-consulte of 4 May 1854 established a special regime for the old colonies that reserved to the Senate control over civil and political rights and property, gave the government power to rule by decree on matters of national or local government, delegated to the governor all powers of local police and administration, and created local councils with some budgetary powers. In addition, it created a special colonial advisory council composed of members designated by the colonists and the minister to consult with the minister on questions relating to the colonies. Representation of the old colonies in the metropolitan Parliament, provided by the Constitution of 1848, was ended. Since no other senatus-consulte was ever adopted, all the other colonies remained under the direct control of the emperor.

Louis Napoleon was also deeply impressed with the success that the British seemed to be enjoying as a result of the adoption of free trade, and for a time he apparently hoped to imitate those results. Hence, his interest in Algeria was renewed during the 1860s, although the result of the various land-grant schemes provided for Algeria left much to be desired when the difficulties of transforming unemployed urban workers into successful farmers in the hostile environment of Algeria finally became evident. In this regard Napoleon shared the illusions of the leaders of the Second Republic who made substantial investments in Algeria in the hope that it would become a port of entry into the heart of Africa and a transit point for the rich resources believed to lie in wait for European exploitation.

The foreign policy of the Second Empire was based largely on an Entente Cordiale with England, which created serious problems for colonial expansion as British and French interests came into conflict along the routes to Asia. In Egypt the British outmaneuvered the French, who were simultaneously involved in conflicts with Italy over Tunisia. As the power of the Ottoman Empire declined, France became an active rival of the other major European states for control over its scattered dependencies. In the process, the more abstract, doctrinal questions concerning the value of colonization tended to disappear under a flood of official rhetoric whose real purpose was to vindicate French prestige at home and improve her relatively lower position abroad. Hence, what one observer has called an "imperial spirit" was proclaimed by the Marquis de Chasseloup-Laubat, minister of the navy from 1860 to 1867, recalling the policy of grandeur typical of the ancien régime: "It is a veritable empire that we must create! A sort of suzerainty, of sovereignty, with free commerce, open to everyone; and also a formidable establishment from where our Christian civilization can spread." [14]

Toward the end of the Second Empire, the liberal writer and diplomat Prévost-Paradol expressed much the same vision when he argued that

> Africa . . . should not be for us simply a trading post, like India, or a camp or training ground for our army; still less should it be a place for the experiments of our philanthropists: it is a French land which as soon as possible should be peopled, possessed, and cultivated by Frenchmen, if we want it someday to count on our side in the determination of human affairs.[15]

This new expansionist spirit was officially inspired, but the actual work of colonial extension was carried on by military commanders, explorers, and missionaries more or less independent of government instructions and totally without any popular sanction. The process of accretion by the action of military commanders was particularly evident in West Africa, where men of vision and great energy like Faidherbe explored and subdued large areas of the Niger Basin and brought them under French authority. Because the financial means were generally lacking for any methodical exploitation of such additions, the gradual extension of French rule into West Africa produced neither great economic rewards nor important political and administrative changes in the colonial system. In fact, throughout the Second Empire colonial expansion drew most of its support from those favored companies whose colonial ventures received state aid, a relatively small number of large European landholders, missionary interests in France and the colonies, and the French military and colonial bureaucracies. Small wonder then that to the republicans of the 1860s, colonialism appeared to be the work of their bitterest opponents—aristocratic bureaucrats, the commercial and capitalist bourgeoisie, and the missionary clergy. Their reaction against these groups, for economic and social as well as political reasons, combined large elements of antimilitarism, anticapitalism, and anticlericalism, each of which provided additional reinforcement for republican opposition to colonialism. And it is, therefore, not at all surprising that the shattering defeat of the emperor's "colonial" army at Sedan in 1870 was seen by many republicans as a confirmation of these anticolonial convictions, as well as the final judgment on the political regime of the Second Empire.

The liberal themes of the colonial myth emphasized the commercial importance of colonies as well as their strategic value to a France now ruled by a stable authority that was obligated to safeguard the basic rights of all citizens, including those Frenchmen who lived in the colonies. These ideas survived the downfall of the regimes that first enunciated them, partly because they were embodied in economic and political institutions, laws, and bureaucratic structures that endured even when constitutions changed. They also endured, however, because over the long period from 1814 to 1870, colonial expansion had become firmly associated with a vision of French greatness that held considerable attraction for the new political elite that came to power after the defeat of 1870 in an era marked by new humiliations and a new outburst of nationalism.

The Radical Republicans

The Third Republic came into being between 1871 and 1875 largely as a result of the inability of the monarchist groups to resolve their mutual differences. It inherited colonial dependencies, but its political doctrines rejected both the policy of colonial expansion and the traditional practices of colonial administration. Later, under the pressure of foreign-policy factors, republican governments turned again to expansion, and colonies, once established, became part of the national patrimony, which they felt obliged to administer. Gradually, the gap between republican doctrine and governmental practice was narrowed, but it was never wholly or permanently overcome. Thus, throughout the first part of the Third Republic from 1871 to 1914, periods of vigorous expansion alternated with powerful movements of anticolonialism. During each expansionist phase, the moderate republicans were opposed not only by monarchists who detested their domestic social policies—particularly their opposition to clerical influence over the schools—but also by radical republicans who objected to colonial expansion in principle and who feared the accumulation of excessive power in the hands of the national executive. Economic interests cut across these social and political rivalries to some extent, but the general pattern just described marked French politics for most of the periods of rapid expansion from 1871 to the end of the century.[16]

Colonial policy during this period was subject to many of the same procedural uncertainties as foreign policy in general. The majority of deputies had no interest in it or knowledge about it. Foreign policy traditionally was the province of the minister of foreign affairs and the president of the republic. It was not discussed in the Council of Ministers, and many times ministers refused to discuss such matters in Parliament. The parties of the Left and the extreme Right often joined to frustrate the designs of the government: Freycinet was driven from office in 1882 for telling the truth about the French expedition to Egypt, and Jules Ferry, the greatest exponent of expansionism during the late nineteenth century, barely succeeded in 1881, with the support of the radical leader Léon Gambetta, in winning support for the Treaty of Bardo giving France extensive rights over Tunisia. The treaty was viewed as a diplomatic success because it demonstrated that, in Gambetta's words, "France resumes her place as a great power." As Gabriel Charmes indicated at the time, "When one rereads carefully the parliamentary debates and diplomatic documents that preceded our defection in Egypt, one perceives that, there again, domestic politics, with its petty preoccupations, caused foreign policy to deviate from the path it should at all costs have followed." [17]

The political faction that eventually came to dominate the first half of the Third Republic was made up of men who are usually identified in the French tradition as "radicals." Broadly understood, the radical label has commonly been applied to all those republicans who, despite their frequent conflicts on economic and social questions, were in basic agreement with Gambetta's formula: the republic—one, indivisible, and secular. Their intellectual heritage differed only in degree from that of their liberal predecessors.

The radicals traced their political ideas from the revolutionary assemblies and the brief experiment of the Second Republic. Their colonial concerns, in particular, reflected the changing role of the urban areas within France and the growing influence of the middle bourgeoisie as well as the shifting international pressures to which

France was subject after 1871. During the 1840s republicans had begun to pay attention to the possibility of colonial expansion as a source of employment for metropolitan workers, although the schemes advanced at that point failed to bring the results expected.[18] Always sensitive to the importance of demonstrating their ability to maintain national prestige, they had also considered the strategic importance of some of the colonies, particularly when expansion was at the expense of England—that perfidious Albion that had fought against the Revolution and won the battle of Waterloo. Most of their attention had been devoted to the island colonies and Algeria, although the Second Republic also supported the establishment of missionary posts in Tahiti, Annam, and along the coast of China.[19]

The republicans of the 1840s had given primary attention to the problem of slavery. Framing their arguments around the humanitarian and egalitarian principles of 1789 and the administrative practices of the Convention of 1792, they had invoked the doctrine of political assimilation as the best means of ending the scandal of slavery. In 1848, just as in 1795, the political and administrative assimilation of the overseas colonies was understood to mean that metropolitan laws and regulations would become the means of extending to the colonies the freedoms associated with the rights of man as they were understood in the metropole.

This abstract, philosophical approach to the problems of human rights was characteristic of republican thought throughout the nineteenth century. It is clearly reflected in the writings and speeches of France's most vigorous exponent of abolition, Victor Schoelcher. Schoelcher's famous report to the Provisional Government of 1848 on the problem of slavery in the West African colonies ended with the declaration that "the republic no longer intends to make distinctions within the human family." [20] His idealism was balanced, however, by a concern for practical reforms, most important of which was the creation of a semiofficial commission of specialists to assist the government in developing a more "scientific" approach to colonial administration.[21]

The republic never succeeded in fully assimilating the colonies, although it did provide for their representation in Parliament and establish a framework for future changes. The Constitution of 4 November 1848 provided that "the territory of Algeria and of the colonies is declared French territory and will be regulated by individual laws until a special law places them under the regime of the present constitution." A decree of 27 April 1848 extended the application of metropolitan laws by appointing "commissioners of the republic" with the power of governors and by creating in the colonies *ateliers nationaux,* or "national workshops," where anyone who was unemployed could find work. A decree of 4 May 1848 abolished the *conseils généraux* in Martinique, Guadeloupe, Guyane, and Réunion and also ended the powers of the colonial delegates, thus giving the metropolitan legislature direct control over the colonies. Since no special law was ever adopted for the colonies under that constitution, the governments continued to rule by decree.[22]

During the brief life of the Second Republic, assimilation encountered serious obstacles in practice, most importantly in Algeria. There a growing colony of European settlers had already become established alongside a rapidly increasing indigenous population, many of whom, at least in principle, were subject to assimilation into the metropolitan political system. An earlier law of 1833 had extended French citizenship to all freemen in the colonies, with the result that, when slavery was finally abolished by the law of 27 April 1848, large numbers of non-Europeans theoretically became citizens. Following the adoption of universal manhood suffrage, they also might have become voters.

In Algeria, however, only European settlers were considered French citizens; therefore, the political and administrative reorganization introduced by the Second Republic affected only the coastal area of European settlement. These changes, together with the inclusion of Algeria in the metropolitan tariff system, were primarily aimed at increasing colonization.[23]

These beginnings were almost entirely obscured by twenty years of opposition to the domestic and foreign policies of the Second Empire during which the anticolonial inclinations of republicanism were revived. Opposition to Bonapartism coincided with resentment felt by many republicans for the "African army" that was sometimes used to put down strikes in the metropole as well as to seek foreign glories in Mexico or the Far East. Radical deputies, most of whom had roots in rural areas, consistently opposed these expeditions, whose costs were more evident than their benefits, which generally fell to the military or to big businessmen.[24] Even Louis Napoleon's gesture of establishing an "Arab Kingdom" in Algeria in 1863 was seen as a petty device to match the prestige of Queen Victoria who had recently assumed the title "Empress of India." It comes as no surprise, therefore, that French republicans came to power with much clearer conceptions of what they wished to avoid in the realm of colonial politics than of what they might achieve.

There were a few specialists in colonial problems whose activities contributed to the education of the political elite. Paul Leroy-Beaulieu published a monumental comparative study, *De la colonisation chez les peuples modernes,* in 1874 which went through five editions, the latest in 1908. "Colonization," he wrote, "is for France a matter of life or death. Either France will become a great African power or in a century or two she will be a secondary power in Europe; she will count in the world for little more than Greece or Romania counts in Europe." [25]

Beginning in 1876, a number of French intellectuals and philanthropists inspired by the International Conference of Geographers, began to encourage a greater awareness of the excitement and adventure of overseas expansion.[26] On the whole, however, the work of exploration and colonization continued to be carried out, as it had been during the July Monarchy and the Second Empire, by military officers brought up in the tradition of Bugeaud and nourished on the experience of the occupation of Algeria.

The most outstanding exponents of this dimension of republican colonialism were Faidherbe, Galliéni, and Lyautey. Faidherbe served as a young lieutenant under Bugeaud in Algeria, from where he went on to become the explorer of the Sudan and the founder of French West Africa. One of his junior officers, Joseph Simon Galliéni, developed the basic notions of colonial rule advanced by Bugeaud and Faidherbe in the Sudan and applied them first in Tonkin and later in the pacification and colonization of Madagascar. Lyautey, who later became celebrated for his success in imposing French rule on Morocco, began his career in Indochina with Galliéni and followed his mentor to Madagascar. All these men developed their approaches to colonial rule in a pragmatic fashion and pursued their policies quite independent of parliamentary sanction most of the time, only turning to the metropolitan government when a military crisis, a colonist's scandal, or a clash with some other European power intervened. Theirs was a spirit of hardy, individualistic adventure, reflecting an important aspect of republicanism that found little room for expression in the socially constricted and politically frustrating atmosphere of the Third Republic. All three were imbued with a profound sense of patriotism, which justified their actions and left them free to speculate on the best means of developing the territories over which they had assumed control for the mutual benefit of France and the colonies.[27]

The strongest impetus behind colonial expansion during the latter part of the nineteenth century, however, came from foreign policy factors.[28] France found herself isolated within Europe after the conclusion of the Franco-Prussian War. For nearly twenty years Bismarck successfully discouraged all the other major European states from contracting alliances with France and encouraged France's rivals on the Continent. Jules Ferry, foreign minister and then prime minister in two governments between 1881 and 1885, responded to Bismarck's strategy with a policy of colonial expansion. For a nation exhausted by war and yet unwilling to adopt a posture of self-abnegation or diplomatic withdrawal, colonial expansion became a national imperative. "Not only should France be present when . . . conflicts arose, to participate in deliberations and interventions, less to gather the advantages than to maintain its positions and establish new connections, all in the interest of peace. But, moreover, it was up to the republic to erase the stigma of defeat first by safeguarding and then by enlarging the fields open to French expansion outside of Europe." [29]

Ferry rejected the complaints of the Right as well as those of the radicals and socialists who favored either a policy of direct opposition to Germany or a pacifist stance. Both implied the acceptance of a "continental" outlook and a policy of passivity, which he condemned. To the jeers of the radicals, who were led at that point by the fiery oratory of Clemenceau, Ferry replied with arguments that stressed the changing strategic situation in the world and emphasized the role of French naval power, the merchant marine, and the colonies: Europe was losing its primacy as the focus of international conflict. The outlying areas of the world were rapidly coming under the influence of the European powers, and they were destined to become the centers of future conflict. The security of the European states would soon depend on their ability to establish control of the seas and therefore a strong navy and a vigorous colonial empire were required. Only a policy of self-extension, Ferry told the Chamber in 1885, could serve the vital interests of France.

That is why Tunisia, Saigon, Indochina were necessary; that is why we need Madagascar and why we are at Diego Suarez. . . . It is neither in the Mediterranean nor the Channel that the decisive battle will take place. Marseilles and Toulon will be defended quite as much in the China seas as in the Mediterranean. Nations, in our time, are great only according to the activity they develop; it is not by "the peaceful extension of institutions" that they are great anymore . . . [Interruptions on the extreme Left and Right]. . . . Extension without acting, without becoming involved in the affairs of the world, by keeping apart from European combinations, by seeing every attempt at expansion into Africa or the Orient as a trap—living like that, for a great nation, is to abdicate, and in a shorter time than you would believe possible to descend from the first rank to third or fourth.

I cannot, gentlemen, nor I imagine can anyone, envisage a destiny such as this for our country. . . . Do not plead attenuating circumstances. . . . Say that you want a France that is great in everything . . . a great country exercising her influence on the destiny of Europe; and that she should extend that influence around the world and carry everywhere possible her language, her mores, her flag, her arms, and her genius.[30]

In turn he accused the radicals of sentimentality for refusing to put the misfortunes of the past behind them and to seize the advantages that could be wrung from the future. Their criticisms of French conduct at the Berlin Conference of 1885 were unjustified, he maintained, since there had been no "colonial compensations" to Germany or to any other power, unless one insisted on treating the Franco-British understanding concerning their respective interests in Cyprus and Tunisia as a compensation. The real issue, as Ferry saw it, was "whether the restrictions which are imposed on nations suffering from severe injuries must result in abdication. . . . Must republican governments, although absorbed in contemplation of a world which will bleed forever, let everything else go on around them?" [31] In particular, did the damages of a cruel war condemn France to a position of such weakness that others might assume her rights and interests overseas? Ferry heatedly refused to acknowledge such a policy.

Ferry also predicted great economic benefits for France as a result of colonial expansion. Explaining to the Chamber that he intended no return to the plantation agriculture of eighteenth-century colonialism, Ferry sought the support of business and financial interests to whom he held out the promise of a protected market for French manufactures and a profitable arena for investment. At that time France was undergoing a period of general economic stagnation; prices were declining, and monetary crises were frequent. Other states including Germany and the United States were erecting tariffs against French goods; hence, the prospect of unfettered access to colonial territories held an understandable appeal for French businessmen who provided much of the support for the moderate republican parties. The fact that most of these benefits were purely hypothetical, since the resources from which they were to be produced had not yet been exploited or in some instances even discovered, did little to reduce the appeal of the rhetoric. Those who opposed Ferry did so because they regarded his policies as capitalist schemes or diversions from the struggle against the real enemy across the Rhine, not because they questioned his economics or even less because they had refuted his strategic arguments.

When pressed to defend his position, Ferry retorted that the radicals were engaging in "political metaphysics" rather than sound thinking. They assumed that colonialism based solely on commerce would be peaceful and humanitarian, but they failed to recognize that men like Savorgnan de Brazza, the naval officer who carried the French flag to Central Africa, could pursue peaceful exploration only so long as conditions remained favorable. He predicted quite accurately that when resistance was encountered, even the radicals would sanction the use of force rather than surrender their undertakings.

There was very little question among any of the republicans that such resort to force was perfectly legitimate. Impressed perhaps by the arguments of men like Herbert Spencer, they were convinced that "the superior races have a right with respect to the inferior races." These rights also implied duties, particularly the duty to civilize the inferior peoples. After all, who could deny that French conquest had put an end to local wars, destroyed feudal oligarchies, brought peace, greater equality, better education, and greater prosperity to the peoples of Africa and Algeria? Even some radicals supported this thesis. As Léon Hugonnet explained: "The grandeur of France is indispensable to the progress of humanity. That is why I support a policy which will unite under the French flag one hundred million defenders of the republic." [32]

According to one authority, only one objection to the principle of colonial expansion was raised during this period. Frédéric Passy presented it to the Chamber on 21 December 1885.

> How is it that, while in Europe you do not recognize the right of any power to deprive another of a shred of its territory, that is to say of its national flesh, you pretend not only to have the right but the duty to dominate, to subjugate, to exploit other peoples who are perhaps less advanced than we in their civilization but who have no less their own personality, their nationality, and like us are no less attached to their independence and to their native soil? [33]

Parliament paid scant attention to this plea for an end to colonial conquest. Nevertheless, support for Ferry's expansionist policy was in no sense unqualified. The Right objected that the government was weakening France in Europe by undertaking colonial ventures that made redress of grievances against Germany impossible. The Left echoed these complaints and protested against "a policy of effacement" in Europe. Colonialism, it was asserted, involved sacrificing moral authority, deluding the nation into a false sense of grandeur, and wasting money and manpower. Even some of Ferry's supporters recognized that colonial expansion might generate diplomatic rivalries that could disturb relations with Britain and Italy as well as Germany. Ferry was finally driven from power in the spring of 1885 by the combined opposition of the monarchists and radical republicans for whom the issue of credits for the Tonkin expedition was primarily a device to defeat a government whose policies each faction disliked for its own reasons.[34]

Even in defeat, however, Ferry's achievements in the realm of colonial expansion had lasting importance for French national policy. In the brief period of five years, from 1881 to 1885, Ferry established France as one of the major European colonial powers. On the Continent, France remained isolated while Bismarck was in office. After 1890, however, she reentered the diplomatic arena with increased power and prestige, thanks largely to her position overseas. As one of Ferry's supporters later commented,

> Everywhere France planted its flag, everywhere she was present in the division of the world. There where her implantations are not terminated, at least they are sufficiently advanced so that the following years permit a definitive installation. There will be no more withdrawal. The impetus given by Jules Ferry to a home-bound people [*un peuple casanier*] made his country a great colonial power.
>
> France is alone in Europe, but she is powerful outside of Europe. The policy of alliances which Bismarck forbade her, she will soon begin, once he is gone. She will do so all the better because she represents a force. Jules Ferry was undoubtedly the one who made possible the achievements of Delcassé.[35]

After the fall elections of 1885 Parliament's interest in colonial expansion languished. The Tonkin occupation, negotiated with China in the Treaty of Tientsin (9 June 1885), came within three votes of being abandoned when the Chamber almost defeated a government appropriation bill. The *Boulangist* crisis divided the monarchists and disturbed French foreign policy on the Continent between 1886 and 1890. With the failure of Boulangism, however, a new wave of expansionism began to swell, building on the discoveries of explorers in central Africa and the shifting efforts of the leading European powers to secure economic and political gains.

The leadership of this movement was provided by another republican, Eugène Etienne. For forty years a deputy from Oran, a friend of Gambetta and Ferry, founder of the Colonial party in the Chamber of Deputies, Etienne was twice undersecretary of state for the colonies between 1887 and 1892. Under his guidance French control over Africa was extended to take in almost the entire western portion of the continent. It was Etienne's dramatic vision of a vast African empire under French control that stirred the Chamber to turn its attention once more to the far side of the Mediterranean.

> If you draw a line from the border of Tunisia past Lake Chad to the Congo, you can say that most of the territories between that line and the sea, except for Morocco and the English, German, and Portuguese coastal possessions that are hidden in the immense circumference, are either French or are destined to enter into the French sphere of influence. We have there a vast and immense domain which is ours to colonize and to make fruitful; and I

think that, at this time, taking into account the worldwide movement of expansion, at the same time as foreign markets are closing against us, and we ourselves are thinking of our own market; I think, I repeat, that it is wise to look to the future and reserve to French commerce and industry those outlets that are open to her in the colonies and through the colonies.[36]

Etienne succeeded where Ferry had failed; he was able to rally some hundred deputies, most of them from the moderate republican majority, in support of expansion. These efforts were supported outside of Parliament by the Comité de l'Afrique Française, a pressure group that included a number of colonial officials, explorers, and businessmen, in addition to members of Parliament. The gradual disintegration of the Bismarckian alliance system after 1890, highlighted by the conclusion of the Franco-Russian alliance, removed one of the chief objections of the Right to colonial expansion. Fed by a hunger for grandeur and an upsurge of nationalist feeling that was shared by all the states of Europe during that period, French colonization became for a brief time a genuinely popular enterprise.[37] French officials preparing for the great Universal Exposition of 1900 could argue with some justice that "in less than one quarter of a century, republican France has rebuilt a colonial empire worthy of the one which the nation had lost a century before. Today, forty-five million men of all races, who have achieved the most diverse degrees of civilization, have entered the French community. . . . The time is past when one doubted the aptitude of our race for colonial ventures." [38]

Many problems remained, however, before the enormous realm claimed by French explorers could be transformed into a coherent community, and many misgivings continued to mark the course of colonial expansion. With the signature of the Entente Cordiale with England in 1905, new strategies were adopted to meet a series of new dangers arising out of the juxtaposition of two rival alliance systems within Europe. As tensions increased between France and Germany, the focus of public policy shifted back once again to continental problems, particularly the defense of France's land frontier. The international diplomatic and military rivalries that preceded the outbreak of World War I permitted France to extend her rule over Morocco between 1900 and 1914. In the process, however, the tide of opinion in Parliament clearly turned against colonial projects once again, and as the possibility of war increased, the political and diplomatic incentives for further expansion declined sharply.[39] In addition, many of the traditional economic arguments formerly advanced by leaders like Ferry lost their appeal during a period of generally expanding business at home and disappointing returns from colonial trade.

The territorial settlement that ended World War I brought the era of expansion to a close by adding to the existing colonial domain the former German colonies of Togo and the Cameroons and the Syrian and Lebanese states detached from the Ottoman Empire. All these areas were placed under French control as mandates of the League of Nations, but in practice they were treated almost exactly as other colonies. Taken as a whole, therefore, the French colonial empire at the end of World War I reflected the haphazard nature of its acquisition. Only recently pacified, the empire was not unified by either common institutions or common doctrines, as one colonial specialist, Jules Harmand, had noted in 1910. None of those shortcomings had been remedied a decade later when the policy of the Third Republic could accurately be characterized as "a mixture of subjugation, administrative decentralization and paternalism." [40] It remained for the governments of the postwar period to undertake the consolidation of this extensive realm under conditions that imposed new burdens and in an intellectual climate that was profoundly different from that of the first half of the Third Republic.

One might summarize this evolution of the colonial myth by noting that during the nineteenth century it served primarily to justify French expansion overseas to several segments of the political elite that previously had opposed colonial conquests for both political and philosophical reasons and that it did so by invoking the libertarian and humanitarian ideals of the French Revolution. The liberal version of the colonial myth emphasized values such as individual liberty and the right to property which, given an implicit conviction of the superiority of French culture, were easily interpreted to justify the imposition of French rule over primitive peoples in the interests of advancing civilization. The liberals also preferred that colonial expansion be limited so as not to weaken the metropole economically or to require the expansion of the state machinery beyond the bare minimum needed to guarantee minimum political rights for all citizens. In practice, the liberal monarchy was quite unsuccessful in its colonial efforts.

The radical republicans developed a somewhat different version of the colonial myth that reflected the increased importance of political participation in metropolitan France during the middle of the century. When coupled with a variety of economic incentives, the radical image of the colonies promised increased national power based on the exploitation of colonial resources. This was a vision that acquired special appeal after the defeat of 1870. It was generous in that it imagined the indigenous peoples of the colonies capable of participating in the common life of the French community, but it also assumed that French governments and legislatures would make all the important decisions and that the colonies would be content with only symbolic representation.

Both liberal and radical versions of the colonial myth were also consistent with a much older tradition that viewed colonial expansion as an expression of national grandeur. Particularly during the latter part of the nineteenth century the republican parties took pride in re-creating a worldwide colonial empire that rivaled the British Empire in size. Their success in a field where both the ancien régime and the liberal monarchy had failed was viewed as tangible proof of the republic's legitimacy and represented an important political advantage for the radicals during a period of domestic turmoil.

World War I marked the end of the expansionist phase of French colonialism. By then a majority of the French political elite had concluded that colonies served both the national interest and the interests of their clientele. After the war a period of consolidation began which was marked by the emergence of new political groupings within the domestic arena and the adoption of a number of reforms in colonial policy. These changes in turn produced some important alterations in the colonial myth.

2. THE REPUBLICAN CONSENSUS

World War I was a turning point in the development of French colonial thought, just as it was in other aspects of politics. This chapter will trace the development of the colonial myth at the hands of those groups who contended for control over the political and administrative machinery of government during the interwar period. Most of those years were dominated by the struggle of the center parties—radicals, moderate democrats, and (toward the end) some socialists—against the political extremes on both the fascist-oriented Right and the communist-dominated Left. The colonial myth was particularly influenced by the criticisms of the socialists, who split, after 1921, into democratic and communist factions, both of which gradually assumed some of the responsibilities of power during the brief interlude of the Popular Front in 1936.

The focus of this discussion remains the relationship between colonial ideas and institutions, and these will be seen to reflect even more clearly than in the earlier period the preferred strategies of the various factions for dealing with other pressing national and international issues. Colonial policy as well as colonial thought remained a secondary area of concern within which various adjustments were contemplated as a means of easing other, heavier international pressures. As the alternatives open to the leaders of the Third Republic at home and abroad became fewer and less attractive, the preservation of the colonial ties took on greater significance, though these ties were justified in different ways by different groups.

The actions taken in pursuit of unity between France and the colonies encountered serious difficulties, however, especially during the years of the Popular Front. Never was the belief in the legitimacy and utility of colonial unity more widely shared, yet already there were disquieting signs of conflict within the French community.

Immediately after the war the prevailing view of the colonial empire was overwhelmingly optimistic and self-confident. The colonies had sent nearly five million tons of goods and half a million soldiers to fight on the battlefields of France between 1914 and 1919.[1] No longer could the radicals argue that colonial expansion would weaken the country rather than strengthen it. Even Clemenceau, one of the few survivors of the colonial battles of the 1880s, was prepared to admit publicly his error in having opposed Jules Ferry. Colonial expansion seemed to have been vindicated by the fidelity of the colonial troops in the hour of greatest national peril. The unity of the metropole and the colonies, it was frequently said, had been "sealed in blood."

At the peace conference France made colonial gains in Africa and the Levant at the expense of the Germans and the disintegrating Ottoman Empire. These arrangements were worked out among the victorious allies on an ad hoc basis.[2] They were readily accepted by the Chamber, where Henri Simon, the minister of the colonies, explained the action as resulting from Germany's *indignité colonisatrice* and recognition of France's superior colonial achievements: "Not a single voice was raised in their [Germany's] favor; humanity in its entirety adjudged them guilty."[3] By the creation of the mandate system of the League of Nations, the fate of the German colonies was reconciled with the twelfth of Woodrow Wilson's Fourteen Points, which pledged that there would be no colonial annexations. Although inspired more by British and American political ideas than by European experience, the mandate system enunciated in the League Covenant was consistent with French colonial thought on most of its essential points. The mandatory powers were singled out as having a special responsibility for the "retarded" states made up of "peoples not yet able to stand by themselves under the strenuous conditions of the modern world," on whose behalf the Covenant confirmed the "sacred trust of civilization" held by the advanced states.

If the principle of international trusteeship created some difficulties, the predominant position of the mandatory powers within the Permanent Mandates Commission and the League Council guaranteed that French control over the mandated territories would not be infringed. In practice the African mandates of Togo and the Cameroons were treated identically to other colonies, and they were presented to the Chamber as further recognition that "we are the natural protectors of the Negro peoples whom we have been colonizing for centuries. *Voilà la verité française.*" [4]

The Policy of Mise en Valeur

The most pressing colonial problem for France in the postwar period was no longer expansion. Instead, consolidation and development became the central colonial concerns of all the parties. In this respect, there was wide agreement that there could be no abandonment of previous acquisitions, whether to some other state or to an international organization whose future was entirely unknown and unpredictable. All the governments of the interwar period acted precisely as Ferry had predicted they would, refusing to consider any change that reduced French authority in the colonies or created any sort of "intermediary bodies" that might challenge the centralized control of the metropolitan ministry. Instead, the governments of the period launched a program intended, in the words of Albert Lebrun, "to unite France to all those distant Frances in order to permit them to combine their efforts to draw from one another reciprocal advantages." [5]

The label given to this policy was *mise en valeur* or "development." Its goals were quite different, however, from those associated with the process of development as expressed in the recent literature on developing countries. It did not seek primarily to create self-sustaining economic growth or to promote the emergence of politically independent states in Asia and Africa. Instead, its aim was to tie the colonies and France together in a cooperative program of economic and social expansion.

The architect of the policy of mise en valeur was Albert Sarraut, governor-general of Indochina from 1911 to 1920, minister of the colonies from 1920 to 1924, and frequent minister in subsequent governments throughout the interwar years. The primary objective of the new policy, Sarraut explained, was "to substitute for isolated, uncertain decisions a method of action that was general and precise." The language of Sarraut's program, presented to the Senate on 27 February 1920 and elaborated three years later in *La mise en valeur des colonies françaises,* provides an eloquent synthesis of the colonial myth as it had developed up to that time.

The wartime experience had underscored the importance of the colonies to the nation and had transformed their role from remote, exotic appendages to areas of vital national concern. Colonial policy likewise became "a national idea, creating a new spirit that discerned more clearly the ineluctable incorporation of that immense colonial life into French life." Colonial troops had defended France and would continue to be needed both to compensate for the demographic consequences of the war and to permit the reduction of military service to eighteen months. "From now on, [France] owes her security to those colonies." [6] Thanks to the colonies, France could escape the financial consequences of dependency on other states for raw materials. Even French diplomacy had come to depend on the strategic advantages assured by the colonies.

But in Sarraut's view it was not the narrow national interest that inspired the policy as much as it was a broad moral and political imperative. Both in his early study and even more explicitly in *Grandeur et servitude coloniales,* Sarraut developed two key themes that he saw as not only justifying modern colonialism but also guiding its scientific development: the need for rational exploitation of the world's natural resources for the greatest good of all and the dangers for European civilization stemming from colonial nationalism. "The profound shudders that are running, in swelling, unseen waves through the immense flood of the colored races, marking the new awakening of aspirations . . . may again bring together the old fanaticisms, the nationalisms, or the mysticisms against the enlightenment that has come from the Occident." [7]

The arguments surrounding the creation of the League of Nations had made it clear, in Jean Morel's phrase, "that colonial questions had ceased to belong to purely national policy." This meant that the economic future of the colonies must be determined with a view not only to the interests of France, but with regard for the universal economic interest of the whole world. That interest, as Sarraut described it, lay in overcoming the gross inequalities that characterized the distribution of natural resources. Europe had most of the capital, the organizational skills, the intellectual and physical strength, but the raw materials were concentrated in the more backward, uncivilized parts of the world where they could not be used effectively. Hence, all the industrialized states were looking toward the virgin lands of Asia and Africa, and it was in the interest of them all that this common fund of resources be exploited for their mutual benefit.

No state had a right to allow its fertile soils to lie fallow indefinitely, and a world in need of raw materials placed certain obligations on the colonial powers. "Under these conditions, should a colonial power be able to hold immense areas of territory out of cultivation, mines without exploitation or waterways unimproved? Is her economic sovereignty totally unlimited by the rights of all and the general utility?" The clear implication was that France had a moral duty to promote economic growth for the common good. The old rationale for colonies, the right of conquest, had been replaced by a new justification, "the right of the strong to protect the weaker. The France that colonizes does not work for herself alone, her advantage is inseparable from that of the world." [8]

This disinterested humanitarian aspect of French colonialism, according to Sarraut, becomes more explicit when viewed against the backdrop of changing international power relations. No longer, he warned, were the world conflicts going to be resolved by the balancing of European states that for centuries had shaped the lives of other races and peoples all over the earth. Sarraut foresaw a day when Europe would find itself under pressure from the very peoples whom it had awakened from centuries of cultural stagnation and isolation. These views, developed at greater length in the 1930s, reflected a theory of the growth and decline of civilizations. Europe, and France in particular, was seen as the source of inspiration for the countries of Asia and Africa. These new states were expanding the ideas and techniques received from their colonial rulers and were threatening to turn them against Europe. By 1931 Sarraut had become convinced that what lay ahead for Europe was nothing less than the decline of its civilization in the face of the rising power of the outlying regions of America and Asia. "The illustrious cradle of everything that was *quality,* Europe feels the heavy menace of *quantity,* the great masses, the huge numbers, weighing upon her life as upon her spirit." [9] It was European colonialism that unleashed these great new forces and armed them, and it was up to French statesmen to conduct colonial policy in a way that would create confidence and order among the native races.

France was in a particularly advantageous position to carry out this responsibility, Sarraut argued, because of "the high and generous moral disciplines that make up her tradition of altruism." According to Sarraut's conception of modern colonialism, the colonies were considered not as areas to be exploited, but as integral parts [*parties solidaires*] . . . of the French state which, through scientific, economic, moral, and political progress, are going to be encouraged to accede to the highest destinies, on the same basis as the other parts of the national territory. . . .

French colonial policy sees in our protected peoples, whatever the color of their skin, however retarded their evolution, *men* and not an anonymous and servile mass; souls, not herds of slaves [*troupeaux d'ergastule*] or "fiscal sponges." France does not oppress, she liberates; she does not exhaust, she enriches; she does not exploit, she shares. If she comes in search of merchandise or outlets, she brings in return—to populations too often given over to barbarism, to misery, to the slavers' whips or to the caprices of bloody despots, to anarchies of every sort—order, security, health, education, justice, the hope of a better future, with the added advantage of new resources, which the genius of the civilizer makes spring from the still virgin soil for the common profit of the protector and the protected.

This policy . . . surrounds and protects the unarmed individual with the formal guarantees of the law. It affirms not only the rights of the colonizing nation, but its duties, and inscribes them in the very first rank. Better still, depending on their level of ability, it wants to associate the protected peoples with this civilizing effort, calling them progressively to manage their country, to fit them by education for that collaboration and, sharing with them the responsibilities as well as the benefits, to raise their awareness little by little, awakened and transformed into the clear sense of their duties, of the obligations that they contract toward us for the increase, the preservation, and the common defense of the common patrimony. From such clay it shapes the primitive multitudes; it models the face of a new humanity.[10]

Here in outline was the radical version of the colonial myth in its entirety. Humanitarian, in the sense that it was founded on the assumption of a universal human nature common to all people, it recognized the need for equality but imagined that equality could exist only among individual men and not among groups. It was libertarian to the extent that liberty meant individual freedom from the crude forms of physical deprivation whether imposed by the forces of nature or by the selfishness of men. It was libertarian also in the degree that freedom was seen to be the product of legal safeguards, to which the individual consented, if only tacitly, thus forming a contractual relationship with his protectors, which in turn imposed both rights and duties on both parties. It was utilitarian in the obvious sense that both the colonizers and the colonized benefited from the relationship, but it was also utilitarian in the more general sense that all of humanity could be regarded as benefiting from the more rational utilization of the "common fund" of world resources that resulted from the combination of European scientific technology and the unused resources of the colonial territories. Finally, this version of the colonial myth was progressive in that it made a clear distinction between the advanced civilizations of Europe and the backward peoples of Africa and Asia and viewed the contact between the two as the best means of raising the colonial peoples to the level of modernization where they would become capable of functioning effectively in the framework of European culture.

This entire system of thought was colored by the philosophical outlook of Comtian positivism, which barely concealed its paternalistic spirit. To a people hypnotized by the beauty of their own principles and inspired by the material achievements of their society, French culture had become synonymous with "civilization" and an object of universal value. The colonial peoples appeared to them as primitive savages toward whom France had a moral obligation to provide both the benefits of its culture and the means for material progress. The fact that France was a democratic state only increased the obligation to see that republican principles were applied abroad as well as at home.

The introduction of democratic institutions in the colonies was not, however, understood to mean the extension of political liberties whether by wholesale naturalizations or by recognizing the autonomy of particular colonies. Naturalization, Sarraut objected, would create opposition by disrupting local civil laws. The extension of political rights would produce chaos in a society that lacked the knowledge to use them.

> Can you see a mass of people in a black or yellow electoral campaign, blindly delivered into the hands of some agitators or some witch doctors, if not some administrators, minor civil servants, mandarins, chiefs, or petty kings of one race or another who could dispose of their votes by an order, just as one assigns the population

> of an entire village or a province to work on the roads, canals, or dikes?
>
> A government worthy of the name could not support a measure that would give over political power in one bloc into the hands of a crowd that is incapable of using it rationally and which, from the very first attempt, would break the instrument that it was given, just as a clumsy child breaks a toy. The protecting state could not favor such a more or less concealed abdication of its sovereignty; that is, the moral superiority of the "sovereign," the force for good, for progress, for science, for order, for civilization that it represents because it brings them to others. To abdicate this force into hands that are ignorant, debilitated, or inexperienced would be to decree a halt to civilization, an end to the benefits that it guarantees, anarchy, and the return of the masses in our trust to their former state of servitude.[11]

Reforms were needed, but there was no question that France must remain in firm control and that whatever changes might be contemplated at the local level were not expected to lead to the creation of politically independent communities. Decentralized administration was necessary, and an end to legislative assimilation was proposed that would leave the local authorities free to act in accord with the needs of the local populations as they saw them. The objective, however, remained unchanged—to tie the colonies closely to the metropole. "Colonial *autonomy* as envisaged above, is neither a synonym for nor a path toward independence. It neither signifies nor prepares the way for any rupture or any relaxation of the ties of solidarity that unite the colonies to the metropole." [12]

The Socialist Opposition

World War I may be said to have put to rest the last reservations that attached to the radical version of the colonial myth, although radical governments continued to press for reforms in administration throughout the interwar period. It did not still the opposition of the socialists to colonialism; however, as the several socialist groups began to assume a larger share of the responsibilities of government, their views also evolved. The socialists, as a general rule, were more critical of colonialism than the radicals and tended to pay much more attention to the specific effects of colonial rule than to abstract generalizations about security and national grandeur.

The pre-Marxist and anti-Marxist socialists denounced the privileges that colonial rule bestowed upon a favored economic elite in the colonies and the metropole and attacked the violence of colonial expansion, but they did not attack the legitimacy of colonialism as such, nor did they advocate disposing of the colonies that already existed. Their attitude regarding reform of the colonial administration was often ambivalent and was always subordinated in practice to the requirements of coalition strategy within deeply divided governments, especially during the Popular Front. The Marxist socialists, while perfectly outspoken in their condemnation of the basic principle of colonial rule, were nevertheless quite cautious in handling the specific colonial issues that frequently cut across their other domestic and international political and ideological commitments.

Socialist thought about colonial questions evolved during the nineteenth century in response to two major factors: (1) the interaction of humanitarian ideas drawn from the Revolution with the experience of a major industrial society and (2) the long struggle against the political movement of revolutionary socialism that grew up around Marxism.

Colonialism played an important role in the thought of utopian socialists of the Saint-Simonian tradition. They welcomed the advent of industrial society as opening the way to a new, universal form of life in which technology made possible the rational exploitation of nature in the general interest of all humanity. By bringing all people regardless of race or background into contact with European culture, expansion of colonial rule opened the way to progress. Moreover, it did so in a manner that tended to minimize violence, at least when it was properly carried out by people with good intentions.

The industrial revolution was seen as the beginning of what Enfantin termed "the era of universal politics," during which Europeans were in contact with Africans, and Asians and Christians with Muslims. Both the complexity of the new era and the frequency of relations among peoples created the need for "a vast plan of civilization," which was to be developed in the colonies. Within this context the socialists had supported the colonization of Algeria in the 1840s, arguing that, in Enfantin's words: "The colonization of Algeria . . . is the achievement of labor, of culture, of industry—the work of civilization—which by itself will be the prelude to the organization of labor in France. . . . Thus it is colonization of the province of Constantine that I consider as the normal school where we may form the real organizers of labor in France." [13]

On a larger scale, colonialism permitted the rational development of the world's natural resources. Most of the important resources lay outside the industrialized countries of Western Europe in the colonies, whose economic development, as Fourier explained in his *Théorie de l'unité universelle,* might lead the way to a total restructuring of national and international relations. A similar vision of a new universal system of politics growing out of colonial experiences was present in the work of Etienne Cabet. His allegorical work *Voyage en Icarie* emphasized the pacific nature of colonial development once it was elaborated in a systematic manner. "Our good deeds have peacefully conquered a whole new Icaria for us and for the savages—for civilization—all while preparing the conquest of the wilderness universe for humanity." [14]

Even Proudhon, who consistently opposed colonial expansion, protested against any abandonment of Algeria in the 1840s, and seems to have held serious reservations about the consequences of ending colonial rule at a later period. He foresaw decolonization coming about as part of a revolutionary change in political organization aimed at the disappearance of the nation-state, which Proudhon and his followers viewed as an obstacle to the development of socialism. Nation-states and colonial empires, particularly the British Empire, would be replaced by loose associations made up of many human groups gathered together in a very loose "federalism." [15] All these schemes reflected the efforts of intellectuals to resolve social issues by elaborating a formula for political change that could reconcile their humanitarian impulses with the technological power of highly developed industrial societies.

Many of the same themes are evident in the thinking of Jean Jaurès, the leader of the French Socialist party after 1905 and a strong critic of colonial expansion during the prewar period. Jaurès did not present anything like a precise doctrine of anticolonialism, and it is obvious from his speeches and other writings that his thought underwent considerable change, especially after 1905 as the socialists began to exert their influence in Parliament. Jaurès perceived the beginnings of national self-consciousness in the colonies and in the non-Western world in general, and he opposed the attempts of European states to impose their domination by force. He did not oppose colonial rule in principle, however, so long as it was peaceful and did not serve narrow private economic interests. Liberty, rather than the progress of socialism, seems to have been the goal that inspired his opposition to the occupation of Morocco.

> I say that there, among all those peoples for so long oppressed or asleep—or separated from Europe by oceans of indifference—I say that everywhere there are new moral forces awakening: an appetite for liberty; an appetite for independence; a sense of right which they borrow our own formulas in order to express. . . . No! The action must not be taken [by violence]. What is needed is the creation of a new order by new methods.[16]

The conviction that colonial conflict would lead to international violence led Jaurès to condemn the trading of colonies as counters in international diplomacy. Employing language very similar to that later used by Woodrow Wilson, he argued that colonial lands "furnish the materials for combinations, for compensatory robberies, shifting thieveries, and the transmission and exchange of violence and falsehoods. This bottomless abyss will swallow up the resources, the real honor, and the conscience of the people." In the context of the Moroccan crisis of 1912 Jaurès proposed that an international consortium "dominated by the disinterested great powers" be created to assure "controlled development" and to replace the traditional balance of power.[17]

The majority of French socialists, like Jaurès, accepted the existence of colonies and devoted their attention to the encouragement of economic and social development, the introduction of administrative reforms aimed at protecting human rights, the construction of more democratic political institutions, and the promotion of better planning for colonial development. Given their humanitarian orientation and the complexity of the social and economic problems to be confronted, it is not surprising that they frequently shifted their colonial policies. Particularly during the 1930s, when they were faced with the pressure of Nazi and Bolshevik versions of socialism, French socialists tended to expand their democratic socialism into a secular religion, which provided a total framework of thought. So broad were its limits and so varied its concerns that colonialism was simply absorbed into the idea of socialism as a fundamental transformation of all social relations. The following observation by Léon Blum indicates how abstract socialism had become by 1945:

> The revolutionary objective is not only to liberate man from economic and social exploitation and from all the secondary and accessory servitudes which that exploitation involves. But also, it is to assure him the full exercise of his fundamental rights and his full personal vocation in the collective society. I believe that the revolutionary objective is to establish a harmony between that social unit that is the person and that social whole which will be collective society.[18]

The central concern with individualism evidenced by Blum's statement also explains the characteristic weakness of the socialist version of the colonial myth. It perceived the dangers and destructiveness of colonial expansion but as solutions could envision only exemplary programs that were expected to inspire emulation by all right-thinking persons. Uncertain whether the ultimate goal was liberty for individuals or groups, the socialists accepted colonial rule as an interim measure that would minimize the dangers of war, limit capitalist exploitation, and encourage international economic and social cooperation. Generally optimistic about the future contribution of international organizations, they saw no alternative to preserving French control over the colonies so long as such organizations did not in fact exist. They consistently urged that such controls be made more humanitarian, primarily by extending to the colonies the progressive social legislation developed in the metropole.

The Communist Viewpoint

The non-Marxist socialists can thus be seen to reflect a mixture of doctrines, many of which seem to reflect temporary political considerations, notably the rise of a strong procolonial spirit among the parties of the Right in the 1890s and the necessity of tailoring colonial policies to the prospect of governmental participation during the interwar years. Both their doctrinal ambiguities and their political uncertainty left the socialists open to violent attacks from the Marxists during the nineteenth century. Following the Congress of Tours in 1921 the Marxist-Leninist faction, which had split off from the SFIO (Section Française de l'International Ouvrière) to form the French Communist Party (PCF), launched its own attack on colonial problems both within France and in the Communist International.

Marx paid considerable attention to colonialism both in *Das Kapital* and in his shorter writings, particularly those dealing with British policy in India, which were published in the New York *Daily Tribune*.[19] His condemnation of colonial rule was unequivocal: colonies formed part of the system of capitalist exploitation to whose development they had contributed and with whose decay they were bound to disappear. In *Das Kapital* Marx pointed to the slave trade, the theft of gold and silver, and the resulting mercantile wars of the sixteenth and seventeenth centuries as characteristic forms of "the idyllic process of primitive accumulation" and important formative influences in the emergence of the bourgeois capitalist state. But the colonies, like the state itself, were simply part of the political superstructure thrown up by the dominant class in an effort to protect its power. Hence, Marx rejected colonial rule not on humanitarian grounds, because it caused suffering, but because it was part of a total system of exploitation aimed at extracting unjust profits from the colonial countries for the benefit of an alien class.

The world was being cut up into protective zones by the capitalists, and the capitalist system was integrating the colonies into a framework of economic relations that contained inner contradictions. But did colonialism really pay, or was it, as Adam Smith and the liberal economists had argued, an infringement on free circulation of goods and therefore an uneconomic allocation of resources? Marx never answered this question satisfactorily. He recognized that on strictly economic grounds, the profits tend to be less than the costs. However, since the costs are borne by the taxpayer, while the profits accumulate to the private capitalist, the imbalance between private and public interest is real even though it may not be apparent. He did not carry out this line of argument to inquire whether there are other costs, either strategic or political, that might under some circumstances justify colonial rule, as the later liberal theorists had concluded.

If colonies were part of the larger process of capitalist exploitation, they nevertheless remained always a subordinate aspect of the system. Marx clearly was convinced that it was the economic development of the most advanced capitalist states that was going to produce the next stage of the revolutionary movement. The colonial actions of these states were peripheral to the fundamental process of economic and social change that controlled the development of the revolution, but they had important consequences for that development. Marx's dialectical view of history led him to conclude that the colonial powers were playing a necessary role in breaking up the old, feudal, preindustrial societies of Africa and Asia much as the capitalist bourgeoisie had disrupted the feudal aristocracies within Europe, opening the way for change and eventually for socialism. Thus, in 1853, he wrote that British policy in India, "the Ireland of the East," had produced "the greatest, and to speak the truth, the only *social* revolution in Asia." Colonialism, although evil in principal, was seen as historically necessary, since Marx and Engels shared none of the illusions of Fourier, Lassalle, or the eighteenth-century utopians about the nature of traditional village life:

> We must not forget that these idyllic village communities [of Asia], inoffensive though they may appear, had always been the solid foundation of Oriental despotism, that they restrained the human mind within the smallest possible compass, making it the unresisting tool of superstition, enslaving it beneath traditional rules, depriving it of all grandeur. . . .
>
> England, it is true, in causing a social revolution in Hindustan, was actuated only by the vilest interests and was stupid in her manner of enforcing them. But that is not the question. The question is, Can mankind fulfill its destiny without a fundamental revolution in the social state of Asia? If not, whatever may have been the crimes of England, she was the unconscious tool of history in bringing about that revolution.[20]

Marx also rejected the radical utopia embodied in the notion of a civilizing mission based on the extension of democratic institutions and motivated by humanitarian concern. He saw in such notions nothing but a self-serving ideology that concealed exploitation. To understand that colonialism is a necessary stage of history does not justify it, but it does explain it and indicates that colonialism is not an absolute evil. But this view also created serious tactical problems for Marxist socialist movements. The imposition of colonial rule tended to produce nationalist reactions from local elites, of which most were feudal in character, a few bourgeois, but none socialist.

How then were the socialists to conduct themselves with respect to these potentially revolutionary forces?

Engels, although clearly aware of the rise of national self-consciousness in colonial territories such as Egypt, Algeria, and the Dutch and Spanish possessions, urged caution in dealing with the new elites. With the French clearly in mind, he wrote to the German socialist Eduard Bernstein:

> We Western Europeans should not be so easily led astray as . . . the Romanic people. Strange. All the Romanic revolutionaries complain that all the revolutions they have made were always for the benefit of other people. This is easily explained: it is because they were always taken in by the word "revolution." . . . I think that we can well be on the side of the oppressed fellahs without sharing the illusions they nurture at the time (a peasant people just has to be hoodwinked for centuries before it becomes aware of [its status] from experience).[21]

Part of the difficulty stemmed from the conviction that revolution was a European export. As Demetrio Boersner has shown: "The idea that the bourgeois-national revolution of the colonies might actually precede the establishment of socialism in Europe never occurred to Engels. The victorious European proletariat would have the task of taking over the administration of the colonies and of leading them to independence as swiftly as possible." [22] Another tactical problem, however, stemmed from the great difficulty in anticipating the consequences of supporting any particular nationalist movement. Marx's own writings illustrate but do not resolve the problem. As a means toward the eventual triumph of socialism, he supported nationalist movements led by bourgeois groups in Poland, Austria-Hungary, and Ireland, whose success would weaken the feudal monarchies of Russia and Austria-Hungary or the bourgeois regime of Britain. He opposed the Czech and Serbian nationalist movements because their victory promised no such advantages. Where the alternatives were less clear, the proper course of action became more uncertain and the role of the socialists more ambiguous.

This tactical concern for nationalism clearly contradicted the more overtly rationalistic proposals of some French socialists for transcending the entire nation-state system. In a scathing denunciation of Proudhon, which nevertheless grasped the unconscious assimilationist tendency of French socialism, Marx asserted:

> The Proudhon clique among the students in Paris [*Courrier Français*] preaches peace, declares war to be antiquated, nationalisms to be nonsense, attacks Bismarck and Garibaldi, and so on. As polemics against chauvinism their doings are useful and explainable. But as believers in Proudhon (my good friends Lafargue and Longuet also belong to them), who think that the whole of Europe should and would sit peacefully on its ass until the gentlemen in France have abolished "*la misère et l'ignorance,*" . . . they become ridiculous. . . .
>
> The Proudhonists propose to dissolve everything into small "groupes" or "communes," which are to form an "association," but not a state. And this "individualization" of mankind with its corresponding "mutualism" is to proceed while history comes to a stop and the whole world waits until the French are ripe for a social revolution. They will then perform the experiment before our eyes, and the rest of the world, overcome by the force of their example, will do the same. Exactly what Fourier expected of his *phalanstère modèle*. . . .
>
> The English laughed very much when I began my speech by stating that our friend Lafargue, etc., who has abolished nationalities, had addressed us in *French!* that is, in a language nine-tenths of the audience did not understand. I furthermore suggested that by the negation of nationalities he quite unconsciously seemed to imply their absorption into the French model nation.[23]

For a time Jaurès was able to bridge the gap between the Marxists and the other factions of the French socialist movement. Largely by the force of his own personality and by his ability to find formulas that were sufficiently ambiguous to be acceptable to almost every faction, he was able to shape the Socialist party into a working political organization. Outside of France, within the international socialist movement, the French were in the minority, and the conflict between the Marxist and non-Marxist factions of the SFIO grew intense as the German socialists joined with the French Marxists to dominate the Second International. At the Stuttgart Congress of 1907 the radical faction, led by Karl Kautsky and supported by Frenchmen like Bracke and LaPorte, took the position that colonialism was equivalent to exploitation and that the task of socialists was to liberate the toiling masses of the colonial countries. They echoed the arguments set forth in 1902 by the Englishman J. A. Hobson and in 1905 by

Paul Louis whose short study *Le Colonialisme* condemned colonialism on economic and political grounds. They argued that the benefits of colonies go entirely to the bourgeoisie, while the high costs are borne by the workers, who pay the taxes. Moreover, colonial development is inefficient, since it leads to overproduction and economic dislocation. Worst of all, colonialism carries with it the risk of international conflict and the twin dangers of foreign war and militarism at home.

The moderate faction in the Stuttgart Congress sought the adoption of a resolution declaring that "the Congress does not reject on principle and for all time every colonial policy, which under a socialist regime could have a civilizing effect." Instead, they condemned the use of force and called on all socialist parties to work for the adoption of administrative reforms.

> To this purpose, they are to advocate reforms to improve the lot of the natives . . . and they are to educate them for independence by all possible means.
>
> To this purpose, the representatives of the socialist parties should propose to their governments to conclude an international treaty, to create a colonial law, which shall protect the rights of natives.[24]

This was the view adopted by most French socialists, including Jaurès, but it failed to carry the majority of the International, which adopted the position set forth in 1916 by Lenin in his pamphlet *Imperialism.* In that work Lenin stressed the intimate relationship between the struggle of the European working class to free itself from capitalist domination and the parallel efforts of the colonial peoples to escape from exploitation. The conception of colonialism as the weakest link in the capitalist system reversed Marx's priorities and led to the conclusion that revolution in the nonindustrialized areas of the world, by depriving the capitalist states of their special privileges, could aggravate the crisis of capitalism in Europe and speed up the revolution there.

Following the Russian Revolution in 1917, these principles were introduced into the policies of the Soviet Communist party in relation to the national minorities within the Soviet Union. At the same time the conception described by Stalin in *Marxism and the National and Colonial Question* of an alliance between the proletarian movement in the industrialized countries and the nationalist movements in the colonial areas became the operative principle of the Communist International. As the prospects for revolution in Europe faded during the 1920s, the Comintern encouraged the communist parties of the developed countries to assist all colonial nationalist movements. Support was urged regardless of the class composition of such movements wherever they were engaged in struggles for independence that "objectively" weakened the imperialist states. This idea of a united front was spelled out in detail at the Sixth Comintern Congress in 1928, where it soon became evident that a new element had entered the picture.

The congress, after reasserting the validity of Stalin's thesis on the national and colonial question noted that

> the establishment of a fighting front between the active forces of the socialist world revolution (the Soviet Union and the revolutionary labour movement in the capitalist countries) on one side and between the forces of imperialism on the other, is of decisive importance in this epoch of world history. The labouring masses of the colonies, struggling against imperialist slavery, represent a most powerful auxiliary force of the socialist world revolution. The colonial countries are the most dangerous sector of the imperialist front. The revolutionary liberation movements of the colonies and semi-colonies are rallying to the banner of the Soviet Union, convinced by bitter experience that there is no salvation for them except in alliance with the revolutionary proletariat.[25]

The French Communist party was specifically instructed by the Comintern to "bring together the genuinely revolutionary elements" of the trade unions and other mass organizations in North Africa "into a fighting bloc of workers and peasants," based on "ever closer cooperation between the revolutionary sections of the white proletariat and the native working class." Within each country the parties must "attract into their ranks in the first place native workers . . . and must formally and in fact become independent sections of the Communist International." In addition the communist parties of the imperialist countries were told that their task was threefold: to establish "lively connections" with the revolutionary movements in the colonies; to organize mass actions in support of colonial nationalist movements; and to struggle against the colonial policy of social-democracy which "has officially adopted the point of view . . . according to which the ruling classes of the developed capitalist countries have the "right" to rule over the majority of the peoples of the globe and to subject these peoples to a frightful regime of exploitation and enslavement." [26] Clearly, in the future, the colonial policies of the French Communist party would have to respond to three quite distinct imperatives: the prospects for gaining power within France; the status of the nationalist movements in the colonies; and the demands of the Communist International, which reflected primarily the interests of the groups competing for power within the Soviet Communist party.

A thorough analysis of the colonial policies of the PCF has not yet been written.[27] The broad lines of its activities, limited as they were during the interwar period by a multitude of other more pressing concerns, emerge quite clearly from the published statements of party policy and the scattered references in the party histories. During the period from 1921 to 1924, when the possibility of a general European revolution seemed good, there was little incentive to pay more than formal attention to colonial questions. From 1925 to 1935 the PCF, despite serious internal divisions, followed a "Leninist policy of struggle against colonialism." It opposed the use of force against Abd-el-Krim in Morocco in 1925 and called for recognition of the Moroccan nationalists as the "Rif Republic." For this the party was congratulated by the Executive Committee of the Communist International at its seventh enlarged plenum: "The party conducted a brilliant campaign against the Moroccan war. For the first time in France, it has applied the principle and tactic of the struggle against imperialist war." However, it had failed to organize North African workers in France, and in response to criticism from the Comintern it established a colonial bureau in 1926.[28] Later during this period it also supported the Djebel Druzes uprising in Syria.

Following Hitler's rise to power the Soviet Union and the communist world adopted the new line of a "popular front against fascism," with the result that PCF activity veered away from rigorous anticolonialism. After the Laval-Stalin understanding of 1935 colonial questions were forgotten as the PCF joined the movement for a Popular Front government in the hope of gaining power legally in France. The program of the Popular Front was very discreet about colonial questions. During the period of the Nazi-Soviet Pact the party returned to the anticolonial posture, urging the colonial peoples "to seize upon the opportunity afforded them by the present difficulties of their oppressors" to gain their freedom.[29] This position lasted only until the German invasion of the Soviet Union on 22 June 1941; after that there were no more calls to the Algerian people to revolt and no more references to "oppressed colonial masses." Instead, the communists, having become anti-Nazi, discovered in the colonies important strategic positions to be defended from the Axis.

The communist version of the colonial myth that emerges from these doctrines and experiences is significantly different from the versions expounded by other French parties in that the communists did envision colonial independence as a desirable goal, and they did unequivocally condemn the colonial system in principle. However, independence was never an end in itself for the communists, and the ultimate objective of an integrated socialist society led by the communist parties of the advanced industrial states always held out the possibility that the revolution would come more quickly to the colonies if they remained closely associated with France. This latter possibility became a virtual certainty once the Communist party found itself on the verge of assuming power within the metropole in 1945.

The Resurgence of Nationalism

The interwar years were for France a period of increasing political demoralization. Conflicts between extremist groups on the Right and Left combined with rapidly changing ministries and arbitrary violence on the part of the executive to generate dangerous clashes, like that of 6 February 1934, that progressively undermined the authority of the republic. More serious for colonial affairs, however, were a number of changes that damaged France's international position.

As a result of the slow disintegration of the peace settlement, the sense of security from foreign attack disappeared, and in its place there developed a frenzied search for substitutes, first in the League of Nations and later in an alliance with Britain. With the quest for security, interest in the colonies revived, heightened further by the attempts of Germany and Italy to reassert colonial claims. At the same time the rise of nationalist movements in the colonies and the activities of the League of Nations in promoting the ideal of national self-determination inspired a new wariness about the future of

France's colonial empire. Taken together, all four of these developments called forth a considerable effort on the part of colonial specialists and interested political leaders to reassess the role of the colonies and to speculate on means for consolidating the unity of France and the colonies. Only a few of the suggestions advanced were acted upon during the short-lived Popular Front government, and most were blotted out by the rising threat of war.

As a reaction to her enduring fear of a resurgent Germany and in response to the British and American refusal to guarantee the rigorous enforcement of the Versailles settlement, France adopted an attitude of nationalistic self-assertiveness in foreign affairs. Acting on the basis of her temporary military advantage, she developed a system of alliances aimed at isolating Germany and sought to impose on Germany a strict interpretation of the Versailles treaty. The failure of the Ruhr occupation in 1923 weakened French prestige, however, and seemed to demonstrate France's incapacity to pursue an independent foreign policy without either the support of Britain or the acquiescence of Germany. The subsequent failure during the "Locarno period" of Briand's efforts to restore Franco-German relations and to encourage multilateral diplomacy, was followed by a new upsurge of nationalistic feelings in the late 1920s and the early 1930s. The rise to power of Mussolini in Italy and of Hitler in Germany and the intervention of the Fascist powers in Ethiopia and later in the Spanish civil war, all added fuel to the fires of French nationalism. Colonial affairs remained secondary concerns, but the framework within which they were considered was shaped by the nationalist spirit of the period.

German and Italian policy made much of colonial claims. The Versailles settlement had deprived Germany of her colonies, but in distributing them among the Allies, the peace conference failed to fulfill the expectations of the Italians, whose wartime agreements with the Allied powers—especially the Treaty of London (1915), which guaranteed Italy compensation for possible Allied colonial gains in Africa—seemed to have been ignored.[30] Italian demands for protection of her citizens in Tunisia and for control over Eritrea, Libya, and Abyssinia, together with German demands for the restoration of her former colony in the Cameroons, remained important, if secondary, causes of the international rivalries that marked the period between the wars. Franco-German and Franco-British antagonism in the Levant gave rise to further concern that the Fascist powers might succeed in undermining the equilibrium in the Mediterranean. In each of these international colonial conflicts, voices were heard on both extremes of the Chamber denouncing, as the case may be, either the thoughtless transfer of subject populations like pawns in a heartless struggle or the surrender of traditional interests, rights, and especially security. It was security, both military and economic, that became the central issue in all these cases; colonial development never received attention on its own merits.[31]

The merits of colonial rule were the focus of attention of a number of groups connected with the League of Nations. In spite of its political and administrative limitations, the League had a special symbolic importance for the colonial peoples, as it did for the small states in general. The League Covenant inscribed the principle of international responsibility for the well-being and development of colonial populations in a document of major international importance, thereby giving stature and encouragement to the small, Westernized elite in those countries who were seeking to advance the cause of national independence.

Moreover, apart from its formal activities, the League provided a focus for the efforts of small groups of writers and scholars in the Western countries who began to cooperate through organizations like the International Institute of Intellectual Cooperation (IIIC) in studying aspects of peaceful change, including colonial questions.[32] Some of the specialized agencies that grew up around the League of Nations, such as the International Labor Office, which in 1927 established the Committee on Native Labor; the League Health Organization; and other bodies dealing with traffic in arms, traffic in women and children, traffic in opium, and even disarmament, occasionally concerned themselves with conditions in the colonial countries. The activities of these agencies were not confined to the mandates; they encompassed all colonial territories and taken together they called attention to the importance of developments in the non-self-governing areas.

It was not the League of Nations alone, however, that encouraged the growth of nationalism in the colonies. The ideals of the Revolution of 1789, which were propagated as part of the colonizing mission of France, were the same slogans that had found enthusiastic support in Western Europe, the Austro-Hungarian Empire, Russia, and much of the Far East during the nineteenth century. These revolutionary, egalitarian, and humanitarian principles were no less attractive to the peoples of the colonial states than they had been in other countries. Because of the economic backwardness of the colonies, however, nationalism grew slowly, and at the end of World War I it attracted little notice in French political and intellectual circles. When remarked, it was often welcomed as evidence that traditional native institutions, most of which were regarded as primitive and pagan, were disappearing in favor of "modern" institutions. Many expected that French national affinities would soon replace the attraction of divisive local traditions, thus creating one great democratic indivisible republic.

Two major stumbling blocks stood in the way of such a development, however—religion and repression. The resurgence of Islam during the nineteenth century and the ability of the Muslim peoples to resist Christianization encouraged them to reject not only French religion but French administration and politics as well. Since to acquire French citizenship a Muslim was required to abandon his rights under Koranic law and thus to reject his entire religious heritage and family tradition, the incentive to avoid assimilation was far stronger than the desire to gain political privileges. The periodic repression that followed nearly every effort of native groups to gain equal treatment with Europeans tended to reinforce this religious incentive to separatism. Then too, national unity was encouraged in the overseas territories, much as it was in central Europe under the Napoleonic Empire, by the obvious foreignness of the officials who brought its message. The resentment against foreign occupation was, of course, greatly magnified by the size of the European community and the distance that separated it in all matters from the natives. The French colonists, especially in North Africa, had secured for themselves comprehensive control of all the administrative machinery at the local level and were unwilling to countenance changes that would give an effective voice in local affairs to the much larger but more backward native populations. Even in the protectorates of Tunisia and Morocco it was impossible, as Julien indicates, for the government in Paris to impose its policy on the European colonists who controlled the local situation.[33] Against such regimes created and supported by French interests and virtually immune from any moderating influences, the nationalist movements began to organize.

Slowly, and in a variety of forms, nationalist movements, clubs, societies, and associations gathered supporters, conducted discussions, published newspapers, raised funds, and occasionally staged demonstrations. In Tunisia, for example, the Jeune Tunisien organization was formed before World War I by French-educated youths who were seeking equal treatment in economic and social matters. Embracing some of the spirit of the pan-Islamism of the nineteenth century and the pan-Arab feeling that accompanied it, the Tunisian movement became more explicitly political in the years after the war and joined with other groups to form the Destour party in February 1920. During March 1934, after having resisted such measures as the citizenship law and after resolving some internal disputes, the Destour was reorganized by Habib Bourguiba into a new, secular nationalist party, the Neo-Destour. It launched a massive campaign of political education, which was met with swift repression. The arrival in power of the Popular Front ended the penalties on the Neo-Destour in 1936, but the fall of the Blum cabinet brought renewed repression in 1937, and the opening of World War II left the nationalist movement at the mercy of French internal and international struggles.

In Morocco, in Algeria, in Indochina, and even in the relatively tranquil areas of West and Central Africa similar movements were underway. From the clubs of young Moroccan religious and intellectual leaders of the 1920s emerged the Comité d'Action Marocaine and, after a spate of repressions, the Istiqlal party. In Algeria, where nothing in the way of traditional political structures such as the Beylic and the Sultanate existed, nationalist sentiment took a less explicit form. Organized resistance to French administrative demands was supported, encouraged, and directed by groups like the Parti Jeune Algérien and the Paris-based movement Etoile Nord-Africaine, whose leaders, after having undergone a period of imprisonment and harassment, regrouped under the Parti du Peuple Algérien in a more explicitly political movement.

The nationalist movements of Indochina differed in their origins from those of North Africa and the Muslim world, but like the rest, they grew most vigorously during the interwar years. Although rivaled by traditionalist groups like the Hoa Hoa sect, whose xenophobic nationalism was an elitist rather than a mass movement, Nguyen-Ai-Quoc (later known as Ho Chi Minh) organized the International League against Colonialism at the time of the Paris Peace

Conference. Following a series of strikes led by supporters of Ho Chi Minh during the period of radical exhilaration that swept across the world in the wake of the Bolshevik Revolution, the nationalist movement was severely repressed. The Vietnam Nationalist party (Viet-Nam Quoc Dan Dang), founded in 1927, was the object of particular violence; many of its members were executed or forced into exile after an unsuccessful attempt on the life of Governor-General Pasquier and as a result of its part in the Yen Bay uprising in 1930. The amnesty granted by the Popular Front government in 1936 proved only temporary, and repression was resumed after its downfall. Therefore, when the Pacific war broke out, most of the nationalist leaders were in prison, and the movement continued to be harassed by the Vichy government administration and by the Japanese. Any nationalists who were able to do so escaped into China.

West and Central Africa presented still a different picture from either the Muslim areas or the territories like Indochina with ancient civilizations for which the people were seeking recognition. In Africa almost all political activity was inspired by groups following the example of the metropole. The political parties, especially the Socialist party, sought to develop local units based on the African elites who constituted the new social and political forces coming into existence in the growing towns. For the mass of Africans, however, political awareness developed very slowly and unevenly. National self-consciousness was hard to discover anywhere in West or Central Africa prior to the mid-thirties; and even then, as might be expected, it was concentrated in the older and more prosperous coastal colonies like Senegal, Guinée, and the Ivory Coast. There the political impact of social change was becoming evident in numerous religious movements, as well as in trade unions and in other educational and self-improvement societies. Typical of the messianic religious movements were Kimbanguism and Amicalism, both of which made a major impact during the 1930s in Equatorial Africa as passive resistance movements aimed at frustrating the forced labor system and opposing the administration. The Kakiste movement, founded by Simon Mpadi in 1941 and built around the "savior" Simon Kimbangou, was a more overtly political movement.[34] Indeed, it was this lack of explicitly political organizations in most of Africa that made it possible for so many Europeans to ignore the political awakening of Africa completely.

In retrospect at least, it is possible to discern a pattern that typified the rise of nationalism in the French colonies after World War I. Discontent bred by economic and social changes was met with administrative action that was more or less severely repressive. As nationalist groups formed, they were dissolved or forced into clandestine reorganization, from which they emerged again to conduct an increasingly explicit political resistance. During this process, however, it is noteworthy that the language of nationalist protest was borrowed for the most part from the socialist and radical vocabulary of French political struggle, and the organizational forms that emerged were more or less consciously those of French political parties. Sometimes, as in the case of the socialist parties, colonial nationalists assumed the form of overseas branches of metropolitan groups. Taken as a whole, these movements, although still in their infancy, represented a fundamental challenge to the traditional centralism of French colonial administration and a much more complex assault upon the paternalistic formalism of French political thought concerning the colonial empire.

Conflicting Attitudes toward the Colonies

During the 1930s conditions in many colonial areas appeared ripe for change. French leaders themselves had been instrumental in arousing great expectations for development through devices such as the monumental Colonial Exposition of 1931. Thereafter local elites waited ever more impatiently for effective action. The first year of the Popular Front government in 1936 seemed to promise at least partial fulfillment for these hopes, but the government's subsequent failure provoked bitter disillusionment among the nationalist movements, and reactions might have been far more serious had not the colonial crisis become submerged by the general disorder of those years.

While there was some complaining about "the disintegration of the empire," many writers showed great concern for the events taking place overseas and stressed the need to reassess the role of the colonial territories in a world that was changing much faster than anyone had thought possible.

It is convenient, as a means of assessing French efforts to confront colonial developments of the 1930s, to distinguish three somewhat different orientations that characterized the writing of that period. The first tended to view with interest the more liberal political forms of the British colonial specialists. The second point of view reflected the more limited experience of colonial administrators, who often appeared to see all colonial problems from the vantage point of the special difficulties encountered in the colonies where they had served longest. Finally, there were the spokesmen for various economic or ideological interests, and particularly for the European colonists in North Africa, who sought action by the metropole to secure or enhance their respective advantages. All three groups had in common, however, a more general interest in combating the increasingly pervasive sense of insecurity that gripped the nation by infusing a new confidence in the colonial accomplishments of the Third Republic and a new mood of national grandeur.

The resurgence of colonial fervor centered around the colossal Colonial Exposition of 1931. Inspired by respected leaders like Marshal Lyautey and encouraged by Albert Sarraut's vigorous polemic against "the spirit of sedition," [35] it produced a substantial wave of reaction against the tendency to depreciate the colonies, while it contributed a new set of illusions about the nature of colonial nationalist movements. In keeping with the general tenor of the exposition, it was the past accomplishments of France, not the problems of the future, that received most careful attention. Characteristic are the writings of Albert Duchêne, then director of political affairs in the Ministry of the Colonies, who reasserted the strategic value of the colonies while underscoring the virtues of a tight administrative structure. "The unity of our outlying empire . . . is the grandeur and the strength of France as was seen during the last war. Nowhere is France merely associated in one of those federations that are always fragile, those large countries, those 'dominions' that Great Britain only holds today by the thread of loyalty." [36]

Among intellectuals and academic specialists on colonial affairs other voices could be heard pleading for a clearer recognition of changing conditions and greater flexibility in both doctrines and institutions. The most important examples of this position were the works of Georges Hardy, whose *Géographie et colonisation* (1933) attempted to place colonial questions in the context of current international conflicts. Hardy's later study *Politique coloniale et le partage de la terre* (1937) stressed the great variation in institutional patterns that could be appropriate under different conditions.

The administrators reflected a much wider range of interests and opinions, but most sought to establish a general direction for French policy based on the conditions in the colonies where they had been active. Few of their works proposed truly comprehensive programs, and even less did they concern themselves with broad political problems, yet a number of these books represent important initiatives toward an empirical approach to the problems of political change. For example, A. R. Fontaine proposed an imaginative program for Indochina, which would have led to full autonomy on a basis akin to that developed earlier by the British as a means of extending self-government to the dominions. Under such a plan the metropole would retain control only over foreign and defense policy.

For Africa the ethnologist-administrator Henri Labouret proposed an extensive reform of the educational system that was intended to build upon indigenous institutions and to promote their development in the direction of a more effective modern state system. A similar need was indicated by Robert Delavignette, then a junior administrator, in a remarkable study, *Les Paysans noirs,* and later explored in several other valuable works. Citing the obvious effects of economic change on social and personal relations, Delavignette pleaded for flexibility in developing new institutions and for careful attention to local needs. "There exists a whole new African world," he wrote, "and it is we who have brought it into being." Yet it was also a world that in his view held serious dangers: "Watch out for racism, on the part of blacks or whites. It is capable even in Africa, of setting the black peoples against the universalism of the French." [37]

In other parts of the empire, however, there were those who sought to apply a system of "indirect rule," even at the risk of holding back further political development. A number of younger administrators protested against such policies on the ground that they would appear aimed at "keeping the colonies in infancy or even pushing them back into their Middle Ages or their prehistory. The colonial powers, perhaps without having wanted to do so, have undertaken to educate the retarded societies of this planet. Let us be good teachers and let us prepare good Europeans." [38]

The situation in Algeria was different in many important ways from conditions elsewhere in the French colonial world, and there the dream of establishing a single unified nation still held nearly total attention. Some of the problems that blocked its fulfillment were well appreciated by only a few, among them the noted sociologist René Maunier, who discussed the complex problems of culture change in his study *Sociologie coloniale,* which appeared in 1932.

It is perfectly clear that this doctrinal ferment did not amount to any systematic reexamination of French colonial relationships, nor did it produce any significant changes in colonial administration at the time. Descriptions of administrative practices and native life during the interwar period have shown that regimentation of native populations was, in fact, typical of the 1930s.[39] What this debate does demonstrate is that the stagnation of French policy in the interwar years was not the result of a lack of ideas or a deficiency of interest or enthusiasm. The colonial bureaucracy remained rigid, but it cannot be seriously accused of lacking imagination or an enterprising spirit, for many administrators as well as scholars and intellectuals were at least partly aware of the shortcomings of the system in which they were obliged to work, and a number of them were able to speak out vigorously on the need for change.

If their pleas were not heeded and if basic structures and doctrines were left unaltered, it was partly because of the fragmentary character of these criticisms; but more importantly, it was because none of the critics ever was able to conceive of the fundamental issue of France's relationship to the colonies in any other terms than those derived from a century or more of a tradition that excluded political separation as a legitimate goal of national policy. Regardless of their other differences, administrators, scholars, and intellectuals all approached the colonial issues of the thirties in the terms proper to the republican heritage—which by then included the conviction that the republic was multinational and indissoluble. The possibility of a contradiction existing between these two elements of the national mythology could not readily be admitted, especially at a time when antirepublican movements of both fascist and communist varieties were maintaining a steady barrage of criticism against the domestic institutions of republican government. Any proposal for change was greeted by the extreme Right as evidence of decadence and by the communists as proof of a desire to perpetuate bourgeois imperialism. Under such circumstances, it is little wonder that the goals of the status quo were usually maintained. The intellectuals were not the only ones, however, who suffered from such limited vision; those who exercised the power of political decision were even more acutely handicapped in their outlook and approach to colonial issues.

The general public remained unconcerned with the colonial world except in its most superficial, symbolic sense. But Parliament and especially the government held the real authority and the power to bring about change. That they did not do so reflects the influence within the Senate, the Chamber of Deputies, and especially in the government of the third group of spokesmen on colonial issues—the representatives of European colonial interests. It is not necessary for the purposes of the present study to undertake a detailed examination of the political struggles that underlay French policy during the 1930s. Neither is it useful to impute to the men involved any special cunning or villainy. It was their position within the National Assembly that gave them the power to make their views effective, and it was the unanimity with which they approached the problems of colonial relations that accounts for much of their success. Finally, it was their ability to appeal to a well-established mythology of French colonial relation, rich in the symbols of nationalism, patriotism, and humanitarianism, and closely connected to well-understood economic interests that assured their successful defense of the status quo.

The outlook and the power of these colonial interests can be seen clearly at many points, but especially in the parliamentary struggle that rendered vain the efforts of the Popular Front government to introduce a measure of social and political change into the colonies. Undoubtedly the most significant aspect of that program in the long run was the Blum-Violette plan, which would have permitted Algerian Muslims who were able to meet certain qualifications to vote on the same basis as French citizens but still to retain their civil rights as guaranteed under Koranic law. This proposal reflected the conviction of Maurice Violette, long a member of Parliament and for several years governor-general of Algeria, that the Algerian crisis was social and political rather than merely economic. The remedy he proposed was to associate the Algerian elite more closely with the European community by permitting them to exercise power jointly through elections that would be free from administrative intervention. This, he argued, was the only real alternative to continued economic dislocation, poverty, and misery for the masses of the Algerian people.[40]

Such a view was wholly unacceptable to the spokesmen for European interests in Algeria and ultimately to the majority in Parliament. With only minor differences of emphasis or tone they denounced the plan as "heresy." In their view the real problem was an economic crisis that had been exploited for subversive purposes through the propaganda of various foreign interests and supported by well-meaning but naïve dupes like Maurice Violette and other left-wing French intellectuals. The rise of Islam and the activities of nationalist groups like the Etoile Nord-Africaine were being supported from Moscow and Berlin in the hope of weakening France. They were convinced that the problem would be quickly resolved by economic aid and vigorous police measures to "restore the authority of France."

These same spokesmen, together with the parties of the Right in general, had viewed the triumph of the Popular Front in the elections of 1936 as a sign that the nation was in the greatest danger. The rejoicing among most Muslims, which had accompanied the electoral victory and their excitement following the introduction of the Blum-Violette bill in Parliament only convinced the rightists of their jeopardy.[41] They lost no time in portraying the entire Blum-Violette plan as an attack on the security of the state which should be vigorously repressed. It was not by argument, however, that the spokesmen for colonial interests succeeded in defeating the bill. Following the discussion of the plan and the adoption of its first paragraph by the Senate Committee on Universal Suffrage on 4 May 1938, all the deputies representing Algerian colonists, except for the Socialists, announced that they would resign if the bill were brought before the Chamber. Their action was followed by similar threats from the local government officials in Algeria at all levels—county councilors, municipal councilors, mayors, and their assistants. When the Chautemps cabinet resigned on 11 March 1938, these threats were withdrawn, but the Blum-Violette bill was never considered by Parliament.[42]

Many other issues of greater importance for the nation were in competition with the Blum-Violette bill for the attention of the Parliament, but its failure was a demonstration of two things: first, the inability of the government to overcome the passionate resistance of the Europeans in Algeria and, second, the continuing tendency for colonial problems to fall victim to the personal animosities and group interests that characterized French parliamentary politics. In the absence of firm leadership and faced with deep divisions on both sides of the Mediterranean, the status quo was left unchanged. The price that was paid, however difficult it was to measure, was great just the same; for the pro-French elite in Algeria was deeply disillusioned, while the European colonial interests had been severely threatened. The main profit in the end accrued to the Algerian nationalists who had either kept silent or opposed cooperation with France all along.

The accomplishments of the Popular Front were only slightly more lasting in other overseas territories. Some limited administrative decentralization was accomplished, and decrees were issued limiting working conditions for women and children, providing for the negotiation of collective bargaining agreements, and establishing procedures for dealing with labor disputes.[43] Most important, from a political standpoint, however, was the decision to permit the organization of trade unions by African workers and to abolish the practice of forced labor.[44]

In their total impact these reforms introduced by the Popular Front had only marginal effect at the time, yet they were of great importance in the long run. In a sense they opened the door to political organization for the peoples of Africa and encouraged the growth of a variety of political movements that were instrumental in bringing about the total independence of those colonies in the brief span of twenty-five years.

These possibilities were recognized at the time by the colonial community, but the actions of its spokesmen, such as Paul Saurin, the deputy from Oran, and the Comité de L'Afrique Française, only served to underscore their importance, not to defeat them. Thus, while not attacking the government directly, the Comité de L'Afrique Française repeatedly expressed concern lest the "principles of humanity" and the "liberations" that France had "sought to bring to the retarded peoples" might become the weapons of unscrupulous demagogues.[45]

The elections of 1936 had indeed brought France to a crossroads in colonial policy, as well as in many other aspects of internal life. And it became clear, if one looked carefully at the turmoil in the colonies and in the circle of colonial specialists, as well as in Parliament, that there were new formations of power taking shape and new issues of policy to be confronted. Within the colonies the commercial and financial interests were increasingly uneasy and defensive as they strove to protect their vested interests from harmful administrative reforms, such as the introduction of a labor code, and from political agitation among native workers. The indigenous political groups, on the other hand, were taking form rapidly, not only around trade unions, but around recognized political leaders and sometimes around charismatic religious figures. Finally, the colonial administration was undecided as to how best to proceed, and, while limited in its immediate actions by the existing procedures, was searching in various directions for more adequate institutional patterns and more coherent doctrines to guide future developments.

In Parliament, and in the metropole generally, opinion was deeply divided over international policy toward Germany, over internal economic conditions, and, most seriously, over the adequacy of the representative institutions of the Third Republic. After the crisis of 6 February 1934 the fissure between the extreme Right and the center Left grew in proportion as animosities mounted within Parliament. So that on the domestic political scene suspicion and distrust arising around the problems of social and economic policy as well as the increasingly serious threats to France's international security and the issues of military policy all combined to discourage any review of colonial administration or any consideration of new political arrangements for the colonies as a whole. In the face of mounting tension the preservation of the colonial status quo tended to become a primary goal of national policy admitting of no inquiry except where circumstances made it absolutely unavoidable. That this should be so becomes all the more readily understandable when one realizes that what was at stake in the colonial crisis was far more than an issue of policy; for in reality the future of the French colonies had become an integral part of the French political mythology and was intimately related to the self-image that French leaders had evolved.

3. THE GAULLIST COLONIAL OUTLOOK

One consequence of France's military defeat in 1940 was the attention it forced upon the problem of French colonial relationships, which had remained latent throughout the 1930s. The collapse of the French army in the metropole swept away many of the illusions of the interwar years, among them the comforting notion of a "greater France" whose combined resources in men and material were equal to those of France's aggressive neighbor across the Rhine. With the metropole disarmed and partly occupied, the unresolved question of France's relationship to the colonies became a matter of pressing national policy.

The official terminology depicted those areas as part of "overseas France," and some preferred the more pretentious label "the empire." But such terms concealed many differences in background and status among the colonies, protectorates, and mandates that had come to be regarded as legally constituting "greater France." Moreover, in June 1940 the precise meaning to be attributed to such terms was not an abstract exercise of formal legal logic. Depending on how one understood the relationship between France and the colonies, quite different patterns of national policy became conceivable. Conversely, depending upon what direction one felt France should take in order to save whatever could be salvaged from defeat, very different images of the relationship with the overseas areas became possible.

Those who were convinced that the most important aspect of the colonial relationship was the preservation of common sovereignty tended to draw the conclusion that the war should continue from the overseas territories regardless of the defeat suffered by the army in the metropole. On the other hand, those who considered the relationship with the colonies as one of colonial subordination to the interests of the metropole found it equally logical that the colonies should share the fate of metropolitan France and abide by the terms of the Armistice of 1940. General de Gaulle and those who later rallied to support the Free French movement vigorously defended the first assumption, while the elites who remained obedient to Marshal Pétain and the Vichy regime accepted the second.

Within the framework thus defined, both the Gaullists and the Vichy regime attempted to utilize the colonial traditions and achievements to support their respective efforts at reviving some semblance of the national identity during a period of nearly total disaster. While both factions necessarily worked within the same broad outlines of prewar colonial thought, each emphasized somewhat different elements of the republican tradition in their efforts to gain or hold the support of particular constituencies and to confront pressing issues of national policy under quite different circumstances. Each faction waged its struggle on three fronts: against the Axis; against its domestic opponents; and against France's allies, Britain and the United States, whose interests often seemed to conflict with her own. But each developed a distinctive strategy and outlook on colonial matters, even though they shared a common view that the colonies offered an invaluable means of regenerating France and restoring her to a position of greatness among the nations of the world.

The Vichy Regime

The Vichy regime bore the stigma of having negotiated the Armistice of 1940, which ended France's military role in World War II and subjected metropolitan France and the colonies to the exactions of the Nazi occupation. The French army had been overwhelmed by the speed and destructiveness of German military might. After concluding that France's allies were incapable of providing any further immediate military assistance, General Weygand, the French military commander, pressed the Pétain government to negotiate an armistice. His objective was to seek a political settlement of the war that would save at least part of France from occupation, protect the still-intact French fleet, and safeguard the colonies. The Constitutional Law of 10 July 1940, which officially created the new regime, brought the colonies under the formal authority of Vichy.[1]

Confronted with German military superiority on the European continent and convinced that a Nazi victory was imminent, some of

Pétain's supporters sought to arrange a place for France in the Europe of Hitler's "New Order." Others, including military strategists such as Weygand, held out some hope that the colonies in North Africa could be used as a training ground to rebuild an army capable of eventually seeking revenge against Germany. Still others, perhaps a majority of the colonial officials among them, were more concerned with preserving discipline within their particular segment of the bureaucracy and avoiding political or even personal disorders than with confronting larger questions of national policy. These concerns of the Vichy rulers were reinforced by a pervasive anglophobia, which found particular favor among the many military and civil officials who were concentrated in North Africa and the Levant.[2]

The attitude of the Nazi occupation authorities toward France's colonial concerns was ambivalent. During the years just prior to the outbreak of the war, Nazi propaganda had vilified the French for their colonial practices and denounced the universalistic goals of French colonial policy. Through the party organization, the NSDAP Kolonialpolitisches Amt, and through the Reichskolonialbund, both directed by General von Epp, the Nazis reproached the French for inefficient administration and gross neglect of the former German colonies. The French conception of a colonial mission based on the rationalist philosophy of the Enlightenment was denounced as a betrayal of the white race and a perversion of the true meaning of nationhood, in which blood, race, language, and civilization were regarded as decisive. At the same time Nazi propagandists depicted France as drawing both economic and military strength from the colonies.[3]

During the summer of 1940, when Nazi occupation officials were optimistic about the prospects for Franco-German cooperation, their propagandists encouraged Vichy's colonial interests as an alternative to France's traditional preoccupation with her eastern frontier and the fate of the annexed provinces. When it became apparent that the collapse of Britain was not imminent, the Nazis became concerned that Vichy maintain its hold on the African colonies, and they later demanded the use of French bases in Syria for attacks on British forces in the Near East. At no time, however, were the Nazi authorities willing to consider giving the Vichy forces either political autonomy or the equipment necessary to pursue an independent policy in the colonies. They maintained strict control over all armaments and confiscated large amounts of the raw materials produced in the colonies when these managed to reach the metropole.[4]

Within the colonies, the primary aim of Vichy was to prevent dissident movements from disturbing administrative controls. Hence, what mobilization was accomplished in Africa during 1940 was aimed less at reducing German influence than at destroying Gaullist prestige and diminishing the growth of British influence. The Japanese victory in the South Pacific in 1941 compelled Pétain to make important concessions in Indochina. At the same time, Vichy came under strong pressure from the Allies, especially Britain, whose positions in India and Burma appeared threatened if the Axis powers were permitted to use French bases in Madagascar.

The ideological appeals of Vichy, summed up in slogans like "the National Revolution," had little impact overseas, although some of the racist and anti-semitic policies of Vichy found favor with French settlers in North Africa. Similarly, the religiosity of Pétainism may have appealed to some French residents in the colonies, but there seems to have been very little effort made by Vichy to develop a coherent colonial doctrine. Instead, Vichy relied heavily upon the bureaucratic traditions of the civil and military authorities to maintain order in the colonies. Aided by a long-standing tradition of anglophobia and a deep distrust of democratic processes that made the colonial bureaucracy unwilling to envisage any transfer of real political power to indigenous groups, the Vichy authorities were able to maintain control over the colonies by invoking professional values.

One can judge how effective these traditions and values were in holding the loyalty of the colonial bureaucracy by recalling the response of Vichy to the Gaullist efforts to rally the territories of Africa and the Levant to continue the war against Germany in 1940. In West Africa Pierre Boisson, newly appointed high commissioner of the French territories of West and Central Africa, recognized the authority of Vichy and agreed to enforce the terms of the armistice, even though he had earlier considered a plan to organize the West African colonies into a bloc capable of continuing the struggle on the Allied side. Boisson's explanation clearly depicts the state of mind of many officials at the time. The first imperative, he later wrote, was to

> maintain unity! Do nothing that will retard the rebuilding of the distant fatherland [*patrie*]. No anarchy; no provocations; no Tol-

> stoyism; fundamental unity! Dissidence is a very contagious disease for which the whites will pay the costs in the end. To advance junior officers, or turbulent métis ahead of career officers, and to arrest them and put them under guard by blacks who the day before were under their orders, is a kind of insanity that would have dangerous repercussions for the future of France overseas. Movements that do not respect hierarchy carry within themselves the ferment of dissolution.[5]

After an initial period of confusion and hesitation, colonial officials in most of the larger territories accepted the legitimacy of Vichy for similar reasons. Where there was uncertainty, Pétain moved quickly to place in power men loyal to himself. As governor-general of Tunisia he named Marcel Peyrouton, a colonial administrator whose successful career had been interrupted when the Popular Front ousted him from the secretariat-general of Morocco and Tunisia in 1936. Elsewhere, the Vichy regime put into power an elite drawn largely from those segments of the military and civil bureaucracies most opposed to the principles and practices of the Third Republic. Under Admiral Jean François Darlan's influence, many of the colonial posts were filled by admirals: Admiral Esteva replaced Peyrouton in Tunis when the latter moved to the Ministry of Interior in 1941; Admiral Decoux was sent to Indochina; Admiral Robert to Martinique; Admiral Auphan was put in charge of the merchant marine; and Admiral Platon was named minister of the colonies. This influx of admirals into important positions in the regime reportedly led Cardinal Liénart to wonder whether after his death there would be enough admirals to replace him.[6]

These appointments underscored the character of the Vichy regime, whose authority depended more upon the professional dedication of the military and upon loyalty to a personal patron than upon the values and traditions of republican government. They also help to explain why Vichy, for all the importance that it attached to safeguarding French national interests, never developed any coherent colonial policies. The leaders who assumed control of the colonial territories lacked any experience or direct knowledge about the colonies and were moved chiefly by fears for their own professional status. Little wonder, therefore, that the Vichy regime's principal concern in the colonies was less to resist the Axis than to prevent those territories from rallying to the support of Free France under the leadership of Charles de Gaulle.

De Gaulle and the Free French

The Free French took quite a different attitude toward the colonies from that of the Vichy regime. While Vichy considered the colonies as a subordinate part of France, subject to the controls of the metropole and sharing her fate, de Gaulle stressed the contribution that the colonies could make toward preserving the integrity of the nation. Both factions shared the assumption that France and the colonies were integral parts of one body politic, but the Gaullists drew from the assumption of national unity the conclusion that France had not been defeated, despite the occupation of part of the metropole by the military forces of its continental enemy. De Gaulle argued repeatedly that as long as major portions of the national territory remained free from Nazi control, France must continue the struggle. As he told the people of France in the historic speech of 18 June, 1940: "France is not alone! She has a great empire behind her. Together with the British Empire, she can form a bloc that controls the seas and continue the struggle." [7]

Once de Gaulle had decided that France's future lay in maintaining her commitment to the Allied cause and fighting on as best she could until Germany was eventually defeated, the colonies assumed a role of primary importance for both political and strategic reasons. In the initial phase of the struggle it was essential to prevent Germany from gaining control over the colonies and, if possible, to secure colonial resources in men and raw materials for the Allied cause. For this purpose de Gaulle first aimed to bring together under his control the commanders of the scattered remnants of French territory that remained free from the direct control of the German army. That effort failed when none of the senior military leaders was willing to reject the authority of Pétain and join de Gaulle in London.

Later, when the Free French found themselves the central focus of the Resistance movement outside France, the colonies provided a political base and afforded de Gaulle's movement a legitimacy that most of the other governments-in-exile in London did not possess. With the liberation of North Africa in 1942 the French National Liberation Committee (CFLN) gained a territorial base that further strengthened its claim to speak for the interests of France on the side of the Allies. This ability permitted de Gaulle to return to France in 1944 at the head of the Provisional Government of the French Republic (GPRF), a regime that had effectively preserved the interests and honor of the nation since the collapse of the Third Republic.

In order to accomplish these ends de Gaulle was obliged repeatedly to confront the question of the traditional role of the colonial territories within the French political system and to improvise new arrangements that would hold the loyalty both of the colonial peoples and of the metropolitan bureaucracy. This task required reexamining many traditional conceptions of the colonial relationship, reformulating political doctrines to do service under vastly changed conditions, and inventing new policies and sometimes new institutions to carry out the decisions necessary to meet the pressing demands of wartime strategy and diplomacy. Those ideas and policies, which were often prompted by temporary conditions, had long-run consequences both for the Gaullist leadership and for the colonial peoples in their later relationship with metropolitan France during the postwar era. To appreciate the stages through which the relationship between France and the colonies developed during the war, it is useful to examine briefly de Gaulle's political doctrines as they applied to colonial questions.

The political ideas that were elaborated by the French Resistance movement reflected the influence of several groups and did not form a coherent political ideology or a consistent social philosophy. Particularly influential were the ideas of Liberal Catholics who, together with the French communists, played an important role in the internal Resistance movement. Also important were the views of democratic socialists whose tradition derived from Proudhon and Saint-Simon rather than from Marx. Most of all, however, it was Charles de Gaulle whose political conceptions and personal style of leadership shaped and colored the policies of the Free French. The framework of ideas that he enunciated provided the principal intellectual context within which critical national policies were formulated. Therefore, it is his work that deserves greatest attention.

De Gaulle himself never formulated an explicit statement of his political or social philosophy. Therefore, the student of French politics is obliged to extract de Gaulle's key ideas from his published works.[8] The most revealing of these are the *Mémoires de guerre* and the occasional speeches, most of which were republished in *Discours et messages*. The earlier works of the prewar period help to reveal the continuity of certain themes in de Gaulle's thought, but even with the assistance of several contemporary studies,[9] the task is difficult.

The most satisfactory way to view the Gaullist colonial doctrines is to treat them as one particular variant of the French republican colonial myth discussed earlier. The themes of the myth that are peculiar to Gaullism or that received especially compelling reformulation at his hands can be seen to reflect de Gaulle's personality and personal philosophy, the tactical priorities dictated by his assessment of the historical situation confronting France, his strategic vision of French national interests, and his constitutional theories and preferences.

Turning first to what may be termed the "idiosyncratic" aspects of de Gaulle's thought, one discovers beneath the dismaying egotism of his style and the rapidly shifting array of policy issues a coherence to de Gaulle's statements and actions that seems to flow directly from the character of the man and to be inspired by his personal philosophy.

De Gaulle's political thought appears to have been colored from the start by a revulsion for routine, formalistic thinking. He was always in revolt against the orthodoxies of the day, whether in political or military matters. Even as a junior officer he was singled out because of his critical attitude toward his superiors. All his works display his profound disdain for the shortcomings of the French political system.

At the heart of de Gaulle's political theory is his concept of the relationship between the uses of military force and the ends of national policy.[10] The importance he assigned to these matters supports the judgments of those who regard de Gaulle as the outstanding modern example of a political tradition that began with Machiavelli. His preoccupation with the role of military force was linked to a historic vision of France that gave de Gaulle a sense of purpose and inspired in him an austere manner of living and a heroic style of leadership that set him apart from the other leaders of his epoch.

De Gaulle's vision of France derived in part from his upbringing. The son of an old, ardent Roman Catholic family, he grew to maturity in an atmosphere filled with the traditional culture of France and under the tutelage of a father whose firm wisdom imbued in him a profound attachment to the values of classical French civilization. De Gaulle was also clearly influenced by his youthful encounter with the ideas of Charles Maurras, leader of the *Action Française,* and those of its leading historian, Jacques Bainville. They inspired in him a profound contempt for republican political institutions and an enduring predilection for a variety of corporatist approaches to political problems. Most of all, he derived from such writings a vision of France as a romantic ideal, a historic cultural unity that possessed a life of its own and which, in its moments of greatness, was the embodiment of universal truth and virtue. It is this ideal, greater than any individual person or faction, that ennobled the acts performed in the name of France.

This special vision of France, as de Gaulle explained in the opening passages of his *Mémoires,* informed all his acts and inspired his conviction that grandeur must always be a primary element in French policy. In his own words:

> All my life I have adhered to a certain idea of France. It is sentiment as well as reason that inspires me. The emotional part of me naturally imagines France, like the fairy-tale princess or the madonna in the frescoes, devoted to some eminent and exceptional destiny. Instinctively, I have the impression that Providence created her for great achievements or exemplary sufferings. If it should happen, however, that her acts and accomplishments should be marked by mediocrity, I experience the sensation of an absurd anomaly, imputable to the faults of Frenchmen and not to the genius of the nation.
>
> But the positive side of my spirit also convinces me that France is not really herself except in the front rank. Only vast undertakings are sufficient to compensate for the ferments of dispersion which her people carry within themselves. Our country such as it is, among the others, being what they are, must look up high and stand erect even at the risk of mortal danger. In brief, to me France cannot be France without grandeur.[11]

A number of important political implications flow directly from these underlying assumptions. The primacy of the nation-state as the effective unit of modern political life, and therefore the supreme political value, derives from his insight into the eternal greatness of France. As a corollary of that principle de Gaulle placed the conduct of foreign affairs at the top of the list of national interests. Moreover, since the world was obviously divided into a hierarchy of states with the great powers shaping the alternatives within which the leaders of the small and middle powers must necessarily choose, de Gaulle concluded that France must at all costs be restored to a role of equality among the nations that are great. Consequently, he tended to minimize France's short-term weaknesses and to stress her past glories and future potential. By viewing the present disaster in the context of a long-term struggle for European security, de Gaulle hoped to persuade the Allies to recognize the continuing importance of France, despite her military defeat. He also aimed to convince Frenchmen that no matter how hopeless the present seemed, the future would provide a role for France consistent with her past achievements. In this effort the colonies were to play a major role. As de Gaulle told a gathering in Algiers in 1943:

> In the end, one is never wrong to believe in France; one never ultimately regrets having aided her or having loved her. . . . For the future France, by her genius, by her experience, and by her capacity, will be one of the best artisans of universal peace. Integrated into the old Europe . . . but spread out over the entire world by its territories and its humanitarian influence, the France of tomorrow will be among the front rank of the nations who are great.[12]

In much the same vein, de Gaulle later reflected on his enthusiastic reception in the United States and commented on the "extraordinary love of France" that it betokened. Such admiration was another justification for the rank and grandeur to which he aspired, regardless of French weaknesses.

Alfred Grosser, discussing de Gaulle's conceptions, has stressed the manner in which such general political ideas were shaped by de Gaulle's peculiar attitude toward history. The subsequent actions of de Gaulle seem to have been deeply influenced by his personal experiences with prewar military and government leaders and with wartime chiefs, and especially by major conflicts on matters of strategy among the Allies. His proclivity for archaic historical analogies and his tendency to formulate current policy in a time frame of centuries, extending back into the era of France's preeminence during the eighteenth century or even to the time of Vercingetorix, gives an oddly Olympian tone to many statements of Gaullist policy. De Gaulle's conception of nationalism, too, as Grosser notes, was a blend of ideas drawn from both extremes of the French political spectrum. "One of the foundations of Gaullism consists precisely in assuming the double heritage of Jacobin patriotism and the nationalism of the Right." [13] Taken together with de Gaulle's self-consciousness regarding his own historic role, these factors tended to produce what some have called a "bifocal" view of history: a nostalgia for the glorious past coupled with a consuming concern for the more or less distant future. So pervasive were these underlying personal convictions that de Gaulle can legitimately be regarded as a "man of the day before yesterday and the day after tomorrow."

One final personal characteristic that clearly marked de Gaulle's style of leadership was his ability to combine deliberateness to the point of total inaction with brutal activity in periods of crisis in a calculated mixture that frequently infuriated even his most essential allies. In this regard de Gaulle followed to the letter Machiavelli's counsel that a successful prince should combine the talents of the lion and the fox, utilizing both cunning and great strength and alternating periods of careful preparation with swift and unhesitating action once the situation has become ripe for change. Much of the decisiveness and intransigence, the dissimulation and adroitness with which de Gaulle conducted the policies of the Free French stemmed from the conviction that, in the "high politics" of nation-states, it is impossible to achieve desired ends directly, and many zigzags may be required before conditions permit a leader to gain his ultimate goals. Of course, he also recognized that the more modest the power at his disposal, the more a statesman must seek to make the best of any opportunities for promoting the grandeur of his state.

This Machiavellian quality of de Gaulle's personality is closely related to a second aspect of his political thought regarding the colonial territories, which can be called "tactical." In the midst of the debacle of June 1940 de Gaulle was confronted with a choice between accepting an armistice with Germany and continuing a struggle that most of his superiors considered hopeless. His decision was for *guerre à outrance,* and it was to involve him and his small band of Free French compatriots in a bewildering complex of diplomatic and military maneuvers. Many of these were designed to take advantage of the potential of the colonies for safeguarding French interests.

De Gaulle had always demonstrated a concern for tactical problems. During the 1930s he had pressed for the formation of a well-trained, mechanized, professional army as the only adequate response to the growing power of Germany, but he had failed to break through the paralyzing fear that immobilized the governments of the time. A similar tactical sense led him to stress the importance of the colonies in planning for national defense. De Gaulle conceived of France not as a European continental power but as a world power with interests in every part of the globe. Consequently, the collapse of armed resistance in metropolitan France led him to envision the organization of a new body capable of rallying the colonies to liberate France. After first seeking to avoid an armistice by encouraging a variety of more or less desperate plans, including a last-minute scheme for the formation of a Franco-British union, de Gaulle escaped to London, where he launched the Free French movement in June 1940.[14]

His most pressing tactical concern after 18 June 1940 was to establish the legitimacy of the Free French as authentic representatives of the nation in the eyes of the Allies, on whom he depended for both economic and military support. The colonial territories played an absolutely essential role in this endeavor. With their support de Gaulle could claim for the Free French a status analogous to that of the other governments-in-exile which were then active in London, even though Britain and the United States both maintained relations with Vichy and recognized it as the legitimate successor to the Third Republic. By establishing himself in control of the French colonial territories, de Gaulle also was able to make good in a modest way on his claim to maintain France's military role in the Allied war effort. As the head of a French army, he enjoyed improved prospects for diplomatic recognition, and his ability to make at least a token contribution to the eventual liberation of the metropole was assured.[15]

The way in which these aims were accomplished also reveals de Gaulle's mastery of the tactics of weakness in an alliance with stronger powers. His initial position, as a brigadier general in the French army who had been replaced as under-secretary of national defense after his dramatic but ineffectual mission to London in June 1940, had little to suggest that de Gaulle was beginning a brilliant career as one of the outstanding statesmen of his time.

In June 1940 rhetorical offensives were all that he could muster. De Gaulle could order no one to serve him; those who obeyed did so of their own volition, because they shared his hopes for the liberation of France and because they admired his intransigence in the face of defeat. Most of de Gaulle's followers during this early phase were men whose liberal convictions prevented them from accepting the rule of Pétain and whose devotion to France's honor forbade them to accept the predominance of Germany. A few were political figures from the Third Republic, notably Pierre Mendès-France and André Philip; some, like Admiral Muselier, were military men. Most were professional people, businessmen, administrators, journalists, or members of the French communities in London, New York, and other large cities abroad. On the whole, very few of the early Gaullists had been closely associated with the political life of the Third Republic. For his part, de Gaulle consciously set about elaborating a myth of Free France capable of sustaining the efforts necessary to keep the nation alive in the midst of its most desperate struggle.

At the time of de Gaulle's first radio broadcast to France on 18 June, Churchill had known him personally for only nine days. Yet with the endorsement of the British government, de Gaulle was permitted the use of the BBC to rally what support he could from metropolitan France and from the colonies in a desperate effort to keep France fighting against the Axis. That famous speech was addressed to soldiers under arms, workers, and engineers, who were urged not to abandon the struggle but to join de Gaulle in London from where they could continue to fight. Once the French government had decided to seek an armistice, de Gaulle spoke out more clearly, opposing not only the Axis enemy but the Pétain government as well.

> At the present hour, all Frenchmen understand that the usual forms of government have disappeared. Confronted with the confusion of French souls, confronted with the liquidation of a government that has fallen under the yoke of the enemy, confronted with the fact that our institutions cannot function freely, I, General de Gaulle, French soldier and leader, am conscious of speaking in the name of France.[16]

On 28 June, after another effort to persuade leading French officials to join in forming a government-in-exile, de Gaulle was recognized by the British as "leader of the Free French." From that point on, de Gaulle asserted authority over all Frenchmen who resided in British territory or arrived there and considered Free France the only legitimate voice of France.

The colonies figured importantly in all these appeals. De Gaulle spoke directly to soldiers and administrators in the overseas areas urging them not to accept the terms of the armistice.

> Every Frenchman who still bears arms has an absolute duty to continue resisting. To lay down arms, to evacuate a military post, to agree to submit one single piece of French territory to enemy control would be a crime against the fatherland. At this hour I speak especially for French North Africa: for North Africa intact. The Italian armistice is nothing but an ugly trap.[17]

The response to de Gaulle's initial call for colonial resistance was encouraging, especially in West Africa, where many local administrators, chambers of commerce, veterans' clubs, officers' clubs, and other local notables dispatched telegrams announcing their desire to resist and their intent to affiliate with the Free French.[18] Most of these quickly withdrew their support, however, as soon as it became clear that Pétain had denounced de Gaulle and intended to apply the provisions of the armistice overseas. Only the most remote of the colonial areas were prepared to maintain their affiliation with the Free French from the outset. British influence was strong in New Caledonia, the tiny Pacific islands of Oceania, and the French towns of India, while in equatorial Africa special economic and political considerations encouraged some local authorities to break with the Vichy regime.

The rally to Free France stopped well short of a complete triumph.[19] De Gaulle's attempt to gain possession of the important naval base at Dakar with British support was met with organized resistance on a large scale. Thereafter, he abandoned further attempts to seize control of other West African territories such as Dahomey, the Ivory Coast, and Guinée and concentrated instead on consolidating the regions that had rallied to Free France. Consequently, from September 1940 until after the Allied landings in North Africa in 1942 French West Africa remained divided, and the Pétain regime, with the Vichy government, controlled the most important areas.

Nevertheless, the Gaullists were in a position to take advantage of widespread pro-French sentiment among the native elite in many of the colonies, especially in Africa. General de Gaulle seems to have recognized from the outset that the indigenous population of Africa was an important factor in the economic and military, as well as in the political future of the Continent, and he was anxious to turn this force into an asset for Free France. Furthermore, the obvious necessity of encouraging self-sufficiency on the part of the colonies once they rallied to Free France made it essential to consider the sentiments of the indigenous elite. Yet, it is apparent from de Gaulle's speech of 30 June 1940 that appealing directly to the local population was seen as a last resort to be employed only if all else failed to persuade Europeans, and especially local officials, to back the Free French.

> High commissioners, governors-general, administrators, residents of our colonies and our protectorates, your duty to France, your duty to those whose interests, honor, and lives depend on you, is to refuse to execute the abominable armistices. You are the guardians [*gérants*] of French sovereignty, which at present has lapsed. Many among you already have joined with me to carry on the war alongside our Allies; those men will be given support. But again I am calling on others. If need be, I will call upon the entire population.[20]

In those colonies that rallied to Free France the Gaullists were obliged by the disruption of normal financial and administrative channels to rely heavily on the cooperation of the indigenous elite in providing for the minimum needs of the territory. While, in practice, the political role of the indigenous peoples remained subordinate to that of the European colonists, the Gaullist movement was instrumental in mobilizing popular sentiment behind the cause of France and the Allies, in the process encouraging an awakening of pro-French sentiment among the non-European population.

The specific policies developed by the Free French to integrate the colonies into a coherent battle plan for the liberation of the metropole will be examined in the next chapter. Before considering that aspect of the Gaullist experience, however, it is well to ask how de Gaulle's outlook on colonial problems changed as the Free French movement gradually assumed the responsibility for governing the French territories. Beginning from a very small territorial base in the colonies, the Gaullists were successful in riding the wave of Allied victory to power, first in Africa and later in metropolitan France. As de Gaulle's sphere of authority widened, he elaborated a doctrine for the colonies that emphasized a third set of considerations.

Colonial questions were highly relevant to what might be called the "strategic" dimension of Gaullist thought. From the Gaullist perspective the most serious long-run danger to France was not confined to the depredations of the Axis powers. The tendency of other states, particularly France's Anglo-Saxon allies, to misconstrue or disregard her vital interests, or even to seek to profit from her distress, was one of de Gaulle's concerns. As he explained to Cordell Hull on the eve of the North African invasion, the war was not just a game of checkers.[21] To those who were fighting, it was a matter of moral duty, which made it impossible for the Free French to comprehend the indulgent attitude of the United States toward Vichy or the coolness of the American government toward those Frenchmen who were fighting alongside the Allies.

President Roosevelt's determination to withhold recognition from the Free French and to deal directly with the local authorities, Gaullist or Vichyite, whichever was most consistent with short-run military requirements, greatly increased de Gaulle's apprehension. From the outset of the war de Gaulle had been suspicious of American intentions vis-à-vis French colonial holdings, particularly those in North Africa, the Antilles, and the Pacific. He based his attitude partly on the character of recent American policy.

For example, in the Havana Resolution of July 1940 the United States and other Pan-American powers declared their intention to oppose actively any transfer of sovereignty over colonial areas in Latin America from one European power to another. Although obviously aimed at preventing Germany from acquiring sovereignty over Caribbean territory, de Gaulle interpreted this move as an indication of American intent to intervene against the interests of Free France in the Americas. American opposition to his seizing control of Saint Pierre and Miquelon on 24 December 1941 was particularly offensive to de Gaulle, who was determined to use the referendum there to solidify his own political role as leader of a legitimate French regime. The nearly unanimous vote of that tiny colonial community had unusual significance because it was the first formal evidence, obtained by overtly democratic procedures, that Frenchmen of metropolitan origin accepted the Free French as the representatives of France.[22]

A similar hostility resulted in 1942 from conflicts between the Free French and American military forces under the command of General Patch, who had been granted permission to establish air bases, station troops, and extract raw materials from the Pacific islands of New Caledonia, New Hebrides, and Oceania. In the French Congo and Madagascar, too, American requests for military bases aroused concern for the sovereignty of France, which frequently seemed to be eclipsed by the enormous military might of the United States.

The continued refusal of formal recognition, even after the liberation of North Africa, implied rejection of the symbolic role of Free France. Even more serious, it bespoke a lack of confidence in France's future. As de Gaulle explained to Harry Hopkins and United States delegate Jefferson Caffery just before the Yalta Conference, "The French have the impression that you no longer consider the grandeur of France as necessary to the world or to yourselves. Hence the cold draft which you sense on our part, even in this office." [23]

An additional factor that encouraged Gaullist misgivings was the attitude taken by Roosevelt toward the end of the war on the role of the colonies during the postwar era. De Gaulle was always suspicious of Rooseveltian internationalism.[24] Because of his own view of international politics was much closer to the so-called realist theories of Clausewitz and Bismarck, he conceived of international politics in terms of national, rather than supranational, relationships. National interests and the power that states could command in order to pursue them dominated de Gaulle's thinking. Consequently, he tended to discount as "unrealistic" the claims advanced by Roosevelt on behalf of an international community and to see in them only ruses aimed at concealing underlying national ambitions. His reaction to the Anglo-American declaration of war aims expressed in the Atlantic Charter was one of distinct coolness, which reflected not only a determination to preserve French claims to parts of the Rhineland, but also a different conception of the problems of European security. The restoration of a balance of power on the European continent seemed to de Gaulle to depend upon the future role of Germany. This, in turn, implied a greater respect for the importance of France, which since 1914 had played a major part in balancing German power and would do so again in the future. It also implied a recognition of France's rights and other economic advantages. Declarations of generous intention counted for little alongside the realities of force. As de Gaulle explained to Roosevelt in 1944, "In the affairs of states, logic and sentiment do not weigh heavily in comparison with the realities of power; what was important was that one took what one knew how to hold." It therefore followed that "France, in seeking to retrieve her place in the world, should not count on anyone but herself." [25]

At the same time de Gaulle was keenly aware that only the United States could supply him with the military equipment and the financial support necessary to mount a major French war effort, and he fully appreciated the vital role played by the United States in the conduct of the war. The disparity between his meager strength and that of the American forces led him repeatedly to accede to American requests for permission to make temporary use of many territories under Free French control in spite of his misgivings. It was de Gaulle's relations with President Roosevelt and some of his advisers that were the most difficult. But even at that level de Gaulle's respect for Roosevelt as a political leader was not lacking. Unfortunately, profound differences in style and outlook separated the two men, and, together with Roosevelt's ignorance of French conditions, disdain for French domestic politics, and insensitivity to the many political changes taking place in Europe, created a gulf between the American government and the Free French regime that gave rise to recurring tension in their relations throughout the war.[26]

Gaullist attitudes toward the British, while still ambivalent, were much more positive for a number of reasons. First of all, in Churchill de Gaulle found a leader of heroic stature from whom it was possible to win genuine compassion and real understanding for France's suffering. Then, too, de Gaulle's sense of the dynamics of world politics told him that Britain and France had come to occupy similar positions in relation to the great powers, the United States and the Soviet Union, on whom the future security of Europe would largely depend. Finally, de Gaulle's appreciation of historic traditions made it unmistakable that Britain and France were linked by the same patterns of social, economic, and political development, and that they, therefore, stood together as defenders of European civilization and bulwarks of liberal democracy in a world faced with revolutionary disorder.[27]

De Gaulle's conception of himself as defender of France's "rights" as a great power made cooperation with the British a matter of exceeding delicacy, especially in matters relating to the colonies. To be sure, there was a long tradition of Franco-British rivalry in Africa and the Middle East, which both Nazi and Vichy propaganda deliberately sought to keep alive. Other aspects of the Franco-British relationship also created friction. De Gaulle soon came to understand that he would never be able to gain the active support of Churchill against the United States, and as the war progressed he realized that Britain was increasingly unwilling to risk offending her most powerful ally. He interpreted this special relationship between the Anglo-Saxon countries as a threat both to France's colonial holdings and to her place as a great power. For it signified to de Gaulle that instead of seeking to become the leader of Europe together with France, Britain had chosen to remain aloof and to seek advantages from cooperation with the United States. Since France was unable to gain predominance over Europe by herself, this meant that France could become just another minor European power. It was this fear—that France, as de Gaulle once put it, "might count for nothing more in the world than Greece does in Europe"—that moved him to strive continuously for the preservation of French colonial authority in order that France might retain the status of a great power despite all her losses. Moreover, it seemed to de Gaulle that the empire alone could restore to France the needed prestige with the victorious Allies to guarantee her a proper role in the postwar European system.

Looking toward the more distant future, de Gaulle posited a central role for France in the creation of a new European power balance—a role that could be effectively filled only if France and the colonies remained united in a coherent, mutual association. As he later explained:

> It is perfectly clear to me that in order to conduct such a policy in Europe, we must have our hands free beyond the seas. If the overseas territories detach themselves from the metropole, or if we allow our forces to become hung up there, how much will we count for between the North Sea and the Mediterranean? Should they, on the contrary, remain associated with us, why then the way would be open for our action on the Continent—secular destiny of France! [28]

Unity between the metropole and the colonies was, consequently, a primary prerequisite to the achievement of the most basic goals of Gaullist foreign policy: the restoration of France's rank among the nations of the world and the preservation of the grandeur that de Gaulle had always considered essential to France's destiny and that had formed such an important part of his own "certain idea of France."

During the latter days of the war, de Gaulle began to pay increasing attention to another set of problems that had always been central to his political thinking. These dealt with what might be broadly described as the "constitutional" aspect of French politics.

De Gaulle's disdain for the French system of party politics was deep and of long standing. It was the circumstances of the war, however, that cast him in the role of a political rebel and finally moved him to seek to restructure those institutions along different lines. An examination of the evolution of de Gaulle's constitutional doctrines greatly exceeds the scope of the present study, but it is necessary to recall here the outlines of his conception of French democracy because it had a direct bearing on de Gaulle's policies in regard to the colonial territories.

Though he had often been critical of them, de Gaulle had avoided suggestions that the Free France movement was in revolt against the institutions of the Third Republic. In a statement broadcast from Brazzaville in October 1940 [29] he depicted Vichy as an illegal regime, first because Vichy had consented to allow France to be ruled by her enemies, and also because the National Assembly had been forced to capitulate to Pétain. Free France was the only legitimate French regime, he argued, because it alone represented the continuation—albeit in an attenuated form—of republican government. De Gaulle's republicanism, however, was certainly not the conventional variety. Its central elements were once again a combination of ideas familiar to both the traditional Right and Left factions of the French republican tradition.

The Jacobin, or revolutionary republican, elements of Gaullist doctrine appear most clearly in the conception of Free France as the embodiment of the national will to resist the enemy. Compelled by circumstances to transcend normal constitutional processes and to seek authority directly from the French people, de Gaulle evoked the concept of the general will elaborated by Rousseau. "It is in the name of France in its entirety . . . that I fulfill my mission," he announced.[30] This conception of a direct but implicit grant of authority from the people as a whole to act in the long-run interests of France is what ultimately provided the political legitimacy for the Free French regime. From time to time it was necessary that de Gaulle's authority be made explicit, and that was accomplished by a referendum in which the entire population was asked, in a carefully worded formula, to endorse or reject his basic policies. This practice of verifying the general will by referendum had firm roots in political theory inasmuch as de Gaulle, like Rousseau, conceived of the general will as something distinct from the claims of any particular faction or party and different even from what might appear to serve the short-run interest of a majority. This process was used successfully in rallying Saint Pierre and Miquelon to Free France and later became a primary tool of Gaullist political leadership.

Under the circumstances of 1940 the general will expressed the nation's determination that, although defeated, divided by her enemies, and governed by traitors, France was still "only one nation, only one territory, only one empire, only one law." As de Gaulle explained to an audience in London's Albert Hall on Armistice Day 1942:

> Among Frenchmen, dispersed by force or impelled by despair, an accord has been reached in the secret of the soul. This accord is now public. The mass of the French people is now united on the three following imperatives: the enemy is the enemy; the salvation of the country is to be found only in victory; and it is with Free France [*France Combattante*] that all of France must unite. . . .
>
> The nation holds plebiscites for Free France every day. It is to her that [the nation] turns. It is in her that she finds herself. It is to her, and to her alone, that [the nation] looks for the direction of her struggle.[31]

De Gaulle's personal role was reminiscent of Rousseau's "legislator," whose responsibility was to frame the laws and lead the people to a fuller understanding of the general will. As de Gaulle explained it, that role lost none of its original ambiguity. "Only the people is sovereign; . . . until the time when it will be capable of expressing its will, I have taken it upon myself to lead." [32] De Gaulle was to continue in that role until 1946 and to repeat it again on a later occasion. Throughout the whole period of his active political life, however, his fundamental conception of his authority remained the same. As he commented some years after the war: "The nation instinctively grasped the fact that, plunged as it was into disorder, it would be at the mercy of anarchy and then of dictatorship were I not there to serve it as guide and rallying point. Today the fatherland attaches itself to de Gaulle in order to escape subversion just as yesterday it did so to be freed from the enemy.[33]

There was also a strongly conservative aspect to de Gaulle's analysis of French politics. It is clear from his earliest writings that he considered the state bureaucracy, rather than the representative organs of government, to be the vital center of the political system.[34] Government, in that view, was primarily a matter of making decisions and imposing rules to accomplish necessary goals, rather than a process of reconciling conflicting interests. While de Gaulle never questioned that France must be restored to the ranks of the democratic countries, he was profoundly concerned with making democratic government compatible with the requirements of national independence and grandeur.

Only a state system capable of making and enforcing decisions that were in keeping with the seriousness of the immense problems confronting France would suffice. A return to what had become the normal pattern of prewar party government was out of the question, since France required a strong executive with clear authority over the bureaucracy. Hence, the need to carefully limit the power of the representative organs and to protect the power of the executive. These ideas were fundamentally at odds with those widely accepted by the moderate and leftist groups, which made up an important part of the Resistance, and they also offended many of the traditional bureaucrats. Nevertheless, they were expounded repeatedly, most notably in the Bayeux speech of 1946. While they did not achieve full acceptance during the wartime period, de Gaulle never wavered from them.

These considerations of doctrine were reinforced by the lessons that de Gaulle drew from his brief experience in the Renaud government in 1940. There he had watched the decay of political power and had seen men of ability and high character ground under by the constant pressure to compromise and maneuver in order to remain in office. The result was the annihilation of the state as a mechanism of government and the total collapse of power, not just in the military, but in every arm of policy-making. Thereafter, de Gaulle remained totally convinced that the parliamentary system based on a multiplicity of parties, which gave free play to petty interests, was synonymous with disaster.[35]

Consequently, one of the tasks he set for himself during the war was to rebuild the state mechanism and, when the circumstances permitted, to remodel France's institutions in order to safeguard the state in future crises. He made an important beginning in the summer of 1943 when, under strong pressure from the Allies to accept a regime in which he would share power with General Giraud, de Gaulle succeeded in imposing his own conception of centralized rule on reluctant authorities in Algiers.[36]

Ironically, it was not only the weakness of the parties that led de Gaulle to act as he did, but the strength of one of them. By the end of 1943, when the liberation of the metropole was in prospect, the Free French were confronted with the necessity of preparing their return to France. The internal Resistance movement had developed largely outside the framework of the Free French, and after 1941 it had come very largely under the influence of the French Communist party. The PCF was the only one of the prewar parties that possessed a strong organization and a coherent ideological position. It had also benefited directly from the support of the Soviet Union and was profiting by the popular enthusiasm that accompanied the heroic struggle of the Red Army. De Gaulle was determined to develop the CFLN into a new political regime for the metropole which could prevent the PCF from taking advantage of the disorganization that was bound to accompany the Liberation.

For its part, the Communist party had opposed de Gaulle until May 1941, asserting that "the unity of the French people behind the cause of national liberation will never be achieved under the leadership of a movement made in the image of British imperialism and led by the defenders of colonial exploitation." [37] True national unity, it had asserted, could only be attained by forming a united front led by the PCF and dedicated to transforming the capitalist war into a social revolution modeled on the example of the Soviet Union and by observing a policy of strict neutrality as stipulated in the Molotov-Ribbentrop Pact. After the Nazi invasion of Russia on 22 June 1941, the French Communists proclaimed a new "national front" and endorsed the Free French. The Soviet Union encouraged this shift when it endorsed de Gaulle as "leader of the Free French" and promised to support the "full and complete restoration of the independence and grandeur of France."

One immediate consequence of this volte-face was an abrupt halt in Communist efforts to encourage colonial revolts. During 1940 the PCF had been actively urging its followers, especially in North Africa, to "seize upon the opportunity afforded by the present difficulties of their oppressors and free themselves." [38] With the liberation of the metropole at hand and hopes running high that the party would be in a position to gain power in the postwar French government, the PCF supported the continuation of France's colonial role. This position was calculated to allay some of the fears of the bourgeois elements upon whose toleration they still depended, and it also corresponded with the Soviet Union's interest in reducing the international influence of the Anglo-Saxon powers in the Mediterranean.

As one party spokesman explained to the Consultative Assembly in Algiers:

> France is now installed in Algiers and in Tunis as well as in Marseilles; France stands guardian over the great interests of civilization and over a necessary equilibrium in the eastern Mediterranean. It would be dangerous for her to underestimate the importance of her role in the Mediterranean. She is and must remain a great power in Africa. [*Applause*] Greater France has 110 million inhabitants and unlimited resources. Thus, we need never feel crushed by any inferiority complex [*cries of "Very Good!"*] which might push us into considering our country as an appendage, a complement to other states, so long as we possess all that is needed to play the role of a great nation in the family of democratic countries, surrounded by the respect and friendship of all our allies. [*Applause*] [39]

While moved by very different concerns, the Communists' analysis of France's international position coincided fairly closely with de Gaulle's own. He too saw France's future bound up with its role as a world power. He also realized that the allied governments were then considering a number of schemes for the future of Europe, and even of the world, that did not necessarily take into account the interests of France and in whose elaboration France had not been invited to participate. He was therefore determined that France should be given an appropriate role in the coming victory and be permitted to assume a significant place in the postwar world. Hence he warned the Communist party and the Allies, even as he sought to rally his countrymen for the final effort of the Liberation:

> French citizens, wherever they are, who are fighting the enemy . . . are doing so at the call of France, to attain the goals of France, and in accord with the wishes of France. Any system that may be established on any other basis than those will lead to adventure or to impotence. But France, who values her life, her grandeur, her independence, does not admit, in this grave matter, of either impotence or adventure. . . . But now the end is in sight for the worst tragedy of our history. Lift up your heads! Let us close ranks in brotherhood! and let us all march together into the fray, through victory, toward our new destinies.[40]

De Gaulle was keenly aware, however, before France could recover her former grandeur a number of steps would have to be taken to assure that the political parties would not return to "the savoury games of illusion and denigration" that previously had led to disaster.[41] To silence these internal demons would require a new sense of self-confidence and a renewed determination. The colonial territories were one important element in meeting this need. As de Gaulle assured the Consultative Assembly on 21 November 1944, "In the rediscovered unity of the nation and empire, we will be sure enough of ourselves to be able to contribute powerfully to the maintenance of peace." [42]

The other essential condition was the reform of the domestic political system to assure that France had a regime capable of commanding confidence in the metropole and acting effectively to safeguard her interest. Thus, de Gaulle asserted:

> Tomorrow everything will be controlled by the question of a central power which the country acclaims and follows. For me, . . . it is no longer a matter of throwing a few troops into combat, or rallying here and there little bits of territory, or of singing to the nation the romance of her grandeur. It is the whole people, just as it is, that I must gather together. Against the enemy, in spite of the Allies, in the face of frightful divisions, I will have to build up around myself the unity of war-torn France.[43]

For these purposes, also, the preservation of unity within the colonial empire appeared essential. In this regard, it is one of the major ironies in de Gaulle's political thought that he repeatedly defended the principle of France's autonomy vis-à-vis other governments, yet never considered that principle relevant to the internal organization of the republic. In this respect, he remained consistent with the republican colonial tradition discussed above. At no time did he imagine France at the center of a network of autonomous states bound together in the fashion of the British Commonwealth, only by ties of economic interest, culture, and tradition. Instead, his attitude took for granted the universalistic ideas of equality and liberty that bind citizens within the historic community of the nation. Where cultural differences and economic conditions made such links inadequate, it was necessary to supplement them with administrative controls and, in some cases, with the use of force. Under the circumstances that prevailed in 1945, and having staked everything on his opposition to any "abandonment" of France's traditional interests, de Gaulle could only conceive of a right of "self-determination" within the existing framework of the republic.

It remains now to examine the specific policies initiated by the Free French in an effort to preserve unity between the colonies and the metropole and to consider the consequences of those initiatives.

4. GAULLISM AND COLONIALISM: DOCTRINE AND PRACTICE

The conditions of war worked many lasting changes on the French colonial system. At best, the colonies were cut off from the metropole and forced to survive on their own resources without economic support, with diminished personnel and uncertain leadership. At worst, they became part of the battle zone. The result was to weaken the hold of the metropolitan bureaucracy over the colonial administration and to reduce sharply the control the latter could in turn exercise over the indigenous peoples of the colonies. The war also reduced the means available for promoting economic development and strongly stimulated the emotional and political movement of the colonial peoples toward independence. In a number of instances these changes were encouraged and supported by France's allies—whether Britain, the United States, or the Soviet Union—for their own purposes.

De Gaulle's response to these conditions was contradictory. On one hand, he was determined that he would return to the republic intact the patrimony it had lost as a result of the collapse of 1940. The crime of Vichy had been to consent to abandon France's most vital interests in a time of danger, impairing her status as a world power and destroying her honor.

> This the nation condemns. If it were ever to come to admit or to practice such deliberate attempts upon her honor, her grandeur, or her independence, she would no longer be France. . . . But she still is! And we, who have never ceased to believe it . . . can say

This chapter originally appeared, in slightly different form, in *France and Britain in Africa,* ed. Prosser Gifford and Wm. Roger Louis (New Haven: Yale University Press, 1971), copyright © 1971 by Yale University; reprinted here by permission of Yale University Press.

today, as Clemenceau once did, *"La guerre! Rien que la guerre! La Justice passe. Le pays connaitra qu'il est défendu."* [1]

On the other hand, it was essential that some limited reforms be introduced to cope with the most pressing needs of the colonies. After the downfall of Vichy—which never ceased accusing de Gaulle of betraying French interests for the benefit of England—it became possible to plan for new institutions. The guiding principles that underlay those reforms remained largely unchanged, as did the policies that were employed in carrying them out. Consequently, the reforms introduced by the Free French encouraged greater expectations of further change on the part of the indigenous elites of the colonies by providing them with a rudimentary political system through which new demands, once legitimized, could be made politically effective. Thus, the Gaullist policies gave a vigorous thrust to the development of native nationalist movements whose ultimate goal of independence the Gaullists had entirely refused to consider.

This fundamental contradiction between Gaullist aims and Free French policies appeared clearly in a number of instances, most critical of which were the reforms inaugurated by de Gaulle at the Brazzaville Conference in January and February 1944; the ordinance of 7 March 1944, conferring French citizenship on tens of thousands of Algerian muslims; and the declaration of 24 March 1945, instituting a new relationship between France and Indochina. The first brought together the principal threads of Gaullist political thought regarding the colonies and attempted to apply them to the problems of sub-Saharan Africa. The second expanded on some of the same themes in the very different context of North Africa and the Middle East, while the third attempted to find a legal solution to a situation in Indochina that had already disintegrated into open violence. Central to all three cases was de Gaulle's determination to hold the colonies within the French orbit as a guarantee of France's world status and as evidence of his own superior stewardship. In every case, the policies he initiated had unintended consequences that were to vitiate and eventually to confound those intentions.

The Brazzaville Conference

The first occasion on which the disparate elements of Gaullist colonial doctrine were brought face to face with the realities of colonial life was the Brazzaville Conference of January and February 1944. This important meeting assembled the governors of all French Africa, now once again united under Free French control, together with members of the Consultative Assembly at Algiers and the ranking members of the Gaullist provisional regime. Its primary purpose was to formulate a plan to coordinate the economic and political development of the African territories. The results of the conference, although difficult to assess in detail, must be accounted impressive by any reasonable standard. For not only did the conference advance a comprehensive program of economic and social improvement, but for the first time—and, indeed, the only time in recent history—the men who were directly responsible for the execution of French policy were given the opportunity to lay out a program of political action as well. This effort at shaping the process of political change and the attempt to maintain a close relationship between political, economic, and social developments within the vast area of French Africa was truly a monumental undertaking.

The grand scope of these purposes was dramatically presented by de Gaulle in his opening speech. After stressing the urgent need for coordinated planning and hailing "the centuries-old civilizing mission of the republic" that had been carried out by France's great colonial administrators, de Gaulle analyzed the changing position of the colonies in French strategy and urged his listeners to take careful account of the enormously accelerated pace that the war had given to the political evolution of the colonies. Such rapid changes created many problems which, he said, France was determined to confront in a generous spirit, for, "if there is one imperial power that has been led by recent events to heed its lessons, to choose nobly, liberally, the way of a new era in which to direct the sixty million people who find themselves associated with the destiny of her own forty-two million children, that country is France." [2]

As one would expect on such an occasion, the familiar themes of Gaullist colonial doctrine were prominently displayed. Special emphasis was placed upon "the immortal genius of France . . . for raising men toward the summits of dignity and fraternity where . . . they may all unite" and upon the "definitive bond" between France and the colonies formed by the heavy sacrifices of blood and treasure on the part of colonial populations "who had not for a moment altered their loyalties." But such ideas were not mere decoration; neither were they invoked to justify inaction. It was change and radical innovation that de Gaulle clearly intended to inspire, for he repeatedly stressed the need for France to look forward to the day when Africa would come of age politically as well as economically and to prepare the way for increased economic wealth, improved standards of living, and much larger measures of political autonomy. He told the conference: "There will be no real progress if men in their native lands do not profit by it morally and materially; if they cannot raise themselves little by little to the level where they will be capable of participating directly in the management of their own affairs. It is France's duty to see to it that it shall be so." [3]

If these admonitions are considered in conjunction with his other statements of policy, discussed previously, it becomes clear that de Gaulle conceived of political change in Africa as part of a larger strategic plan whose ultimate purpose lay outside the realm of colonial problems altogether. In his view, the African colonies, like the rest of the colonial empire, were but a means to a greater end, which was embodied in de Gaulle's own strategic vision of France's national purposes.

The amount of innovation that the Brazzaville Conference could accomplish was limited by two important factors, one constitutional and the other economic. Primarily an assembly of civil servants, the conference was empowered only to recommend action to the Consultative Assembly and the Provisional Government, and even these organs had no constituent powers; therefore, any structural changes that the conference proposed had to await action by a competent national assembly. This meant that structural reforms were to be excluded because "it is for the French nation, and for her alone, to proceed when the time comes, to the reforms . . . which she, in her sovereignty, will decide." Meantime the conference was asked "to study what social, political, economic, and other conditions seem to you to be capable of progressively being applied in each of our territories in order that, through their own development and the progress of their populations, they will integrate themselves into the French community with their interests, their aspirations, their future." [4] It would be a mistake, however, to underestimate the extent to which plans adopted to meet immediate problems tended effectively to shape the future. This had happened before in the course of French history, most notably under the National Government of M. Thiers in 1870, and de Gaulle was fully aware of this possibility, *"en at-*

tendant il faut vivre, et vivre c'est chaque jour entamer l'avenir." [5] A second important limitation stemmed from the conditions under which it was necessary to operate and the poverty of the means available. Hence, de Gaulle advised against trying to conceal how long and slow development was bound to be.

At the heart of the problem of colonial reform lay the tangled web of political and administrative institutions that held together the prewar colonial empire. These were substantially the same ones created by Napoleon III in 1854, although the senatus-consulte of 1854 no longer possessed constitutional force and hence could be altered by ordinary law. Since no general law was ever adopted during the Third Republic, the senatus-consulte amounted to a broad grant of power under which the executive governed the colonies by administrative decrees except for the Antilles and Réunion, Algeria, Tunisia, and Morocco, each of which enjoyed special legislative arrangements. Occasionally, metropolitan laws had been extended by the government to meet particular colonial problems. Generally, however, these had been treated by ministerial decree or by special local regulations issued by the colonial governor.

As long as colonial interests were confined to the local European community, this system worked reasonably well, since it was usually possible to shape policy in consultation with commercial groups in the colony or, in the case of parliamentary acts, through the auspices of ministers and deputies who were indirectly interested in colonial questions. With the rapid expansion of economic life and a consequent increase in the importance of non-Europeans within the colonies, a more effective system of policy-making was essential. Such a system had to be based upon four broad groups of existing institutions: (1) the predominantly European economic organizations such as the *chambres de commerce,* producers' syndicates, and employers' organizations; (2) traditional local authorities, including religious leaders, tribal chiefs, local notables, occasional intellectuals, or indigenous farmers' or workers' organizations; (3) the colonial administration, which traditionally operated to coordinate and balance the influence of the first two groups as well as to take charge of most local policy-making; and, finally, (4) the representative institutions of metropolitan France, which traditionally had remained apart from any direct role in colonial affairs.

The Gaullist provisional regime approached the problem in a

manner consistent with the French colonial tradition. Unlike the British, who usually sought to establish responsible local governments by integrating local elites into the civil administration and by emphasizing its responsibility to locally designated legislatures, the French stressed the need for community-wide political representation and administrative centralization. By putting the issue in such terms, they raised a number of exceedingly difficult problems, such as the nature of French citizenship and the related questions of participation in local and metropolitan assemblies, as well as the thorny problems of civil rights in regard to both the executive and the judiciary, and the distribution of power between the central and local government bodies. Characteristically, it was assumed that there existed sufficient underlying consensus—an effective "general will"—to prevent conflict between the people and the policy-making elite, provided sufficient opportunity for local expression could be provided. One writer notes:

> The politicians of that period did not conceive of the empire, even under the more liberal and egalitarian form of the French Union, as an association of autonomous peoples or dominions. Convinced of the rightness of her cause and of the utility of her presence, France did not believe that a single one of the colonial peoples was sufficiently advanced to govern itself without her protection. Lacking any sort of powerful dynastic bond such as England and the dominions possess in the king, France and her possessions, in order that their association or their union be durable, needed to develop between them a bond as strong if not stronger, but a republican bond.[6]

In confronting the problem of political change, the Brazzaville Conference followed the lead given several years earlier by Félix Eboué in a report entitled *La nouvelle politique indigène pour l'Afrique Equatoriale Française.*[7] The substance of Eboué's position was that "assimilation," which in Central Africa had never been more than the official facade behind which traditional chiefs continued to rule under the formal authority of a French administrator, the *commandant de cercle,* should be abandoned in favor of a regime that would recognize openly the important role played by the local elites both European and non-European.

Eboué insisted that French policy explicitly renounce any intention "to remake native society according to our image or our mental habits." He argued that the French administration should strive "not to disturb any tradition nor change any habits." Rather, they should remember the secret of successful colonial rule enunciated by L. H. G. Lyautey, who once had written that in every society there exists a ruling class [*class dirigeante*] born to command, without which nothing can be done: "Let us get it on our side." Following the example of Lyautey, Eboué hoped to induce the traditional African elite to cooperate with the colonial administration in its efforts to improve economic and social conditions. He proposed political and administrative changes calculated to give the educated elite —the *notables évolués*—an active role in the administration of the larger towns. More important, however, it freed this group from the penalties commonly imposed under the *indigénat,* or native code, which permitted local officials to impose punishment for infractions of discipline, and from compulsory labor service which was required of most non-Europeans. The purpose of such liberality toward the African elite was to associate them with the colonial administration in order to encourage them to assume more responsibility for local affairs. It was not aimed, however, at developing the sort of autonomy that would replace French administration with local self-government.

Similarly, the Brazzaville Conference in the preamble to its "recommendations" pointedly observed that no such move, even in the long run, was to be considered. "The goals of the task of civilization accomplished by France in her colonies rule out any idea of autonomy, any possibility of evolution outside the French bloc of the empire; the eventual creation, even in the distant future, of *self-government* [sic] for the colonies is to be set aside." [8]

It was within this rather narrow, traditional framework that the conference took up the questions of greater autonomy for the colonies and increased political participation for non-Europeans both in the colonies and in the metropole. The recommendations it offered on these matters, although not entirely unprecedented, nevertheless went a considerable distance toward recognizing the political personality of the colonies. And despite a general lack of precision in the choice of language, it is evident that what was intended was a substantial change from existing practices.[9]

Within the colonies, the conference sought to gain the support of indigenous leaders by encouraging progressive development toward a system of effective representation: "It is indispensable to create the means for political expression that will permit the governors . . . to rely, on the side of both Europeans and natives, upon a perfectly balanced and legitimate representative system." [10] Specifically, it recommended that existing consultative bodies be abolished and replaced by a set of new organs. At the lower administrative levels, the subdivision and region, councils were to be formed from existing indigenous organizations, supplemented by other members, and were to enjoy the right to consult with the administration. At the territorial level, representative assemblies were to be instituted in which both Europeans and Africans participated. Members of the territorial assemblies were to be elected "by universal suffrage everywhere and under all conditions where the possibility will have been recognized." [11] Where election was impracticable, members might be chosen by cooptation or, in exceptional cases, appointed. The powers of the territorial assemblies were primarily consultative, but they were to have the right to deliberate on the budget of the territory. The budget was always prepared by the colonial administration and customarily contained two parts: the budget for existing expenses, which were primarily costs of administration, and the budget for new programs, including most economic development projects. The only area in which any freedom of choice could be said to exist was the second of these. All decisions required administrative endorsement.[12] The Conseils d'Administration, which were composed entirely of civil servants, were to assist the governor only in matters relating to the application of regulations, and all other representative bodies within the colonies were to be disbanded.

At the metropolitan level, too, the link between France and the colonies was to be strengthened by increasing the role of non-Europeans in the development of colonial policy. The most important step taken by the Brazzaville Conference was to call for the inclusion of overseas representatives in the Constitutional Assembly that was expected to follow the end of the war. It was assumed by everyone in the Free French movement that extensive constitutional reforms would be required in order both to wipe out the repressive legislation of Vichy and to strengthen the feeble institutions of the Third Republic. The precise role of the African and other colonial peoples in such an assembly would, of necessity, have to be determined by a higher political authority. Therefore, the Brazzaville Conference sought merely to lay down general guides for government action. Although the conference did not ignore the choice of means, it was much more explicit about the ends to be sought.

That such participation was "desirable and even indispensable" appeared beyond question in view of "the importance of the colonies in the French community, an importance that should no longer need discussion after the service they have rendered to the nation during the course of this war." [13] In an effort to assure that colonial representation would be more effective than it had been in the past, the conference declared that "a priori any reform is to be rejected that would tend merely to ameliorate the system of representation existing on 1 September 1939 (colonial deputies and senators in the metropolitan Parliament with new seats being granted to those colonies not presently represented)." [14]

Instead, a new representative body was recommended. The Colonial Parliament or, preferably, Federal Assembly, was intended to meet several specific needs: "to affirm and guarantee the infrangible unity of the French world" and to "respect the life and the local freedom of each of the territories that constitute the bloc France-Colonies —or if one may use the term, in spite of the objection it may raise, *la fédération française*." Exactly what powers were to be exercised by this new body could not be determined, since they would reflect the division of authority between the central (metropolitan) government and the colonies. Similarly, the separation of powers among the legislature, the executive, and the local administration would depend on the exact form of the federal system, but the conference wanted it clearly noted that "it is desirable to see the colonies make their way by stages from administrative decentralization toward a political personality." [15]

By these actions, the Brazzaville Conference explicitly recognized the need for the colonies to establish their own political identity. It sought a new institutional framework for the empire that would permit such a development, thereby breaking out of the traditional mold of "assimilation" and "association" and carrying the debate over France's colonial relationship far beyond the point reached by any prewar government. In this regard, Brazzaville is rightly considered a major turning point in French colonial politics. Nevertheless, in order to understand subsequent controversies, it is essential to note the deep ambivalence that marked the conference's recommendations on several levels.

First, on the political level, the Brazzaville Conference assumed that by encouraging the political development of the colonies, those indigenous forces working for political change could be controlled and channeled into constructive economic and social fields with results that would be mutually beneficial to France and the colonies. At the same time, the criterion by which political reforms were to be judged was explicitly understood to be the reestablishment of French national grandeur, and where metropolitan interests and colonial interests might conflict, the interests of the metropole took precedence. Thus, what began as a concern for local autonomy ended with a reassertion of metropolitan predominance.

> It is to be emphasized that the only criterion to be adopted is the necessity, *from the national point of view,* of forming strong, coherent groupings which can be compared with other important foreign colonies in Africa and *bring to the metropole their aid and their economic and political strength. . . .*
>
> France places not only her honor but her interests in having the colonies endowed with their own prosperity, and access to the riches of all that bears the French name is the most certain measure of our country's return to grandeur.[16]

On the administrative level, too, there was ambivalence. On one hand, the conference emphasized the need to involve larger numbers of Africans in local administrative positions as a step toward effective local government. On the other hand, it called for strengthening the financial controls of individual colonies and urged the "modernization of the administration in the domain of material installations and methods as well as the revaluation of the civil service." [17] Lateral recruitment, which would be necessary if Africans were to be brought into the local administration in large numbers, was approved, subject to "reasonable limitations." Given the vagueness of the language employed, it remained unclear which took precedence: the africanization of cadres or the modernization of the existing services.

A similar ambivalence characterized the treatment of economic questions. For example, the conference stressed the need for raising standards of living for the masses of Africans and hence for increasing economic productivity. To this end, it proposed to break with established patterns of colonial agriculture by promoting industrialization in areas where resources were available. Yet this departure, which certainly constituted a major step toward economic self-sufficiency, was hedged about with conditions and limitations. It was to be carried out "by steps, with method and prudence, within the strict limits resulting from the application of a general plan of production." [18] It was taken for granted that the colonial administration would control the plan.

More important, none of the recommendations contemplated any fundamental change in the structure of the colonial economy. As one critic noted at the time,[19] the conference remained silent about the central role of French banks, shipping concerns, and trading companies which exercised a quasi monopoly over the commerce of French Africa. It also ignored the interlocking relationship between such firms and the colonial administration which provided them with subsidies, controlled prices, and sometimes recruited their labor. This typically colonial pattern of economic organization had many disadvantages: it restricted the supply of capital for the native economy; it distorted the market within which local goods were traded; and it encouraged plantation agriculture and extractive industries, causing both social and ecological dislocations. It was precisely this pattern of economic organization that needed to be broken if the generous aims set forth in other recommendations were to bear fruit.

Any lingering doubts about whose interests were the controlling ones in the economic sphere were removed by the recommendations concerning the closely related issue of customs regulations—customs duties being one of the principal sources of revenue for the local treasuries and a prime factor in determining economic growth. After first objecting to the inflexibility of the existing customs regime, the conference recommended that individual colonies exercise greater control over customs duties and import and export licenses in order to promote more stable and rapid economic growth. Hence, they urged that initial decisions on these matters be made by local representative bodies. However, such decisions had to be approved by a decree signed by the minister of the colonies after consultation with the other ministerial departments concerned; thus, there was no danger that metropolitan interests would be harmed in the process. Only if the central government failed to act within a period of three months did local decisions become operative directly. Obviously, then, the thrust toward local economic self-sufficiency stopped well short of a complete transformation of traditional economic relationships between the metropole and the colonies.

A somewhat different sort of ambivalence was evident in the recommendations relating to social and cultural matters. Here the conference found itself caught between the desire not to change African customs and values or to attempt to make over Africans in the image of Frenchmen and the necessity for social change as a prerequisite to economic and political modernization. Furthermore, since modernization meant developing the capacity to function in the world of Western bureaucracy, it was inevitable that the conference should have recommended the introduction of French values in many areas of civil and private life. Hence, there appears to be a direct conflict in the conference recommendations between the desire to preserve and strengthen the role of African customary law and the need to introduce more modern concepts and practices derived from French civil law.

Three examples will illustrate these difficulties.[20] The conference adopted the general principle that "the development of the indigenous population" should guide social policy. In line with this view, it was recommended that Africans become more directly involved in the adjudication of local conflicts and that the system of administrative punishments prescribed by the *indigénat* be "progressively abolished, as soon as hostilities are ended." Civil and commercial conflicts would continue to be decided locally in accordance with customary law as interpreted in the first instance by African judges. At the same time, however, the conference called on administrators "to intervene constantly in the domain of public law and of the family in order that the evolution of customary law may be controlled and guided according to the principles [of women's rights and freedom of marriage] which were set forth at the time of marriage."

In relation to labor practices, too, the conference envisioned reforms that would eliminate the system of forced labor, "conditionally maintained in force by reason of the war effort." It was to be replaced with a "free labor market" which, however, was to be "really effectively controlled" by the creation of a body of "labor inspectors" dependent on the Ministry of the Colonies. The inspectors, would be charged with applying a comprehensive labor code, which would extend to the colonies many of the rights and practices that had become established in French labor law: the right to organize unions and professional organizations, wages and hours limitations, vacations, working conditions, and so on. Thus, the changes that were proposed as a means of "ameliorating the condition of the native worker" carried with them the prospect of greater personal liberty and security, but also of closer conformity to French standards of work and more elaborate supervision by the colonial administration.

Finally, in the area of education, the conference recommended a dual approach that would provide a general education that would both "reach and penetrate the masses and teach them to live better" and "result in a rapid and reliable selection of elites." The possibility of conflict between these aims was not examined, and most emphasis was devoted to plans for training primary school teachers and organizing professional training programs. On one point, however, the conference was unequivocal: "Instruction is to be given in the French language; the use of local spoken dialects in teaching being absolutely forbidden, in private schools as well as in the public schools." Thus, while education was clearly seen as the necessary means toward the further progress of the African peoples, there was no disposition to relinquish control over any phase of it to local, indigenous authorities or to permit local interests to influence its methods or direction. Nothing was even mentioned about the content of basic education in the recommendations.

Looking back at the record of the Brazzaville Conference, it is clear that its members were for the most part unaware of the ambivalence inherent in their recommendations, probably because it was concealed by the tone of paternalism that pervaded both the discussions and the final report. This paternalistic attitude, which French writers seldom seem to recognize, reflected a set of underlying assumptions and experiences. Most obviously, it coincided with the long-standing French tradition of bureaucratic centralism that tended to reduce all problems to questions of administrative procedure capable of direction from the center according to a common plan. Similarly, the spirit of *dirigisme,* which is inherent in all modern economic planning, also was conducive to a paternalistic approach to public issues.

The Gaullists' paternalistic attitude also concealed the implicit assumption that specific policies for reform would remain more or less indefinitely within the control of the colonial administration. Political, social, and economic change, from their point of view, was seen as the consequence of French generosity and liberality, or at least as means of fulfilling enlightened self-interest. In no case was change regarded as the outcome of political struggle. Perhaps most important of all, the assumptions and attitudes that underlay the recommendations of the conference were consistent with the strategic goals of the Free French at that moment: to promote the development of the African colonies within a political and administrative framework that contributed to the restoration of French grandeur.

Symptomatic of the contrast between the overt and latent dimensions of the Brazzaville Conference were the spirit of optimism and the romantic aura of unity that pervaded its recommendations, largely obscuring the seriousness of the underlying political conflicts. Because of its location and timing, the conference met with no organized political opposition from any groups either in the colonies or in the metropole. In such an atmosphere, it was possible for the participants to confront the prospect of political change with considerable confidence in the outcome, and whatever lingering doubts may have existed were outweighed by the hope that the enunciation of general principles of reform would satisfy all existing discontent.[21] A vivid example of the "spirit of Brazzaville" generated by the conference was offered by Félix Gouin, veteran Socialist parliamentarian and president of the Consultative Assembly, who declared:

> More and more there emerges among Frenchmen of the metropole a very keen feeling of increased and reinforced responsibility toward our colonies; those creations of our own flesh and blood that we owe it to ourselves to protect, to aid, and to assist more each day in order to bring them slowly toward a better future. . . .
>
> We are deeply convinced that after the gigantic tidal wave of the war, the relations between the metropole and the colonies should be based on a policy that is realistic but disinterested. . . .
>
> Let us, therefore, be careful in the period that we have now reached not to aggravate the sense of right that is awakening nor the susceptibility to insult on the part of those spirits newly promoted to civilization.
>
> I know already that along this general line, your thoughts and ours are the same and that like all of us you have the feeling—I should say, the certainty—that the best civilizer is he who knows how to find the words that join hands and unite hearts.[22]

More than words were required, however, to bring unity between the metropole and the colonies. During the course of 1944 a number of decrees were issued putting into effect some of the most important recommendations of the conference, including the suppression of forced labor,[23] the promulgation of a uniform penal code to replace the indigénat, the reestablishment of trade unions, and a wholesale reorganization of the educational system.

It should be noted that elimination of the excesses of the native labor system in force during the interwar period was an important part of the programs advanced by the Popular Front government in 1936 and that the first concrete steps in that direction had been taken by the socialist minister of the colonies, Marius Moutet. Most important of all was the decree of 11 March 1937, applying the metropolitan laws regarding the organization of trade unions to all of French West Africa. This effort at reform remained incomplete, however, and other aspects of the labor system, particularly the recruitment of African workers, was left largely unaltered until after World War II.

The most important questions of political organization remained to be decided by the Constituent Assembly, but these partial reforms, together with the decision that Africans should be represented in the Constituent Assembly, changed both the context and the content of the political discussions when they were reopened in 1946. They are also important because in the interim they gave rise to two sets of conflicting expectations. De Gaulle, like many other Frenchmen, seems to have regarded the recommendations of Brazzaville as a maximum concession to local interests in the form of a limited federal system that left the essential constitution unity of the republic unaltered. Many Africans, however, soon began to look upon Brazzaville as but a short step in the direction of complete local autonomy. These expectations, although not sufficiently at odds to openly disturb the unity of the colonies and the metropole, were to make it much more difficult to find a workable formula for unity in 1946 than was the case at Brazzaville.

Free France in North Africa

The efforts of the Free French to build colonial unity by timely reforms were not confined to Tropical Africa. In North Africa, too, they sought, under very different conditions, to promote political changes that would encourage close relations between the local populations and metropolitan France. As at Brazzaville, the preferred avenue of approach was that of enlarged representation. The most noteworthy example is the decree of 7 March 1944, which extended considerably the voting rights of Algerian Muslims.

General de Gaulle had been deeply impressed by the support given to the Free French by the colonial populations, but he was well aware that he could continue to hold their confidence during the crucial period of the Liberation and the difficult months that would follow only if the colonial territories were not forced to remain in their former roles.[24] Summing up his attitude in a speech to a large crowd of Muslims in the Place de la Breche in Constantine on 12 December 1943, he declared:

> By proving their profound unity throughout these last four agonizing years, all the territories of the French imperial community have been a credit to France. To France—that is, to the evangelist of racial brotherhood, equality of opportunity, and the vigilant maintenance of order to assure the liberty of all. . . .
>
> All the peoples have lavished upon France the proof of a fidelity to which the extent of her own suffering gives a decisive character that is not only deeply moving, but that places her under obligation from now on.
>
> Yes, it places her under obligation; and especially toward the Muslims of North Africa. . . . What better occasion could I find to announce that the government . . . has just adopted a number of important resolutions concerning Algeria? The Liberation Committee has decided to extend immediately to several tens of thousands of Federal Muslims their full rights as citizens without allowing the exercise of these rights to be interfered with or limited by objections based on personal status [that is, the retention of their rights under Koranic law].[25]

These declarations were given official form in the decree of 7 March 1944, which enlarged the noncitizens' electoral college by extending voting rights to all Muslims twenty-one years of age or older (about 1.6 million) who were not French citizens and by increasing the number of seats apportioned to noncitizens in the selected assemblies of Algeria to two-fifths of the total. It further abrogated all special administrative measures applicable to Muslims who were assured "equal rights and equal responsibilities" with non-Muslim French citizens. Finally, the decree granted French citizenship to a number of specified categories of Muslims (about fifty to sixty thousand) in recognition of their individual achievements. This grant was limited to voting rights, and it was strictly personal in its scope. These changes, which were not contingent on the renunciation of any existing rights under Koranic law, were substantially those that had been proposed in the rejected Blum-Violette plan of 1936.

The clear intent of the decree was to maintain unity by providing a larger outlet within the French community for the expression of local Muslim opinion. But its real significance can be seen only after examining some of the circumstances surrounding its adoption, for Algeria enjoyed a very special role in the French colonial system.

Algeria was regarded by most Frenchmen as an extension of metropolitan France, and it had been described as such even in the nineteenth century, despite the fact of its large Muslim population and the special political institutions that were provided for it. The large urban areas were governed in much the same way as metropolitan departments, whereas the rural sections were under various forms of colonial administration. Algeria was very different from other colonies in Africa because of the size of its resident European community and the extent of European landownership and commercial activity. It was also distinguishable from other North African territories because it lacked an indigenous, Muslim political authority. The Algerian Muslim community, nevertheless, had developed a degree of political self-consciousness during the years before 1940 that gave its local politics a flavor very different from that of Tropical Africa.

During the war, Algeria had been, first a center of pro-Vichy, anti-Gaullist sentiment among the European population, and, later, the temporary capitol of the Free French Provisional Government. More important, it had been for a time part of the war zone, and during that period French authority was overshadowed by the military might of the American armed forces and undermined by the political maneuvers of American diplomacy. President Franklin D. Roosevelt's personal representative in North Africa, Robert Murphy, was said to have been instrumental in consolidating the efforts of the several Muslim nationalist organizations which up to that time had remained divided into opposing factions. With encouragement from the American authorities, a group of Algerian Muslims under the leadership of Ferhat Abbas drafted a "Manifesto" urging drastic revision of the relations between France and Algeria and recognition for the predominant interest of the Muslim population in Algeria. Its issuance, on 12 February 1943, according to Charles-André Julien, marked "the beginning of a new era of nationalist activity," [26] for it was the first occasion on which anyone had demanded explicit autonomy for Algeria in a form that commanded public attention.

The Gaullist response to the Manifesto was one of total opposition. In an effort to counter its effects, General Georges Catroux, who had been named by de Gaulle in June 1943 to be governor-general of Algeria and commissaire d'état for Muslim affairs in the Provisional Government, issued a series of decrees aimed at integrating Muslims and Europeans still more closely. These decrees were bitterly resented by the Algerian Muslim leadership, and they elicited massive opposition on the part of the Muslim elite, many of whom threatened to cease all participation in public bodies unless consideration was given to the issues raised by the Manifesto. This time the Gaullists responded even more vigorously, placing Ferhat Abbas and a number of other nationalist leaders under house arrest or compelling them to issue public apologies.[27] Yet the seriousness of these events, especially the threat of public demonstrations, led the Gaullists to reconsider their policies, and ultimately to take the steps embodied in the decree of 7 March.

That decree seems to reflect the same political frame of reference and to have been inspired by many of the same calculations as the Brazzaville recommendations. Although conditions in Algeria were drastically different, the Gaullists clearly assumed that increased representation would allay the resentments and capture the imaginations of Muslim leaders bringing them and their followers into line behind a new French regime. As at Brazzaville, de Gaulle was prepared to consider new local institutions and to grant a wider range of personal rights. By removing the stigma of colonial subjection, he hoped both to restore confidence in French administration and to encourage economic and even military support.

Yet some of the same ambivalence was also present in the decree, for more liberal institutions were again considered only as a reflection of French generosity, in response to acts of heroism on her behalf. Greater political participation was not intended to open the way to separation, rather it was supposed to unify the Muslim and European populations within the same political system. In the case of

Algeria, however, the Free French reforms were instituted among peoples who had already entered a phase of national self-consciousness, whose leaders were fairly well established, ready and willing to organize resistance to continued French domination.

Consequently, both in sub-Saharan Africa and in the Maghreb, Gaullist Free French policies encountered a variety of unintended consequences. Greater administrative autonomy and enlarged representation were permitted to function only as unifying structures within the French community. Wherever political consensus was inadequate, in practice, to sustain continued cooperation, the Gaullists quickly asserted the rigorous administrative controls of the past. The result was that the Gaullist Free French frequently sought to affirm a new ideal of unity between the colonies and the metropole, but when reforms proved ineffective, they resorted to repressive methods that generated deeper hostilities and provoked greater antagonism. Both in the Maghreb and in the sub-Saharan colonies, the consequences of Gaullist reforms were often the opposite from what was intended or desired.

Free French colonial policy in Africa, as elsewhere, was dominated by the determination to safeguard French sovereignty and to restore national prestige. Many of the actions taken by de Gaulle, however, bore little relationship to the real grievances or the political demands of the indigenous population. In North Africa, particularly, the conflict was severe, for there, as Ferhat Abbas later wrote, "France was late not by a war but by a revolution." [28]

Muslim nationalism, grounded in the social and economic impoverishment of the great mass of the indigenous population, made most of the Gaullist reforms empty gestures. On the other hand, the Free French determination to maintain full control over the colonial territories led directly to violent conflicts that quickly reduced the credibility of the government's liberal declarations. The end result, as the past twenty years have demonstrated, was to create hostility and encourage mounting violence on both sides. This was particularly the case in Morocco and Tunisia, and most tragically in Algeria.

French rule in Morocco operated through the authority of the sultan, the traditional sovereign. In January 1943, at the Casablanca Conference, Sultan Sidi ben Youssef discussed the future of his country with President Roosevelt and was reported to be encouraged by

Roosevelt's criticism of France's colonial claims and by his suggestion that the United States would support the efforts of colonial countries to gain full independence.

Sultan ben Youssef later cooperated with the Moroccan nationalist party, the Istiqlal, which was organized during December 1943. The Istiqlal program demanded that France immediately recognize Morocco's independence and grant political autonomy to the traditional governmental institutions of the sultanate. It denounced the French administration for infringing on the sultan's authority in violation of the protectorate agreements, proclaimed the need for a number of social and economic reforms, and promised to use every legal means to achieve these ends.[29]

The French responded to the Istiqlal demands with repression. The party's leader, Ahmed Balafrej, was arrested and deported to Corsica, an act that provoked major disorders in Rabat and Fez, in which more than forty lives were lost and hundreds were injured or imprisoned. Throughout most of 1944 French troops patrolled most of the country.

In Tunisia there was also strong nationalist feeling expressed by the Neo-Destour party which evoked similarly repressive reactions from the French authorities. General Alphonse Juin, acting under orders from General Henri Giraud, deposed Moncef Bey on 13 May 1943 on charges of conspiring with the Axis. The bey was forced into exile, and a number of administrative changes were introduced that effectively subordinated the nominally sovereign Tunisian government to the French authorities. These hasty and ill-considered acts not only violated the terms of the treaty of 12 May 1881, which guaranteed the bey's authority; they also created new sympathy for the nationalist movement and provided it with a powerful impetus toward unity.[30]

General Juin later declared that he regretted having been forced into "an impolitic act to the detriment of a sovereign against whom there was nothing serious to reproach and who had always been loyal." According to Roger Le Tourneau, the real reasons behind his removal had nothing to do with collaboration:

> The bey who was being deposed was the same one who stood up to the resident-general of France, whoever he was, who had formed a government on his own initiative (January 1943) contrary to all the

accepted usages and without prior negotiations, who on many occasions affirmed his desire to profoundly change the political habits acquired during sixty years of the protectorate. In sum, the French authorities jumped on the opportunity to rid themselves of an extremely inconvenient partner.[31]

Throughout the war, the attitude of the Tunisian elite had remained generally tolerant toward France and favorable to the Allies. Despite its antipathy to French colonial administration and some pro-Nazi sentiment among the young intellectuals of the Neo-Destour, the ruling group in Tunisia was conscious of the threat to Tunisian independence posed by Italian ambitions, and most of them assumed a neutral stance, awaiting an Allied victory. Habib Bourguiba urged the Neo-Destour leaders to cooperate actively with the Gaullist Resistance in 1942, and in a declaration to the people of Tunisia in May 1943 he proclaimed the need to "form a block today together with France: without France there is no salvation."[32]

The removal of Moncef Bey and the attempt to reassert control over the affairs of Tunisia had the principal effect of creating a powerful new movement of nationalist opposition. Rather than capitalizing on the personal influence of Moncef and the realism of Bourguiba in an effort to arrive at a compromise that would protect French interests in Tunisia, de Gaulle installed a puppet who could not command respect from any segment of Tunisian opinion. Lacking any valid spokesman with whom to carry on negotiations, the French administration was forced to confront strikes, demonstrations, and public manifestations of discontent. Once the nationalists took to the streets, however, repression was swift and severe. Hence, the pattern of disorder and recourse to force was repeated in Tunisia just as it occurred in Morocco. The last chance for a peaceful resolution of Franco-Tunisian conflicts thus passed even before the Free French had established their authority in North Africa. From 1943 on, feelings grew more hostile on both sides.

The limited reforms proposed by the Gaullists in 1945 and 1946 failed to meet the demands of the Tunisian nationalists. In an effort to bring pressure on France, their spokesmen, especially the Neo-Destour leader, Habib Bourguiba, presented the Tunisian case to many official and unofficial figures in the United States. At the same time, greater freedom to conduct internal affairs permitted the nationalists to organize popular support through trade unions, particularly the Confédération Générale du Travail Tunisien, and to develop an institutional base from which to press for further changes. Reflecting on his experiences at this critical period, Bourguiba later testified that he now knew that nothing was to be expected from France. "Nothing more from Free France than from the other one, and nothing more from the Fourth Republic than from the Third. Relying on the good sense of the French for the liberation of Tunisia was a waste of time. . . . Between France and us, it has become a question of force." [33]

In a revealing letter to Ferhat Abbas written from exile in Cairo, 29 June 1946, Bourguiba set forth the details of his strategy to gain international support for Tunisian independence and emphasized the common links between his experience and that of the Algerian nationalists. Even in the face of French intransigence, however, he was not vindictive, and if he was convinced that conflict was unavoidable, it was more out of despair than anger.

> If only France made an effort to understand us! If only she got around in time to changing her policy, we would hold out our hands to her with genuine relief, and we would form a real bloc with her against whatever sorts of foreign undertakings. But where is the French statesman who is able to make the French colony listen in Tunisia (or Algeria) and make them understand and accept the necessary concessions? The only time a French minister wanted to do something in Tunisia (Vienot), he was swept away like a wisp of straw before he could even begin to put his policy into action. It's unfortunate, but that's the way it is." [34]

In Algeria, the unintended consequences of Gaullist policy were even more tragic. The Muslim population reacted to the decree of 7 March with derision. Only the moderate, urbanized évolués endorsed it because, like the Blum-Violette plan of the thirties, it recognized their long-standing claims to greater participation in local government. The Communist party, a group that included a number of Europeans and Algerian Jews as well as Muslims, took a more qualified position because it saw possibilities for political propaganda and electoral support.

As if in response to the assimilationist intent of the decree, Ferhat Abbas announced on 14 March the formation of a single, unified nationalist organization, the Amis du Manifeste, which brought together the three major factions within the Algerian nationalist movement: the Islamic reformers of the ulemas association, the impoverished urban working-class supporters of Messali Hadj's clandestine Parti du Peuple Algérien (PPA), and middle-class supporters of the Manifesto. The Association of the Reformist Ulema of Algeria was a group of Muslims connected with the Salafiya movement, which sought to promote a reformed, puritan version of Islam that left room for modern technological developments. As David Gordon noted, "The reformers wanted the best of two worlds. They were adamant in rejecting all the superstitions and saint-worship that came under the rubric of *maraboutisme* in Algeria, and they insisted on a strict, puritan pattern of behavior, the revival of Arabic as the official language of the nation, and its purification (according to the standards of the language of the Koran)." [35] In 1945 the ulema strongly supported the founding in Algeria of an independent Islamic state aligned with other Islamic communities in North Africa.

The Amis du Manifeste took advantage of the newly restored liberties to organize a campaign among the évolués enfranchised by the decree of 7 March aimed at discouraging them from registering on the electoral lists of French citizens in order to demonstrate Algerian determination to refuse assimilation. Membership in the Amis du Manifeste grew rapidly; by September 1944 it claimed 500,000 adherents, and in December, Ferhat Abbas's newspaper, *Egalité,* attained a circulation of 30,000 copies.

As agitation continued to spread, the Muslim population became more and more restless, stirred on by the excitement generated by the founding of the Arab League as well as by the emotional speeches of their own leaders. At its first national congress in March 1945, the party, by then under the influence of Messali's PPA, adopted a program that called for "an Algerian parliament and Algerian government," abandoning the more cautious language of Ferhat Abbas who earlier had advocated autonomy for Algeria within "a French federation of nations." The consequence, as Roger Le Tourneau observed, was that "the young people, scouts, high school and university students, and pupils at the reformist [Koranic] schools, followed the activities of their political chiefs with passionate interest and egged them on to intransigence. In short, the political climate was like nothing Algeria had ever known." [36]

Tension was further increased during the spring of 1945 by the shift of military operations from North Africa to Western Europe, which deprived Algeria of important economic resources and drastically reduced the strength of French garrisons, leaving the country's internal security in the hands of the police and local militia. In this highly explosive atmosphere it required very slight provocation to evoke the worst fears and the most bitter hatreds among both French and Muslim Algerians. The first intimations of serious disorder occurred on May Day when the PPA sought to turn the traditional workers' parade into a nationalist rally in the large cities of Algiers, Oran, Bone, and Bougie. The police intervened and order was restored, but not before several dozen casualties had occurred, including three or more killed.

During the week of 8 May 1945, a major uprising began as a result of riots that occurred when groups of Muslims attempted to demonstrate in favor of Algerian independence during V-E Day ceremonies. The worst of these occurred in the small, provincial cities of Sétif and Guelma, as well as in the surrounding Constantine region. In a semi-organized outburst, set off by a policeman in Sétif, thousands of armed Muslims roamed the towns and countryside indiscriminately killing Europeans. The French authorities, urged on by terrified, outraged colonists, launched a vicious repression that lasted until the middle of June, in which the armed forces were used, including naval bombardment of the coastal villages and aerial attacks on the interior towns, in addition to administrative and judicial executions.

Losses on both sides were heavy. French sources list 97 killed and more than 100 wounded among the Europeans in the region, and 1,500 Muslims killed. Nationalist sources estimated that as many as 50,000 Muslims may have died. The true number will never be known, but the bitterness engendered by these events became evident in 1954.

An official investigation failed to discover any direct connection between the nationalist parties and the uprisings, but there was strong public pressure from European colonists and in the metropolitan press for their suppression and a demand for the recall of Governor-General Yves Chataigneau, a socialist criticized for dealing too leniently with the nationalists. De Gaulle refused to replace Chataigneau and went ahead with the municipal elections scheduled for July 1945. Ferhat Abbas and most of the leaders of the Amis du

Manifeste were arrested and convicted, together with about two thousand other participants in the uprisings. Forty-eight persons were executed, and most of the rest remained in prison until March 1946 when they were liberated under an amnesty voted by the First Constituent Assembly. A number of the nationalist leaders, including Abbas, were elected to the Second Constituent Assembly under the banner of the Union Démocratique du Manifeste Algérien.[37]

Most authorities agree that May 1945 marked a critical turning point in the relations between France and Algeria. To cite just one example, Le Tourneau has concluded:

> From May 1945 on, there developed a profound break between the two communities who, nevertheless, had lived together for a century. The scope and severity of the repression and the fact that it was only a very small proportion of the Muslim population that took up arms, made it unlikely thereafter that a new explosion would occur right away. But if the two communities did not confront each other again immediately, each remained deeply distrustful of the other. The Muslims feared that any political decisions taken by the metropole were inspired by the French Algerians or would strengthen their domination; while these same Frenchmen were convinced, especially after the uprisings of 1945, that force alone would protect them, and they put all their confidence in it.[38]

Free France in West and Central Africa

The situation in the two colonial federations of West and Central Africa was less tense than in Algeria, but even in relatively remote areas like Guinée and the Ivory Coast, new movements were developing in the aftermath of the wartime reforms. There was very little discussion of "independence" anywhere in French West Africa, but demands for social, economic, and administrative changes emerged quickly after the announcement of the recommendations of Brazzaville. Until then, Africans had been divided into two groups: those born in the "four communes" of Senegal, who enjoyed civil and political rights granted by metropolitan legislation during the Third Republic; and the rest, who were without any guarantees of civil or political liberty. The vast majority of the African population was ruled by the indigénat, which gave the local administrative officer general authority to maintain discipline, define offenses, and prescribe punishment. In practice, the local commandant de cercle exercised virtually total discretion over the lives of Africans in his district.

In matters of military service and forced labor, the ordinary African was subject to special liabilities not imposed on French citizens, whether African or European. In addition to a longer period of military service, noncitizens were subject, as part of their military obligation, to assignment to the *deuxième contingent,* which provided labor for the maintenance of roads and construction of public works. The administration also had the power to requisition labor for use on European plantations and to establish wage scales that would assure a profit.

On the other hand, the personal lives of the subjects in regard to matters such as marriage, divorce, and inheritance were left to local tradition and, where applicable, to Koranic law rather than to French civil law. Hence, political liberties were available only to a tiny fraction, about 80,000 out of a total population of roughly 14.5 million in West Africa, prior to World War II.[39] Explicitly political organizations were almost totally lacking until 1945. During the interwar period an assortment of economic and cultural groups had emerged whose activities, though primarily directed at other goals, often verged on the political. The most important among these were trade unions, veterans' organizations, and school alumni associations (the Anciens de l'Ecole Normale William Ponty in Dakar included many of the most dynamic leaders of the African elite from all of French West Africa), youth groups, tribal societies formed to aid those who had migrated sometimes from great distances to the growing towns, and cultural societies of many types. These quasi-political groups, as Thomas Hodgkin and Ruth Schachter have noted, provided a basis for the subsequent development of organized political movements.[40] They were not mass organizations, but they provided a source of experienced militants for the rich assortment of political movements and parties that sprang up after World War II.

Beginning during the Popular Front period, more explicit political education was provided for some of the elite by missionaries or teachers with connections among the leftist parties—Socialists or Communists—of the metropole. In 1943 the French Communist party established Groupes d'Etudes Communistes (GEC), with centers in several large towns of West Africa. Although they produced few orthodox Marxists, the GECs afforded access to Marxist language and modes of analysis.[41] The emotional shock that followed the French military defeat in 1940 was felt even in the most remote corners of French Africa. Yet, it did not precipitate any overt opposition to France among the African elite. This tiny group tended, for the most part, to show great sympathy for France and, initially at least, to echo the sentiments of the colonial administration with which a substantial proportion had very close economic or professional ties. However, the announcement of the armistice produced a wave of sympathy for the dissident Gaullists, with the result that a greater degree of political awareness began to emerge, and some Africans openly opposed the local administration. Admiration for the venerable Marshal Pétain and the Vichy officials diminished rapidly as it became clear to Africans that "restoring the authority of the state" provided the basis for a new, brutal policy of exploitation and repression. What was not accomplished by racial discrimination and forced labor was achieved by the anti-Negro, racist propaganda of the Nazis.

The impact of the disputes among Vichy and Gaullist colonists is difficult to estimate, although it did create an impression of administrative confusion. Where Vichy officials were in firm control, that is, in nearly all of West Africa, Africans who took part in pro-Gaullist activities were treated as subversives, and some who were caught were subjected to torture and imprisonment. Nevertheless, some Africans did participate in the Gaullist Resistance groups, and in a few instances whole tribes or villages fled into neighboring British colonies until the end of the war.[42] The most dramatic gestures of resistance were those of Ora Ashedi, chief of Porto-Novo in Dahomey, who committed suicide for fear his subjects would be turned over to German authorities, and of the Mogho Naba, ruler of the Mossi kingdom and the most powerful traditional chief in French Africa, who ended his life in an elaborate ceremonial at his capitol of Ouagadougou. Such gestures generated considerable emotion among the masses of Africans who had remained generally impassive.[43] For the peoples of West Africa as a whole, however, the decline in French authority was far less dramatic than in North Africa.

During the closing phase of World War II, Free French policy in

Africa suffered as a consequence of the diminished role that the African region came to occupy in the military strategy of the Allied powers. As the centers of conflict shifted to Western Europe and the Far East, the Gaullist regime was forced to realign its strategic concerns. Particularly after 1944, the Free French found themselves confronted both in the Levant and in Indochina with acute threats to the political unity of the French Empire and to its grandeur.

The collapse of German power in North Africa brought British and French forces into a bitter confrontation over the control of the Levant. That crisis, which was almost simultaneous with the end of the war in Europe, found the troops of the two allies on the verge of open conflict.

Free France in the Middle East

In seeking to maintain a foothold for France in the eastern Mediterranean, de Gaulle found himself plunged into a dispute that had raged intermittently since the turn of the century, inciting international enmities on many sides. To abandon France's claims in Syria and Lebanon would have been impossible, however, given de Gaulle's political stance and France's historic role in that region. With the lines of rivalry and policy so long established, there was a sort of fatalism surrounding both de Gaulle's policies and their ultimate failure. Yet, the events surrounding the Levant crisis of 1944–45 are of special interest as an indication of the potential for discord that lay concealed within the framework of Gaullist colonialism.

France's interests in the Middle East, especially in Syria, have been thought by some Frenchmen to date from the time of Charlemagne, and a continuous link had existed with the region ever since the first Crusades. From protecting the holy places and supporting Christian minorities in Lebanon, French interest gradually spread throughout Syria as mission schools were founded and as trade and commerce expanded, especially during the nineteenth century. For long periods French claims to dominant interest were unchallenged, but during the last quarter of the nineteenth century, particularly in the complex diplomatic exchanges that preceded World War I, other nations began to advance rival claims.[44] First Italy and Britain and later, during the Balkan wars and the series of diplomatic crises of 1900–14, Germany, Russia, and even Austria-Hungary sought to challenge the primacy of France in the eastern Mediterranean. With the partition of the Ottoman Empire into spheres of interest, France succeeded in obtaining recognition from Italy, Britain, and Germany of her superior role in Syria and Lebanon. At the same time, a movement for national independence began to gather momentum within Syria as the control of the Ottoman Empire crumbled.

French-British rivalry was rekindled by a series of disputes during the course of World War I, but in the Treaty of San Remo of 25 April 1920 France once again gained formal recognition for her interests. At the peace conference after World War I both Britain and France asserted their willingness to grant eventual autonomy, in conformity with the language of Article 22 of the League Covenant, to the national governments of Lebanon and Syria. No immediate national unity was possible, however, and the French were recognized as the administering power under the League of Nations mandate system. During the 1920s France was confronted with strong pressure both from Britain and from Arab nationalists who were demanding immediate independence. Only after some heavy fighting, in which several thousand Arabs were killed (five thousand reportedly died in the siege of Damascus, 24 July 1920), were the French able to compel Emir Faisal to consent to the mandate, officially established in 1924 by the Treaty of Lausanne, which detached the area from the Ottoman Empire.

Nationalist opposition continued to grow in both Syria and Lebanon during the interwar years. In the most serious incident of that period, the fierce Djebel Druses uprising of 1925, French authority was severely shaken, and riots and demonstrations followed year after year only to be suppressed by colonial troops drawn from Senegal and from among the despised Armenians who had fled into Syria from Turkey. Finally, in 1936, the French governor, Martel, acting under instructions from the Popular Front government, negotiated an agreement with the nationalists providing for Syrian independence, subject to certain military advantages retained by France. A similar agreement was negotiated with Lebanon. Before these could be brought to a vote, however, the Popular Front government had been reconstituted, and the French Parliament refused to ratify the treaties. Hence, French troops still occupied Syria and Lebanon at the outbreak of World War II.

The French garrison in the Levant, under the command of General Dentz, remained loyal to Vichy in 1940, despite efforts by the Free French to rally support for de Gaulle. In 1941 a major conflict arose in the Levant when, as a result of an agreement between the Vichy foreign minister (Admiral Darlan) and Hitler, Nazi aircraft were permitted to land at Syrian airfields while they were engaged in operations against British forces in the Middle East. The British retaliated by moving their army into Syria and ousting the Vichy authorities. De Gaulle hoped that the British would permit him to assume full control over the region at once and to deal with Dentz and the Vichy forces, from whom the Free French expected to gain new supporters. Instead, the British insisted on retaining control of the military forces in Syria, and they refused to allow the Gaullists to recruit among the interned French troops, most of whom were later allowed to return to France. De Gaulle was permitted to assume control of the administrative affairs of the region, however, and mindful of France's earlier difficulties in limiting the expansion of British influence, he immediately sought a political countermove to offset the British military advantage, all the while protesting vigorously against the British infringement on French authority.[45]

Faced with the presence of British troops and wholly dependent at that point on British financial support, de Gaulle responded by naming General Georges Catroux, a senior officer with a distinguished record of colonial service, to administer French interests in the Levant. In his first major policy decision Catroux announced the independence of Syria on 27 September 1941 and that of Lebanon on 26 November, thereby putting Free France publicly on record as favoring the fulfillment of the agreements of 1936 and attempting to forestall any swing of local opinion to the side of the British. The force of this initial move was largely mitigated, however, by de Gaulle's subsequent explanation that these proclamations, while representing a decision in principle, could not have the effect of terminating the mandate, since that would require a new international agreement, which would have to wait until the end of the war.

The British, who continued to enjoy considerable influence over local opinion as a result of their control of trade and commerce throughout the region, began to press the Free French to hold elections in Syria and Lebanon. Although extremely reluctant to do so, de Gaulle was forced to consent to the announcement of elections in Lebanon after an agreement in principle to that effect between

Catroux and the British representative in Cairo, Mr. Casey, was leaked to the press. The elections were delayed until July 1943, but when they were completed, the results showed an overwhelming victory for the Lebanese nationalists—Bechara Khoury, who was chosen as president, and Riad Solh, the prime minister. Within three months the anti-French sentiments that underlay the Nationalist party led to a demand that the French Délégation Générale turn over full sovereignty to Lebanon and convert itself into a diplomatic mission. The delegate-general, Jean Helleu, was under instructions from de Gaulle to refuse any change in the French mandate's status until a new treaty had been negotiated and not to permit any changes in the Lebanese constitution without the approval of the CFLN.[46]

The Lebanese National Assembly had acted to amend the constitution, however, during the delegate-general's absence in November 1943. Helleu returned from Algiers in great haste, after apparently extensive consultations with de Gaulle and other members of the CFLN. Acting on his own initiative, without formal orders from Algiers, he suspended the constitution, dismissed Parliament, arrested Bechara Khoury, Riad Solh, and a number of other members of the Lebanese government, and appointed the defeated, pro-French candidate, Emile Edde, as provisional president. In the furor that followed this *coup de force* the Free French were obliged to compromise. Catroux was returned to Beirut to replace Helleu and, without disowning Helleu's actions, to undo as much mischief as possible. He first freed Bechara Khoury and the other ministers and then reconstituted the Lebanese government. Later the Lebanese Parliament was recalled, and conditions returned to a more normal state. However, feelings had been injured on every side.

De Gaulle regarded the whole affair as the outgrowth of British propaganda and nationalist perfidy. He accused the British of having "strongly influenced" the elections of July 1943 and of seeking then to "put them to good use" to make themselves the unrivaled suzerains of the entire Middle East.[47] In the midst of the crisis the British had in fact intervened to demand the recall of Helleu and the convening of a three-power conference to resolve the incident. At one point British General Spears confronted Catroux with a demand for the immediate liberation of the Lebanese government under threat that British forces would declare martial law and take over the country to maintain order. Catroux's reaction was one of exasperation: "Here we are back at the time of Fashoda!" But as de Gaulle was well aware, this was Fashoda with a difference. France and Britain were no longer military equals; moreover, the other interested parties were far more influential.

Outcries against French policy were heard from every quarter. From Nahas Pasha, then prime minister in Cairo, from Noury Said in Baghdad, and from Amman, where British influence over Abdullah was very strong, the protests were violent. More important, however, was the fury in Washington. Enough has already been said about relations between de Gaulle and the American government to indicate that understanding was lacking at all times on both sides. The Levant crisis, coming at the very time President Roosevelt was preparing to meet with Churchill at Cairo and with Stalin at the Teheran Conference, severely strained the already tense relations between the American president and de Gaulle. It seems likely that this crisis directly affected Roosevelt's decision at Cairo not to support Gaullist efforts to regain control of Indochina,[48] since the president's sympathies lay entirely with the Lebanese government. Secretary of State Cordell Hull had informed Robert Murphy on the eve of the president's departure for Cairo that the State Department was anxious that the United States not become involved in any such repressive actions and that Hull was contemplating a public denunciation of de Gaulle unless steps were taken quickly to correct the situation. On November 20 Roosevelt informed Hull that he favored vigorous support for the British position in Lebanon.[49]

Most important of all, the Lebanese crisis convinced Roosevelt that regardless of de Gaulle's increased power in North Africa and in the French colonies, he could not be trusted to cooperate with the Big Three Allies. Consequently, Roosevelt was confirmed in his judgment that the Allies should continue to refuse to recognize the Free French regime as the legitimate government of France.[50] This was unfortunate for the Allies because it came at a crucial point in the planning for the final phases of the war in Europe when French interests were deeply involved and French cooperation was of great importance. But it was doubly disastrous for de Gaulle, since it not only denied him the possibility of participating in important decisions that were to have an impact on the political future of the CFLN after the Liberation, but it also imperiled the primary aims of Gaullist policy: recognition by the Allies of France's status as one of the world's great powers and restoration of a sense of national grandeur.

Free France in Indochina

De Gaulle's decision during the closing days of the war to proceed with plans to reoccupy Indochina had tragic and far-reaching consequences for the future of France and for the peoples of Southeast Asia. Yet it was inconceivable to de Gaulle to do otherwise, for Indochina was an important part of the republic's colonial heritage, and he was determined to prove that "whether it be at Brazzaville, Algiers, Hanoi, or even at Nantes, Lyons, or Paris, nothing has been able to make French unity cease to be indivisible." [51]

The Free French were unable until the very last months of the war even to prepare their return to Indochina, for nowhere else in the French world were conditions so unfavorable. General de Gaulle had declared war on Japan on 8 December 1941, and despite his total lack of military means he repeatedly asserted France's support for the Allied cause in the Pacific theater of operations, but he had been cut off from direct communication with Indochina throughout most of the struggle. As the war in Europe was ending, the Vichy authorities whom de Gaulle had allowed to remain in Indochina after the Liberation were imprisoned by the Japanese. In place of the French rulers in Vietnam the Japanese installed an indigenous regime headed by the traditional emperor Bao Dai, but his authority was challenged by guerrillas associated with the revolutionary movement of the Vietminh. The resulting disorder was further multiplied by the disruption of the local economy and an acute food shortage, which produced inflation in the towns and widespread discontent in the countryside.[52]

Still more injurious to the Free French cause were the plans formulated by the other Allied powers for the removal of Japanese forces from Southeast Asia. De Gaulle considered France a formal equal with the other great powers of the alliance, and he demanded a voice for the Free French in any dealings with the Japanese. In his view this meant that with the surrender of Japan, "from one day to the next Indochina again became accessible to us. . . . We will not lose a day in returning there. Moreover, it must be done as recognized participants in the victory." [53]

These feelings were not supported by the United States, Britain, or China, however, and the disarmament of the Japanese went ahead as planned, with the Chinese and British armies (together with American observers) taking charge north and south of the sixteenth parallel, respectively. These events caused de Gaulle another severe loss of face in Indochina. But he refused to accept such a diminution of French sovereignty and sought to counter it with all the means at his disposal. Since the formation of an expeditionary corps required time and great effort, he was confined by the circumstances to political and diplomatic responses for the immediate future. And it is in this context of internal and international disorder that the notion of a new political system, a French Union," was officially enunciated.

The declaration of 24 March 1945 was the Provisional Government's immediate official response to the bloody uprisings of 9 March inspired by the Japanese. After recalling the general tenor of the Brazzaville Conference, M. Giacobbi, the minister of the colonies, affirmed that "Indochina is called to occupy a special place in the French community. . . . The Indochinese Federation will form, together with France and the other parts of the community, a French Union whose interests abroad will be represented by France." [54]

Although the meanings of these terms remained highly ambiguous, the intent of the declaration was clear enough. Its primary aim was to rally support among the traditional Vietnamese ruling class for the restoration of the French protectorate by offering them new safeguards for local autonomy. Specifically, the French sought to block the attempt of the Vietnamese nationalists to unite the three *Ky,* or provinces (Tonkin, Annam, and Cochin China), into an independent state and to win back the support of the governments in the kingdoms of Laos and Cambodia by recognizing the cultural autonomy of each region and increasing the prestige of the traditional rulers. If he could secure the continued support of the traditional sovereigns, who themselves were coming under increasing pressure from popular revolutionary groups, de Gaulle reasoned that it would still be possible for France to preserve her control over the foreign, military, and trade policies of Indochina. And despite the radically changed conditions of the world, he was confident that such an arrangement would permit France "to regulate relations for at least a generation." [55] This conclusion followed logically from de Gaulle's conviction that political alignments, whether alliances or protectorates, were the product of historical circumstances; that is, they were matters of fact or necessity, not volition. The only choice involved, as far as Indochina was concerned, was a choice of protectors, and here the historic links with France gave it a large priority. Indeed, rather than permit some other state to replace France in Indochina, de Gaulle was prepared to use force if necessary. For certainly no other country was in a better position than the French republic to provide for the development and "civilization" of such overseas territories. As for the Vietnamese nationalists, it was easy to dismiss them as demagogues, for most people in France were fully convinced that "the real guarantee of independence in the countries where our action has been extended is their incorporation into the French community (*la collectivité française*)." [56]

De Gaulle summed up these feelings in an emotion-packed speech to the people of France on 14 March 1945, in which he declared:

> Not for a single hour did France lose the hope and the will to recover free Indochina. . . . In the suffering of all and in the blood of the soldiers a solemn pact is at this moment being sealed between France and the peoples of the Indochinese Union. . . . In truth, never has the Indochinese Union been more committed to finding within herself, with the help of France, the conditions for her own development in every area: political, economic, social, cultural, and moral where her future awaits her. From now on, the veils are torn away and the French government is going to make known without delay the ways and means by which that will be accomplished.[57]

Yet, if the existence of the protectorate seemed to de Gaulle beyond negotiation, the means by which it was to be implemented were not. And the declaration of 24 March made it clear that France was prepared to extend to the peoples of the various territories of Indochina rights and privileges previously granted to none of the overseas areas. These included a promise of citizenship, both in their respective states and in the French Union that carried with it a right to "access to all posts and all federal employment in Indochina and in the union." Indochina was to have its own federal government headed by a governor-general and a council of ministers responsible to him and chosen from among both Indochinese and resident

French communities. There was to be a Conseil d'Etat, composed of the highest ranking officials (*"les plus hautes personnalités"*) of the federation, to prepare the laws and regulations, and an Assembly ("elected by the form of suffrage most appropriate to each of the states of the federation") with power to debate the laws, vote the budget, impose taxes, and regulate commercial relations within the federation. The federation was guaranteed the right to economic autonomy from France and the freedom to plan its own economic development. The declaration set forth a variety of other personal civil liberties as well as a number of general pledges of continued social reform along the lines of Brazzaville: educational improvement, trade union organizations, health and cultural development, and so on.

In short, the declaration of 24 March proposed to establish a federation within a federation. It was fairly specific about the nature of the first but completely obscure about the second federal system. By implication, a large degree of administrative centralization was expected to continue, otherwise it would have been impossible to promise the Indochinese equal access to employment throughout the union. But what sort of political structure could accommodate both a large measure of local political autonomy and a highly centralized administration? Even more difficult was the question of how to reconcile such a superfederation with metropolitan political institutions. This troublesome issue was passed over in silence by the declaration, but it remained at the heart of the colonial problem.

Looking backward at the major Gaullist efforts to adjust French colonial policy to the new realities of the wartime era in Africa, the Middle East, and Indochina, it seems clear that they followed a common pattern. For, despite de Gaulle's willingness to contemplate numerous far-reaching administrative and social changes and his determination wherever possible to provide legitimate outlets for the expression of political opinion, the Free French never openly confronted the problem of reconciling political autonomy for the colonies with the unitary, centralized structure that was the French republic. Instead, they tended to discuss colonial autonomy within the context of concepts like universal suffrage and the indivisible republic which, at heart, denied both the possibility and the desirability of autonomous subdivisions within the body politic.

Moreover, in an effort to restore French grandeur for the future, de Gaulle juxtaposed immediately necessary reforms and a myth of a transcendent national unity. This was a difficult combination to sustain, even in the short run, for it tended to treat grants of autonomy to the colonies as matters purely for French initiative and hence to prolong the same attitude of paternalism whose elimination was one of the primary goals of those who sought autonomy for the colonies. In this respect the declaration of 24 March 1945 was no different from the earlier statements of Gaullist policy. Consequently, one effect of this declaration was to encourage Indochinese nationalists to support the most extreme groups, such as the Vietminh, who accused France of resorting to the old imperialist trick of divide and rule and who were preparing to wage a guerrilla war to prevent the French from returning to Indochina. In the metropole the declaration elicited little interest among leaders who were preoccupied with other pressing problems. By dispatching an expeditionary force to regain Indochina, however, de Gaulle committed France to a course of action that was to have far-reaching and disastrous consequences for both countries. It also seriously complicated the problem of finding acceptable political solutions to increasing nationalist demands in other French territories where conditions were more favorable.

Thus the involvement in Indochina, which was only dimly perceived at the time by most French leaders, including de Gaulle, had a doubly destructive influence on the fate of the wartime reforms in Africa. Confronted with mounting costs of military intervention, the Gaullists and their successors were compelled to defer badly needed and repeatedly promised plans for educational improvements, economic development, and social changes that formed a vital part of the Brazzaville recommendations.

Perhaps more important in the long run, however, was the fact that the defeat suffered in the Levant and the bitter struggle with the Vietminh in Indochina generated deep anxieties both within the metropolitan French political elite and among the general public. As a result, the spirit of optimism that characterized the Brazzaville Conference was replaced in the Constituent Assemblies by a deep sense of distrust on the part of many metropolitan deputies. On the other hand, those nationalist groups within the colonies that had viewed Brazzaville as a sign of hope and a promise of further change were progressively disillusioned by these evidences of French determination to preserve every shred of French authority.

The absence of integrated, modern political communities in most of French Africa and the lack of an effective political consensus among the small, indigenous, modernizing elite in those countries tended to obscure these developments, while economic dependency further discouraged interest in radical political change. Nevertheless, local self-consciousness had been aroused throughout French Africa, and the need for internal reforms was clearly felt by a growing African elite, which waited impatiently for an extensive reform of the French colonial system.

The Paradox of Colonial Reform

Gaullist wartime efforts to restore France's grandeur by assuring the unity of the colonies and the metropole take on an aspect of mounting paradox when viewed from the perspective of the postwar period. The Gaullists always thought of themselves as preserving and developing the heritage of republican colonialism, yet their policies of reform and repression contributed significantly to its transformation. The myths of French colonialism supplied the Gaullists with a framework of ideas so familiar that they could be taken for granted in shaping policy, even if the ideal of a reborn republic that was "one and indivisible" with its colonies did not correspond very closely to the desires of important segments of the colonial population. In drafting a series of electoral reforms for choosing the National Constituent Assembly, the Gaullists completed their last major act of the wartime period, and this innovation, like the political changes discussed earlier, provides a sharp insight into the paradoxical character of Gaullist colonialism.

The electoral reforms of 1945 were in large part the culmination of the policy that began at the Brazzaville Conference and that aimed to encourage unity with the colonies by giving the peoples of the overseas areas a direct and substantial voice in the making of French policy. The Brazzaville Conference had reached a decision in principle to permit the colonial population to participate in the eventual reorganization of the institutions of the republic; but it had been unable to agree on the implementation of this policy. The events leading up the Liberation of the metropole and the transfer of the Gaullist government from Algiers to Paris prevented further action on the question during the ensuing year. By the spring of 1945, with the war in Europe nearly over and elections scheduled for fall, decisions on the matter of colonial participation could wait no longer.

The decisions that had to be made were, nevertheless, exceedingly complicated because of the great variety of conditions existing in the colonies, the short amount of time available for the preparation of voting lists, the lack of administrative personnel, and the enormous distances and difficulty of communications. The continuation of hostilities in Indochina made it impossible even to attempt to hold elections there. As a first step, the Ministry of the Colonies appointed a committee under the direction of Gaston Monnerville to study the problem of colonial representation and to present specific proposals.

Under existing laws, the so-called old colonies (Guyane, Guadeloupe, Réunion, Martinique) and Saint Pierre and Miquelon were fully represented in the National Assembly. The four communes of Senegal had been represented by African deputies since 1914, but the rest of West Africa had no representation, and the Senegalese seat had remained vacant following the death of the incumbent Galandou Diouf in 1942. The only other colony to send a deputy to the last Parliament in 1936 was composed of the tiny French enclaves in India. In addition, ten deputies represented the French colonists in Algeria.

The principle of colonial representation having been established, the Monnerville Commission had to determine what proportion of the seats in the Constituent Assembly were to be allocated to the overseas areas and how the seats were to be filled in each case. Since no decision had been reached by the late spring of 1945 on the form of the Constituent Assembly—whether it was to be bicameral, like the parliaments of the Third Republic, or a new unicameral assembly specially chosen to draft the constitution—the commission had to formulate alternative plans to fit both possibilities. Its composition assured that the recommendations of the commission would represent primarily the opinion of the ministries concerned. An additional factor that may also have exerted some influence was the pressure generated by a group of African students in Paris who resented what they took to be governmental indifference toward the sacrifices made by the colonies for the war effort and repeatedly intervened to demand enlarged colonial representation.[58]

The Monnerville Commission completed its report on 5 July 1945 while de Gaulle was still seeking agreement among the various metropolitan parties on a plan for the forthcoming elections. The commission proposed that, in the case of a bicameral parliament, the colonies should be represented in the lower house by sixty-six members and in the upper house by twenty-nine. The members of the lower house were to be allocated approximately according to population, whereas each colony was to have a single member in the upper chamber. In the event of a unicameral parliament, the colonies were to have ninety-five seats out of a total of six hundred. These totals did not include any seats for Algeria because that area was considered part of metropolitan France, but they did provide for representation of the mandated territories of Togo and the Cameroons, despite the fact that these areas were not, strictly speaking, "French territory." No provision was made for representing those French citizens residing in the protectorates of Morocco and Tunisia for fear of alienating the sovereigns of those countries.

A second proposal, stemming from a conference of Resistance groups called the Etats Généreaux de la Renaissance Française, and largely influenced by communist and socialist opinion, urged more extensive assimilation of the colonies and proposed to set aside one-fifth of the seats in the Constituent Assembly for overseas representatives.[59] On the whole, however, there was little public comment in Paris on either of these proposals. In fact, their importance seemed to be generally ignored in the midst of more urgent and dramatic incidents concerning the fate of the new economic program, the bloody struggle in Indochina, the bitter incidents in the Levant, and the deepening government crisis over the constitution.

In characteristic fashion, the Provisional Government, after deciding to leave the form of the Constituent Assembly to be determined by a referendum, resolved the problem of colonial representation in a manner different from both the Monnerville proposal and the plans of the Resistance groups. De Gaulle's plan, set forth in a series of decrees during August and September 1945,[60] was significantly more modest than either of the other two proposals. It provided for twenty-nine deputies to represent Algeria, sixteen of whom were to be chosen by noncitizens, while in Morocco and Tunisia French citizens were permitted to select three and two deputies respectively. In most of the other colonies French citizens and native subjects voted in separate colleges. Thus, the French citizens in the colonies (not more than about 10 percent of whom were non-Europeans, apart from the four communes of Senegal and the Antilles) controlled better than half the overseas seats. Noncitizens held twenty-three seats out of a total of sixty-four provided for overseas areas. In some very small colonies like New Caledonia, the islands of Oceania, and the Indian enclaves, both citizens and noncitizens voted together in a single, mixed college. It is clear from the figures in table 1, that substantial inequalities existed within both electoral colleges as well as between citizens and noncitizens.

TABLE 1

Overseas Representation in the First Constituent Assembly, 1945–46

Constituency (No. of seats in 1936)	*Citizens' Voters*	*College Seats*	*Noncitizens' Voters*	*College Seats*	*Mixed Voters*	*College Seats*
Algeria [a]	(501,724)	(13)	(1,341,978)	(13)		
Algiers (4)	209,222	5	460,826	4		
Constantine (3)	103,026	3	586,322	6		
Oran (3) [b]	189,576	5	294,830	3		
Morocco	91,451	3				
Tunisia	75,526	2				
Martinique (2)	114,543	2				
Guadeloupe (2)	106,528	2				
Réunion (2)	107,120	2				
Guyane (1)	12,309	1				
St. Pierre et Miquelon	2,487	1				
Oceania					19,294	1
New Caledonia					9,829	1
Indian Establishments (1)					3,141	1
Somalia (Djibouti)					620	1
Senegal-Mauritania (1) [c]	44,292	1	25,188	1		
Ivory Coast	3,646	1	31,384	1		
Soudan-Niger	3,243	1	33,626	1		
Guinée	1,944	1	16,233	1		
Dahomey-Togo	1,279	1	11,599	1		
Cameroons	1,991	1	12,468	1		
AEF						
Gabon-Moyen Congo	2,803	1	5,873	1		
Oubangui-Tchad	1,361	1	6,858	1		
Madagascar	(16,604)	(2)	(72,473)	(2)	(4,447)	(1)
1st District	11,271	1	46,426	1		
2nd District	5,333	1	26,047	1		
3rd District					4,447	1
Totals (64 seats)	1,088,941	36	1,557,680	23	37,331	5

SOURCE: Raoul Husson, ed., *Elections et referendums.*

[a] Algeria was represented in 1936 by ten deputies elected by French citizens only.

[b] Three deputies from Oran were never seated.

[c] Africans born in the four communes of Dakar, Rufisque, Gorée, and Saint Louis were citizens.

These decisions of the Provisional Government concerning the electoral system make it clear that, although the spirit of Brazzaville was still part of the prevailing doctrine, General de Gaulle was not prepared to expose the fragile unity of the recently liberated metropole and the colonies to serious threats from overseas. Most of the outspoken opponents of colonial unity were excluded from the First Constituent Assembly, since the nationalist groups in Morocco and Tunisia were not represented, nor were the sovereigns of these states involved in any direct way in the reorganization of the French colonial system. Indochina, although on the minds of many people, was not directly represented either. The Algerian leaders of the Amis du Manifeste were still in prison following the Sétif uprising. Thus the only possible organized opposition to the policy of a continuing union was to be found among the two deputies from Madagascar who represented a growing movement in favor of greater autonomy for their island colony. While a few such isolated individuals might exert some personal influence within the Assembly, it was certainly not expected that the colonial deputies as a group would wield very much power. On the contrary, it was hoped that by their presence the colonial peoples would be brought to identify themselves more fully with the new political system that was to be created.

By their doctrines and their policies the Gaullists had largely succeeded in preserving the forms of France's colonial system, and by important reforms in sub-Saharan Africa and the Maghreb they had maintained and possibly increased somewhat the political consensus that supported a strong, renovated French community. But none of the wartime Gaullist reforms was either very novel or very precise, and most important of all, none was able to resolve the crucial issue of political structure. What was needed above all by 1945 was not a more complete set of doctrines, but a new pattern of political institutions that could assure further and more liberal changes.

The problem was put very concisely by Governor Henri Laurentie in an address at the Palais de Chaillot. "The colonies having passed through the test of war—their war—are not quite the same as before. They have grown up. . . . They have confidence in the intentions of France, but now it is necessary that those intentions be carried into actions." [61]

The reforms adopted by the Gaullist Free French regime guaranteed that when those actions were determined, the opinions of African and Muslim groups would, at least in part, be taken into account. However, the policies pursued by the Gaullists in applying the reforms frequently served to divide the new politically conscious elites overseas from the metropolitan leadership and hence tended to defeat the underlying goal of unity. In the end the reforms of the wartime period did indeed contribute both to the desire for independence within the colonies and to the creation of a political system that tended to legitimate the pursuit of that aim. Yet nothing could have been further from the intentions of those responsible for Free French policy, especially Charles de Gaulle. To him, the unity of the empire and the metropole appeared, in that prenuclear era, to hold the key to the restoration of French grandeur and to provide tangible evidence of her rank as a world power.

5. THE POSTWAR POLITICAL MILIEU

Constitutional reform was the first order of business for France in 1945. After the humiliation of 1940 a return to the constitution of the discredited Third Republic was unthinkable. The Vichy regime had effectively discredited those who demanded a more authoritarian form of government for France, while the experience of the Resistance and the Liberation inspired a hope for fundamental political and moral transformation. As Léon Blum explained,

> If the idea of a constituent assembly has such a hold on people, it is because they see in it one of the remaining means of realizing the hopes which, though in many respects already betrayed, nevertheless remain alive. If the return to the old constitutional formulas inspire such a strong reflex of withdrawal and opposition, it is because people understand instinctively that this return would close the gates of the future before them, perhaps in an irreparable fashion.[1]

A year after the Liberation there were only two organized political forces in France: General de Gaulle and the French Communist party. Around those two poles all the other political groups calculated their actions and took up their positions. The Constituent Assembly was to become the principal battleground between those two forces, and, although their rivalry was a major factor in determining the character of the French Union, each was primarily interested in shaping metropolitan institutions.

The strength of the Communist party lay in its nationwide network of tough, disciplined cadres and its immense popular prestige. The party's wartime record of resistance was well publicized—the PCF called itself *le parti des 75,000 fusillés*[2]—and this, together with the immense prestige then enjoyed by the Red Army and the Soviet

Union, enabled the Communists to exercise what one writer called "a sort of moral dictatorship over the country." [3] The fact that from 1939 to June 1941 the party had attacked British imperialism rather than Nazism was conveniently forgotten. This popularity was reflected in an enormous increase in party membership, from about 340,000 in 1939 to 906,000 in 1945, and in the wide circulation enjoyed by its press—the Paris daily *L'Humanité* distributed 450,000 copies. By virtue of its control over the Confédération Générale du Travail (CGT) the Communists exerted a major influence over the nation's five and a half million trade union members.

By far the largest political party in France, the PCF had managed to consolidate its control over many local government agencies. In the areas where it was strongest, such as the mining regions of the North, the suburban industrial areas around Paris and in some of the rural areas of the South, this position made it attractive to many civil servants whose traditional allegiance had been to the Socialist party. The Communist leadership stressed the Party's patriotic action and disclaimed any intention to seize power by revolutionary violence. Instead, its objective was to gain power in France by democratic means, as Etienne Fajon explained to the Tenth Party Congress in June 1945. "Marxism-Leninism teaches us that it is essential to discover what can be done in a given period. For example, this babbling about the establishment of socialism in France is nonsense or else it is the work of provocateurs who seek to divide the democratic forces, because the indisputable conditions for that establishment have not been created." [4]

The new constitution was a key element in the Communist strategy. It aimed to create a unicameral legislature that was free from any institutional checks on its power and within which the PCF had good reason to anticipate that it would predominate. Since 1943 the party had participated in the Provisional Government, and it was confident that no government was possible without its support. After the elections of 21 October 1945 the Communists received five ministerial posts, including the appointment of their secretary-general, Maurice Thorez, as vice-president of the Council of Ministers in charge of the civil service. In the First Constituent Assembly theirs was the largest group of deputies—160 out of a total membership of 586.

The party's domestic policy was to win electoral support wherever it could be found, among left-leaning catholics as well as among farmers and small businessmen, in addition to the traditional backers of the Marxist parties. For this purpose it supported government policies aimed at promoting economic recovery, but at the same time opposed any fundamental reforms that might tend to strengthen the existing regime. In its foreign policy Thorez guided the PCF according to what he knew to be the priorities of the Soviet Union. Only recently returned from his wartime refuge in Moscow where he shared the home of Nikita Khrushchev, Thorez was well aware that Soviet priorities placed the consolidation of Russia's wartime territorial gains and its internal reconstruction far above revolution in Europe. By cooperating with de Gaulle's efforts to rebuild French international power, the Communists could also hope to effectively bloc the expansion of British and American influence in the Mediterranean and to prevent the formation of an anti-Soviet alliance in Western Europe.[5]

Unlike the Communists, General de Gaulle had no organized political movement behind him. He owed his power to his unique ability to incarnate the spirit of France and thus to capture the imagination of the French people and the loyal support of voters and public officials. As head of the Provisional Government he exercised great influence over the state machinery, particularly the army and the foreign office. De Gaulle repeatedly disclaimed any intention to use the army to impose his rule on France; nevertheless, he had the strong loyalty of many military officers whose opposition to communism was very profound. Therefore, no one could be certain how the army would react in the event of a Communist political victory. The additional fact that numbers of American troops were still in France in 1945 increased the chances that such an outcome might lead to a civil war similar to that in Greece.

De Gaulle was determined to rebuild French national power in the world and for that he was convinced France needed a strong, effective leadership at home. He therefore considered the new constitution a matter of utmost importance and sought to shape it so as to give France the type of political institutions that would be capable of overcoming past misfortunes and avoiding present dangers. On the basis of his prewar and wartime experience with the political parties, de Gaulle despaired of fundamental changes in the electorate and profoundly distrusted the French political party system. Since it could not be replaced, he sought to limit its divisive effects by providing a strong, independent executive. De Gaulle proposed that the president be elected by an electoral college that included the national legislature, local government councils, representatives of various economic organizations and the overseas areas. The legislature was to be bicameral, and only the lower house was to be directly elected. The president's powers were to include the appointment of ministers, dissolution of Parliament in the event of a deadlock, and the possibility of appealing directly to the people by referendum.

Between de Gaulle and the Communists the other French political factions were relatively powerless. The traditional Right was in total disgrace after having in various degrees supported Vichy and collaborated with the Nazis. Of the older parties that survived from the Third Republic, the Radical Socialists elected only 27 deputies and the other moderates held 67 seats in the First Constituent Assembly. Much closer to the PCF in numbers were the Socialists and the Mouvement Républicain Populaire (MRP), a new party that grew out of the Christian Democratic Resistance movement. The former won 142 seats and the latter 152, but neither had the organization or the mass base to permit it to compete on equal terms with the Communists. Both were essentially electoral machines rather than mass organizations, hence, it was only through control of the state bureaucracy that they were able to balance the power of the Communists. The Socialists were most aware of this situation and were never willing to govern with the Communists alone. The MRP was often tempted to withdraw from the government but never actually did so for fear of opening the way to rule by a Communist dominated majority.

The referendum of 21 October 1945 created a Constituent Assembly empowered to draft a new constitution which was to be submitted for ratification by a new referendum in seven months. The Assembly also had the power to legislate and to vote the budget but not to initiate expenditures. Its power to oppose government bills or to pass motions of censure was limited by special provisions. De Gaulle took no part in the election campaign and did not seek office openly; neither did he resign. Instead, he remained aloof from party quarrels until, after failing to agree on another candidate, all three parties supported his reelection as president of the Provisional Government. Following a series of further negotiations between de Gaulle and the party leaders and among the leaders themselves, a new government was approved unanimously on 23 November. The price for his retention as provisional president was de Gaulle's agreement to divide the governmental posts equally among the three major parties, thus seriously limiting his freedom to choose his own ministers. Two other actions at the same time reduced de Gaulle's control over the government policy still further. The Communist and Socialist parties both decided that their parliamentary parties would not be bound by governmental decisions even when their own party leaders accepted such decisions. Thus, both Marxist parties rejected the practice of collective responsibility and claimed a right to participate in governmental decisions but to oppose those same actions in the Assembly if they wished. A second and equally problematic decision was adopted by the Assembly barring the government from any direct role in drafting the constitution. Only the Constitutional Committee was entitled to receive proposals or to discuss alternative schemes prior to the completion of the preliminary draft.

These limitations on the presidential powers made an open confrontation between de Gaulle and the parties unavoidable, as one party after another launched bitter attacks against the policies of the government to which all belonged. The major issue on which the fate of de Gaulle's government finally depended was military appropriations. Against de Gaulle's insistence that the army be maintained and enlarged—at one point in 1944 he had requested American aid to equip fifty divisions—the Socialists argued that domestic social and economic needs were more pressing and accused the military of wastefulness. It was said that two million rations per day were being paid for when only seven hundred thousand men were under arms; uniforms were bought but not used, and the army even purchased ten thousand khaki brassieres for the Women's Army Auxiliary. A move to reduce defense appropriations by an exemplary 20 percent was narrowly defeated after de Gaulle warned the party leaders:

> The point that divides us is a general conception of the government and its relations with the national representatives. . . . There are two conceptions, and they cannot be reconciled. Do you want a government that governs, or do you want an omnipotent Assembly that delegates power to the government to carry out its desires? Personally, I am convinced that the second solution does not respond to the needs of the country in which we live or to those of the period in which we are living.[6]

De Gaulle attempted to overcome the objections to his form of leadership by announcing his retirement from active political life on 20 January 1946, fully expecting that within a short time the parties would be forced to recall him to power on his own terms.[7] He was mistaken, however, in thinking that without his leadership the parties would be incapable of agreeing on a successor. In fact, the prospect of de Gaulle's return to power was sufficiently objectionable to all the parties that it encouraged them to preserve the formula of tripartism throughout the remainder of 1946.

The significance of de Gaulle's resignation for the constitution was considerable. It meant that the three major parties had a free hand in shaping the constitutional draft. It also meant that the Tripartite Government could not escape the primary responsibility for economic reconstruction. As a result, foreign policy issues received a lower priority, and domestic social and economic questions gained in importance.[8] In view of these changes, one cannot help but wonder whether some foreign policy issues such as Indochina would not have been treated more decisively had de Gaulle remained in power. The fact that he was not in command certainly seems to have encouraged some lower ranking officials to make decisions on their own responsibility that would never have been tolerated by de Gaulle. In the case of Indochina, in particular, such actions proved severely damaging to French interests.[9]

Even though he was absent, de Gaulle continued to influence the government's decisions and the actions of the Assembly. Deliberations among the parties in the Constitutional Committee turned on the issue of unicameralism. What was really at stake in these negotiations, however, was a double concern: first, to prevent the adoption of a system that would favor de Gaulle's return; and, second, to avoid domination by the Communists. To achieve the first goal it was necessary that the National Assembly be subject to no institutional limitations, while the second objective required that it be structured in such a way that no single party could dominate it. The outcome was a draft constitution that reinforced the role of the parties by giving them the right to determine who would be a candidate and by allowing the single Assembly to elect the government and approve its policies. Dissolution was automatic after two ministerial crises, and the president of the republic, who was designated by the Assembly and the Council of the French Union, had few real powers. In case of a conflict over the meaning of a law, a referendum was possible and the Assembly could be dissolved, but otherwise it was not subject to any controls.

The Socialists and Communists endorsed this plan, but when the MRP failed to win approval of a larger role for the consultative Council of the French Union, they opposed the April draft in the referendum of 5 May. More than twenty million Frenchmen voted, of whom 53 percent opposed the April Draft and 47 percent approved it; 21 percent of the registered voters abstained. As Gordon Wright later observed, "The referendum, in the minds of many citizens, had turned into a plebiscite for or against the Communist party. Frenchmen ranging from right-wing socialists to the PRL had decided that a 'yes' majority might open the way to eventual totalitarian control by a single party." [10]

The elections of 2 June returned a new Constituent Assembly in which the MRP, with 28 percent of the vote and 160 seats, replaced the Communists, who held their 26 percent of the electorate but won only 146 seats. The biggest loser was the SFIO with 21 percent and only 115 seats. The remaining 62 seats went to the Rassemblement des Gauches Républicains (RGR) and the moderates. Within the Assembly the pattern of interparty rivalry was similar to that of the preceding period except that this time the Socialists aligned with the MRP instead of with the Communists. After extended negotiations the Constitutional Committee framed a new draft that incorporated many of the suggestions made earlier by the Socialist leader Vincent Auriol. While retaining the principle of parliamentary sovereignty, the new scheme imposed a variety of restraints on the Assembly. There was to be a bicameral legislature, the president had broader powers, the judiciary was separated from the control of the Assembly, but control over the government still rested in the lower house. The principle of dissolution was maintained but was subject to severe limitations.

The Communists strongly opposed the new draft and would have voted against it had de Gaulle not chosen to attack it even more bitterly. After having remained completely aloof from the constitutional debate since leaving office in January, de Gaulle spoke out on 16 June in a ceremony at Bayeux condemning both the April Draft and the party system that produced it. He recalled the humiliations of 1940–45, which he attributed to "the weakness of our traditional institutional structure," and observed that during the crisis "salvation had to come from elsewhere." In place of the warring parties, de Gaulle called for a strong president equipped with enough power to be able to conduct national policy without restraint.[11]

De Gaulle's plan conflicted with the ideas of all the parties, including the MRP, and the Constituent Assembly ignored most of them. When the new draft was presented to the Assembly in August, de Gaulle again attacked it declaring that it did not provide the sort of executive which alone could offer an effective check on the Assembly and the parties.[12] Despite the entreaties of many MRP leaders he refused to endorse the revised text.[13]

The effect of de Gaulle's opposition was paradoxical. Instead of convincing the MRP, whose leaders were anxious to put an end to the provisional regime, to oppose the constitution, he persuaded the Communist party to support it. The Socialist party was equally anxious to see the constitutional problem resolved because it was undergoing a severe internal crisis as a result of the efforts of Guy Mollet and some younger party militants to unseat the older supporters of Léon Blum and party secretary Daniel Mayer at the Thirty-eighth Congress in Paris. Under the joint pressure of de Gaulle and the conservatives, the government parties resolved their outstanding differences and brought in a compromise text which was finally adopted by 440 to 106. Unwilling to concede defeat, de Gaulle took his case to the public urging Frenchmen to vote "No" a second time. "If the draft were approved by the majority . . . there is reason to believe that the consequences would be first impotence, next anarchy, and finally dictatorship." [14]

The second referendum became something of a plebiscite for or against de Gaulle. On 13 October eight million voters endorsed his views while nine million defied him and supported the constitution. Another eight million abstained entirely. Thus, the constitution of the Fourth Republic was adopted by a minority of 35 percent of the electorate against 34 percent opposed and 31 percent abstaining, and the victory gave no assurance of support for the new institutions, from either the Communists or the Gaullists.

In all these constitutional negotiations the conflicting interests and ambitions of the various parties centered on metropolitan political institutions. Colonial questions played a very marginal role, and, as will be shown in chapter 7, the institutions of the French Union in particular became stalking horses for the larger ambitions of all the parties. To recognize this fact is not to condemn those party leaders but to appreciate how the tripartite formula—essential as it was for French internal unity—served to distract the Constituent Assemblies from confronting the problem of decolonization at a time when it was still possible to imagine a variety of solutions to native demands. This was an opportunity that was never to recur, and it might not have arisen at all had it not been for the presence in the Constituent Assemblies of a number of deputies representing the colonial territories.

The New Colonial Elite

The mass of French public opinion was never deeply concerned about colonial problems before World War II, and in 1945–46 it was totally preoccupied with the rehabilitation of the metropole. However, there were always a few individuals and small groups that maintained a consistent interest in colonial matters. These included military officers who had made their careers in the colonies, missionaries, businessmen with connections overseas, journalists and a few legal and political specialists from the universities, and a tiny assortment of writers and intellectuals. The nucleus of this loose body of opinion was formed by the senior officials of the Colonial Ministry, the minister himself, and a few members of Parliament. The parliamentary members of the colonial elite never formed a distinct faction or party; instead, they participated in the making of colonial policy as individuals who were often recognized by their parties, because of their presumed expertise, as spokesmen on colonial issues.

This loose group, which has been termed the "colonial elite," underwent a number of important changes toward the end of World War II. Most significant was the addition of a substantial number of representatives from the colonial territories brought about by the electoral decrees of the Provisional Government. This change altered the character of the colonial elite by destroying its relative ideological homogeneity and dividing it into two adamantly opposed blocs: those who favored increased autonomy for the colonies and those who insisted on preserving their unity with the metropole.

The Brazzaville Conference had urged that all the peoples of the overseas areas be permitted to take part in the rebuilding of French political institutions once the war was over. The Provisional Government accepted this recommendation, and as a result it substantially altered the composition of Parliament. The contrast is most marked if it is recalled that in the last prewar election, that of 1936, colonial areas were represented by a total of nineteen deputies. All of them were elected by French citizens—noncitizens took no part in the elections—and in fewer than half of the colonial constituencies were non-Europeans in the majority. In short, the colonial deputies were for the most part the spokesmen for French settlers' interests.

The Provisional Government's plan gave the overseas areas 64 seats out of a total of 586. Of these 64, there were more than 30 constituencies where non-Europeans formed a majority. Some parts of the overseas empire were not represented, however. Conditions in Indochina prevented elections. In Morocco and Tunisia, the native populations were theoretically subjects of their respective sovereigns rather than French subjects; therefore, the electoral law applied only to French citizens residing in those countries.

Who were the overseas deputies, and whom did they represent? These are difficult questions to answer, especially for the First Constituent Assembly, for a number of reasons. Elections were hastily organized overseas, which meant that the results inevitably tended to reflect the preferences of the local administration [15] and to favor those parties or individuals that had already established a public position before the war or during the Resistance. In only a few areas were there any effective party organizations to provide candidates or organize voters; consequently, there was a great deal of unavoidable confusion.[16] The choice of candidates was particularly limited in Algeria where virtually the entire leadership of the Algerian nationalist movement had been imprisoned following the uprising at Sétif in 1945.

The electoral system had been constructed to assure representation for two small groups in the colonies: the settlers, who together with a relatively small number of naturalized native citizens formed the "first" or "citizen's" college, and the mass of native subjects, who voted in the "noncitizen's" or "second" college. In a few small territories these were combined into a single mixed college, but to have done that for the overseas areas as a whole would have meant that a small minority of French citizens would have been swallowed up in the mass of noncitizen voters. Thus, a clear advantage was retained by French settlers.

The results of the elections of October 1945 and June 1946 attest to the dimensions of the change in the colonial elite. Table 2 shows the party affiliations of the overseas deputies during the two Constituent Assemblies (ANC-1 and ANC-2) and during the first Legislative Assembly (AN-1) of the Fourth Republic elected in November 1946. It reveals that the first-college voters, far from returning an overwhelming majority of conservative deputies, actually divided in much the same way as did metropolitan voters, with the Communist and Socialist parties each collecting large blocs of votes. The exception was the MRP, which did much less well overseas than in the metropole, primarily because it was entirely a metropolitan party without roots overseas until 1944 when some of its members were appointed to administrative posts in Equatorial Africa. The extreme Right, which united under the label of the Parti Républicain de la Liberté (PRL), initially had only one overseas member, Louis Dumat of Morocco, although it picked up strength in the Second Constituent Assembly.

TABLE 2

Party Affiliations of Overseas Deputies
1945–46

	Citizen		*Noncitizen*		*Mixed*		*Totals*		
Party	*ANC-1*	*ANC-2*	*ANC-1*	*ANC-2*	*ANC-1*	*ANC-2*	*ANC-1*	*ANC-2*	*AN-1*
PFC-URR	10	4	4	2		1	14	7	17
SFIO	6	8	12	6			18	14	13
MRP	7	8	1	1			8	9	8
RGR [a]	12	6	1	1	5	3	18	10	9
PRL & Right	1	9					1	9	6
No Party			2	13			2	13	21
Others		1	3 [b]			1	3	2	1 [c]
Totals	36	36	23	23	5	5	64	64	75

SOURCE: Husson, *Elections et referendums.*

[a] In the First Constituent Assembly the Radicals (6) and UDSR (12) were separate; they joined to form the RGR in June 1946.

[b] Muslim Conservatives (Oran).

[c] Deputy from Indochina never elected.

Most spokesmen for French settler interests turned initially not to the PRL and the far Right, but to the older and more moderate Radical party and especially to the new Union Démocratique et Socialiste de la Résistance (UDSR). The citizens'-college deputies from

North Africa played a particularly important role in Radical party affairs throughout the Fourth Republic. They included, in addition to Auguste Rencurel, Léon Deyron, and Paul Cuttoli, who had served in the First Constituent Assembly, a number of prominent Radical figures. Senator Henri Borgeaud was reputedly the richest man in Algeria; Emile Roch, later president of the Conseil Economique, was an influential resident in Morocco; Martinaud-Déplat of Tunisia later became one of the presidents of the Radical party from 1948 to 1955; and René Mayer, deputy from Constantine, was later responsible for the defeat of the Mendès-France government in 1955 on the question of Algeria.

The UDSR, which joined with the Radicals in 1946 to form the RGR, was an outgrowth of the non-Communist Resistance movement, and most of its members, nearly one-third of whom were overseas deputies, were fervent Gaullists. Some of these had become known as prominent Gaullist resisters, such as General Chevance, elected first-college deputy from Guinée where he arrived in 1945. Others, like François Quilici from Oran and Antoine Colonna from Tunis, were elected by local parties representing French interests and may have found the protective coloring of a Resistance party politically rewarding.

The situation in which the non-European deputies found themselves was more complex than that of the settlers' spokesmen. Part of the problem lay in the widely differing character of the deputies themselves, and part stemmed from the absence of firmly established party habits and allegiances. In effect, there were three different subgroups within the bloc of non-European deputies: radical nationalists, who sought election only in order to present their territory's case for independence before the French Parliament; "administration nominees," who owed their election to favors extended by the local colonial administration; and moderate reformists, who were prepared to work through the existing parliamentary institutions in order to bring about changes in keeping with their particular interests or principles.

It was clearly impossible for all these deputies to work together in harmony. Even if they had been willing to forego their differences, they were too few to gain formal recognition as a "group" under the bylaws of the Constituent Assembly; hence, they could not gain a voice in organizing the work of the Assembly nor would they have been assured of representation on the various committees, which actually did much of the work. By themselves, they would have found it extremely difficult even to gain a hearing for their positions. This was, in fact, the experience of the Malagasy deputies, who did refuse to enroll in any parliamentary group. Their occasional speeches fell on an empty chamber, and their two or three votes were not enough to be decisive.

The radical nationalists were more effective in the Second Constituent Assembly. In the elections of 2 June 1946 the Union Démocratique du Manifeste Algérien (UDMA), under the leadership of Ferhat Abbas, won eleven of the thirteen second-college seats in Algeria, displacing a number of Muslim conservatives who, as administrative nominees, had been allied with the SFIO in the First Constituent Assembly. With the support of the eleven UDMA and the two Malagasy nationalists, the Communist and Socialist groups held a narrow two-vote majority in the 586-member Assembly. The importance of this position is indicated by the fact that Abbas, the UDMA leader, was appointed to the vital Constitutional Committee, despite the fact that the UDMA was far too small to qualify as a regular group under the rules of the Assembly. Within that committee Abbas also played a vital role, for his vote gave the Communist-Socialist majority exactly enough to balance the opposition.

In addition to the effect of their numbers, the mere presence of their leader in the Assembly brought the UDMA more public attention than any of the radical nationalists had been able to secure during the seven months of the First Constituent Assembly. The UDMA, and Ferhat Abbas in particular, were looked upon by French officialdom as conspirators. They had been accused of organizing the uprising at Sétif in 1945 and had been interned for nearly a year. In fact, the general amnesty granted in the spring of 1946 liberated them just in time to seek election to the Second Constituent Assembly. Hence, they all came to the Assembly more or less directly from prison, with enough of the aura of convicts about them to gain the affection of the Communists and the intense distrust of the Right.

Paradoxically, Ferhat Abbas had been an active proponent of assimilation until about 1943. His background was that of a middle-class, European-trained Algerian. The son of a caid, he received a degree in pharmacy from the University of Algiers and practiced his profession in Constantine. In his first published work, *Le Jeune algérien* (1931), he pleaded for full participation of Algerians in the

French political community on an equal basis that would recognize the cultural accomplishments of Islam and the personal dignity of the Muslim population. His goal was not a separation of Algeria from France but a society which would recognize that "we are Muslim and we are French. We are natives and we are French." He ended one moving chapter with a desperate plea to the people of France: "Help us to regain our dignity, or take back your schools!" [17]

In 1943 Abbas abandoned the thesis of integration, and in the *Manifeste du peuple algérien* he explained that "the Algerian problem is essentially racial and religious. . . . The French colony will allow but one sort of equality with the Algerian Muslims: sacrifices on the battlefield. Even there, the native must still fight as a 'native' with a mercenary's pay and pension even if he is a professional or a specialist." He therefore concluded:

> The identification and the formation of a single people under the same paternalistic government has failed. . . . The European bloc and the Muslim bloc remain separated from one another, without a soul in common. . . . The systematic or disguised refusal to give the Algerian Muslims access to the French community has discouraged all the partisans of the policy of assimilation. That policy appears today in everyone's eyes as an inaccessible chimera, a dangerous device put in the service of colonialism. . . . From now on the Algerian Muslim will ask to be nothing else but an Algerian Muslim. . . . Algerian nationality and citizenship offer him more security and provide a clearer and more logical solution to the problem of his evolution and emancipation.[18]

In May 1944 Abbas formed the Amis du Manifeste et de la Liberté devoted to promoting the idea of an Algerian nation and the formation of an autonomous Algerian republic, federated to a renovated, anticolonialist and antiimperialist France. But the repression that followed the uprising at Sétif in 1945 led him to adopt a more cautious stance in order to avoid unnecessary provocation. On his release from prison in March 1946, Abbas issued a statement that retained the essential points of his previous position, but expressed them more guardedly.

> No assimilation, no new masters, no separatism. A young people, . . . associated with a great, liberal nation; an infant democracy, guided by the great French democracy: such is the clearest image

> of our movement of Algerian renovation. Algeria must be liberated from the old system of colonial domination, regardless of what form that domination takes, while respecting the nationality principle.[19]

Abbas's position was still tantamount to a demand for full independence in the eyes of his followers for, as Thomas Oppermann correctly observed:

> It is difficult to say exactly to what extent the constitutional formulas that one finds in the party programs were destined for the use of a segment of French opinion it was convenient to reassure. The mass of ordinary people, in a native population that had little familiarity with juridical subtleties, understood it only as a call for independence from foreign domination.[20]

As a means of defending this position Abbas organized the UDMA and chose the path of legal resistance. He refused, however, to become part of the traditional parliamentary system. Rejecting Governor Chataigneau's suggestion that he accept an appointment as undersecretary of state, he insisted: "What interests us is the promotion of a new policy responding to the profound aspirations of the population and the respect for nationalities. It is a denunciation of the policy of assimilation in all its forms. For this reason, I could not participate in a French government. But I was prepared to press the idea, however modest, of an Algerian government." [21]

Parliamentary participation brought some rewards in the form of direct contact with the responsible ministers and with the prime minister, which, on occasion, had results in Algeria. For example: the Amis du Manifeste, which had been outlawed by the administration, was rehabilitated; Messali Hadj, leader of the prohibited PPA, was transferred from his exile in Brazzaville to Paris; Abbas's newspaper, *Egalité,* which had been suspended after the Sétif uprising in 1945, was allowed to resume publication; a bill was introduced enabling the PPA to operate legally; the minister of finance was persuaded to approve the credit of 500 million francs to pay indemnities to the victims of the Sétif uprising.[22]

With respect to its basic goal of persuading the French Parliament to adopt a new attitude and recognize the existence of a new autonomous community in Algeria, the UDMA was completely frustrated.

On 2 August 1946 they introduced a bill to provide a large measure of autonomy for Algeria within the French Union. Its most important articles were the following:

1. The French republic recognizes the complete autonomy of Algeria. She recognizes at the same time the Algerian republic, the Algerian government, and the Algerian flag.
2. The Algerian republic is a member of the French Union as an "associated state." Her foreign relations and national defense are in common with those of the French republic and are the responsibility of the authorities of the union in whose exercise Algeria will be associated.
3. The Algerian republic possesses full and complete sovereignty over the entire extent of its territory for all matters of an internal order, including the police.

4 and 5. Every metropolitan French citizen enjoys the status of an Algerian citizen while in Algeria. As a consequence, within Algerian territory he possesses the same rights as Algerian citizens including the right to vote and access to public service.

7. The official languages of the Algerian republic are French and Arabic. . . .

30. Property rights, both French and Muslim, will be respected. . . . Agrarian reform and the social policy of the peasantry . . . are included in the realm of public concern.[23]

In style and tone as well as in content the UDMA bill reflected the thought of Abbas. It stressed Algerian national identity, but balanced the tendency toward separatism with a radical, egalitarian formula of unity. It was reformist regarding the social and economic interests of the peasantry, but gave assurances that property rights would be respected. It asserted an equal status with French for Muslim culture and Arabic language, but was totally opposed to Pan-Islamism and in favor of creating a modern state system. As Abbas himself later reflected, "I don't see how anyone could have been more considerate of the interests of a young people anxious to exercise their own sovereignty, and of those of the French people, from whom none of the overseas people dreamed of a divorce." [24]

This parliamentary initiative in the direction of legal reform within the framework of a loose, but still explicitly French, political system also reflected the relatively moderate character of the UDMA within the Algerian nationalist movement. The UDMA was basically a bourgeois, reformist party, rather than a revolutionary peasant movement like the PPA or an Islamic, traditionalist movement such as that led by the ulemas. Its leadership came primarily from the middle classes in eastern Algerian and from the Westernized intellectuals in the large cities.[25] With the PPA outlawed and Messali Hadj in exile, the UDMA had no rival for the allegiance of the peasantry in 1946, and it therefore became the undisputed spokesman of Algerian nationalist ambitions. Abbas and his followers, keenly aware that the time for a peaceful adjustment of the relations between the French and Muslim communities was fast running out, pleaded with Parliament, the government, and French public opinion for a major change in Algeria's legal status while there was yet a possibility of compromise. The metropolitan response was total incomprehension and on occasion blind fury.

As Abbas observed, "The French bourgeoisie, bound up in its paternalism, inhibited by its defeat in 1940, and more colonialist than ever, attributed to us black designs and treated us as 'enemies.' "[26]

Abbas was driven to this bitter conclusion after repeated efforts to induce the Constituent Assembly to accept a flexible view of the French Union had failed. That failure is important because it demonstrated the total absence of communication that existed between the metropolitan and Algerian deputies. Jean Lacouture is certainly right when he concludes that

> more than the often irritating and sometimes provocative words spoken by a Bey Lagoun or an Ahmed Saadane, their interventions demonstrated that over and beyond political tactics or the ambitions or rancors of any leader, something had broken down between the elites of Algeria and the metropole. When one gets to the place where it is no longer possible to speak the same language; when what seems to one a naïve expression of the truth is, for others equally sincere, totally unheard of; when a single language thus expresses two distinct sociological affiliations, asserting two forms of national behavior, then Parliament is no longer a crucible for fusion but an arena for irremediable confrontations.[27]

The Algerian nationalists had come to be considered as "enemies" not because they were demagogues, for they were not; not because their proposals endangered established interests, because there was never the slightest chance that they would be adopted; rather, they became enemies because they explicitly questioned the myth of unity between France and the colonies. They rejected the universality of French citizenship in principle, even though they admitted the practical value of maintaining fairly close connections with France for political and economic purposes and stressed their commitment to French cultural values as a basis for constructing a modern, Western-oriented society in Algeria.

The extent of the UDMA's challenge to the colonial myth and its impact on the institutions of the French Union will be examined later, but it is important at this point to underscore the change that the introduction of such conflicting attitudes worked in the atmosphere of cordiality that initially characterized the attitude of the Constituent Assembly toward colonial problems. By the middle of the summer, the acrimony reached a level that is difficult even to imagine.

One particularly ugly incident occurred during September that revealed the extent of the hatred that many metropolitan deputies had come to feel toward Ferhat Abbas and his followers. As the UDMA leader rose to address the Assembly during the closing hours of the final debate on the French Union sections of the constitution, Abbas was met with murmurs from the benches on the Right where someone yelled, "What is that *salaud* doing here?" Other remarks were drowned out in the shouts of protest from the Left. When, after considerable difficulty, the president of the Assembly finally restored order, Abbas began speaking. He talked briefly of the objections that had been raised by the colonial deputies to the French Union articles, but then he moved on to denounce "the colonial system of yesterday." Departing somewhat from his subject, he heaped scorn on the Radicals, who, he said, were responsible for the conquest of the empire, and on Daladier, whose government had been incapable of defending it in 1940. At this point, the benches in the Center and Right exploded with insults, shouts, and noise: "There was de Gaulle!" cried one voice, "Did you fight with de Gaulle? You collaborated with Pétain!" shrieked another. Abbas tried to continue, but even the Socialists joined the chorus of catcalls and derision as he announced that the disorganization of colonial policy under the Third Republic was one of the main faults of the prewar system. As desk tops slammed and shouts flew from all sides, the president despaired of restoring order and suspended the session. Just at that moment, there was a rush of angry centrist and rightist deputies, among them such figures as the normally gentle, dignified Maurice Schumann, onto the floor of the hemicycle and toward the doors on either side of the speaker's rostrum leading out of the chamber. A bottleneck occurred between the front benches on the Right and the steps leading to the speaker's rostrum where Abbas was still trying to address the rapidly emptying chamber. As the volume of shouts increased, he descended a few steps toward the Right benches and appeared ready to hurl himself on his antagonists. He was prevented from doing so by two bailiffs who rushed up the opposite stairway and, seizing Abbas by the arms, succeeded in drawing him back to the relative safety of the Communist benches while a platoon of bailiffs linked arms to prevent the rest of the UDMA and their sympathizers from joining the fracas.[28]

The very personal nature of this violent episode would seem to underscore the distinction between the radical nationalists from Algeria and Madagascar and the moderate reform-oriented deputies who represented the other overseas territories, especially those in West Africa. It is impossible to discuss the situation of the West African deputies here in detail; [29] nevertheless, it is important to stress two aspects of their role. First, they all operated within the ideological framework of the colonial myth, never seriously raising the question of "independence" or sovereignty. At this period they all sought political reforms within the French system and without challenging its general validity. The West African deputies demanded to participate in the political life of the French Union on equal terms with other Frenchmen—at least in principle—rather than to establish a separate community. Second, the African deputies, because they represented a number of distinct territories with special problems and interests, were much less organized among themselves than the radical nationalists of the UDMA. Their internal differences set them at odds with one another even when their colonial interests brought them together to oppose the representatives of the metropole. Thus their presence in the Constituent Assembly had a double impact: it introduced new perspectives peculiar to the African territories, even though these were usually expressed in the accepted vocabulary of the colonial myth, and it injected an additional set of rival interests into the complicated pattern of existing conflicts and added to the confusion surrounding constitutional issues.

A rapid glance at several leading figures among the group of African deputies will perhaps help to clarify their role in the Constituent Assemblies. Unlike Ferhat Abbas and the Algerian nationalists, the African deputies had no single leader and no single organization. Most of them were elected not by parties but by groups that included a variety of local organizations whose members differed greatly in their ideologies, interests, and activities. Ruth Schachter Morgenthau has termed these "party nuclei" or in some cases "pre-war cliques," and, as she explains, only in Senegal and the Ivory Coast were they organized in time for the elections of 21 October 1945.[30]

In Senegal, where numbers of Africans were "citizens," Lamine-Guèye was elected deputy from the first college and Léopold Senghor was chosen by the "subjects" in the second college. Both men were at that time members of the Senegalese section of the SFIO. The Senegalese SFIO was the first African branch of a metropolitan political party, and it remained the only non-European party of this type. Organized in 1936 at the time of the Popular Front in France, it received the encouragement of the minister of the colonies of that day, Marius Moutet.

> The prewar Senegalese federation was Socialist far more in principle than in practice. The party had the same structure and policy as any French section of the SFIO. . . . The party took positions against fascism, was anti-clerical, and favored raising the status of women. Yet, Socialist terminology, and French Socialist problems, were the province of but a small educated group in the SFIO—led by Lamine Guèye—who also attended the Socialist Congresses in France. There Senegalese delegates were accredited as the representatives of 3,000 members, and generally voted with the established leaders of the party. . . . But the SFIO federation of Senegal represented privileged African citizens, included few workers or peasants. The limited franchise, and its own constitutional outlook, made it, necessarily, also an alliance of "clans." It included ethnic associations such as the Lebous of Dakar, many of whose *notables* were illiterate; its electoral position was stiffened

> by such informal bodies as the *Amis de Lamine Guèye*. It was after all, the *parti de l'opposition* to Galandou Diouf and his *Dioufists* [who were backed by the local administration]. The SFIO federation favored reforms, and the spread of citizenship as a consequence of its assimilationist doctrine. But it was careful not to attack the system.[31]

Lamine-Guèye was probably the best known political figure in any of the French African territories in 1945. As the first African to receive a doctorate of law from the University of Paris, he quickly became a celebrated personality in Dakar and in 1925 was elected mayor of Saint Louis. He was one of the founders of the Senegalese SFIO and in 1938 had been instrumental in bringing into the SFIO a majority of the Parti Socialiste Sénégalais. He further strengthened the party through his personal contacts with local notables, trade union leaders, and war veterans whom he defended in numerous judicial proceedings, especially those arising out of the tragic incidents at Tiaroye in December 1944 when a demonstration by returning Senegalese war prisoners resulted in riots that cost many lives. By 1945 Lamine-Guèye had become the recognized spokesman for a large part of the educated, urbanized Senegalese elite, and with his reputation as the opponent of Galandou Diouf and the local colonial administration at its height, he was the obvious choice as first-college candidate.

As the ranking Socialist colonial deputy, and probably the most experienced African political leader in the Assembly, Lamine-Guèye chose to work within the parliamentary system in order to secure a number of concrete changes in the African territories. As he later observed, "The first objective of the overseas representatives in coming to the Constituent Assembly was [to secure] the abolition of the indigénat and the equality of political rights for their electors." [32] He became a member of the Committee on Overseas Territories which, although it lacked the formal authority to make decisions on constitutional matters, had the general power to examine all legislative and administrative actions concerning the overseas areas under the jurisdiction of the minister of overseas France. Colonial deputies occupied twenty-two of the forty-two seats on the committee under the chairmanship of aging Socialist Marius Moutet. When Moutet moved up to become minister for overseas France in the Gouin cabinet in January 1946—a position that he retained in the Bidault and Blum governments until 24 November 1947—Lamine-Guèye assumed the chairmanship of the Committee on Overseas Territories. From this vantage point, and with the relatively easy access he enjoyed through his personal friendship with the minister and with Governor Laurentie, the director of political affairs in the ministry, Lamine-Guèye was able to exert considerable influence over administrative matters involving the West African territories.[33] Even on constitutional issues, Lamine-Guèye was one of the primary spokesmen for the colonial deputies, and his committee made frequent proposals to the Constitutional Committee for new institutions for the French Union.

The second-college deputy from Senegal, whom Lamine-Guèye chose and the local SFIO invested, was the leading African intellectual of the day, Léopold Sédar Senghor.

> About twenty years younger than the Wolof "citizen" Lamine Guèye, Senghor was the son of a prosperous "subject" Serer shopkeeper from Joal, in the Sine-Saloum, the heart of the peanut growing area of Senegal. A Catholic, partly mission educated, he spent many years in France where he became the first African to obtain the coveted *aggrégation,* and taught grammar in *lycées* in Paris and Tours. He became a naturalized French citizen. Mobilized in 1939, he spent a short time in a German prison, but spent most of the war teaching at a *lycée* in Joinville. In France and Africa he was a recognized man of letters, and a poet. He was spokesman for African art and culture, for *negritude,* and became one of the patrons of *Présence Africaine.* While Lamine Guèye, used to living in the towns, traveled in the interior with difficulty, dressed formally in well-pressed suit and tie, Senghor wore khaki and sunglasses, sat on the floor of huts and ate what he was served. Some of the "citizen" Socialists disdainfully called him "the deputy in khaki," while the numerous Senegalese war veterans, who were also voters, applauded Senghor's deliberate attempt to identify with them.[34]

Newly elected and wholly inexperienced, it was not to be expected that the African deputies would play important roles in the Constituent Assemblies. Senghor, however, became something of a symbol of successful assimilation when he was appointed by the SFIO as one of its spokesmen on the influential Constitutional Committee, where his talents as a literary stylist won him the job of rapporteur for the colonial clauses of the April Draft Constitution. The forty-two members of the Constitutional Committee were designated by their parties on the basis of proportional representation, with the Communists and MRP each holding twelve seats, the SFIO eleven, and the remaining seven distributed among the minor parties. The strategic position of the SFIO, whose eleven votes could assure a majority either to the Communists or to the MRP, did not afford Senghor as much leverage as might be expected, since most basic decisions on constitutional issues were taken by the party executive committees, rather than by the Constitutional Committee itself. The records of the Constitutional Committee make it clear that the parties all used committee debates as a forum for exposing their respective positions rather than as a place for negotiating and resolving differences.[35]

Furthermore, overseas deputies held only four seats on the Constitutional Committee; the other two besides Senghor and Viard in the First Constituent Assembly were occupied by two Communist back-benchers, Mme. Alice Sportisse (Oran) and M. de Lepervanche (Réunion). The elections of 2 June 1946 altered the membership of the Constitutional Committee in two respects. Ferhat Abbas was given a seat from which he could present the demands of the Algerian nationalist groups, while two citizens'-college deputies—René Malbrant, UDSR (Algiers), and Marius Dalloni, Socialist (Oubangui-Chari-Tchad)—defended the views of the European colonists. Senghor remained the leading spokesman for the African territories, but P. E. Viard was not reappointed by the MRP, which was then starting to shift its position on the colonial constitution. Several other colonial deputies, including Dr. Aujoulat, MRP (the Cameroons), and M. Rencurel, Radical (Algiers), appeared before the committee in their personal capacities to discuss colonial questions.[36] In general, however, the colonies were not strongly represented on the Constitutional Committee, and this seriously weakened the committee's ability to formulate meaningful proposals for colonial reform.

In addition to the two Senegalese Socialists, the group of African deputies also included two leaders of the nascent Rassemblement Démocratique Africain (RDA), which was to become the leading force behind the movement for greater autonomy in French West

Africa in the next ten years. Both Félix Houphouët-Boigny and Gabriel d'Arboussier were members of the Committee on Overseas Territories, and both took active parts in the drafting of various portions of the constitution dealing with the colonies.

Houphouët was one of the founders of the Syndicat Agricole Africain (SAA), which was formed in 1944 with the blessing of the governor of the Ivory Coast to enable African planters to compete on more nearly equal terms with European coffee and cocoa growers. Governor André Latrille described Houphouët, who was then forty years old, in a report dated April 1945.

> A direct descendant from the family of traditional chiefs of the Baoulés of Yamoussoukro, Félix Houphouët is a young man who is active, cultivated, and anxious to do things that will benefit his people. . . . He graduated number one in his class from the Ecole de Médecine in Dakar and at first practiced as a medical auxiliary. On the death of his brother Augustin, he was unanimously designated as chief (*chef coutoumier*) and acclaimed by everyone for his personal authority and character.[37]

Houphouët's political strength stemmed from his role as president of the Syndicat Agricole Africain. With the cooperation and encouragement of Governor Latrille, the SAA obtained significant improvements in the working conditions of migrant field laborers and exemption from forced labor for resident African planters (including their wives and children) with productive holdings of more than six acres. In 1945 Houphouët defended the interests of African planters in their unsuccessful attempt to secure a share in the subsidy authorized by the Ministry of Overseas France to European coffee planters in the Ivory Coast.

As a member of the First Constituent Assembly, Houphouët chose not to join the SFIO, perhaps because Governor-General Cournarie and the minister of the colonies, Paul Giacobbi, were associated with it. Instead, he became a member of the small group of the Union des Republicains et Résistants (URR), which was allied with the Communists. Houphouët later explained the reasons for his affiliation with the PCF and emphasized their tactical significance.

> It is true, Houphouët told Georges Monnet in 1948, that we have good relations with the PCF. But to be *apparenté* does not mean,

> in any way whatever, that we ourselves are Communists. Could I, Houphouët, a traditional chief, a doctor, a large landowner, a Catholic, be called a Communist? But our *apparentement* to the PCF has been very valuable to us in the sense that we have found some parliamentary groups in France that gave us a friendly welcome, while others took no interest in us at all. And with them, we have found it possible to win out in matters that are close to our hearts.
>
> Our colleagues from Madagascar, who also were only two or three, when they defended proposals that favored their great island, never found any echo. Every time that we of the RDA defend a proposal we can count on the 183 votes of the Communist party.
>
> And thus we have been able to make our viewpoint known and appreciated.[38]

The support of the PCF was not confined to votes in the Assembly. At rallies in the industrial centers of France the African deputies affiliated with the PCF could count on an audience of thousands to applaud their programs. Overseas, the Communists were willing to provide assistance to the infant RDA, which Houphouët helped to organize in 1946 to bring together and coordinate the actions of local parties in the Ivory Coast, Guinée, the Sudan, and elsewhere. The PCF did not hold any of the ministerial portfolios dealing directly with the colonies, but as a member of the government coalition its voice was influential on some matters of local administration. For example, when Minister of Overseas France Moutet was under pressure from European planters in the Ivory Coast to remove Governor Latrille, Houphouët intervened, and with the support of the Communist ministers Latrille retained his position.

Houphouët was also able, as a member of the Committee on Overseas Territories, to promote changes in the Ivory Coast by encouraging such major administrative reforms as the suppression of forced labor and the abandonment of the indigénat. More important, from the point of view of the new constitution, however, was the work of his fellow URR deputy from Moyen Congo, Gabriel D'Arboussier, who became the rapporteur of the Committee on Overseas Territories for the problem of local assemblies and one of the most skillful parliamentary tacticians among the non-European deputies.

Gabriel d'Arboussier, like Senghor, was a synthesis of French and

African cultures, but unlike the Senegalese leader, he had chosen to express himself in the political rather than the literary realm. His father, a former governor of the Sudan, came from an old Gascon family, and his mother was a direct descendant of El Hadj Omar and belonged to a distinguished African family that includes the powerful Senegalese religious leader El Hadj Seydou Nourou Tall. D'Arboussier's education included studies at the Dominican College of Sorèze, where Montalembert had taught, and at the Ecole Coloniale, then under the direction of Robert Delavignette. As a student in Paris at the time of the Popular Front, like Senghor, he was strongly attracted to Christian-democratic ideas. He was appointed as an administrator in Haute Volta and later in Equatorial Africa from where he was elected as deputy to the First Constituent Assembly. One of the founders of the RDA, he resigned from the colonial administration to devote full attention to African politics and did not seek reelection in June 1946. Soon after that he became the first secretary-general of the RDA and a leading advocate of full autonomy for the territories of French West Africa.

The constitutional views of the African leaders will be examined in detail later, but it is apparent that their presence injected a new sense of realism into the proceedings of the Constituent Assemblies. In spite of the differences in emphasis or conflicts of interest on specific issues, they brought to Paris a contact with the native peoples that had never existed previously. Moreover, unlike the radical nationalists, they were willing to accept the framework and the symbols of French parliamentary government as the best means for advancing the interests of their supporters. To be sure, the commitment to French institutions was tactically sound; the African deputies had no large, well-organized body of followers who, like the Algerian UDMA or the MDRM in Madagascar, could bring pressure directly on the local administration. For them the best means of controlling European interests was to influence the central administration, and that could only be done through the ministry in Paris, which meant, in effect, through the government and Parliament.[39]

At the same time, theirs was not a purely tactical commitment to "unity" with France, for in most cases the myth of a democratic French Union had a genuine appeal to African leaders, even when they differed on its precise form or meaning. "We would be the last ones," Houphouët explained,

> to underestimate the profound meaning of our presence in this Assembly. No power, before you, has admitted a native from its colonies to its Parliament. But understand us well: the mandate of a deputy, as honorable as it may be, is not for us an end in itself . . . but a means for contributing effectively to the evolution of the territories that we represent. We refuse to sit beside you simply for symbolic purposes.
>
> We intend to be the artisans of a sincere union between the people of France and the other peoples of the union. . . .
>
> We are not attached to France by money, by the franc—that poor franc that has lost a great deal of its value—this material bond would be too fragile. But there is a powerful bond, capable of resisting the tests; a moral bond that unites us: it is the ideal of liberty, of equality, and of fraternity for whose triumph France has never hesitated to sacrifice the most noble of her blood.
>
> It does not seem at all foolhardly to us to say that, with the inevitable evolution of the peoples who compose it, the French Union will one day be a multinational state which will lose none of its cohesion if this sacred love of liberty and equality is sustained. . . .
>
> United in peace as we were in the liberating war, let us work with all our hearts for a French Union which is grander, stronger, more beautiful and where we can live happily, different but together.[40]

Thus, it was ideology as well as tactics that led the moderate autonomist deputies to participate in the work of the Constituent Assemblies. Furthermore, it would appear that the democratic themes of liberty and equality that formed an essential part of the myth of unity were powerful enough to encompass the widely varied interests of a Senghor, a Lamine-Guèye, and the leaders of the RDA, giving them an intellectual and emotional basis for cooperation that would not otherwise have existed. By endorsing the myth of unity and adopting its democratic symbols, the autonomists had the added advantage of placing a large part of the metropolitan elite in the position of having at least to tolerate their criticisms, or else denying one of the primary principles on which the legitimacy of the republic was founded. At best they might succeed in convincing a majority to support important reforms, and at worst they would continue in the existing dependent relationship, with the chance of restraining the arbitrariness of the local administration.

Despite their repeated affirmations of faith in the future of the French Union and their declarations of fidelity to the principle of unity with the metropole, the moderate autonomist deputies, like the radical nationalists, were often attacked as demagogues and denounced as ingrates by metropolitan deputies who doubted their professed commitment to the French Union or who found their vocabulary as well as their tactics incompatible with traditional conceptions of professional dignity or national honor. The referendum of 5 May 1946 revealed a deepening split between the native representatives and the spokesmen for French colonists and their metropolitan supporters. The April Draft Constitution had made important, if vague, gestures in favor of giving natives a larger share in the administration of local affairs and in the conduct of the political life of the French Union. As table 3 indicates, the April Draft Constitution was strongly supported in all the overseas constituencies where natives were permitted to vote. Unlike the elections to the Constituent Assembly, however, only those natives who were French citizens were qualified; hence, the power of French settlers was predominant.

TABLE 3

Referendum of 5 May 1946, Overseas

Constituency	*"YES"*	*"NO"*
Algeria	175,049	185,992
Morocco and Tunisia	43,706	71,572
AEF and AOF (except Senegal)	5,780	11,465
Overseas departments ("Old Colonies")	90,912	37,942
Senegal	28,915	2,666
Indian settlements	2,037	325
Other colonies (Saint Pierre and Miquelon, Oceania, N. Caledonia, Somalia)	1,726	4,431
Total Overseas	348,135	314,392

SOURCE: Husson, *Elections et Referendums.*

In Algeria, a sizable portion of the Muslim population had been granted citizenship, with the result that the margin of defeat was small. In Tunisia and Morocco the only voters were French settlers, and they opposed the constitutional draft by nearly two to one. The results in other overseas areas followed the same pattern, and the majorities in favor of ratification were large enough to suggest that if the noncitizens who were permitted to vote in the second college in the elections of 21 October 1945 and 2 June 1946 had also voted in the referendum, then the April Draft Constitution might have been adopted.[41]

French colonists reacted strongly against the spirit of colonial reform that had permeated the First Constituent Assembly. Opposition was particularly vehement among planters and merchants from West Africa and Madagascar who met in Paris in July 1946 to form the Etats Généraux de la Colonisation Française. The aim of the Etats Généraux was to impress upon the Provisional Government the view that the primary task of the Constituent Assembly was "to guarantee the perpetuation of the superior interests of the country and of civilization in the territories of the French Empire and to maintain, over and above all parties and all local or temporary contingencies, *the sacred principle of French sovereignty*." [42]

Within Parliament, the views of the Etats Généraux were defended by some of the right-wing parties and by some first-college deputies like Castellani from Madagascar and André Schock from the Ivory Coast. The leading personality in the Etats Généraux was Jean Rose, president of the Ivory Coast Chambre d'Agriculture and head of the Association des Colons de la Côte d'Ivoire.[43] Its members were drawn mainly from among the large planters and commercial interests of the Ivory Coast, Equatorial Africa, and Madagascar. The program of the Etats Généraux condemned the colonial clauses of the April Draft Constitution as "partisan ideology" and asserted that the *fait colonial* was more complex than the constituents realized. Hence, it was impossible

> to assimilate a coolie to a Senegalese, a Pahouin to a West Indian, a Moi [i.e. the "montagnard" tribes of Vietnam] to M. Ho Chi Minh, and all of these to a farmer from the Saintonge or a Parisian worker, by a simple legislative act [without] shocking reason and denying the fact of stages of evolution of the overseas peoples.[44]

Inspired by a determination to "save the empire" and to ensure that "French influence in the overseas territories will not be contested," they warned against the dangers of "separatism" and denounced the native deputies, many of whom, they claimed, did not represent the real interests or genuine desires of the native peoples.[45] One resolution cautioned that

> the agitations provoked by a few autonomist évolués, who are considered by who knows what irony as the authentic representatives of the overseas populations when, in fact, they are generally nothing but the expression of yesterday's feudalisms or tomorrow's tyrannies, should not make [the government] forget the true wish of the native masses for *la paix française dans l'ordre et le travail.*[46]

Another resolution expressed particular indignation at the language of the proposals presented to the Constitutional Committee by the African deputies. According to the Etats Généraux, those proposals, if adopted, threatened to destroy "the admirable work accomplished by the Third Republic in all the territories of the empire and to abdicate a sovereignty which was still necessary and in the self-interest of the peoples who still look to France for the order and tranquillity indispensable to their evolution toward freedom and independence."

The Etats Généraux met from 20 July to 24 August at exactly the time the Constituent Assembly was considering the problem of the French Union. At the close of the session, a proposal was made public calling for the creation of a "federal" system for the French Union. While it did not receive formal endorsement from any of the groups in the Assembly at that time, this plan deserves attention because the scheme eventually adopted by the Assembly bore a close resemblance to it.

The plan called for the creation of three bodies: a president of the French Union, who was to be the president of the French republic; a "High Council," which would be composed of delegates from the protectorates (now dubbed "associated states") that had not been previously represented in any proposed assembly and an equal number of metropolitan delegates; and an "Assembly of the Union," in which all the overseas areas would be represented together with the metropole. The plan made no mention whatever of any representation for the colonies in the metropolitan Parliament.

The Etats Généraux also proposed that the Constituent Assembly abandon the notion of a single citizenship for all persons living in the French Union. They insisted on the need to distinguish between French citizenship and the more inclusive—and ambiguous—citizenship of the French Union.

> The acquisition of French citizenship cannot be a matter for collective action, extending in an obligatory fashion to all the inhabitants of the empire rights whose sense and grandeur most of them would be incapable of comprehending or which some would even deliberately reject. Rather it is an individual matter, open broadly to all who are able to grasp its moral, social, and political significance.

The underlying reason for this attitude was not wholesale opposition to political change so much as a desire to gain control of local administration, especially of economic policy. Thus, the Etats Généraux supported the creation of local territorial assemblies with extensive financial powers and imposed no limit on the political role of these bodies. Moreover, the Etats Généraux was especially distressed by the effects of the governments' policy regarding the suppression of forced labor, which they foresaw as having dire consequences for the future economic viability of the European community in Madagascar and West Africa. "Work is a social duty" became a leading slogan, and one of their leaders spoke openly of the probability that "coercive measures" would have to be employed if the cocoa and coffee crops were to be harvested in time. The Etats Généraux, in short, represented the French settlers' reaction against the natives' demand for greater autonomy. Although some of their proposals were cast in liberal rhetoric, they seemed intended to preserve the settlers' economic interests and to safeguard their sense of superiority from attack by the rising native elite. The outlook and program of the Etats Généraux functioned for the French colonists as both an economic and psychological defense against the forces of social change.

The native deputies, too, received some support from groups outside of the Constituent Assembly, which, at least on occasion, took public positions favoring greater autonomy for the colonies. The range of attitudes reflected by these groups was great, however, and their positions were often poorly articulated and their actions uncoordinated, with the result that their total impact was negligible. At one extreme they included organizations like the Association

France-Vietnam and the Comité Franco-Malgache, both predominantly Communist inspired, although they included a number of non-Communist intellectuals and some Vietnamese and Malagasy students and professional people who lived in Paris. Their programs called for recognizing the independence of Vietnam under the government of Ho Chi Minh or creating "a free Madagascar in the French Union." [47] Among the moderate groups there were also some liberal Catholics who favored basic reforms overseas, including eventual independence for Indochina. As one writer argued in the columns of the left-wing Catholic weekly *Témoignage Chrétien,* "The question today is no longer whether or not we will grant Indochina the complete autonomy which some people are now demanding, but to see how we can bring them to full independence." [48] Similarly, in November 1945 *Témoignage Chrétien* published the declaration of the Vietnamese bishops favoring independence for Indochina and calling on the peoples of the world to recognize that "our dear country is presently being invaded and is defending its independence, the cause of justice and liberty." [49]

Témoignage Chrétien and a few other journals, such as *Esprit* and *La Quinzaine,* remained highly critical of the Indochina war, but they did not attempt any broad analysis of colonial problems or express any new alternatives until the next decade. In this respect they mirrored the silence of the Church hierarchy and the Vatican on colonial questions.[50] As a general rule, however, it was the colonial administration, rather than the settlers or the native groups, who decided questions of colonial policy.

The postwar reforms, in addition to giving more power to both settlers and native leaders, changed the composition of the colonial bureaucracy in some important respects. The purges that were carried out after the Liberation resulted in some changes at the higher levels of the navy and the colonial service, two agencies of the state that had remained obedient to Vichy until the war was almost over.[51]

At lower levels in the administrative hierarchy some Vichy officials were transferred to less important posts, censured, or forced into early retirement. Generally speaking, they were replaced by others whose devotion to the Gaullist movement had been demonstrated during the war by service in the colonies under Free French control. Peyrouton, the Vichy governor-general of Algeria, was replaced by Gaullist General Catroux after the formation of the National

Liberation Committee. He in turn was succeeded in September 1944 by Yves Chataigneau. Pierre Boisson was dismissed as governor-general of French West Africa in 1943 and was replaced by Pierre Cournarie who was later succeeded by René Barthes. Both Cournarie and Barthes had been active Gaullists, and Cournarie as governor-general dismissed the governors who had been most antagonistic to the Free French. Among these was Governor Rey in the Ivory Coast who fled to Liberia at the end of 1943 to avoid prosecution. He was replaced by the former governor of Tchad and a supporter of Eboué, André Latrille. Similarly, Auguste Marcoin became governor of the Sudan in 1944 and a non-European, Wiltord, was named governor of Senegal. In Morocco, the very conservative Gabriel Puaux was replaced by Erik Labonne, a strong advocate of social and economic reform and a close friend of the sultan.

Several of these new Gaullist officials brought with them fresh political views and a clear appreciation of the need to give speedy attention to the demands of native groups. Especially after the Brazzaville Conference had put the Gaullist imprimatur on colonial reform, men like Latrille in the Ivory Coast and Labonne in Morocco undertook major programs directed at improving the condition of the native population. The central issue in the Ivory Coast was forced labor; and Latrille, with the support of his assistant Lambert, took direct steps to end the practice of forcing African planters and their families to leave their own fields to work the European settlers' plantations. He also encouraged the formation of an agricultural cooperative, the Syndicat Agricole Africain, which enabled African planters to compete more effectively with Europeans. On the political level, Latrille protected the newly developing African parties and permitted them to carry on their electoral activities without excessive interference from the local administration.[52]

Erik Labonne made a determined effort during his two years as resident-general in Morocco to build confidence among the nationalists and trade unionists as well as with the supporters of the monarchy. He attacked illiteracy, improved agricultural production, encouraged the growth of trade unions, and liberated political prisoners. In July 1946 Labonne proclaimed his desire "to give the people of Morocco the feeling and the certainty that life, in all its aspects, is wide open to their labors, to the deployment of their intelligence, to the exercise of all their faculties." [53] A committee on regional organization was constituted which was empowered to draw up new provinces that would be administered with advice of local assemblies having power over economic and social affairs. Municipal reforms were proposed that would affect some twenty-five municipal assemblies, and finally, the government council itself was to be reformed to include in one single body the representatives of all elements in the country. "Morocco, it has been said, is growing sullen and divided between dependence and independence. This is a false dilemma that gives an impression which is mistaken and distressing. It is that of disunity, dissension, and ruin. On the other hand, our course is clear and sure; it is that of a powerful, creative development for Morocco." [54]

Labonne's efforts and those of others including Latrille, Marcoin, and Chataigneau benefited from the presence in the Paris ministry of leading Gaullists who gave sympathetic, if not always effectual, support to overseas reform. A series of ministers including René Pleven, Paul Giacobbi, Jacques Soustelle, and Marius Moutet directed colonial affairs from 1944 to 1947. During most of this period they were assisted by Henri Laurentie, the director of political affairs. Their influence, while subject to many limitations from other ministries and from considerations of government strategy, was usually on the side of reform, and they favored liberal social and political policies.

Nevertheless, while generally favoring the creation of new institutions and sympathizing with many of the goals proclaimed by the nationalists—even General Juin claims in his *Mémoires* that had he been a Moroccan, he too would have been a nationalist—none of them considered the native nationalists capable of running their countries, and all looked forward to a fairly long period of transition. Moreover, most of the new officials remained extremely cautious in dealing with the nationalist groups, and most were prevented by their sense of professional honor from countenancing any diminution of their own authority or any challenge, even symbolic, to what they regarded as French sovereignty.

This state of mind seems to have been particularly characteristic of the military commanders during the immediate postwar period. Generals like Leclerc, Juin, Valluy, the commander of the French Expeditionary Force in Indochina, and Morlière, the commandant of the Tonkin region, all expressed a willingness to see political reforms in North Africa and Indochina. But their sense of duty led them to conceive of reforms as initiated by France and carried out by the army in such a way that the prestige of the nation, and especially of the army, would not suffer. In their view, "France grants reforms, she does not yield to rebellion." [55] Inspired by such a rigid conception of honor, French military leaders struck back with extreme violence when French military units were attacked by nationalist bands.

There were many, of course, in both the military and the colonial bureaucracies who were not sympathetic to social or political change in the colonies. In almost every colony there were middle-level officials who did their best to limit the influence of reforms and to defeat the rise of the local native elite to power. This was certainly the case in both Morocco and the Ivory Coast, and it was probably also true in varying degrees of all the colonial territories. With the support of local European groups, especially the Chambres d'Agriculture or the local producers' syndicats, these officials were in a position to control the lives of a large part of the native population, and there is some evidence that they even went so far on occasion as to foment incidents in order to repress nationalist movements or to embarrass a superior whom they considered "dangerous." [56] In other cases, such as Tunisia, where Gaullist Resident-General Mast ordered the congress of the Neo-Destour party disbanded and the party itself suppressed in August 1946, administrative hostility was overt.

The picture that emerges from this short sketch of the changes in the colonial elite is necessarily a cloudy one. New organizations were beginning to appear that for the first time were voicing the demands of native groups and working, both within Parliament and outside it, for their satisfaction. These groups were not united, however, and they differed among themselves on local interests as well as on strategies for the future.

There were some within the colonial bureaucracy who saw the need for eventually transferring a large part of the administrative responsibility for the colonies to the local populations and who wanted to begin immediately with what they knew would be a long, slow process of training. They too, however, were uncertain how to begin or how to deal with the emotional forces of nationalism that had been let loose in many areas by the impact of the war and the appearance of a new indigenous political elite that was anxious to win reforms but unskilled in operating modern institutions.

Finally, there were those who denied the need for reform or the possibility of any rapid change at all. For them the nationalists' claims held only threats, and their first reaction was to deny the legitimacy of any move toward autonomy as an affront to French sovereignty and then to repress any groups that proposed such action. Their attitude reflected what Paul Mus characterized as *"la stratégie du pfuitt,"* which consisted primarily in denying the existence of an enemy and then concluding that, since he did not exist, he could easily be eliminated.[57]

It is essential to recognize, however, that in the year immediately following the end of the war, when opinions were not yet fixed by partisan conflicts nor policy-making paralyzed by intragovernmental wrangling, an opportunity did exist to bring about colonial reforms. Many of those charged with the responsibility for shaping French policy in the bureaucracy and in Parliament were men of intelligence, high dedication, and profound sympathy, while the spokesmen for the new native elite were by and large sensitive, articulate, and in close touch with the desires of their peoples. Both metropolitan and colonial deputies evidenced much good will, especially at the beginning, and it would have been exceedingly difficult to discover more "valid interlocuters" on either side.

A willingness to consider reform in principle is not, of course, the same thing as actual political change. And if new men are to put new ideas into practice, they need new institutions. During the year following the surrender in Europe, French colonial affairs were in a state of flux that might have permitted fundamental changes. If France had been in a position of relative security at home and if her role in the colonies had not been directly challenged, it is possible that the spirit of gratitude toward the colonies and the concern for democratic principles that accompanied the Liberation, together with the new realism that marked part of the colonial bureaucracy as well as some intellectual and journalistic circles in the metropole, might have produced new institutions flexible enough to permit an orderly transition to eventual autonomy. In practice, that did not happen, and part of the reason must be sought in another aspect of the political milieu of 1946.

6. THE INTERNATIONAL CONTEXT

The colonial constitution was not simply a domestic affair; neither was it purely a matter between the metropole and the peoples of the colonies. Its importance exceeded the framework of the French community of peoples, for in a basic sense it dealt with the very existence of that community in the postwar world.

Enough has been written about the subject elsewhere to make it unnecessary to dwell upon the disappearance of French power during the course of World War II. What is not so well understood is the extent to which the French Union, as envisioned by the Constitution of 1946, was itself a reaction against the world situation in which France found herself. France was weak and disorganized in 1946—preoccupied with internal reconstruction, the future of Germany, and the formation of suitable relations with the two victorious superpowers, the United States and the Soviet Union. Yet these concerns came to be focused on the colonial constitution in a strange way, as the colonies became partly a symbol of France's past greatness and partly a guarantee that her present eclipse would be no more than temporary. Furthermore, the French Union articles of the constitution were the product of an Assembly grown bitter and disenchanted at least in part because of developments in the world at large. Thus, the French Union had a dual character. On the positive side it contributed to the preservation of the myth of France's greatness and to the belief that French status and prestige would reappear in the postwar era. Its negative side reflected the determination of the Gaullist government and its successors to refute in principle and rebuff in practice a number of concrete threats to the integrity of French sovereignty.

This dual character of the French Union can be seen most clearly in two sets of challenges that confronted France during the constitutional period. The first was the challenge to the entire principle of colonial authority, which the French saw stemming from the institution by the United Nations Charter of a system of trusteeship. The second was a direct challenge to the fact of French sovereignty in Indochina subsequent to the end of the Pacific phase of World War II.

France and the United Nations Trusteeship System

France's relationship to the United Nations trusteeship system was extremely complex, reflecting many factors that had little or no bearing on colonial problems, and these deserve to be analyzed in depth in a separate study. It is sufficient for the purpose of the present argument to recall that all the major provisions of the United Nations Charter were first explored at the conferences of Moscow, Yalta, and Teheran from which France was absent. The preliminary proposals prepared at Dumbarton Oaks did not deal specifically with the territories to be included in the trusteeship system; instead, they concentrated on basic principles and mechanisms. The objectives of the trusteeship system were—

1. to further international peace and security
2. to promote the political, economic and social advancement of the trust territories and their inhabitants and their progressive development toward self-government
3. to provide for non-discriminatory treatment in the trust territories with respect to the economic and other appropriate civil activities of the nationals of all member states.[1]

As originally conceived, the system was to apply to all territories then held as League of Nations mandates, plus any other territories that might be detached from the enemy states as a result of the war and any other territories that administering states might choose to place under international administration.

The scope of the trusteeship system was much broader than the mandate system of the League, since it applied in principle to all non-self-governing areas. The idea that all peoples had a right to choose their own form of government had been embodied in the Atlantic Charter, and various wartime conferences had elaborated it to the point where many people got the impression that the end of the war would mean the end of the entire colonial system.

The Charter of the United Nations provided, in Article 1, that among the general purposes of the organization was "to develop friendly relations among nations based on respect for the principle of equal rights and self-determination of peoples, . . ." and in Chapter 11 this principle was specifically applied to the remaining colonial territories.

Declaration regarding Non-self-governing Territories

Article 73

Members of the United Nations which have or assume the responsibility for the administration of territories whose peoples have not yet attained a full measure of self-government recognize the principle that the interests of the inhabitants of those territories are paramount, and accept as a sacred trust the obligation to promote to the utmost, within the system of international peace and security established by the present Charter, the well-being of the individuals of these territories, and to this end: . . .

a. to ensure, with due respect for the culture of the peoples concerned, their political, economic, social and educational advancement. . . .
b. to develop self-government, to take due account of the political aspirations of the peoples, and to assist them in the progressive development of their free institutions, according to the particular circumstances of each territory and its peoples and their varying stages of advancement.

The initial reaction of the French government was hostile to the entire conception of the trusteeship system and skeptical with regard to the United Nations as a whole. De Gaulle viewed the United Nations proposals "with sympathy but not without circumspection," and he was quick to recall that during his conversations with President Roosevelt the previous year, the two had discussed the matter and the president had "made me see how close to his heart this monumental edifice was." De Gaulle then reflected, "Besides, although he did not mention it, Roosevelt expected that the crowd of small nations would assault the position of the 'colonialist' powers and assure the United States an enormous political and economic clientele." [2]

As for the trusteeship system, de Gaulle was convinced that, like all ideologies, it was simply a façade meant to conceal the true interests of its sponsors, whom he suspected of harboring "malevolent intentions toward the French Union." [3] A similar opposition to any international concern with French colonial matters was voiced by Colonial Minister Giacobbi, who declared that the idea of trusteeship or a mandate system for the French colonies was out of the question.

> Those are ideas that are current in the press. The government attaches no more importance to them than it ought; but the government owes it to itself to say that the territories that have been shaped, civilized, enriched [*fécondés*] by the blood and the sweat of its children are out of the question and could not in any way become the object of other attentions than those which emanate from French sovereignty, which intend to exercise themselves for the good of all those who live in those territories.[4]

The French delegation at the San Francisco Conference supported a number of amendments to various articles in Chapters 9 and 12, particularly those that limited the portent of Article 73. That article finally took the form of a unilateral declaration to which each of the member states subscribed, and it omitted any mention of "independence" as a goal of national policy for the administering state. France also insisted on a narrow interpretation of the provisions in Article 79 governing the negotiation of trusteeship agreements between the United Nations and "states directly concerned" with the administration of non-self-governing territories. Finally, the French delegate to Committee II/4, which drew up the proposals for the trusteeship system, made the following declaration concerning the committee's report:

> The French delegation considers it necessary to make it clear that none of the provisions submitted for the approval of this committee implies total or partial renunciation by the French government of the right to take advantage of Article 8 of Chapter 2, by virtue of which, subject to certain provisions of Chapter 8, nothing in this Charter shall authorize the organization to intervene in matters that are essentially within the domestic jurisdiction of any state or shall require the members to submit such matters for settlement under this Charter.[5]

When the General Assembly met for its first session in London on 10 January 1946, none of the mandatory powers had yet drafted the trusteeship agreements provided for in Article 77, Section 1a, of the Charter. The French government had announced its intention to do so at San Francisco but had taken no action during the intervening months. When British Foreign Minister Bevin announced, on 18 January, that Britain would soon submit a trusteeship agreement for Tanganyika, British Cameroons, and Togoland, the French government let it be known that it no longer planned to place its mandated territories under the trusteeship system. Under strong pressure from other members of the United Nations, France qualified her opposition.

In a speech to the General Assembly on 19 January 1946, Foreign Minister Bidault restated his government's position as follows:

> For twenty-five years the French government has administered these territories in conformity with the spirit and with the letter of the mandate conferred upon it by the Council of the League of Nations. It has used its best endeavors to acclimatize methods of cooperation with the populations. Togo and the Cameroons recently appointed, by democratic elections, representatives to the French Constituent Assembly, and, in the first months of this year, their inhabitants will be electing a local representative assembly through the same medium of free elections.
>
> The French government intends to carry on with the work entrusted to it by the League of Nations. Believing further that it is in the spirit of the Charter that this work should henceforward be carried on under the trusteeship system, it is prepared to study the terms of the agreements by which this regime could be defined in the case of Togo and the Cameroons, on the understanding, however, that this shall not entail, for the populations concerned, any diminution in the rights that they already enjoy by reason of their integration into the French community, and further that these agreements will be submitted for approval to the representative organs of these populations.[6]

The government, on 9 February, announced its decision "to conclude with Great Britain, as the power directly concerned, the agreements to establish for the Cameroons and Togo the regime provided for by the San Francisco Charter." These negotiations dragged on for the next nine months, and it was only on 5 November that the French delegate finally submitted to the Trusteeship Committee the proposed agreements for the Cameroons and Togo. The text was criticized severely by India and the Soviet Union because it included a provision that "France shall have full powers of legislation, administration, and jurisdiction in the territory and shall administer it in accordance with French law as an integral part of French territory, subject to the provisions of the Charter and of this agreement." [7]

The French delegate, M. Naggiar, defended these terms as part of the original mandate. However, he maintained that "the French government does not consider itself authorized by these words to diminish the personality and individuality of the trust territories in any way." And he asserted categorically that "France does not consider herself the sovereign of the trust territories, that she never claimed that sovereignty in the past and does not intend to in the future." [8] Furthermore, both Belgium and Britain shared these views, and the Australian agreement also used similar language.

The trusteeship agreement was finally accepted by the General Assembly on 13 December 1946, but only after an extended debate in the Fourth Committee during which Douala Manga Bell praised the French administration and supported the draft agreement, declaring that it had been submitted to the population of the Cameroons and had full popular endorsement.

Within the Constituent Assembly there were repercussions of the conflicts in the General Assembly. In January 1946 Marius Moutet explained the situation to the Constitutional Committee, underscoring the government's misgivings by greatly exaggerating the impact of the trusteeship system.

> Insofar as general policy is concerned, it must not be forgotten that it is a matter of submitting the colonial territories to a manner of internationalization, or trusteeship. The Trusteeship Council will designate a mandatory power for each territory which, in reality, will merely execute the decisions taken by the council. It is thus a question of whether France will preserve her sovereignty over the overseas territories.[9]

On February 21 the first-college deputy from the Cameroons, Dr. Louis Aujoulat, initiated an interpellation concerning "the current situation in the Cameroons and the economic, social, and political consequences of the trusteeship agreements." [10] During the subsequent discussion, Aujoulat made it clear that what was disturbing was the manner in which the trusteeship was being arranged, rather than the principles underlying it. These, he asserted, were in keeping with France's traditional concern for the welfare of the native peoples; but he regretted that the agreements were being negotiated by the Foreign Ministry without ever consulting the elected representatives of the territories concerned.

> Not for a moment did my colleague Douala Manga Bell and I think of doubting the superior reasons that inspired the decisions taken at London before the United Nations Organization by the French delegation. We have, it is true, had occasion to say that its action could have been facilitated by the presence within the delegation of representatives of the mandated territories. At the very least, may we be permitted to regret that the government had resolved to negotiate a trusteeship agreement concerning Togo and the Cameroons without deigning to consult the deputies sent by these territories to the Constituent Assembly. . . .
>
> I am willing to believe that our intervention would not in any way have changed the final result, but I think that the use of parliamentary institutions would have paid off. It would thereby have given those who sent us a moral satisfaction that they had the right to expect.[11]

Both Aujoulat and Soustelle commented on the conflict between the government's current willingness to negotiate a trust agreement and its earlier reluctance to admit any change from the terms of the mandate. In addition, Soustelle found that "a decision was taken which, perhaps, replaces a regime that was leading toward the French Union with an international trusteeship about which the most we can say is that we don't really know what it conceals."[12]

Aujoulat was able to rationalize the position by pointing out that

> the real question is whether for certain the trusteeship represents a regression, a stabilization, or an advance in relation to the mandate, as far as the interested populations are concerned. If we stick to the clauses set forth in the San Francisco Charter, the answer is very clear: it can only be a question of an advance. . . . We are willing to believe . . . that the trusteeship system represents nothing other than a change of words in relation to the mandate and that in the same degree that the United Nations Organi-

> zation equals the League of Nations, trusteeship equals mandate. But we do not feel that there is any reason to minimize, as has been done, one important point, which is the following:
>
> In the new regime born at San Francisco, the controls appear to be more strict and more rigorous than before. The United Nations Charter provides, notably, in Article 87, the sending of international control committees. No doubt, this control will not be specific to Togo or the Cameroons. No doubt, too, France had nothing to fear from a control that only represents an additional reason to remain faithful to her obligations.[13]

In his response to his questioners, Bidault rejected the view that some of his critics had taken, especially those who accused him of having compromised the French position by accepting the trusteeship agreements at London. He indicated that regardless of the inclinations of some, it was impossible for France to do otherwise than to accept the system and act in accordance with the provisions of Article 77. To have refused to negotiate the trust agreement or to have sought the prolongation of the mandate would have meant violating the Charter. And unless France were willing to go so far as to annex these territories by force—something no one even remotely suggested—"I don't see how we could have refused to negotiate the trusteeship agreements." [14]

The government's decision formally closed the question of France's participation in the trusteeship system. Nevertheless, a certain uneasiness persisted in the Constituent Assembly about the relationship between the commitments to the Charter and the aims of the French Union. The cultural and economic goals announced by the Charter were regarded as wholly consistent with French policy, and they were readily supported. The political framework of the trusteeship system, on the other hand, was difficult to reconcile with French constitutional theory or practice.

What was at stake was a fundamental conflict of political outlook and administrative traditions. The Charter explicitly undertook to organize the process of decolonization by establishing an intermediate status between full independence and colonial dependency, which would recognize the legitimate desires of many territories for separate political existence and still provide for their political and economic support. It asserted, as one French writer later argued, that "politically, colonial imperialism and classical colonization no longer have any international support; legally, colonization is no longer a purely national matter; it has been transformed into an international public service." [15] To the French, however, the idea of international administration was unacceptable; partly perhaps because no international administrative machinery then existed and partly because the obvious conflicts already developing within the Security Council and the General Assembly between the Soviet and American governments made it unlikely that any international consensus could be found on colonial problems. But most of all, they realized that any form of international control over colonial administration would interfere with traditional French administrative procedures and disrupt the lines of authority that, in principle at least, linked the various governors, governors-general, and local administrators to the Paris ministry. In particular, the French delegation vigorously opposed the General Assembly's decision to broaden the scope of its concern beyond the mandate to include all colonial areas by establishing the ad hoc Committee on Non-self-governing Territories with power to examine the reports submitted to the secretary-general by the administering powers under Article 73(e) of the Charter.

The advent of the United Nations trusteeship system challenged the widely held view of France as the patron of civilization in the colonial world. As François Borella noted, the Charter provisions regarding the treatment of non-self-governing territories constituted "an official and definitive condemnation by the most solemn international act of the oldest French colonial tradition in favor of the collective emancipation of the colonial peoples." [16] By its explicit endorsement of national independence as the appropriate objective toward which all the colonial territories should strive, the trusteeship system challenged the comfortable assumption that the colonial peoples were anxious to cooperate with France in building a close-knit French community. Therefore, many French leaders who accepted the social and economic purposes of the trusteeship system nevertheless rejected it as a threat to French political unity.

The moderate and conservative groups were convinced that the benefits obtained by the colonies as a result of French rule justified its continuation. The socialists and communists were more critical of France's past colonial involvements, but they too believed that the colonial peoples would fare better under French administration—

especially a French administration they controlled—than under a system of international controls that would inevitably be subject to the influence of the capitalist countries, particularly the United States. Even the native deputies, for whom the principle of national self-determination had undeniable appeal, did not look upon the trusteeship system as an immediate alternative to a reformed French Union whose language, traditions, personnel, and institutions were already familiar.[17] Hence, the immediate impact of the trusteeship system was to incite the Constituent Assemblies to increase their efforts to find an acceptable solution to the colonial problem within a French framework.

Reoccupation of Indochina

The single most important international development that influenced the formation of the French Union was the struggle for control of Indochina that began in the spring of 1945 and continued throughout the next nine years. This increasingly costly conflict began as the last phase of World War II was coming to an end and mounted in intensity as the Constituent Assembly met. Hence, it coincided with the diplomatic embarrassment suffered by France in the Levant and with the difficulties encountered at the San Francisco Conference, leading some journalists to speculate whether France would be able to maintain her position as a colonial power any longer. For the French government, however, Indochina was a part of French territory, and therefore, was to be liberated as soon as conditions permitted. Once French troops were attacked by the Japanese on 9 March 1945, the government's only option was how to relieve its forces from an untenable position. The events that followed the Japanese coup and resulted in the proclamation of an independent republic of Vietnam on 2 September 1945 produced a series of French military and diplomatic moves aimed at unseating the Vietnamese nationalist regime and restoring French rule over Indochina.

A brief review of those events will make clear how tenaciously the French leaders clung to the colonial myth as a justification for their policies and will help to explain some of the reasons for such tenacity. An appreciation of the problems confronting the French government in relation to Indochina also helps to illustrate how the French

Union—a concept first officially employed in relation to that territory—was intended as an alternative to national independence that could be used to bargain with native nationalists.

The Vichy government had signed a series of agreements with Japan in 1940 that permitted the Japanese to occupy Vietnam and Cambodia.[18] Japan recognized French sovereignty over the area and allowed French administrators to remain in place subject to Japanese control. After the Liberation of France, the Provisional Government confirmed the Vichy governor-general Admiral Jean Decoux at his post in the hope of safeguarding what remained of French authority, despite the severe limitations imposed on it by the presence of Japanese troops.

The decline in French power, as well as the need to exploit to the fullest the economic resources of the territory to meet its needs and the demands of the occupation for food and raw materials, led to an increase in the power of the traditional Vietnamese elite. The Vichy administration introduced a number of changes favoring the mandarinate and increasing the prestige of the Annamite emperor Bao Dai. Together with economic reforms and improvements in education, these changes stimulated the growth of nationalism and led to the creation of organizations like the League for the Independence of Vietnam (Vietminh). Because these nationalist groups opposed both the Japanese and the Vichy French authorities, they attracted some military and financial support from the Nationalist Chinese and American forces operating in China.

French rule in Indochina came to an abrupt end, however, when the Japanese launched a brutal attack on French garrisons throughout the country on 9 March 1945 and completely overwhelmed them. The Japanese then encouraged Bao Dai to denounce the French protectorate and declare Vietnam independent, which he did on 11 March. During the weeks that followed Bao Dai proved incapable of consolidating his regime. Shortly before the Japanese surrendered to the Allies on 15 August, the government of Premier Tran Trong Kim resigned under heavy pressure from nationalist groups in Tonkin. On 13 August the Vietminh, which had seized power in Hanoi, launched a revolt that quickly secured control over Tonkin and parts of Annam and Cochin China for the National Liberation Committee headed by Ho Chi Minh, Vo Nguyen

Giap, and other leaders of the prewar Indochinese Communist party. Emperor Bao Dai abdicated on 25 August after issuing a letter to the heads of the Allied governments asserting Vietnamese independence. He then assumed the position of "political adviser" to the National Liberation Committee, which in turn proclaimed the independence of the Republic of Vietnam on 2 September. Thus, as Philippe Devillers observed, "Ten days after the Japanese capitulation, the Vietminh dominated the entire Vietnamese country. With disconcerting ease, and through the joint effect of negotiation, infiltration, propaganda, and intimidation, and thanks especially to the "neutrality" of the Japanese, they had seized power. Their flag now floated everywhere."[19]

The French response to these events was one of shock followed by a denial of the reality of defeat and a policy of military and diplomatic actions aimed at reasserting French sovereignty. Part of the explanation for these reactions was the brutality of the Japanese and Vietnamese assaults on the French population. But part of the reason also seems to lie in the profound illusions that virtually all French leaders in Paris held regarding the French role in Indochina.

There had never been the slightest question in de Gaulle's mind that Indochina would remain French. He pointedly reminded journalists after his conference with President Roosevelt in Washington on 10 July 1944 that even after four years of war and suffering, including foreign occupation and betrayal from within, not a single French colony had refused to do its utmost to support the war effort of France and the Allies. "France is certain to recover intact everything that belongs to her. . . ," he declared, when asked about the future status of Indochina; but the colonies were to be organized in a new manner following the ideas set forth at Brazzaville.[20]

In a message addressed to "the sons of the noble, intelligent, and faithful Annamite people" on the occasion of the festival of Tet, 15 February 1945, de Gaulle underscored "the obscure harmony" which, he said, united all the supporters of liberty on the eve of the great victory over "those who wish to enslave others." France, he asserted, was aware of the sufferings of the Indochinese, "who are temporarily subjected to enemy occupation but whose liberation, with increasing support from our arms, is now a certainty." For the future there were also new projects in store.

> Proud of what she has accomplished here already with the devoted cooperation of the population, especially that of an elite that reveals so many aptitudes, [France] intends to make the political, economic, social, and cultural development of the Indochinese Union one of the principal goals of her activity in her reborn power and her refound grandeur.
>
> France, who is and will remain her own mandatory, will carry out that undertaking with respect for the rights, customs, and traditions of the peoples of whom she has taken charge. She will know how to accomplish that by associating them themselves not only with their own progress but also with the organization and the life of that ensemble of distinct entities and human values which, in the four corners of the earth, is formed by so many men united around her by the same ideal and the same fidelity. . . .
>
> Honor and happiness to the noble Annamite people! Confidence in the great French association which tomorrow, in so many countries of the earth, will form 110 million valiant, hard-working men living under our flag. That is the wish of France for the festival of Tet.[21]

In Paris the Japanese coup of 9 March was explained by the Provisional Government as part of the final battle against the Axis. On 12 March Minister of the Colonies Giacobbi spoke of the "sometimes touching loyalty" of the Indochinese people to France and stressed that "soon our flag will again float over a free Hanoi, Hué, and Saigon just as over Strasbourg and Metz." [22] In a radio address two days later de Gaulle elaborated on the same theme, explaining that even though the fate of French forces in Indochina was dim and depended on help from the allies, the political significance of their resistance was great. It assured France a place of honor among the victors in the imminent triumph of the United Nations forces in the Pacific war—something that Vichy had seriously jeopardized when it signed the agreements giving Japan access to Indochina. Moreover, de Gaulle maintained that resistance also strengthened the future of French Indochina.

> Yes, the future of French Indochina, because, in the trials of all and in the soldiers' blood a solemn pact is at this moment being sealed between France and the peoples of the Indochinese Union. . . . From now on, the veils have been torn away and the French

> government will make known how [the development of Indochina] will be accomplished.
>
> In Indochina, as everywhere, the ordeal of this war is like a boiling crucible. Certainly one might have feared that it would seal our decline, but now it can be hoped that in it our renewal will be forged. It is our acts that will decide.[23]

De Gaulle derided the attempts of the Japanese to establish a nationalist puppet regime as "feints and artifices" aimed at spreading dissension by creating a "paper tiger" of Vietnamese nationalism. At no time, he declared, had Indochina been more determined to go its own way with the aid of France.

This appreciation of the events in Indochina was further amplified by de Gaulle in remarks made to the Consultative Assembly on 20 March at the close of a lengthy debate on the colonial budget. First, he noted that during the course of the debate the Assembly had reached "a common, though subtly nuanced thought concerning what has been called . . . the French community," that reflected "an awareness of . . . the cohesion definitely established between the old metropole and the overseas territories."

The bloody events taking place in Indochina were cause for reflection, de Gaulle warned, though he assured the Assembly he paid no particular attention to the interpretations given to those events by foreign journalists. Thereupon, he read a cable from one of the besieged French garrisons praising the morale of the troops, pleading for immediate aid, and ending with a patriotic flourish: *Vive la France!* An emotional response followed as the Assembly rose to its feet amid shouts and tears.[24]

In less dramatic style, several speakers had earlier expressed the same confidence in the unshakable loyalty of the colonies of France. Thus, Hettier de Boislambert asserted:

> France's position in the world from the viewpoint of the colonies is good . . . because you know the faithfulness of those who live overseas whether they are Frenchmen or natives . . .
>
> —Albert Darnal. There is no difference.
>
> —Boislambert. None but geographical. You know that all those hearts beat in unison.[25]

Later, in another debate concerning the troubled conditions in Morocco and Tunisia, a motion was adopted calling on the government to initiate a plan of reforms based on democratic principles capable of achieving "the indissoluble and necessary union of the Moroccan and Tunisian peoples with the people of France in an atmosphere of affectionate confidence and reciprocal comprehension." [26]

All these statements asserted the existence of a community of French peoples around the world linked together by a common interest in French war aims and by a desire for French rule to be restored so as to guarantee the future welfare of the colonies. In the case of Indochina, however, that assertion was based upon three serious misconceptions. The French government greatly exaggerated the size of the pro-French Vietnamese elite and overestimated the relative power of that elite in relation to the more aggressive nationalist groups in Indochina. It also failed to appreciate the stimulus given to Vietnamese nationalism by the Japanese. Finally, as a consequence of the two previous errors, the government grossly overestimated its own power to control the political changes already under way in Indochina.

There are several factors that clearly contributed to these errors, and although it is impossible to show that they were the only significant influences, they provide a plausible interpretation of the events. One obvious factor was the lack of clear information about what was taking place in Indochina, especially after the 9 March coup. Most of the political and diplomatic missions dispatched to Indochina by the Provisional Government in 1945 were either destroyed or captured by the Japanese and Vietnamese armies. Only an unofficial mission led by Jean Sainteny, a Free French commissioner in China, succeeded in reaching Hanoi from Kunming. When Sainteny returned to Paris in July, he attempted without success to warn members of the government of the dangers already confronting France in Indochina and urged them to reassess their policy.

> I pointed out the opposition that we must expect on the part of Annamite [Vietnamese] nationalism. In vain. The warnings that I gave repeatedly on this subject met with nothing but skepticism. Far too many Frenchmen imagined that the Indochinese were awaiting our return with impatience and were preparing to welcome us with open arms.

> In the absence of a powerful expeditionary corps . . . and without the full support of a powerful ally, there was only one thing left for France to do to maintain itself in Indochina: reach a settlement with the Indochinese themselves—and it was already clear that they were going to drive a very hard bargain.
>
> I did my best to explain this reasoning to the people I could meet; it was received with a great deal of reserve, and each new conversation confirmed my feeling that if the Indochinese problem preoccupied a few people, it was, as a general matter, placed very far down in the order of innumerable metropolitan concerns.
>
> In reality, if the question was not entirely neglected, at least it was dangerously underestimated.[27]

One of the factors that discouraged the government and the Assembly from reevaluating its attitude toward Indochina as Sainteny had urged was the widespread conviction that the colonies were essential to France's future grandeur. The debates in the Consultative Assembly offer abundant evidence that the colonies were considered indispensable to the restoration of French power and the revival of national grandeur; consequently, the growth of native nationalism was perceived only as a vague threat to metropolitan interests. The most extensive discussion of colonial problems took place on the occasion of the debate over the colonial budget before a virtually empty house. The government's preoccupation was stated bluntly by the rapporteur Hettier de Boislambert: "Either we want France to resume her place as a great nation or else we don't. If that is not what we want, then there is nothing else for any of us to do here." Gaston Monnerville, the president of the Assembly Committee on Overseas France, echoed the views of his colleague.

> France must make a choice: to remain a second-rank nation or instead, thanks to the contribution of her overseas territories, to become once again a great power. . . . France is at a crossroads. Let her hesitate no longer. Let her follow the only path that conforms at once to her well-understood self-interest, to her highest traditions, to the eminence of her humanistic philosophy, and which, moreover, is that of her grandeur.[28]

The conviction that Free France must liberate Indochina also reflected de Gaulle's concern to protect his own political legitimacy.

One of the principal bases of that legitimacy was the claim that de Gaulle had never consented to any sacrifice of French sovereignty. With the Liberation of the metropole accomplished and the return to more normal existence underway, de Gaulle found his authority beginning to decline as the political parties reformed and the Consultative Assembly made plans to elect a new Constituent Assembly. One means of forestalling such a shift of influence was to make Indochina a rallying point around which all factions could be united by patriotic appeals, at least for a time. This seems to be what de Gaulle intended when, for example, he climaxed his speech of 20 March with the declaration: "Gentlemen, I conclude by calling on you all to recognize with me that, when essential questions are at issue—and without a doubt those are the only things that will be at issue for the next several months—we are all perfectly united [*nous sommes parfaitement rassemblés*].[29]

The decision to restore control over Indochina was dictated by a number of domestic political factors, but the manner in which it was executed reflected primarily the conditions that existed in Indochina itself. The French could not immediately invade Indochina because they lacked the means of doing so and because the area was occupied by Chinese and British forces that had entered Indochina to disarm the Japanese. Moreover, when the army commanded by the Chinese Nationalist general Lu Han arrived in Hanoi on 9 September 1945 it found the Vietminh regime in de facto control of much of Vietnam. Neither Lu Han nor the Vietminh was willing to permit the French to reoccupy their positions in Tonkin. The British, whose army occupied Cochin China and the southern part of Annam below the sixteenth parallel, were more cooperative. However, it was not until 3 October that the expeditionary force under General Leclerc reached Saigon and, with British aid, was able to reoccupy the capital. With the arrival of armored units under the command of Colonel Jacques Massu, Leclerc launched a series of daring raids that enabled the French authorities to regain control over the larger towns of Annam and Cochin China.

The restoration of French control over Cambodia was facilitated by conflicts between the traditional ruler, King Norodom Sihanouk, and the leader of the Khmer Issarak or "Free Cambodia" movement, Son Ngoc Thanh, who had served as minister of foreign affairs in the short-lived Japanese puppet government formed in March

1944. In addition, Cambodia and Laos had both lost territory to Thailand following the Japanese conquest, and King Sihanouk was anxious to have French support to regain it. When a joint British-French military mission arrived in Phnom Penh in October, there was no resistance, and the Khmer Issaraks fled into Thailand after their leader, Thanh, was seized. On 7 January 1946 the French entered into an agreement with Sihanouk that granted Cambodia a measure of formal autonomy as a member of the French Union and of the Federation of Indochina, both of which at that point still existed only on paper, in the very vague language of the declaration of 24 March 1945. It reserved to France de facto control over most of Cambodia's internal administrative services as well as over police and foreign affairs, but it also provided for substantially increased participation by Cambodians in local administration as well as formal recognition of Cambodia's status.

Laos, which remained under Chinese occupation until the middle of March 1946, was reoccupied by French forces from Cochin China between 17 and 25 March when Vientiane was taken. The northern capital of Luangprabang was finally reached on 13 May 1946. A modus vivendi was signed on 27 August recognizing the unity of the Laotian provinces and their autonomy within the Indochinese Federation and the French Union. The Laotian nationalists who made up the small but active political elite had resisted the return of the French, and their organization, the "Lao Issara" (Free Lao), was driven into exile in Thailand after the fall of Vientiane.

Despite their military successes in Cochin China, Laos, and Cambodia, the French were still barred from Tonkin and northern Annam by the combined presence of the Chinese and the Vietminh. By January 1946 Leclerc's plans for an armed assault on the Vietminh stronghold were complete, and they depended on taking advantage of the semiannual flood tides, predicted for early March, to move large transports into the port of Haiphong. Leclerc and the high commissioner, d'Argenlieu, preferred, if possible, to smooth the way by negotiation, both with the Chinese and with the Vietminh. Leclerc was particularly anxious to avoid creating a situation in which the Vietminh might flee to the interior where, with Chinese aid, they could continue to wage a guerrilla war for many years. Moreover, there were 30,000 French settlers living in the North, surrounded by the Vietminh, the Chinese army of 180,000, and 35,000

Japanese troops. Against these the French could muster only the armored column of Colonel Massu, the 5,000 troops imprisoned at Hanoi, and a few thousand troops under General Valluy that could be transferred from the South.[30]

The first step was the Franco-Chinese agreement of 28 February 1946. In this agreement, negotiated directly with Chungking, the Chinese nationalists consented to remove all occupation forces from Indochina by 31 March 1946, to transfer to France all the responsibilities for maintaining order and removing the Japanese, and to permit the immediate landing of a French military force for these purposes. In return, the Chinese received possession of the Yunan Railway within the borders of China and duty-free use of the entire rail line and the port of Haiphong; the cancellation of French leases and extraterritorial rights in Shanghai, Tientsin, Canton, and Hankow, as well as special guarantees for Chinese residents in Indochina. Detailed plans for the application of the agreement were to be arranged by local military staff committees. Unfortunately, these dragged on so slowly that no formal agreement had been reached with the Chinese garrison at Haiphong by the time French forces arrived on 5 March, resulting in a bloody exchange of fire—the first of many—between the French and the Chinese in Tonkin.

Meanwhile, the second part of the French strategy required reaching an agreement with the Vietminh that would permit French forces to replace the Chinese. For their own reasons, the Vietminh were as anxious as the French to see the Chinese depart. The country was being systematically looted by the occupation army of General Lu Han, who seemed content to stay in Tonkin forever. There was an imminent threat of a French assault. There was also doubt about the ability of the Vietminh leaders to control the other nationalist groups in Tonkin or the doctrinaire revolutionary faction within its own ranks. Under these conditions Ho Chi Minh chose to enter into negotiations with the French, but it is clear from Sainteny's account that he did so reluctantly. Furthermore, Ho first took the precaution of reshuffling his government to bring in representatives of the other Chinese-backed nationalist groups, especially the Dong Minh Hoi and the violently anti-French Viet Nam Quoc Dan Dang (VNQDD) so as to spread the responsibility for a decision that was certain to evoke deep resentment among the populace.

By the terms of the agreements of 6 March 1946:

> The French government recognizes the Republic of Vietnam as a free state having its own government, its parliament, its army, and its finances, belonging to the Indochinese Federation and to the French Union. Insofar as the unification of the three Ky is concerned, the French government undertakes to carry out the decisions reached by the population, consulted by referendum.
>
> The government of Vietnam declares its willingness to give a friendly welcome to the French army when, in conformity with international agreements, it will relieve the Chinese troops. . . .
>
> The stipulations formulated above will come into force immediately. Immediately after the exchange of signatures, each of the high contracting parties will take all necessary measures to bring a complete end to hostilities, to maintain the troops in their respective positions, and to create a favorable climate necessary for the immediate opening of frank and friendly negotiations. These negotiations will concern notably: the diplomatic relations of Vietnam with foreign states; the future status of Indochina; French economic and cultural interests in Vietnam. Hanoi, Saigon, or Paris may be chosen as the place for the conference.

The adjoining military agreement detailed the arrangements for the Franco-Vietnamese force that was to replace the Chinese. It specified, among other things, that:

> The relief forces will be composed of:
>
> 10,000 Vietnamese, with their own Vietnamese cadres, responsible to the military authorities of Vietnam.
>
> 15,000 French, including the French troops currently residing in the territory of Vietnam north of the sixteenth parallel. The said elements shall be composed exclusively of Frenchmen of metropolitan origin, except for the troops charged with guarding the Japanese prisoners.
>
> All of these forces shall be placed under the French High Command, assisted by Vietnamese delegates. . . .
>
> Mixed commissions shall be created at all levels to assure, in a spirit of friendly collaboration, liaison between French and Vietnamese troops.
>
> The French elements of the relief forces will be divided into three categories:
>
> The units charged with guarding Japanese prisoners of war.

These units will be repatriated as soon as their mission has been completed, and in any case within a maximum delay of ten months.

The units responsible, together with the Vietnamese army, for the maintenance of order and security of the territory of Vietnam. These units will be relieved, by fifths, each year by the Vietnamese army; this relief having thus been effectively completed in a delay of five years.

The units responsible for the defense of naval and air bases. The duration of the mission assigned to these units will be defined in subsequent conferences.[31]

The agreement of 6 March 1946 served the immediate purpose of postponing a showdown between France and the Vietminh, and it enabled the French Expeditionary Corps to reach Hanoi on 18 March. However, it was only a preliminary agreement, and it left all the main political issues to be resolved at future meetings. France had recognized that Vietnam was a "free state," but the government had refused to use the term "independence" in relation to it. Vietnamese assertions of national unity had also been rejected, at least until a referendum in Cochin China demonstrated the desire of its populace to participate in a state run by the Vietminh.

Discussions between the local French and Vietnamese authorities resumed at Dalat on 17 April amid widespread incidents of violence involving both Vietminh and Chinese forces. The Vietminh still insisted that France recognize the full sovereignty of Vietnam, and they interpreted membership in the French Union to mean a purely voluntary association that would not interfere with the right to maintain a separate national military and diplomatic service. As for the plan for an Indochinese federation, this too was acceptable only if confined to economic cooperation. The future of Cochin China, or the Nam Bo as the Vietminh called it, caused particular concern, since the French continued to hunt down Vietminh forces there in violation of the terms of the 6 March agreement. For the Vietminh, the Nam Bo soon became "a veritable Alsace-Lorraine of Vietnam." The Dalat Conference ended on 11 May without reaching agreement on any of the major substantive issues, but it was agreed that these would be reexamined at a new conference at Fontainebleau, in which the members of the French government would take a direct part. A "friendship" mission of Vietnamese *parlementaires,* which returned from Paris on 16 May, had reported favorably on their reception by members of the French Assembly and the government.

The intentions of the local French administration in Indochina, however, were cast into serious doubt when, immediately following Ho Chi Minh's departure for Paris on 31 May, Admiral d'Argenlieu, acting on his own responsibility and without instructions from Paris, announced the formation of an autonomous Republic of Cochin China using the identical formula employed by the agreement of 6 March: "a free state, having its own government, parliament, army and finances and forming part of the Indochinese Federation and the French Union." This action technically changed nothing, since it was dependent on ratification by the French Assembly and by the people of Cochin China in the referendum provided for in the 6 March agreement. Nevertheless, it was altogether contrary to the intent of that agreement, and the Vietnamese, both in Hanoi and at Fountainebleau, regarded it as a direct challenge to national unity.

When the Fountainebleau Conference finally met in July 1946, the positions of both sides had hardened to the point where any possibility for compromise had been virtually eliminated. The government had assumed a distinctly more cautious outlook following the elections of 2 June. The new premier, Georges Bidault, while anxious to find a solution to the increasingly costly war, was committed to the position taken by de Gaulle, which the MRP, as the *parti de la fidelité,* could not abandon. The Vietminh delegation, for its part, quickly became deeply embroiled in domestic French partisan struggles as they actively sought the support of the French Communist party and went out of their way to fraternize with the Algerian nationalist deputies who were also newly arrived in Paris. Personalities also played a part in the breakup of the conference, but the final showdown came when d'Argenlieu convened a second conference at Dalat, ostensibly to plan the future of the Indochinese Federation, to which he invited representatives from Cochin China, Laos, Cambodia, and South Annam, but not the Vietminh.

From 1 August to 13 September 1946 exchanges between the French government and the Vietnamese delegation continued in an effort to salvage something from the wreckage of the Fontainebleau meetings. In the end it was apparent, however, that there was no longer any basis for agreement between the French and the Vietminh on the future of Vietnam. Ho Chi Minh, anxious not to return to Vietnam empty-handed, finally signed a modus vivendi in which the French government agreed to cooperate with Hanoi in ending hostilities in Cochin China and to institute a more liberal regime there "based on democratic liberties." In exchange, the Vietminh leader promised to permit a resumption of French commercial and cultural activity in the North and to join an Indochinese monetary and customs union. The modus vivendi said nothing about Vietnamese "independence" or the scheduling of a referendum in the Nam Bo, and it was for these reasons that Ho is reported to have expressed the fear that in accepting it he was "signing his death warrant."

Such fears were well founded, for the Vietminh leaders in Hanoi, influenced increasingly by extremists such as Giap, were growing increasingly resentful over the long delays. Within a few weeks of his return, and only two days after the modus vivendi was scheduled to take effect, Ho was forced to form a new government from which all the moderate nationalists were dropped, together with the representatives of the VNQDD. On 12 November the Vietnamese Assembly, after first ousting all its non-Vietminh members, adopted a constitution that omitted any reference to the French Union.

Barely one week later, violence erupted in the Haiphong region, culminating in an order by the local French commandant, Colonel Dèbes, acting on instructions from General Valluy, for French naval vessels to shell the city of Haiphong. Official estimates of Vietnamese casualties reached six thousand killed.[32] Despite frantic efforts by the newly formed government of Léon Blum to restore the status quo, the Vietminh, convinced that further negotiations with the French were futile, launched a full-scale assault on French garrisons throughout the North on 20 December 1946. Ironically on that very day, as the First Indochina War was beginning, the British government announced its decision to offer immediate independence to Burma.

The developing crisis in Indochina had a profound impact on the political milieu within the Constituent Assembly. The frustrating confrontations between the Vietminh and the French government at

Fontainebleau coincided with the reconsideration of the French Union articles of the constitution in the Constitutional Committee of the Assembly. As these events unfolded, the Assembly found itself trapped between the desire to bring an end to the Indochina crisis and complete the drafting of a new constitution for the French Union, and the need to support the government in negotiations with a difficult, demanding opponent. The immediate result was to force the Assembly to abandon the ambiguous language of the April Draft Constitution, which described the French Union as an association of states and territories "based on free consent" in favor of a much more explicit, and therefore less commodious, structure of rights and obligations attaching to membership within the French "bloc" of nations.

The government's conception of the French Union, as set forth in a note delivered to the Vietminh on 11 July, emphasized its unitary character and left no room for doubt concerning the direction in which they expected it to evolve.

> The French Union is not a simple association of interests. It is more than that, and it will only really exist to the degree that its members are infused [*pénétrés*] with the desire to serve a common ideal, the democratic and socialist ideal which is the common heritage of our two nations. . . .
>
> It is the conjoining of our military and economic potential which will assure the solidity of the system as a whole. Consequently, the external defense of Vietnam can only be organized jointly and simultaneously by the forces of Vietnam and those of the French Union. . . . The diplomatic relations of each of the members of the French Union with foreign states can only be conducted through the qualified organs of the French Union, each of them having the possibility of making its voice heard within that union. . . . It is logical that each member of the French Union address itself to the qualified organs of the union to receive counselors, experts and technicians that may be needed in any domain. It will call upon foreign states only if the French Union cannot respond to its needs in a particular case.

"Our conception of the French Union," declared Max André, the head of the French delegation at Fontainebleau, "is not that of an alliance, but that of states closely united by common institutions." [33]

The government's position regarding a settlement in Indochina was further expounded in a memorandum drafted by the Interministerial Committee on Indochina [34] and approved by the Council of Ministers on 14 August. While retaining the formula of a "free state" embodied in the 6 March agreement, it also asserted that the federal government of Indochina (including Laos, Cambodia, and Cochin China, in addition to Vietnam) would exercise sweeping powers over all common economic, diplomatic, and defense matters. It went even further than the earlier statement in specifying that all tariffs and currency matters would be under federal (that is, French) control and that the status of French commercial properties could not be altered except by common agreement. Finally, it postponed the plebiscite on the future status of Cochin China that had been a primary aspect of the 6 March agreement "until public order has been restored." [35]

This position was itself a compromise between the views of the local French administration and the demands of the Vietminh. The Saigon French community, especially the local civil service, had as its chief spokesman Governor-General d'Argenlieu, who urged the government to avoid any political commitments to the Vietminh and to stall for time until French forces could regain control of the North.[36] The compromise was unacceptable to the Vietminh, however, since they were unwilling to yield control over the economic, political, or military affairs of Vietnam, which they then exercised, and they particularly objected to French efforts to divide Vietnam by creating a separate state in Cochin China. Once the failure of the Fontainebleau Conference became certain, the Assembly found itself in the embarrassing position of repudiating commitments undertaken by the French government if it adopted a less precise version of the French Union than the one proposed by the Interministerial Committee on Indochina. Certainly, to have done so would have meant provoking another government crisis only a few months after the bitterly contested elections of 2 June.

Furthermore, the atmosphere within the Assembly became embittered by the enthusiasm with which the extreme Left adopted the Vietminh and by the unsubtle efforts of the Vietminh to recruit support from the Algerian and Malagasy nationalists. The result of this close identification was less to strengthen the hand of the Vietminh than to discredit the colonial views of the Left, especially the Socialists.[37] An important reason for this reaction lay in the continuation of terrorist attacks upon French forces in Indochina during the spring and summer—especially the bloody ambush at Bacninh on 6 August—which brought a flood of angry letters and telegrams from the French community in Indochina, urging the government to take strong measures against the Vietminh.

All these circumstances combined to dissipate the feelings of optimism that had marked the discussion of colonial reforms in the First Constituent Assembly and to undermine once and for all the confidence of the moderates that a French Union based on free consent would win overwhelming support overseas. Instead, the fear began to grow that a French Union conceived along such loosely structured lines would be nothing but an *anti-chambre de sortie*. The fact that the policy of negotiation with the Vietminh had been initiated by men of the Right such as Sainteny and Leclerc in no way relieved the skepticism of the MRP and the moderates concerning the ultimate aims of Ho Chi Minh and his followers. Public opinion was deeply influenced by the apparent danger to traditional French interests and ideals to the point where, as Devillers later explained:

> National feelings, whipped up by the war, were becoming extremely irritable as soon as it appeared that France's future as a great power was at stake. Public opinion, while ready to accept any transformation—even a radical one—in the colonial system, was, on the other hand, absolutely unwilling to permit the slightest attempt at secession (especially after the Syrian affair). But to the public, the word "independence" inevitably evoked the idea of secession.[38]

The extent of the anxiety can be gauged by the fact that it was the leader of the RGR, Edouard Herriot, generally considered a man of the Left, who spoke out in the Assembly on 27 August in an emotional appeal for the reconsideration of the French Union articles of the constitution. Citing the importance of the negotiations then under way at Fontainebleau and Dalat, Herriot insisted that the form of the French Union be more precisely stipulated in the constitution. If the April Draft Constitution were to be adopted in its existing form, he protested, not only would it fail to take into account the position of Indochina, but if successfully applied elsewhere, it might well have unforeseen dangers.[39]

Responding to Herriot's speech, which clearly had touched a vital chord in the emotions of many deputies, Overseas Minister Moutet acknowledged the importance of the Indochinese negotiations and went on to explain:

> When we are demanding respect for the agreements of 6 March—that is, the integration of the Republic of Vietnam into the French Union—it is even more indispensable that we be able to tell them precisely what the French Union is: what the rights of Vietnam will be; but also by correlation, what the rights of the French republic will be. [*Applause on the Left, in the Center, and on the Right.*] [40]

There can be no question that the vast majority of metropolitan deputies shared these sentiments, for they had endorsed the concern voiced earlier by Marius Moutet when he told the First Constituent Assembly:

> In colonial matters, France is at the crossroads. It makes me think of that character in ancient tragedy, of Oedipus, who was to be king and whose destiny was decided there, where the road divided into three.
>
> What then is the problem facing us? Simply this: Will France remain a great world power because she will be present in every part of the world and will gain from it political prestige, economic power, and cultural enlargement? Will she remain united to those populations who have all, even when some have turned against her, contributed to save France when she was in the greatest peril? Or will she see them slowly drift away, attach themselves to some other ideology, and seek to make their way in other ethnic or political groups? This is the hour of decision.[41]

Moutet recommended a policy of conciliation toward the native nationalists. "Either we give satisfaction to the legitimate aspirations of these [colonial] populations, or we will have to resign ourselves to seeing them drift off." [42] De Gaulle insisted on a policy of authority. Under existing circumstances he was convinced that the answer to nationalist demands lay not in satisfying "legitimate aspirations" but in imposing unity from above. It was not enough just to assert general principles, he argued:

> The constitution should, on the contrary, affirm and impose solidarity with France on all the overseas territories. It should, in particular, put beyond any question the preeminent responsibility, and consequently, the rights of France in matters concerning the foreign policy of the entire French Union, the defense of all its territories, common communications, and economic measures involving the group.[43]

The second draft constitution came much closer to adopting de Gaulle's views, and it seems probable that an important part of the explanation for this shift is to be found in the experiences of France during the preceding year, both with colonial nationalists in Indochina and inside the Constituent Assembly and with the larger world as embodied in the disputes over the Trusteeship Council. No conscientious observer could escape the recognition that the French world was shrinking and that some of the most cherished symbols of French grandeur were under attack and in grave danger of being destroyed.

7. TWO PERSPECTIVES ON UNITY

The colonial myth depicted France as the center of a worldwide community of racially and culturally diverse peoples and states united by ties of historic experience and broad, very general political objectives. The situation confronting France at the close of World War II, however, was dominated by the increasing demands of native groups for local autonomy. If the unity of the French colonial system was to survive into the postwar period, it was necessary for the Constituent Assemblies to devise new links between France and the overseas areas capable of giving real substance to the broad general principles contained in the colonial myth. What were needed were new political institutions; hence, metropolitan and overseas representatives had to agree on a number of concrete organizing principles which, at least for the immediate future, would regulate relations within the new French community. One French writer stated the problem in these terms:

> World War II has led us to recognize one fact: "France is an empire"—some prefer to say a "union" or better still a "community of peoples." And it is this fact that it is essential for us now to translate into institutions in order to make it a permanent reality. We say that it is absolutely necessary, for doubtless none of our compatriots will contest the fact that the metropole cannot revive in the years ahead except through her empire—with it and within it. Above all, by becoming fully aware of the strength represented by the possession of immense territories, spread out all over the globe, and by honoring the responsibilities which that situation imposes upon us, we will deserve to retain the rank of a great power and reconquer the full confidence of our allies. If we want to participate in the reorganization of the world, our first

> duty is to show that we are capable of organizing ourselves, inasmuch as we constitute a nation of a hundred million men, conscious of its riches, its strength, its grandeur, its spiritual radiance and moral unity.[1]

Viewed from this perspective the constitution appeared to provide a new bond to unite France and the colonies. It was also possible, however, to view the constitution somewhat differently. The native deputies tended to regard it as a formal guarantee of equal status for colonial peoples and a means of acquiring greater autonomy for the colonies in relation to metropolitan France. The colonial myth provided both metropolitan and colonial deputies with appropriate symbols to justify conflicting constitutional proposals tailored to serve their respective conceptions of unity.

The reader will recall from the previous discussion that the colonial myth embodied an egalitarian conception of political authority and embraced the institutions of parliamentary democracy even when it assumed the continued existence of a centralized state bureaucracy. Preceding chapters have also shown how the belief that France and the colonies formed a single, united republic was embodied in the composition of the Constituent Assemblies.

Turning now to the drafting of French Union articles of the constitution, it will be seen how they were shaped by the concepts that formed the colonial myth and how in turn the myth of unity became altered as metropolitan and native deputies tried to agree on explicit rules and institutions for governing future relations. In that bargaining process each group tried to obtain rules consistent with its particular conception of the colonial myth and favorable to its own clientele. Hence, in assessing how the colonial myth was used to justify different versions of the French Union, one must ask what each group stood to gain or lose and how its supporters would fare.

The records of the Constituent Assemblies, together with party records, contain abundant evidence regarding the strategies pursued by most of the parties. In each instance it is useful to ask: (1) What did the leaders see as the primary purpose of the Union, and which themes of the colonial myth did they use to justify their choice? (2) What institutional arrangements did they advocate and how did they stand to gain from adoption of those plans? (3) Correspondingly, how did they stand to suffer if the plans put forward by their opponents were adopted? (4) Finally, what alternative rewards were available that may have provided incentives to accept compromises? The multitude of political, social, economic, and even psychological variables involved in such an analysis make it hard to identify specific causes of party behavior. Nevertheless, several reasonable explanations can be offered consistent with our knowledge about the events.

One way to assess the influence of the colonial myth is to examine the priorities assigned by the parties to the various elements of the colonial constitution. Citizenship was by far the most extensively debated issue. The difficulties encountered in attempting to define it in a manner satisfactory to both native and metropolitan deputies underscored one of the key ambiguities in the colonial myth. What was the bond that linked the colonial peoples to France? Did it unite individuals or governments? Was the French Union to be a community of peoples or an association of states? The problem of political participation was also troublesome because the colonial myth clearly required some form of representative government. But how, and in what proportion, were the native peoples to take part in the government of the union either at the local or the central level?

These were difficult issues at best, partly because the concept of citizenship and its relationship to representation were very confused in metropolitan usage. For historical reasons that can only be suggested briefly here, French constitutions have tended to view citizenship from two distinct vantage points, one juridical and the other political.[2] Furthermore, since France adopted a revised form of the Roman law system, there are additional difficulties arising out of the distinction between civil-law rules (i.e. private law) and public-law rules, which have no real analogue in common-law countries. Thus, for a time under the Third Republic the terms *citizen, subject,* and *national* were not synonymous, as they usually are considered to be in Britain or the United States. Rather, they designated differences in status between those inhabitants of metropolitan France or the overseas areas who were fully subject to French law in civil as well as in public matters (*citoyens français*), and those who did not enjoy political or private-law protection but were instead subject to local, traditional laws (*sujets*). The term *nationals* (*nationaux*) referred to the distinction between foreigners and persons enjoying French nationality regardless of civil status. To further confuse matters, the Constitution of the Fourth Republic uses the term *ressortissants* as a euphemism to avoid speaking directly of natives as "noncitizens" or "subjects" who were, nevertheless, French nationals.[3]

The dual character of French citizenship stems mainly from a combination of revolutionary and prerevolutionary political theories. To be a citizen, under the ancien régime, meant simply to be a full member of the community, and it referred to the bond of allegiance between the individual and the sovereign. Hence, citizenship was indistinguishable from nationality. The main impact of citizenship was personal, that is, it determined what system of laws governed matters like inheritance, landholding, and similar obligations, so that being a citizen meant that one was fully subject to all the laws of the state.

The French Revolution introduced two important changes in the meaning of citizenship. The first followed closely on the elimination of the monarchy and the transfer of sovereign authority from the king to the nation, and it involved the introduction of a new criterion of citizenship derived from the political theories of Rousseau. To be a citizen, according to Rousseau, meant to participate in the exercise of sovereignty, which was the formulation of the general will. This principle was loosely interpreted in such a way that participation in the election of deputies came for a time to be the distinguishing mark of citizenship. But since suffrage was restricted to a small minority, the concept of "citizen" was no longer the same as "national." Thus, in the Constitution of the Year III (1793–94) and again in the Constitution of the Year VIII (1799–1800) a distinction was introduced between electors, who were *citoyens actifs,* and nationals. Even the Code Civil of 1804 treated citizenship strictly as a matter of political status; thus, the broader meaning of the term, which implied an individual's acceptance of the state's laws and his allegiance to it, had apparently been completely displaced.

Revolutionary legalists, in the course of their efforts to codify French law, further separated civil-law rules from public-law rules in a manner that had serious consequences for the meaning of sovereignty. If citizenship were viewed strictly from the perspective of Rousseau, it became a matter of public law rather than one of primarily civil importance as had been the case under the ancien régime. Nationality then determined whether or not a person was subject to the civil law irrespective of whether he might also be an active citizen.

Even the revolutionary constitutions were not entirely consistent in their usage, however, and later constitutions did not preserve these distinctions. In fact, during the nineteenth-century none of the various constitutions gave an explicit definition of citizenship. Moreover, in actual practice citizenship was widely regarded as having both a political meaning, expressed as a right to equal suffrage, and a juridical meaning conveying protection under the civil law. The Code Civil in its edition of 1889 abandoned the view that citizenship was strictly a political status and asserted instead that it carried a recognition of civil rights as well, thereby returning to the broader meaning that had been associated with it earlier.

The French tradition, therefore, has been to treat citizenship as a legal status that includes rules of public law as well as rules of private law, much as the older notion of Roman citizen included all persons subject to the laws of Rome, the *jura publica* as well as the *jura privata.* In its modern usage citizenship carries two implications: the right to vote and submission to the civil laws of the state. With the growing acceptance of socialist thought during the present century, there has been a further shift away from the exclusive concern with abstract civil rights toward a greater awareness of social needs in a modern industrial society. Hence, the idea of citizenship has taken on the additional implications of a right to unemployment insurance, education, family allowances, safe working conditions, paid vacations, assured retirement, and all the other protective services associated with modern social welfare legislation.

When viewed from within this tradition, the problem of unity with the colonies posed serious difficulties. In theory, these difficulties could have been surmounted either by subjecting all citizens to the same laws and according them all the same political and civil rights or by creating a union of states, each with its own distinctive system of public and civil law. In practice, however, neither "integration" nor "federation" (as these alternatives were sometimes called by their proponents) could avoid imposing a measure of cultural assimilation and a degree of political equality that were unacceptable to many metropolitan and overseas deputies. In either case, the practical difficulties were overwhelming, and all parties were aware that some middle ground would have to be found, but each group was also determined to shape the compromise to fit its own conceptions as closely as possible.

A third aspect of the union that raised serious problems was the role of the bureaucracy. In the past French military and colonial officials exercised de facto control over local administration. The Constituent Assemblies unanimously favored altering this role; but how was the administrative machinery to be changed? [4] Here again the conflict among the parties' differing interpretations of the colonial myth became intense as they began to discover how dissimilar the perspectives of the metropolitan and native deputies really were.

At the start of the First Constituent Assembly, however, the general euphoria of the Liberation, together with the near universal ignorance of colonial conditions, inspired a spirit of optimism concerning the colonies. Most deputies seem to have approached the problem of defining the French Union with a sense of moral duty toward the overseas peoples who had been faithful to France during the war. A few, it is true, detected threats to French rule from the United Nations or from local nationalists, but they were a distinct minority.[5] Most of the metropolitan deputies, in particular, seemed ready to make a clean break with the old pattern of colonial rule and looked forward to a new union of the colonies and the metropole based on common interests and shared values. As Gaston Monnerville explained,

> There is a sort of spiritual revolution taking place in relation to the overseas territories. France has finally arrived at an understanding that the overseas territories were not made solely for the metropole. [The April Draft Constitution] constitutes a denunciation of the *pacte colonial* . . . and leads to a conception of the French Union that should tend in the direction of a general agreement . . . on the basis of equality between the metropole and the overseas territories.[6]

Behind this optimism lay feelings of both moral obligation and self-interest. One contemporary writer stressed that the moral obligations of the past implied unity for the future.

> The empire, like the nation, but infinitely larger than it, today displays a will to live, to move, to raise ourselves up together. The peoples associated with our destiny feel strongly that they

> have but a single destiny, and that they accept. Do we ourselves know how much we owe to each of them? And how much stronger and richer we will be if we know how to bring them together in this active union that we have given them and that they have returned to us? [7]

Other writers, like Robert Lemaignen, emphasized the need to preserve unity with the colonies out of considerations of self-interest and patriotism.

> In the face of the decline that menaces us, forty generations of Frenchmen adjure us from the depths of their tombs, which are spread around the world, with all the fervor of their national faith to rediscover the traditional awakening that, in their own time, almost all of them knew. It is that which makes us rebound from the deepest depths toward the zenith. Today, as far as we can see, it is from the imperial concept and from it alone that we can find support for that reestablishment. . . . The option is not between the status quo ante bellum and reform. It is really between the construction of the empire and its loss.[8]

In such an atmosphere it was reasonable to consider colonial reforms as gestures of generosity rather than as the price of agreement among groups with conflicting interests. This feeling lasted throughout the First Constituent Assembly even though the consensus on which it was based had by that time begun to disintegrate.[9] In its place there emerged two fundamentally different perspectives on the French Union. The native deputies generally took the view that unity between France and the colonies was necessary and advantageous. But they saw it as essentially temporary and felt it would be best served by creating institutions designed to minimize metropolitan control over local affairs and to encourage a gradual transition toward full autonomy, especially in those territories that already had some prior experience with political independence. As the implications of the native deputies' proposals became clear, many metropolitan deputies and representatives for French settlers overseas became incensed at what they increasingly regarded as an attack on the unity of the republic. In turn they insisted that a hierarchical system of institutions was needed to protect French interests overseas. When viewed from these two contrasting perspectives, it will become apparent that the ideal of unity put forward by the colonial myth could lead to entirely different solutions to the constitutional problems of citizenship, representation, and administration.

The Native Perspective

The April Draft Constitution embodied a vision of the French Union that reflected the preferences of the native deputies, particularly those from the African territories who wanted a loose, decentralized union between France and the colonies. The Preamble invoked "the principles of 1789" and followed the example of the Constitutions of 1793, 1795, and 1848 by inscribing a declaration of "the sacred and inalienable rights of man" which, it asserted, "the republic guarantees to all men and all women living in the French Union." [10]

Beginning with the principle that "all men are born and remain free and equal before the law," the Declaration of Rights said that, "all sovereignty resides essentially in the people," and concluded that "the law is the expression of the national will," which is elaborated by the elected deputies of the people. Among the thirty-nine articles in the declaration, nineteen dealt with traditional civil liberties and seventeen with social and economic rights. Two articles referred directly to the colonies:

> 12. On penal matters, identity of jurisdictions within the framework of a single territory is guaranteed to all members of the French Union.
>
> 18. Access to the public service is open to every subject [*ressortissant*] of the French Union enjoying political rights attached by the present constitution to the status [*qualité*] of citizen, without other conditions than those of ability, aptitude, and talent.
>
> Access to all professions, posts, and private employment is open under the same conditions to all subjects [*ressortissants*] of the French Union. . . .
>
> For equality of work, service, grade, category or responsibility, everyone has a right to equality of moral and material position.[11]

The institutions of the French Union were outlined in title one under the heading, "On Sovereignty." The relevant articles were as follows:

40. France is a republic, indivisible, democratic, and social.
41. France forms with the overseas territories, on one hand, and with the associated states, on the other hand, a union of free consent [*librement consentie*].
43. Sovereignty belongs to the people. It is exercised in conformity with the constitution.
44. All subjects [*ressortissants*] of the French Union enjoy the rights and liberties of the human person guaranteed by articles one to thirty-nine of the present constitution.

    All French nationals and subjects [*ressortissants*] of the metropole and the overseas territories enjoy the political rights attached by the present constitution to the status [*qualité*] of citizen.
45. The natives [*originaires*] of the overseas territories, to whom the law recognizes a personal status, preserve that status so long as they themselves do not renounce it.

    That status cannot in any case constitute a cause for refusing or limiting the rights and liberties guaranteed by articles one to thirty-nine of the present constitution.[12]

The April Draft thus created a union of three communities: France; the associated states that already enjoyed formal autonomy, subject to a French protectorate; and the overseas territories that occupied an intermediate status for the present but would probably move in the direction of becoming associated states as they developed their own political life. In the interim the peoples of the overseas territories were assured of the rights necessary to such political development. Léopold Senghor, the special rapporteur for the French Union articles, justified this arrangement to the First Constituent Assembly by referring directly to the egalitarian and libertarian ideals of the colonial myth.

> The principal innovation of the Constitution of 1946 is the explicit recognition of the rights of man and of the citizen not only to women in the metropole but to men and women overseas. . . . The Fourth Republic, faithful to a tradition already long, felt it more imperative than ever to liberate the overseas peoples from the modern slavery of the indigénat. . . .
>
> Taking into account the historical and geographical realities, [the constitutional committee] has sought to establish a system

> that preserves not only the equilibrium of the union as a whole, but also the internal and individual balances. This system is supple. I was going to say that it is a transitional system; I prefer to say that it is a dynamic system which leaves the door open for the future, permitting the most diverse alterations and expansions while still preserving the harmony of the whole.

Consequently, Senghor urged the Assembly to adopt the French Union provisions of the April Draft with the same unanimity that had finally emerged within the constitutional committee. Such an accord, he emphasized, "would be in the republican tradition, or more exactly, in the French tradition" exemplified by the unanimous support for antislavery in the Assembly of 1848. The French Union would also stand out, he maintained, as an example to the rest of the world that peoples of many races, cultures, and religions could live together in freedom, equality, and brotherhood. Thus, the constitution is "an act of faith in the republic." [13]

The concept of a union based on free consent reflected the desire of the native deputies to incorporate those territories that already were autonomous states or that previously had been independent, such as the mandates and the protectorates of North Africa and Indochina, or Madagascar, as well as the African colonies that were just beginning to aspire to autonomy. In view of the variety of different societies that made up the union, the native deputies wanted the ties between their communities and France to remain flexible in order to assure that as the capabilities of the colonies increased, they would also gain greater political autonomy. The result was to be a union of peoples rather than a unitary state, within which the overseas territories were free "to assimilate without being assimilated." [14]

The April Draft provided for a system of counterbalancing legislatures within the French republic. The National Assembly included deputies from all the overseas departments and territories in addition to the metropole. The number of seats to be filled by overseas voters was much smaller than the metropolitan share, but that inferiority was offset by the creation of territorial assemblies overseas with much greater power over the local administration than their metropolitan counterparts. An advisory body, the Council of the Union, was to coordinate the affairs of the union. The local assemblies in the overseas departments and territories were to elect one-third of the union councilors, and the departmental councils in the metropole selected the other two-thirds. The April Draft also changed the machinery of colonial administration by making the governors more directly responsible to the metropolitan government. It made no provision for the representation of Morocco, Tunisia, Indochina, or the mandates at any level, since such matters required new international accords.

Despite its flexibility, this version of the union did not satisfy all the native deputies equally. As Senghor indicated in his report, it was a compromise between two quite different proposals. One, labeled "federalism," aimed at the eventual creation of autonomous states. It was put forward in explicit form by the Malagasy deputies Joseph Ravoahangy and Joseph Raseta, who introduced a bill to recognize Madagascar as "a free state having its own government, parliament, army, and finances, within the French Union." This was the same formula that had been adopted in the Franco-Vietnamese agreement of 6 March 1946, and they defended its application to Madagascar by formulating their own version of the colonial myth.

France, they argued, had committed herself to the concept of universal human rights, thereby implying

> support for peoples who have accepted her republican ideal in order to lead them toward the full flowering of their genius and their special qualities. . . .
>
> It is only being true to the French tradition to accomplish a still more revolutionary act toward those nations like Madagascar that already know the worth of all those values.
>
> In reality, Madagascar exercised full sovereignty before the island was conquered by France and declared a colony on 6 August 1896. In the new spirit that animates her, and without denying the works that she has undertaken, France intends to satisfy all the aspirations and all the wishes of the Malagasy people within the French Union. The recognition of a Malagasy state within the French framework signifies the will of Madagascar to respect and guarantee the economic, cultural, and moral interests of France.[15]

The Constitutional Committee refused to discuss this proposal, which, therefore, became a dead letter. In a move that appeared to be partly related, the government introduced an amendment to the

Territorial Assemblies Bill that divided Madagascar into five districts, each with its own local council, in addition to a *conseil général* for the entire island. Raseta and Ravoahangy objected strenuously that the government was trying to divide their constituency and was using parliamentary sleight-of-hand to accomplish it. Minister of Overseas France Marius Moutet protested that there was no trickery involved and argued that the amendment, proposed originally by another Socialist, Jean Pierre-Bloch, but rejected by the Committee on Overseas Territories, simply established consultative assemblies in the provinces to assure representation of all regions on the immense island.[16]

The second alternative, favored by the native deputies from the old colonies of the Antilles, Guyane and Réunion, involved the integration of their territories into the republic as overseas departments with roughly the same status as the metroplitan departments. However, this "unitarist" solution was clearly not in the interest of the majority of territories where French settlers numbered only a handful in the midst of an immense native population. The special problems of Martinique, Guadeloupe, Guyane, and Réunion, were settled by a separate law of 19 March 1946.

Underlying that action were a number of historical and ideological factors. As Aimé Césaire, the rapporteur for the bill, explained, all four territories had become largely assimilated to metropolitan practice in political matters. Under the Third Republic they elected deputies to the Chamber and for many purposes their inhabitants were considered French citizens. However, the social legislation of the metropole had not been applied in those colonies, because of objections from French settlers, whom Césaire called *"une féodalité agissante."* Changing status of the colonies to overseas departments, he maintained, would benefit the metropole as well as the colonies by curbing the settler's monopoly over the local economy.[17]

In support of these changes Césaire could again point to the long tradition of revolutionary colonial doctrine that extended metropolitan laws to deal with social and political problems in the colonies. He also argued pointedly that in taking such a step France would be making a gesture that had profound international significance—presumably for the United States, with whom the Antilles had developed important economic ties during the war. "At a time when, here and there, doubts are raised about the solidity of what has conventionally been called the empire, at a time when the foreigner echoes the rumors of dissidence, this demand for integration constitutes a homage rendered to France and to her genius. This homage assumes singular importance in the present international situation."[18]

A number of advantages accrued to the native deputies from the old colonies as a result of the adoption of departmental status. The application of metropolitan labor laws and social legislation by the end of 1946 promised renewed support for the Socialist and Communist parties that divided the seats in Martinique, Guadeloupe, and Réunion. In Réunion there were special economic considerations, resulting from the postwar monetary reforms that forced the sale of exports—mainly sugar and rum—in the metropole at a low rate of exchange to pay for foodstuffs imported from Madagascar at inflated rates, which complicated but did not prevent assimilation.[19]

The Algerian Muslim deputies were less successful when they attempted to gain acceptance for the idea of an Algerian constitution as a separate part of the French constitution. One of their primary objectives was to enlarge the scope of French citizenship to include all Algerian Muslims who were not granted that status by the ordinance of 7 March 1944. Another was to establish a new system of representation in the local assemblies in Algeria so that every voter would have the same voice in local affairs. Such a change would have put an end to the situation in which one million French settlers and Muslims who possessed French citizenship voted in a separate electoral college that controlled more seats in the local assemblies than the eight million Muslims who voted in the noncitizens college. When these questions were raised in the Constitutional Committee, all three metropolitan parties agreed, no doubt because the issues at stake were potentially explosive, to reserve discussion on Algeria.[20] In fact the First Constituent Assembly never discussed the matter; and when it was revived in the Second Constituent Assembly, conditions had changed so drastically, in France as well as in Algeria, that rational consideration of Algeria's relationship to France proved virtually impossible.

The primary beneficiaries of the April Draft were the deputies from the colonies in black Africa. This was partly a result of the vigorous activities of Lamine-Guèye, Gabriel d'Arboussier, and Félix

Houphouë-Boigny in the Committee on Overseas Territories and of Senghor in the Constitutional Committee. Many people considered these African deputies to be symbols of the fusion of French and African values and traditions that the French Union was expected to promote. As individuals the African deputies also possessed a knowledge of colonial realities that most metropolitan leaders lacked, and all had the skills to use such knowledge to good political effect.

Given the profound differences in culture, tradition, economic development, and political consciousness that separated the African colonies from the Antilles, and given their dependence on France for technology and public investment, the African deputies rejected both the "unitary" and "federalist" approaches to the problem of union. Nevertheless, they were determined to achieve a larger measure of autonomy. The most pressing need was to put an end to the arbitrary system of colonial administration typified by the indigénat and the practice of forced labor. As Lamine-Guèye later explained, "The essential problem which arises everywhere is that of equal rights, which must not be confused with that of political assimilation. . . . In coming to sit in the National Constituent Assembly the overseas deputies had as their primary objective the abolition of the indigénat and the establishment of equal rights for their constituents." [21]

D'Arboussier put the same point in different language in his report on the Territorial Assemblies Bill. What the overseas deputies wanted was local autonomy, and he explained that

> when one speaks of autonomy it immediately becomes apparent that the situation of the overseas territories, other than the four old colonies, is entirely different from what one might imagine when, in the discussions, some tend to link the question of assimilation to the unitary thesis or the question of autonomy to the federalist thesis.
>
> I think there is a confusion there that needs to be clarified. One can be a partisan of a unitary system and at the same time support the development of the special character of the countries comprising this unitary system, just as one can sometimes be a federalist and tend, in reality, to assimilate without wanting to say so.
>
> The present bill tends, on one hand, simply to affirm the auton-

omy of the administered populations with regard to the local executive and, on the other hand, to assure democratic representation of all the elements of the population.[22]

It became evident from these debates that the African deputies were intent on obtaining real political power at the local level, rather than gaining recognition of a national identity which, unlike the Malagasy or Algerian deputies, they neither possessed nor felt called upon to assert. A primary device for securing such power was metropolitan law, which was used on at least three occasions to reinforce the grant of citizenship, to abolish forced labor, and to define the powers of the territorial assemblies. In each case it was their intention to guarantee that the formal principles of citizenship set forth in the constitution would become more than gestures.

The law of 7 May 1946, called the *Loi Lamine-Guèye* in honor of its sponsor, guaranteed that regardless of how the constitutional provisions relating to citizenship might later be interpreted, natives in the overseas territories including Algeria, would enjoy the same rights as Frenchmen living in the metropole. It declared them to be "citizens on the same basis as French nationals of the metropole," but provided for special laws to determine how the rights of citizenship were to be exercised.[23] Forced labor was abolished in the overseas territories by a decree of the Council of Ministers, 11 April 1946.

More than either of those acts, the Territorial Assemblies Bill went to the heart of the question of local autonomy in the overseas territories. At that time, elected local-government bodies had existed only in the municipalities of Algeria, parts of Senegal, the coastal towns of French India, and in some islands of the Pacific. In most cases such local councils had worked intermittently and were not meeting in 1945. There also had been advisory bodies such as *conseils d'administration* that gave European settlers a voice in local affairs, but as an adjunct to the colonial administration. The Territorial Assemblies Bill, which became the law of 9 May 1946, was intended to give real political power to native voters by creating assemblies in which they had substantial representation and through which the local administration could be partially controlled. Under the terms of that law the territorial assemblies that were established in the overseas territories had the power to vote the local budget and to impose taxes, subject to certain limitations. The law also gave the territorial assemblies power to control mining, forestry, and land concessions as well as the acquisition and exchange of personal property and real estate and all other public finances. The decisions of the assemblies were final unless the governor requested and the Conseil d'Etat ordered that they be annulled for exceeding their authority or violating metropolitan laws.[24] This law reflected the determination of the native deputies to secure real autonomy, not just to win pro-forma acknowledgment of abstract rights, as Saïd Mohamed Cheick explained,

> The institution of local assemblies with power to decide important questions such as mining, forestry, and agricultural concessions illustrates and makes concrete in our eyes the need for total renovation which has presided over the elaboration of the present constitution.
>
> It is vain and even dangerous to grant to the overseas peoples political rights identical to those exercised by the citizen in France if one does not wish to grant them the same sort of rights in regard to economic decisions.[25]

When some complained that the territorial assemblies were being given too much power, the rapporteur, d'Arboussier, reminded his metropolitan colleagues that the National Assembly retained the right to legislate on the most significant financial questions and on all matters of national security, including conscription. Moreover, he argued,

> The overseas representatives . . . are well aware that there is no advantage for the populations they represent in attempting to embrace too much. They even fear excessive attributions for these assemblies, whose inexperience they are well aware of, but whose wisdom they are fully confident is adequate to the duties of the present moment.
>
> As it stands, this bill takes account of the present and reserves the future. It is in this spirit of realism and equally of idealism that the Committee on Overseas Territories asks you to approve the bill.[26]

Although the law never took effect because the April Draft Constitution was rejected, it clearly demonstrated the priorities of the native deputies and clarified their understanding of the place the overseas territories occupied within the French Union. Moreover, it seems evident that, having gained assurance of effective local political power, the native deputies were prepared to compromise on other issues. For example, they accepted a plan to elect deputies to the metropolitan Parliament that substantially departed from the republican ideal of universal suffrage. Under that plan natives and French settlers would have voted in a single college, but the balloting would have been done by party lists without *panachage,* that is, without the voter being permitted to reorder the names or to make substitutions on the list presented by each party. The anticipated result would have been to permit some Europeans to be included on each list to guarantee that some "good Europeans" would be elected along with the native candidates.[27]

If further assurances were needed regarding the value of the union, the native deputies may have found them in another law of 30 April 1946 creating an Investment Fund for Economic and Social Development (FIDES). As the acronym suggested, faith in France would be rewarded with tangible economic gains for the overseas territories. The debate that accompanied the enactment of the FIDES reflected the general recognition that, in the future, unity between France and the colonies was going to depend on increasing the welfare of the native population. Earlier efforts to create such a program had failed because, as the rapporteur Gaston Monnerville explained, "That mercantilist spirit of the *pacte colonial,* that colonialist spirit which had been denounced at this platform, still had not disappeared." [28] Now, however, the Assembly was prepared to take a new approach, as the former colonial commissioner Jacques Soustelle attested. "The French Union as a legal entity would amount to nothing if it did not become a reality on the level of technology, with the material base which we must give it. Therefore, I ask the Assembly to manifest its unanimity on this point as a means of showing the peoples who are associated with the destinies of the French republic that we know what we must do for them and with them." [29]

A major objective of the FIDES was to enable local governments in the overseas territories to undertake social welfare expenditures —including investments in health, sanitation, and education as well as the development of transportation—that were not directly related to the exploitation of raw materials. It also aimed to expand trade with the metropole, which had been sharply reduced during the war years, and to promote economic growth in the overseas territories generally. The FIDES financed such operations by using funds appropriated in the metropolitan budget and in the budgets of the territories to guarantee loans at low interest.

The FIDES was administered by the Caisse Centrale de la France d'Outre-mer (CCFOM), subject to the control of a steering committee made up of the minister for overseas France and his director of economic planning, representatives of the Ministry of the National Economy, the Ministry of Finance, and the planning commissioner. The director of the CCFOM plus four members of the National Assembly and two persons appointed jointly by the Overseas and Finance ministries completed the eleven-member board that reviewed all development plans and loan applications.

Primary responsibility for preparing development plans rested with the local authorities, including the territorial assemblies, in each territory. The plans were then reviewed by the Ministry of Overseas France and those approved were sent to the CCFOM. Thus, control over the formulation of plans as well as over expenditures was firmly vested in metropolitan hands. Local assemblies could request and native deputies could plead for funding, but neither had any direct control over money. Therefore, it is probably most appropriate to view the FIDES as a promise to the natives of the overseas territories that the metropole would finance improvements in living conditions when the pressures on the metropolitan budget permitted. As Marius Moutet explained,

> Today it is extremely difficult to assure the budgetary allocation of these funds . . . at a time when the equilibrium of our finances and the stability of our currency constitute the government's primary preoccupation. . . . However, it is necessary to find the means not to limit ourselves to a vote of principle, but to establish a text that will permit us to grant the colonies certain resources.[30]

The financial limitations were very severe at the time. Initial funding for the FIDES was supplied from the residual balance in the Fonds de Solidarité Coloniale, established by Vichy in 1940 to promote development in the colonies it controlled, which amounted in December 1944 to just over 228 million francs. By the end of 1945, however, newly authorized expenditures had reduced that balance by 45 million francs, and projected expenditures of 167.9 million francs for 1946 were expected to leave a balance of only 21 million francs. Moreover, continuing costs attributable to projects already underway were estimated to amount to over 100 million francs, so that, according to the Finance Committee rapporteur, René Malbrant, the FIDES would inherit a deficit of almost 80 million francs. Since the Assembly authorized only 17.5 million francs in 1945, the total deficit inherited by the FIDES amounted to nearly 100 million francs.[31] This shortage was made up in 1946, and by 1948 the program was fully operative.

It is impossible to give a complete picture here of the financial relationships between the metropole and the colonies,[32] but the reader should realize that apart from the FIDES there were many other types of subsidies being paid from the metropolitan budget for various purposes that benefited the overseas territories. In addition to military expenditures there were appropriations for the operation of overseas railways plus a number of direct subsidies to cover deficits in the budgets of the overseas areas. For example, Togo and Guyane received 12.75 million francs and 27 million francs respectively in 1946, and five other territories got subsidies ranging as high as 44.5 million francs. The total of all such payments budgeted for 1946 was 126.7 million francs.[33]

It is difficult to say just how important these economic arrangements were to the native deputies in 1946. Since the vast majority of natives were only marginally involved in the money economy of the colonies, it seems probable that most of the benefits from metropolitan subsidies accrued to French businessmen and colonial officials.[34] In the years that followed the war that situation no doubt changed dramatically, but in 1946 it seems reasonable that the native deputies considered the FIDES largely as a symbol of metropolitan concern for their welfare rather than as a source of immediate tangible gains.

Two additional observations are appropriate regarding the version of the French Union that emerged from the First Constituent Assembly. The first concerns the harmony that existed within the Assembly regarding the union. The native deputies seldom encountered any opposition from metropolitan spokesmen during the debates on the union and on related enabling legislation. A few metropolitan deputies criticized the electoral law and the election procedures in the Territorial Assemblies Bill; however, only once was there a serious confrontation among the major metropolitan parties over constitutional provisions relating to the French Union. That case also confirms the impression of harmony, since the real issue at stake was unicameralism and not the structure of the union. It was only because the MRP, having been defeated earlier, attempted to expand the powers of the Council of the Union in order to dilute the power of the National Assembly that the major parties divided on the question. Otherwise, the native deputies were able to count on the votes of the Socialists and Communists plus many MRP and other center party deputies on most issues.

Because of that apparent consensus the native deputies were willing to leave many aspects of the French Union to be determined later. Even the matter of citizenship was left intentionally vague, on the assumption that the issue could be settled better after the overseas territories had organized their own affairs. This attitude clearly suggests that the native deputies shared the metropolitan assumption that there was an underlying harmony of interests linking the colonies to France, at least for the immediate future. Their efforts to secure a second referendum to permit the new citizens of the overseas territories to endorse the constitution of the French Union provide still another indication of their confidence that the relationship would endure.[35]

Despite the broad consensus that united the native and metropolitan deputies, at least in their public utterances, it is also worth recalling that by the end of the First Constituent Assembly serious divisions had appeared among the major French parties. These conflicts, which were not related to colonial issues, nevertheless threatened the agreement that had been reached on colonial reform because they seriously jeopardized the ratification of the April Draft Constitution. There was nothing the native deputies could do to improve the prospects for ratification because only those natives who were French citizens in October 1945 were allowed to vote in the referendum. Nevertheless, they attempted to obtain assurances from the Assembly that the accords that had been reached concerning the French Union would not be questioned by a new Assembly with a different majority. As Lamine-Guèye declared, "We desire that . . . despite the divergences which have manifested themselves in the metropolitan field, the constitution should seal an engagement that would not permit a new Assembly, that might not be an exact replica of this one, to once again place our status in question; for your Assembly has unanimously decided that the overseas territories will no longer be treated as poor relations." [36]

Such misgivings proved to be well founded. The Constituent Assembly adopted the draft constitution by a vote of 309 to 249 with the MRP and center-Right parties opposed to the Communist-Socialist majority. However, in the referendum that followed, the constitution was defeated by a margin of about 1 million votes, with 9.5 million affirmative and 10.6 million negative ballots out of a total electorate of 25.8 million. The French Union provisions were scarcely mentioned during the referendum campaign, though they were a factor in the decision of the UDSR to oppose ratification.[37]

The attitude of the native deputies changed in several important ways following the elections of 2 June 1946. On one hand they found the MRP had replaced the Communists as the largest party and that its views concerning the French Union had become far more critical following de Gaulle's speech at Bayeux on 16 June.[38] The ranks of their critics were also increased by the arrival in Paris during July of a number of spokesmen for French settlers who called themselves the Etats Généraux de la Colonisation Française. On the other hand, the elections also returned a new group of native deputies from Algeria led by Ferhat Abbas. Their vigorous demands for Algerian autonomy made them the center of a new controversy and in large measure eclipsed the more moderate African deputies. The presence in Paris of Ho Chi Minh and the Vietminh negotiating team also gave a renewed impulse to the movement toward autonomy for the colonies within the Assembly.

One immediate result of these developments was to focus attention on the problem of the French Union and to force the native deputies to develop new strategies, if not an entirely new and more radical vision of their relationship with France. Their first step was to form an Intergroup of Native Deputies which, although neither an official parliamentary group nor a formal party, enabled them to coordinate their actions in the Second Constituent Assembly. The next was to seek adoption of a text that preserved the essential advantages of the April Draft. When the first exchange of views within the newly reorganized Constitutional Committee revealed that the MRP intended to force a complete overhaul of the French Union Articles to make them coincide with the ideas of de Gaulle, the native Intergroup decided that the best strategy was to increase its demands.[39]

The Intergroup plan had been endorsed by the Committee on Overseas Territories and was adopted by a narrow majority in the Constitutional Committee. It consisted of six short articles beginning with a resounding declaration to be added to the Preamble. "France solemnly denounces systems of colonization based on conquest, annexation, or domination of the overseas territories. She renounces all unilateral sovereignty over the colonized peoples. She recognizes their freedom to govern themselves and manage their own affairs democratically."

Having renounced "unilateral" sovereignty in favor of a more basic right of self-government, the Intergroup plan provided for a union between the French republic and the overseas peoples "based on equality of rights and duties, without distinction as to race or religion." Unlike the earlier proposals, however, the new plan embodied the "federalist" approach to union.

> The French Union is a federation of nations and peoples who freely agree to coordinate or combine their resources and their efforts to develop their respective civilizations, to increase their well-being, to perfect their democratic institutions, and to assure their security.
>
> Its formation unites the one, indivisible French republic, the associated states, and the overseas territories including Algeria, erected into federated states.

The ultimate goal of the union was also stated unambiguously, and for the first time in any official document the Intergroup proposed that the constitution stipulate a time limit within which the essential reforms were to be completed. "The progress that the peoples of the union will accomplish, together with the French people, should lead them to self-determination [*la libre disposition d'eux-mêmes*]. Consequently, within a delay that may not exceed twenty years, each people will be able either to leave the union or opt for the permanent status of a freely federated state or, if it wishes to do so, to be integrated purely and simply into the French nation."

The institutional framework of the union proposed by the Intergroup also reflected the native deputies new and more radical vision of the union as a transitional stage in the process of decolonization.

> The formation of the French Union involves the establishment in each country of a constitution formulated by a local assembly elected by universal suffrage.
>
> Once having voted these divers constitutions, the peoples of the French Union will elect an assembly: the Assembly of the Union that will meet in Paris. They will be represented there in proportion to their population.
>
> The Assembly of the Union will be charged with establishing the constitution of the French Union.
>
> For the territories represented in the Constituent Assembly, that representation, which should be in each case proportional to its population, will be maintained in the French Parliament until the day when the constitution of the French Union will have been adopted.

Perhaps sensing that even if adopted, such a constitution might be ignored in dealing with some colonial nationalists or possibly in an effort to include a provision that would have some value for the Vietnamese nationalists, the Intergroup plan concluded with a declaration barring the use of force by France "with a view to conquest" or "against the liberty of any people that is a member of the union." [40]

The discussion of the Intergroup plan in the Constitutional Committee led both the African and Algerian deputies to clarify their views of the French Union. The conception of a voluntary union implied a right of secession, but Ferhat Abbas, Senghor, and Lamine-Guèye all declared that secession was not their intention. Abbas explained,

> We reject separatism for sentimental reasons and for reasons of a practical nature.
>
> The sentimental reasons! We do not recognize for ourselves a right to separate from France at a time when she is in distress.
>
> Practical reasons: We think, as M. Pierre Cot recently said to the delegation from Vietnam, that we have no right, through a

> hasty separation, to leave the door open to the return of certain feudalisms or to the intervention of certain foreign states that would attempt to take the place of France.
>
> We therefore believe that it is wise, as the Intergroup proposal suggests, to provide a twenty-year delay. Twenty years! That is the space of two generations. That will permit the French Union to consolidate.[41]

They all insisted, however, that the constitution provide for the introduction of democratic political institutions in the colonies immediately. Moreover, the native deputies demanded that whatever formal institutions were created for the union be determined in such a way that the constitution would not be, in Senghor's words, "a charter granted to the overseas territories." [42]

The perspective that gradually emerged from these deliberations was one that continued to draw upon the concepts of the colonial myth insofar as they were consistent with the goal of greater local autonomy. The egalitarian emphasis which had been evident in the April Draft was still present, but other themes reminiscent of the republican tradition of nationalism were also present. Most significant of all, the ideal of unity was coming to be viewed as a means toward the end of decolonization, rather than as an end in itself. At the same time that the colonial myth was being revised by the native deputies, some of its central themes, such as the primacy of the legislature as the expression of national sovereignty, continued to inspire both their proposals for local government bodies and their schemes for central institutions such as the new, superparliament that was to draft the constitution of the union. Clearly, the native deputies recognized the need for continued French support, and some could not imagine their territories as independent states for years to come.[43] The African deputies, in particular, seem to have consciously refrained from any flat rejection of the colonial myth because of their own political and economic weakness. Nevertheless, they also understood that once democratically elected assemblies began to function at the local level, they would be in a position gradually to assume control of the overseas territories. In such a situation they stood to gain in prestige and influence by invoking the ideal of colonial unity that allowed them to share in French grandeur.[44]

In the case of the Algerian UDMA deputies such gestures of

solidarity with France were less convincing. Despite the repeated affirmations of Ferhat Abbas, many moderate and conservative metropolitan spokesmen were convinced that support for the French Union was merely a smoke screen behind which the UDMA hoped to gain power in Algeria and oust the French. That is what eventually occurred, but it is difficult to find any evidence to support the view that such was the initial intention. Nevertheless, it is clear that the colonial myth was drastically revised by the Algerians and that Abbas used some of its themes in quite unprecedented ways.

For example, the UDMA program which was summarized in an earlier section, did not abandon the notion of unity between Algeria and France, but Abbas repeatedly used the assumption of unity to justify both greater equality for Frenchmen and Muslims in Algeria and complete autonomy for Algeria vis-à-vis metropolitan France. Granting autonomy to Algeria, he argued, was not a violation of the ideal of unity; rather it should be considered as the fulfillment of the French tradition and the best means of establishing lasting ties between France and Algeria. The draft constitution for an "Algerian republic" proposed by the UDMA affirmed that Algeria would become "a member of the French Union as a federated state. Its diplomatic relations and national defense are in common with those of the French republic." [45]

In defending this proposal Abbas maintained,

> No one pretends that recognition of the Algerian republic would be a renunciation for France, or an end. That's an error! The renunciation would be, on the contrary, in the maintenance of what is called a policy of authority. There is no renunciation when one applies justice. There is no renunciation when one installs in the young republic equality, liberty, and Franco-Muslim fraternity in the old capital of the Regency where the Janissaries made and unmade autocratic deys.[46]

On many other occasions he made similar gestures to mollify those in the Assembly who were fearful of secession. Thus, for example, he told them that

> no one demands that France leave. I have said it before, and I will say it again. We need France. . . . A Parisian weekly—I

> cited *Climats*—alluding to my recent declarations, conveyed the idea that I wanted French technicians and French money, without France. The truth is quite different. In reality, if one wants to express my sentiments it must be said that we want France without colonization and without colonialism.[47]

Abbas continued until the very end of the Assembly session to assert that what he sought for Algeria was in keeping with the basic intent of the French republican tradition. Thus, he insisted that

> you have no right to say that the overseas peoples are against you. They are for you; they are for the metropole, and, to the extent that you show confidence in them, they will have confidence in you.
>
> These people are, in reality, for democratic France. In revolting against colonization, they remain in reality faithful to the French revolutionary tradition.

But in the end he was obliged to admit that his views were in complete opposition to those of the Constitutional Committee and the government, and all he could do was to urge the deputies to take a closer look at France's long-run interests and basic values. These could only be served, he maintained, by

> . . . a vigorous and generous policy that will group around France the peoples inspired by the same ideal of liberty and progress. . . . It is not a matter of distilling freedom a drop at a time, but of setting an example and acting on a level with our responsibilities.
>
> The world is watching us. Generations of Frenchmen have died for liberty. They have imposed a duty on us. Let us not betray them. Let us be worthy of them, and we shall be worthy of France.[48]

Here was the key to the Algerian deputies' strategy. They hoped to persuade the Assembly to grant full autonomy to Algeria by invoking the radical, egalitarian principles of the colonial myth that had played a vital part in the development of democratic government within the metropole at an earlier period. The formalistic reliance on parliamentary institutions that characterized the colonial myth was also present in Abbas's project for a French federation and in the plan for dual citizenship for French and Algerians living and working in the two states. What the Algerians rejected was "French preponderance" which meant that "every bit of sovereignty, every aspect of authority, every lever of command must . . . remain in the hands of the Europeans of Algeria." [49]

Abbas and his followers were in the position of addressing two totally distinct constituencies. One, in the metropolitan Assembly, had the power to restructure Algeria's political institutions. The other, among the Muslim population of Algeria, held the power to determine the fate of those changes. Consequently, their perspective on the French Union was ambivalent, but there was no doubt that the Algerian constituency was the more influential. On the other hand, the metropolitan deputies, including a number of Socialists, were unwilling to countenance "full autonomy" for Algeria or to recognize its "full and complete sovereignty for all internal questions," much less to admit that such sovereignty resided "entirely in the Algerian nation." [50]

Consequently, the most important effect of the Algerian deputies' efforts to elaborate their own perspective on the French Union was to underscore the fragile quality of their vision of unity. Even Abbas's effort to reconcile the aims of native nationalists in Morocco, Tunisia, and Vietnam with the concept of a federal union built around France could not overcome the growing fear of decolonization.[51] What most native deputies considered as the logical fulfillment of France's colonial mission—the recognition of national equality and local autonomy—was seen by most of the metropolitan deputies as a threat to French national unity. The reason for this reaction lay in the fact that the metropolitan perspective on unity with the colonies had also changed.

The Metropolitan Perspective

The construction of the French Union was a secondary issue for all the metropolitan parties, and as a result their conceptions of the problem of unity remained quite ambiguous, even contradictory. The reformist spirit that marked the First Constituent Assembly obscured many underlying differences among them. Most probably agreed with Daniel Boisdon (MRP) when he urged his colleagues to concern themselves with the problems of the overseas areas, "whom we so ardently desire to gather together into what we now call the French Union. We would hope that the Declaration of Rights might be the cement which will bind that union in a manner that is indestructible." [52] Certainly there appeared to be general approval of the principle of juridical equality between natives and Frenchmen, even though there was disagreement about the practical consequences of such a gesture. The goal of the move was seen as the creation of an effective union. The minister of the colonies Marius Moutet, explained that

> there must be an end to racism, whether conscious or unconscious. The natives of the overseas territories want to be considered as inferiors no longer. . . . Does France really consider herself as uniting 110 million souls, or does she instead wish to retire into herself, looking upon herself as a nation of only 40 million people? Will France be a great power or not? . . . It is in our interest to demonstrate to [the overseas peoples] that they can become members of a great nation whose actions are capable of carrying some weight in the world. A consideration of that nature can incite them to give their total support to the French Union.[53]

The failure of the April Draft and the bitter electoral campaign of June 1946 destroyed the earlier feeling of optimism and revealed deep underlying differences among the metropolitan parties regarding the French Union. Even then, however, many ambiguities remained—partly because none of the parties was in very close contact with colonial realities and partly because the sheer volume of pressing domestic political and economic issues that required attention prevented all but a few individuals from devoting attention to colonial questions. In the end, party attitudes toward the French Union reflected a combination of preexisting doctrinal commitments and a variety of situational factors.

As indicated earlier, there was no clear division between metropolitan and native deputies during most of the Constituent Assembly. The Socialists and Communists frequently relied on their African members or affiliates to present party positions on questions relating to the union. Even after a break came between the two groups, there was a considerable range of views within the metropolitan faction with some deputies endorsing the native Intergroup positions and others strongly opposing them. These differences can be explained in part by the differing interests of the rival metropolitan parties, but they also reflect the deep differences that marked the parties' interpretation of the colonial myth.

The Communist party has always maintained that it alone among the metropolitan parties steadfastly supported the desires of the native peoples. According to the official party history, "The position of the Communist party is clear. Its fundamental demand concerning the colonial peoples remains their right to independence and to free self-determination. This position, conformable to proletarian internationalism, coincides with the national interest which commands the fulfillment of the national demands of the peoples who up to now have been oppressed." [54]

In reality, however, the PCF viewed the French Union as just one aspect in a much larger strategy aimed at achieving a peaceful, parliamentary seizure of power in France and supporting the goals of Soviet foreign policy. Consequently, its attitude toward colonial nationalists was quite equivocal. The party never abandoned the principle of national independence, but it was not prepared to back those deputies who wanted an immediate end to French control over the colonies. Only during the brief period of the Nazi-Soviet Pact had the PCF given unqualified support to colonial nationalists, especially in sensitive areas like North Africa. With the opening of the Resistance phase of their wartime activity, and particularly after the formation of the CFLN, which included two Communist representatives, the PCF became concerned about the unity of the French world.

When nationalist uprisings took place in the Levant and North Africa in 1945, the Communist press portrayed them not as part of the struggle against imperialism but as reactionary Fascist plots. The Communists claimed that reactionaries among the local population were in league with British and American imperialists to split the French and Muslim communities and to undermine the traditional position of France.[55] In February 1945 Joany Berlioz attacked the "pro-Hitlerian and anti-French activities in North Africa." He referred to the activities of "pretended nationalists who babble about 'independence' or a 'pan-Arab' union that are impossible to imagine in the present economic state of North Africa except as a shift to a different domination." And he denounced native nationalists as "Muslim feudalisms" who were aiding "the trusts" and "exploiting the legitimate desires of their people for liberty and well-being in order to lead them into anti-French adventures." [56]

At the Tenth Party Congress, Caballero, the secretary of the Algerian Communist party, was vigorously applauded when, according to a report in *L'Humanité,*

> he explained the causes and the methods of the Fascist plot in North Africa that led to the provocation at Sétif. He concluded by underlining that the Algerian people have the same enemies as the French people and do not wish to separate from France. Those who demand independence from France, he explained, are the conscious or unconscious agents of another imperialism. "We don't want to exchange a one-eyed horse for a blind one," he cried. . . . On the contrary, the Algerian Communist party struggles for the reinforcement of the union of the Algerian people with the people of France on the basis of their common struggle against the power of the trusts and the hundred colonial landlords, against the fifth column, for a true democracy.[57]

The central committee of the PCF had published a communiqué on 12 May 1945 calling for "the pitiless and rapid punishment of the organizers of the revolt [at Sétif] and their henchmen who directed the riot." A joint delegation of the PCF and the Algerian PC called on the *chef de cabinet* of the governor-general to discuss the "provocations" and to demand "rapid and pitiless punishment of the provocateurs." [58]

Those who accused the French Communists of abandoning their principles were wrong, according to Henri Lozeray, because

> our doctrine and practice for more than twenty years has been that there can be no question of any improvement in the lot of the colonial peoples without a close union between them and the people, the working masses of the metropolitan countries. That union was always stated as the indispensable condition for the realization of a just policy in national and colonial questions.

Moreover, in keeping with the principles of Marxism-Leninism, Lozeray asserted that "national and international situations of the moment" had to be taken into account. Under the circumstances, the Communists were convinced that it was not in the interest of the colonial peoples to separate from France because—

> 1. the French nation, struggling against the trusts who betray her at the same time that they pillage the colonies, wants to install a true democracy that alone can bring democracy to those colonial populations.
> 2. the lands inhabited by these populations are the object of frightful designs, while they are in no condition to guarantee a really independent existence. No one has any doubt that the French colonies . . . are absolutely incapable of existing economically, and consequently politically, as independent nations.[59]

These political judgments reflected an attitude on the part of the PCF which Alfred Rieber characterized as "nationalist in spirit and assimilationist in content."[60] While largely inspired by Stalin's writings on the national and colonial question in Russia and the Soviet experience with "federalism," such conclusions followed directly from the cynical attitude toward nationalism that has always characterized Marxism. They differed little, in fact, from the arguments of Engels in a letter to Karl Kautsky in 1882.

> The countries inhabited by a native population which are simply subjugated—India, Algeria, the Dutch, Portuguese, and Spanish possessions—must be taken over for the time being by the proletariat and led as rapidly as possible toward independence. . . . Once Europe is reorganized, and North America, that will furnish such colossal power and such an example that the semi-civilized countries will of themselves follow in their wake; economic needs, if anything, will see to that.[61]

Because they were confident that a harmony of interests underlay the relations between the colonial peoples and the metropolitan working class, the PCF was prepared to accept a constitution for the union that guaranteed the basic rights of the native peoples and created democratic local government bodies in the colonies but left most of the central institutions of the union to be defined later. On occasion this attitude produced a curious ambivalence in the Communist positions. For example, in Algeria the PCF attacked the policy of assimilation branding it "contrary to the customs, history, and aspirations" of the Algerian people.[62] Yet they voted in favor of extending citizenship to Algerian Muslims.

Partly as a result of such equivocation, and no doubt because of their earlier condemnation of Algerian nationalist leaders, the Communist candidates were all defeated by the UDMA in the elections to the Second Constituent Assembly. André Marty explained the significance of that defeat and proclaimed the new party line on Algeria.

> The national movement is . . . a progressive factor, in Algeria as in all the colonies. It is one of the essential forces of all real social improvement. On condition, of course, that the independence of the popular movement be preserved. That requires that the workers, the peasants, and the intellectuals have the opportunity to organize freely in their own groups.

He urged the PCF to recognize that they were dealing with *la nation algérienne en formation* and called for large grants of internal autonomy to Algeria within a framework of "federative links, freely decided by the people of France and the other peoples federated in the French Union." [63]

Once legitimate grievances had been met, according to Henri Lozeray, the colonial peoples would refuse to separate from France. Moreover, he asserted that effective local assemblies would provide an "apprenticeship in democracy" for the overseas territories.

> This certainly should not disturb true democrats; those who place their confidence in the people, whichever they may be, and who believe in man's reason and his love of liberty. Because . . . the attachment of the overseas peoples to France is to be found less in the formal ties, which only disguise the continuation of constraint, than in their freely expressed desire to link their destiny with that of France.
>
> We Communists have constantly affirmed the right of self-determination. But the right to divorce has never signified an obligation to divorce. [*Applause on the extreme Left*] Contrary to some, who see only their own interests and not those of the country, we have confidence in the overseas peoples because we want to give them reasons to love France.
>
> Let's be reassured. We know by the fraternal contacts that we

have never stopped having with the men from overseas that they do not confuse the faces of certain reactionaries and colonialists with that of the France of the Rights of Man, the abolition of slavery, and the liberation from fascism.

To that France, the overseas peoples, imbued with the spirit of liberty, will always be attached.[64]

One Communist intellectual, reflecting on this experience more than a decade later, observed that the party leadership had been caught up in "a euphoria of reasonableness" that caused it to lose touch both with its basic ideology and with the actual conditions in the colonies.

> The euphoria of the Liberation grew into a euphoria of hopefulness, and the euphoria of hopefulness crystallized into a euphoria of optimism. I saw only the good side of things. . . . *C'était de l'éthylisme ideologique!* . . . I ignored the fact that the party permitted the persecution of the Algerian nationalist movement and even participated in that persecution. For that matter, I altogether forgot about the colonial problem. The salvos of victory had deafened our ears to the massacres at Sétif. . . . Our anticolonial principles were enough. . . . We were ready to salute with enthusiasm the ruin of the white empire, the yellow revolution, or black liberty. We were so sure of our universalism that it quite naturally became quiescent. It was so perfectly clear to us that our cause was the cause of all mankind that, even if we had been knocked over by Warsaw or Sétif, we would immediately have brought ourselves back into balance by throwing the counterweight of the human race as a whole into the other scale.[65]

The reason given by the PCF for supporting the constitutional draft was its desire to put an end to the provisional regime and to "enter a period of stability." [66] Party spokesmen complained because the new draft eliminated all references to a union based on free consent, but the PCF voted with the MRP and the Socialists in favor of its adoption, thus indicating that other issues took precedence over colonial problems. Another indication that the PCF attached minor importance to such issues is the fact that principal party officials seldom spoke about them. Instead, relatively minor figures like Alice Sportisse from Algeria or Césaire, the poet-politician from Martinique, often presented the party line on colonial questions, although it is very doubtful they had any influence on its formulation. The result was that their speeches seemed to reflect the influence of the French colonial myth as much or more than the doctrines of Marxism-Leninism. This was particularly true in regard to spokesmen like Pierre Cot whose rhetoric owed more to radical-socialism than to communism.

For example, Césaire proclaimed the beginning of a new era in the relations between France and the colonies distinguished on one hand by a new spirit and on the other by the close alliance of the colonial peoples and the metropolitan working class, that is to say, the Communist party.

> It is a spirit whose beneficial force is no less great for what it destroys than for what it builds. What it destroys is . . . the colonial myth. It is this convenient myth, on which Europe lived for several centuries and which the Third Republic itself lacked the courage and the wisdom to renounce. . . . This myth, which is the colonialist myth, this myth of the white man's burden, this myth of the colored man's inferiority has been renounced by the Fourth Republic, and it will be the great merit of our constitution to affirm it boldly. . . . This will be the glory of the new republic to have believed that if, after all, man needs a myth, a myth in the sense that Sorel gave to that word . . . , that myth can only be the revolutionary myth of liberty, equality, and fraternity.[67]

Again during the final debate on the French Union articles of the constitution Césaire stated the position of the PCF in a way that made clear its continuity with the republican colonial myth, even while he criticized that myth. After recalling the contribution of the colonial peoples to the Liberation of the metropole and the obligations undertaken by France in regard to them under the United Nations Charter, he concluded:

> I come to . . . the most important argument. . . . I think that colonialism can no longer subsist because it is contrary to the very principles of the republic you are attempting to construct.
>
> How is it that you want to build a social republic, a demo-

cratic republic, a republic that will admit no differences of race or color, and at the same time, you are trying to conserve, to maintain, to perpetuate the colonialist system, which carries within its flanks, racism, oppression, and servitude? . . .

We ask you to maintain the committee's text and condemn every system of colonization founded on oppression and domination. In doing this, we are convinced that you are acting within a French tradition that is still the glory of this country.[68]

The most innovative proposals to emerge from the Communist group came not from a regular party member at all, but from Pierre Cot, the dissident Radical-Socialist who quit his own party and affiliated with the PCF during the First Constituent Assembly. On many occasions Cot argued forcefully for a fresh approach to colonial matters, and he was prepared to go much further than any other metropolitan party figure toward granting formal independence to the colonies. His reasoning was at once more candid and less dogmatic than that of the official PCF leaders. He urged his colleagues to recognize that

> the colonial era has given way to a great new human movement. Hundreds of millions of men are marching toward a new national consciousness, and through it toward international life. The question that we must resolve is how we will participate in this great movement. . . . France owes it to herself not to engage in one of those rearguard combats in behalf of colonialism that are always lost. France should furnish the formulas of liberation.[69]

The best way to express France's devotion to liberty, Cot argued, was to leave the future form of the French Union open so that the parties directly concerned could settle it by "completely free discussions." But if that possibility were no longer open, then he favored making explicit provisions in the constitution for changes in status within the union so that the colonial territories would not be "frozen" into the status quo. If that was done, he expected that within a very few years, as soon as they had become politically mature, the colonies, "in full agreement with France, would become our equals, our associates." [70]

The only other requirement for unity, the PCF asserted, was that the constitution impose no barriers between French and native citizens. Schemes such as the double-college electoral system contradicted the pledge of equality contained in the Preamble and, therefore, should be rejected.

> Under the French flag, at least, there can be no difference between men within the same territory. Whether that territory be peopled with whites, yellows, or blacks, all men are equal; they have the same political rights; we want them all, without any differences, within the great French family. . . .
>
> It is to the honor of France when, in any part of the globe whatever, a man becomes free or a people arouse themselves and wish to become free; that man or that people are the pupils and disciples of the French Revolution. Let us remain true to that great tradition of equality among men.[71]

These and other statements by PCF spokesmen demonstrate two things about the Communist perspective on the colonies. First, their image of a freely consented union between the metropole and the colonies was perfectly consistent with the prevailing colonial myth, which took for granted an underlying harmony of outlook and interests between France and the colonies. Even the language used by the Communists was drawn as much from the Jacobin tradition of revolutionary egalitarianism as from Marxism-Leninism. The institutional arrangements that the Communists proposed for the union also reflected the predominance of the legislature at both the local and metropolitan levels of government and transferred metropolitan institutions overseas.

Second, the PCF stood to benefit directly from these positions in several ways. Domestically it could anticipate increased support from new native voters and from sympathetic native deputies who would provide valuable leverage within the National Assembly. Given the existing distribution of party strength, such support could significantly improve the Communist's chances to participate in any future cabinet and to shape future governmental coalitions. Internationally the PCF clearly intended to maintain French national power and to use it to block any increase in British or American influence in the colonial areas. As a result they might reasonably have expected to gain the approval and the support of the Soviet Union in the international Communist movement.

It is clear, therefore, that despite its endorsement of the principle of complete autonomy for the colonies, the PCF qualified both its public statements and its political actions so as to remain well within the limits of the metropolitan consensus on colonial matters. Indeed, it is striking how similar both the assumptions and the policies of the PCF were to those of de Gaulle.[72] Needless to say, it required considerable verbal dexterity to reconcile the original anticolonial principles of the PCF with its concern not to disturb the status quo.

One way that this was accomplished was by blaming "the trusts" and the capitalist "imperialists" for the conditions that made an immediate move toward independence impossible. As Lozeray maintained,

> If our colleague Aimé Césaire is absolutely right to proclaim that "the colonial problem will not be resolved so long as capitalism has not been destroyed," it would be politically false and dangerous to hold to that affirmation. Insofar as the French people develop democracy in the metropole, by enlarging it to the overseas territories they create there better conditions for a satisfactory solution to the colonial problem.[73]

Another means of reconciling this apparent contradiction was to emphasize the risks of independence for the colonies. Thus Raymond Barbé defended the actions of the PCF in the Second Constituent Assembly with the argument that it had defended the true interests of the native peoples.

> At this time, faced with the imperialist aims, the common interest of the overseas peoples and the French people is to remain united and to arrange everything so that the liberty of the peoples, the equality of rights, and the fraternity of the various races shall really be guaranteed. In a world where, the war having barely ended, and leaving aside the fifth of the globe where socialism is being built, the great powers of the world are searching for new prey, any attempt to leave the French Union could only lead to an illusory and momentary pseudo-independence and the reinforcement of imperialism.[74]

Finally, the Communists turned to the symbols of the colonial myth to justify their policy, juxtaposing them with Stalin's tract on the "National and Colonial Question."

> Worthy heirs of the revolutionaries of '89 and '93, of the "abolitionists" of 1848, we remain faithful to the principles of the Declaration of the Rights of Man, according to which "men are born and remain free and equal in rights." And we estimate it to be contrary to the interests of the overseas populations and dangerous for France to seek to dodge . . . their legitimate national aspirations. Marxism-Leninism teaches us that "the interests of the proletarian movement in the developed countries and of the national liberation movement in the colonies demand the union of these two aspects of the revolutionary movement in a common front against the common enemy, against imperialism." [75]

The PCF later claimed credit for having saved the native Intergroup plan from total defeat, even though the Communists voted with the MRP and SFIO in favor of the revised plan for the union submitted by the government and opposed by the native Intergroup. In fact, the Communist party did not press for increased colonial autonomy until after the Communist ministers were ejected from the government in May 1947. When there was still a chance that the PCF would control government policy, the French communists were unwilling to endorse any reduction in French control over the colonies. Even after May 1947 the PCF simply demanded that the government "carry out the provisions of the French Union"; it did not advocate formal independence.[76]

The opposite pole of the metropolitan political spectrum from the PCF was occupied by the PRL, the UDSR, and the Radical-Socialists. The latter two groups joined together for electoral purposes to form the RGR. Each group had its own special concerns but all had many characteristics in common, and along with a scattering of Independent Republican, Republican Peasant Action, and other conservative fringe groups, they made up the right wing of the Assembly. Together they accounted for 114 votes in the Second Constituent Assembly.

All the conservative groups were concerned with preserving French sovereignty over the colonies, but they were by no means consistently opposed to all reforms. The PRL, for example, was especially anxious to see changes made that would allow French settlers in Morocco and Tunisia to retain the representation in

Parliament they had acquired under the law establishing the Constituent Assembly. The PRL opposed the conception of a union based on free consent because that implied a loss of sovereignty. Its vision of unity reflected a hierarchical conception of the relationship between France and the colonies which, as Julien Brunhes explained, involved three central concerns.

> First, the texts [of the constitution] should permit the free development, the growth, the evolution of the overseas territories. France has guided them in this evolution, and she is prepared to continue doing so.
>
> But, the second principle, France should maintain her sovereignty over these territories. We have taken account here . . . of how much the members of this Assembly were determined to maintain national sovereignty. We believe that it is not enough just to say it; measures must be taken to allow it to be done.
>
> Finally, we must also provide the articulations and connections between the metropole, the overseas territories, and the associated states, in order that out of that ensemble, made up of metropolitan France and the territories in the five parts of the world where the French flag flies, there may be made not something heterogeneous, but a true union, which corresponds in every domain, to the great world power that France with the French Union should be.[77]

It followed from these principles that the tiny majority of Frenchmen living in the overseas territories should be granted separate representation on account of their "moral, cultural, spiritual, and intellectual importance." Moreover, to insist on uniform suffrage would mean not only that French settlers would be submerged in a sea of native voters, but that the newly promoted, native citizens would quickly find themselves at the mercy of demagogues who might seek to arouse the masses against France and even against "those natives who have had the courage to make common cause with metropolitan Frenchmen." Looking ahead, the PRL could see a danger that such "demagogues" would find ready support from foreign powers, "whether in the East or in the West," who were anxious to displace France from the overseas territories.

Many conservatives, therefore, opposed extending French citizenship to anyone who did not fully meet the requirements of metropolitan law and proposed instead that the constitution create a "citizenship of the French Union" to link the peoples from all parts of the union. French citizens (whether native or metropolitan) would elect representatives to the French Parliament, but the Assembly of the French Union would be the proper body for non-citizen representation. The most basic problem in their view, however, was "the tragedy of the decay of French authority."

> It would be infinitely painful . . . if it could one day be said that the Fourth Republic, by its errors, had run the risk of losing that colonial empire created by the preceding regimes, particularly by the Third Republic.
>
> Let us not forget that France has already lost one colonial empire and that the disgust which many people feel for the name of Louis XV is due above all to his inability to uphold French influence in all parts of the world.[78]

In retrospect, it would seem that Léon Noel, the Gaullist critic, was justified in his harsh judgment of the PRL.

> Insofar as they have been aware of the evolution of the world, they preferred to convince themselves that it would go away without their having to consent to innovations or to the sacrifices necessary for them to adjust to the change. . . . Whenever in one of the three parts of North Africa there was calm, they opposed reforms, calling them useless or premature, since the people remained peaceful. When blood was flowing, they saw in that another reason not to decide anything. According to them, order had to be reestablished first.[79]

On the whole, however, most metropolitan parties favored at least a measure of reform, and it is only after one examines their positions in some detail that deeper conflicts begin to emerge. For example, the UDSR included a number of deputies elected by French settlers in Africa who favored increasing local autonomy but strongly opposed giving natives equal political status with Europeans. To do that, René Malbrant argued, would eventually result in excluding Europeans from the territorial assemblies altogether; besides, in his district, Oubangui-Chari-Tchad, he asserted that it would be impossible to find thirty-six qualified native councilors. By giving some power to local assemblies, especially in regard to economic and financial matters, the local French settlers hoped to improve their own bargaining position vis-à-vis the colonial administration.

The conservative groups pushed hard to gain acceptance of the double-college electoral system, which would have guaranteed representation in local assemblies as well as in the metropolitan parliament for French settlers and natives with French citizenship. Natives who did not possess the same status as citizens of the metropole were to vote in separate electoral colleges. The importance of the double college to both French settlers and native deputies can hardly be exaggerated, for control of local assemblies in the overseas territories was going to depend entirely on how those assemblies were chosen. In both Constituent Assemblies the conservatives were prevented from inscribing the double college into the constitution, but they were finally successful, despite strong opposition, in inserting it into the electoral laws.

Some conservatives would also have preferred to see the central institutions of the French Union spelled out clearly in the constitution in a manner that assured the continuation of France's pre-eminent position within the new structure. This preference for a hierarchically structured union built around metropolitan France was very explicit in a proposal advanced by Jacques Bardoux and prepared by the Académie des Sciences Coloniales.

1. The French Republic is one and indivisible. The territories of the French community are held to be integral parts of the territory of the French Republic. No cession or transfer of territory is to be permitted without prior approval by a two-thirds majority of the legislative assemblies.
2. The constitution reaffirms that French nationality is held by all inhabitants of the French community. . . .
3. French citizenship, or French nationality under internal law, can be acquired, whether automatically or on request, by French nationals. The conditions for this acquisition are fixed by regulations of the governors and residents-general approved by the grand council of the French community.[80]

These ideas were rejected, as noted earlier, by both the First and Second constituent assemblies. Nevertheless, they continued to hold great appeal for the moderate and conservative groups, and numerous efforts were made to introduce them into the constitutional texts by way of amendment. All of these efforts were unsuccessful until very late in the bargaining process. Alongside the discussion of constitutional texts some other actions were taken by the government, however, that seemingly were intended to compensate the conservatives for their failure to obtain formal protection for the interests of their constituents.

In the preceding discussion of the FIDES program it was noted that the principal beneficiaries of the overseas investment plan were French businessmen who dominated the modern sector of the colonial economy. Another action taken by the government in December 1945 also resulted in windfall gains for overseas businessmen and colonial civil servants. The revaluation of the French franc that took place when France adhered to the Bretton Woods Agreement on international monetary affairs produced a huge bonus for the colonies. In place of a single interchangeable franc, French monetary regulations created a special currency for the French African colonies (CFA franc), another for the Pacific colonies (CFP franc), while the money in circulation in Algeria, Tunisia, Morocco, Guyane, and the Antilles remained at parity with the metropolitan franc. The Indochinese piastre was also revalued at the same time along with the French Indian rupee and the Syrian pound. The rates established (1Fr.CFA = 1.7Fr. metropolitan, 1Fr.CFP = 2.4Fr., 1 piastre = 17F.) roughly doubled the value of a civil servant's salary in Africa and an exporter's cargo in Indochina in relation to the metropolitan franc. At the same time the colonial exchange rates maintained the value of the local currencies at or close to that of the dollar, thus avoiding the 140 percent devaluation of the metropolitan franc that occurred under the Bretton Woods Agreement.

The justification given by the government for abandoning a uniform rate for all French franc zone transactions was that the metropole had suffered much more than the colonies from the war and that separation from the metropole during the war had resulted in very different price structures in the two areas. Some economists argued that these conditions had already largely disappeared by December 1945, more than a year after the Liberation of the metropole. In any case, the real reason was to avoid imposing on the colonies a devaluation that would have sharply increased the price of imported goods at a time when the African colonies were importing 76 percent of their total external commerce from outside the franc zone. The Pacific colonies would have been particularly hard hit because there the dollar and the franc circulated freely at the legal rate, and 89 percent of exports and 98 percent of imports were from the dollar area. What was feared most were the social and political consequences of a move that would injure those who had held their assets in francs rather than in foreign currency or gold and would inevitably exacerbate relations within the business community, especially between producers and traders. As one economist observed, "It would have engendered a climate of demands that were not at all propitious for restoring order to the economy or cohesion to the French Union." [81]

The real effect of this system of multiple internal exchange rates was limited by virtue of the controls over imports and exports exercised by the metropolitan regulations on foreign exchange. Moreover, like the investment programs, these measures favored European businessmen in the colonies and administrators who received their salaries in local currency. For the natives, the only perceptible effect was an increase in the cost of living.[82]

Unfortunately it is impossible to make any accurate assessment of the relative costs and benefits to the metropole from the colonies during this period from 1944 to 1946. The data available prior to 1947 is not reliable, and the system of controls on trade, payments, pricing, and production makes any findings misleading. Several points can be asserted with reasonable assurance, nevertheless. The pattern of trade established during the war, with foreign commerce greatly exceeding trade with France, gradually was altered as trade with the metropole resumed the predominant position it had occupied before the war. Trade among the territories of the union had also increased, and many territories had begun to export semifinished products rather than solely raw materials. As a whole the overseas territories in 1946 exported more to France than they imported and imported more from foreign sources, chiefly the United States, than they exported abroad. Hence, the internal balance of payments for the French Union, if it could be constructed for those years, would show a trade surplus for the colonies within the franc zone and a deficit outside. Increased salary payments under various wage and price equalization laws also increased the cost of colonial administration, as did the supplements to the colonial budgets mentioned in an earlier section.

These costs were relatively modest in relation to the total metropolitan budget and probably amounted to no more than 1 percent of metropolitan national income in 1946.[83] However, in the circumstances of that time the added burden was significant, since the metropolitan budget was in deficit by 320 billion francs in December 1945. More serious still, gold and dollar reserves in the Bank of France fell from $2.5 billion in December 1944 to $1.8 billion a year later, and further trade deficits were anticipated. Ultimately, of course, the costs of maintaining the colonies were passed along to the metropolitan consumer, who paid more for colonial products than he would have under a system of free exchange rates and whose taxes increased to cover other subsidies. Finally, since total expenditures in the colonies probably exceeded production, at least in the money sector of the economy, metropolitan inflation was fed by colonial demand pressures. In exchange for such costs France received the benefits of international prestige and cultural influence plus the important satisfaction of having safeguarded French sovereignty.

While it is impossible to demonstrate beyond doubt the connection between economic and political interests, it is quite plausible that the reason why some of the moderate and conservative deputies were willing to omit the central institutions of the French Union entirely from the constitution and to defer consideration of them indefinitely was that they already had obtained important economic guarantees. Others, particularly some French settlers whose stake in the colonies was increased as a result of the postwar economic reforms, may have renewed their determination to preserve French control over the colonies.[84]

The conservatives were not the only group to show concern for the preservation of French sovereignty and a determination to shape the French Union along lines that clearly emphasized the traditional role of France as suzerain within the French community. Paul Bastid, speaking for the RGR at one of the early sessions of the Constitutional Committee following the June elections, demanded that a special section of the constitution be set aside for the French Union and he called on the Assembly to "define it and indicate its nature, since the accession of the overseas territories to an authentic national life is the great fact of our epoch. I would even say that it constitutes in my view the principal justification for remodeling our regime." [85]

The moderate RGR group then proposed a ten-point plan for the union that brought together many of the ideas circulated earlier by others and wove them into a pattern that clearly revealed their hierarchical view of French colonial relationships. The French Union, Bastid asserted, should be constructed first, before the institutions of the republic were organized, so as to respect the sovereignty of the associated states and to take account of the needs of the overseas territories. The French republic was to be comprised of metropolitan France plus the overseas departments and territories; and it, together with the associated states, formed the French Union. The central organs of the union were to be the president, who was by law to be the president of the republic; the Council of States, composed of representatives of the republic and the associated states; and the Council of the Union in which the associated states, metropolitan France, and the overseas departments and territories were all to be represented.

The position of each of the associated states would depend on treaty arrangements. The internal organization of the overseas territories, on the other hand, resulted from metropolitan laws that were to take account of "economic and ethnic affinities . . . in order to create future federated territories and to accentuate their political personality." The overseas territories were to be represented in Parliament by two deputies, one elected by French citizens and one by noncitizens according to provisions of the electoral law. Larger representation would be set aside for the overseas territories in the Council of the Union.

Metropolitan legislation was not to apply automatically to the overseas areas, and special organic laws were to prescribe the powers and mode of election for local assemblies within the overseas territories. Executive powers were to remain in the hands of a high commissioner in each territory or group of territories who was to be "depository of the powers of the republic." Finally, a special "citizenship of the French Union" that was distinct from French nationality was to apply to everyone within the union, leaving each individual free to seek French nationality if he could meet the conditions set forth by law.[86]

The Constitutional Committee rejected the RGR proposal in June, but RGR spokesmen continued to criticize the texts put forward by the native Intergroup and supported largely by the Communist and Socialist groups. Finally, on 27 August, the veteran

Radical-Socialist party leader, Edouard Herriot, made a celebrated speech attacking the draft articles on the French Union. He first denounced the majority for criticizing the colonial accomplishments of the Third Republic. "Without wanting to say . . . that the history of colonization has been an idyll, it can be said, at least insofar as France is concerned, that it has been a work of benevolence [*bonté*], a reaction of the spirit against the obstacles of nature." [87]

Next he assailed the commission's decision to leave the definition of the French Union so loose that it appeared to many to encourage secession. Earlier in the constitutional debates Herriot elaborated his colonial outlook and had urged that the constitution include portions of the declaration formulated in 1936 by the Ligue des Droits de l'Homme that asserted: "The Rights of Man condemn colonization accompanied by violence, by contempt, or by economic or political oppression. They only authorize a fraternal collaboration undertaken with a view to the common good of humanity." [88] However, the Rights of Man, as practiced in the metropole, did not include the right of secession. "Here at home in the metropole secession is summed up by a word that I do not even care to use, but which the French Revolution dealt with by a trenchant procedure. . . . [The need was for] federalism as you write it; federalism as you discuss it; but a federalism that is not going to be 'headless,' that will not be anarchic; a federalism that replaces the existing state of things with a better system." [89]

Moreover, the proposals adopted by the committee, extending French citizenship to natives in the overseas territories, held the most serious dangers for France. Unless revised, Herriot declared, they would create a situation in which "France would become the colony of its former colonies." The constitution contained explicit guarantees for native interests, but "What has been done for France?" he asked. "Nothing! How are her interests defended? They are not defended." Consequently, Herriot called on the Constituent Assembly to reexamine the entire French Union draft in order to "revise these texts, to complete them, to fill up a gap that is simply enormous, inconceivable." Finally, he admonished his colleagues to consider the impact of their actions on the future destiny of France.

> If by complacency, which would be truly blameworthy and beneath the dignity of anyone here, or by a lack of reflection, of

> study, we allow a text to be adopted which . . . for our national defense and even for our economic defense would risk leading us to asphyxiation, hence to death, if we permit such a text to be adopted without its being revised and reshaped, that will be the end of it; it would be impossible to rebuild a second time the overseas community.
>
> The world today is divided up, completely divided up! There is no frozen land around the poles or burning Pacific isle on which some nation has not planted its flag. Where will there remain a place for France? Am I then wrong in saying to you that the problem that I have just discussed is for our country and for the overseas territories as well as for the metropole, a question of life or death? [90]

Herriot is reported to have made this speech at the urging of two fellow RGR deputies, René Mayer and Vincent de Moro-Giafferri. The former represented French citizens in the Algerian constituency of Constantine while Moro-Giafferri, who had served as minister of education in the Herriot cabinet, 1924–25, and was a veteran of Verdun as well as a prominent résistant, headed the RGR list in the first district of the Seine. Radical party spokesmen proudly recalled this speech at subsequent party congresses and claimed that Herriot's timely intervention had "saved the French Empire." [91]

The immediate result of Herriot's speech was to draw from Marius Moutet, the minister for overseas France, a formal declaration that French sovereignty would be protected in any future constitutional plan for the union and a warning that the government would take a direct part in future negotiations relating to the union.

> It is perfectly clear that if the constitution of the republic is a matter of political organization, and it is entirely within the power of the Assembly to decide this matter, it is still true that the government bears a responsibility to the country for everything having to do with French sovereignty, and that we cannot accept certain texts which would in effect endanger that sovereignty.

In addition, Moutet demanded that the Assembly detach the French Union articles from the rest of the constitution and return them to the Constitutional Committee for further action, failing which, in

Moutet's words, the government would be obliged "publicly to affirm its position" in the matter.[92]

The preceding chapters examined some of the political factors that brought about this confrontation over the nature of the French Union. Herriot's speech and the reactions it evoked also indicate, however, that the moderates and the Radical-Socialists were becoming conscious of another level of conflict at the heart of the colonial myth. For while that myth held up French democratic principles and precedents as a model for the colonies, it also cast those principles in a political and administrative framework of subordination. Once one attempted to carry into practice the democratic principles of common citizenship and equal suffrage, it was apparent that the existing metropolitan institutions would simply be overwhelmed. The tradition of highly centralized political and administrative control made any effort at instituting local centers of political power appear to be an attack on sovereignty, and hence, akin to treason. Furthermore, if one were to admit that the French Union could not be brought together into a single unitary democratic state—as indeed most of the constituents were prepared to grant, at least insofar as the associated states of Morocco, Tunisia, and Indochina were concerned—then what was to guarantee that the union of separate states would remain French?

The RGR and other conservative groups recognized the problem, at least to the extent of rejecting as illusory any kind of voluntary association. Instead, they were prepared simply to impose French sovereignty in the conviction that if France left the colonies, her place would soon be taken by others less generous. Furthermore, they believed that the established tradition legitimized France's control over the colonial territories, and no invasion of French sovereignty could be tolerated whether from native nationalists, subversive Frenchmen working in the interests of "another power than France," the self-interested Anglo-Saxon powers, or even the United Nations.

In order to secure the sort of constitution they wanted for the union, however, the moderate and conservative groups had to persuade the two noncommunist parties to agree to the change, since without that support they could not hope to muster a majority in the Assembly. As it happened, the MRP had altered its outlook on the issue of the French Union for other reasons, and by the end of August its leaders were expressing views that closely resembled the misgivings of the conservatives. The plans for the union that were developed by the MRP also echoed many of the concerns of the RGR and the small factions to the Right.

The MRP was slow in recognizing the importance of the French Union as an issue in the Constituent Assembly, largely because its leaders had not yet defined their own views on colonial problems very clearly. This was not surprising since the MRP was a completely new political party founded in the aftermath of the Liberation by men who had been active in a variety of prewar organizations that included Marc Sangnier's Internationale Démocratique pour la Paix, the Nouvelles Equipes Françaises, La Jeune République, the Parti Démocrat Populaire, and several others. None of these, including the group led by Francisque Gay, the founder of the Parisian daily *L'Aube,* had been particularly concerned about colonial problems. Since it lacked a distinctive doctrine on such questions, the MRP tended to reflect the ideas common to the republican parties of the center Left. If their ideas differed at all from the traditional colonial myth it was because, in the immediate postwar months, their outlook was colored by what Alfred Grosser termed "a somewhat naïve generosity" toward the colonial territories.[93]

At the party congress on 8 November 1945, the MRP adopted a program calling for "a unified approach" to the problems of rebuilding French political life in which "democracy in the French Union" took its place together with "political democracy," "economic and social democracy," and "international democracy" as part of a very murky global analysis of France's political problems. Exactly what "democracy in the French Union" implied was not clear. The congress adopted three "principles" that give some indication of its approach to colonial problems.

1. The progressive application of the Declaration of the Rights of Man and of democratic principles by the recognition to all the inhabitants of [the overseas] territories of equal rights, by raising the standard of living and by the extension of social legislation.

2. Advancement toward a federative union of these territories and the metropole by the immediate creation of a Council of the French Union and by the participation of the inhabitants in the political affairs of their territory.
3. Granting of extensive autonomy to the most highly developed of these territories within the framework of the French Union.[94]

By using terms like "the Rights of Man" or "social democracy" and "equal rights," the MRP program conveyed a sense of liberality and reform. However, the greatest stress was placed not on political changes so much as on "raising the standard of living and extension of social legislation." The principal thrust of the MRP position was humanitarian rather than revolutionary, and the political reforms were hedged about with legal restraints. Thus, a proposal for "granting extensive autonomy" to the more highly developed territories was offset by the implied, but clearly understood, reservation that it was metropolitan France that would determine which territories were sufficiently "highly developed" to warrant such autonomy. Hence, behind their humanitarianism lay the familiar assumption of metropolitan predominance, which was carried over intact from the established colonial myth. The MRP favored building a French Union, but it was to be built from the top down, according to metropolitan plans developed in accord with metropolitan requirements.

This hierarchical conception of the union was also reflected in the MRP's attitude toward citizenship, which stressed the identity of citizens and nationals. Since practically all the colonial peoples were French nationals, they were already citizens. If they enjoyed the rights of citizenship, however, that did not mean they were entitled to exercise those rights. As Paul Viard, one of the leading MRP colonial specialists and dean of the Faculty of Law at Algiers explained:

> We believe that we are continuing the work of the Great Revolution. . . . Up to now, in effect, the overseas population, for the most part, lived in the situation of subjects. These subjects did not participate in national sovereignty; they were, in a way, the subjects of a many-headed sovereign: the French Parliament.
>
> But the great reform that we are asking aims, on the contrary,

> to reorganize sovereignty in such a way that each man, in each territory, participates in that sovereignty—participates as a result of the elaboration of the law, so that he will be transformed from a subject into a sovereign.[95]

"Transform subjects into sovereigns" made an impressive lapidary formula, and it gained wide acceptance in the First Constituent Assembly. Significantly, it left all the most important issues unresolved, for it did not explain where the primary loyalties of the colonial peoples were to be vested. Were they to become part of a single, giant unified state or part of a new unit, linked only indirectly to France?

The MRP attempted to rationalize its position by referring to party doctrine concerning "pluralism." In its metropolitan usage, pluralism evoked a medieval conception of society in which "natural" groups such as the family combined with the Church, the various professions, the universities, and other corporate bodies, to form an organic unit. The state, being but one of its parts, could not claim to represent the entire community. Each of the other intermediate groups had a right to exist and develop according to its own rhythm.

It was never absolutely clear just what implications the MRP saw in pluralism, but one early scheme for family voting was explicitly derived from it. For the most part, however, pluralism remained an obscure slogan, and there was never any suggestion that it would lead to the decentralization of real political power. In this the MRP was just as faithful to the tradition of centralized control as were all the other major French parties. In Viard's words, "The entire question is summed up in this: How is French sovereignty to be organized?"

Apart from party ideology, however, the vagueness of the MRP colonial views also coincided with the political interests of its followers. On one hand, its spokesmen included several prominent colonial notables who had a direct stake in preserving French colonial relationships. In the Constituent Assembly the party was often represented by men like Max André, who had made a career in banking in the Far East and was considered to be expert on affairs of Indochina. George Le Brun Keris and Alfred Vignes filled somewhat similar roles in relation to North Africa, as did Paul Viard until he was removed from the Constitutional Committee because his views were too liberal for the party after the election of June 1946. More in tune with the later positions of the party was Paul Coste-Floret, who as rapporteur at a critical stage in the constitutional debate played a part in shaping the colonial constitution. Even the small group of overseas deputies who joined the MRP, including such figures as Abbé Boganda, Chief Douala Manga Bell, Father Bertho, and Dr. Louis Aujoulat, seems to have been moved as much by humanitarian concerns or sentimental ties to native populations and republican principles as by an appreciation of the growing influence of native nationalism.

More important, however, the MRP's ambiguous colonial program lent itself to more immediate party interests. During the First Constituent Assembly, when one of the primary MRP objectives was to defeat unicameralism, the party spokesman endorsed the extension of French citizenship to the colonies and criticized the Socialists for introducing distinctions between the peoples of France and those of the overseas areas. There could be but one "French people," it was argued.[96] Similarly, the MRP proposed for a time that the Council of the Union (as it was labeled in the early drafts) be a large body, composed in equal parts of metropolitan and overseas representatives and that it be empowered to examine bills, propose amendments, and give its advice prior to action on any colonial matters. At one point they even argued that the Council of the Union should participate in the election of the president of the republic. The Socialists and Communists rejected these proposals and denounced the MRP for attempting to restore the Senate through the back door.[97] Faced with certain defeat, the MRP conceded the point but insisted that even if it were to have no powers in relation to the National Assembly, the Council of the Union should at least be dignified with the title "House of Parliament." It is possible to gain some sense of the MRP's interest in the matter from Paul Coste-Floret's observation that this move would give the council greater public prestige and "the more one decreases the powers of the second assembly, the more it is necessary to confer on it prestige in the eyes of public opinion." [98]

Finally, in a last effort to eliminate unicameralism from the April Draft, Coste-Floret demanded that the Constituent Assembly accede to the MRP's proposal that the Council of the Union be given full status as a second chamber of Parliament, failing which the MRP refused to ratify the constitution.[99] The subsequent failure of the April Draft to secure approval in the May referendum, as noted earlier, was unconnected with its colonial provisions, and the MRP's attitude in relation to these matters, at least on the surface, remained unaffected by the fate of the constitutional draft. Thus, Paul Viard assured the overseas deputies: "Our committee wants to make it clear to our colleagues from overseas that in spite of the positions that have been taken with regard to the constitution as a whole, the support of the members for everything that has been envisioned for the French Union was unanimous." [100]

From the earliest meeting of the Second Constituent Assembly it became apparent that the MRP leaders were shifting their outlook on the question of the French Union. Two factors were largely responsible for this change. The referendum campaign had sounded a warning that a more conservative outlook was gaining strength in the country and if the party leadership wanted to retain the support of the rank and file members, a greater degree of caution was needed especially in relation to colonial issues. The second factor that also emerged from the election struggle in June was the necessity for the MRP to preserve its advantage as "the party of fidelity" to General de Gaulle. Since de Gaulle had openly criticized the French Union provisions of the April Draft in a speech at Bayeux on 16 June, the MRP presented the Constitutional Committee with a proposal modeled on his ideas.

De Gaulle concentrated most of his attack on the political parties, denouncing "the perpetual effervescence" of French politics and stressing the need to restore the authority of the state and the unity of the nation. However, he also placed heavy emphasis on the need to pay more attention to the fate of the French Empire, and to provide appropriate constitutional safeguards for its future. "The fate of the 110 million men and women that live under our flag lies in an organization of a federal type which time will spell out little by little, but of which our constitution should mark the beginning and regulate the development." [101]

Faced with great dangers at home and abroad, de Gaulle insisted that France needed a strong executive and a bicameral legislature whose second chamber would be indirectly elected in order that it might bring to bear the stabilizing influence of the civil administration, the professions, and other economic interests that would lend balance to the decisions of a "purely political" body like the National Assembly. That second chamber would also include representatives chosen by the local assemblies in the overseas territories and as the Council of the French Union it would have the power to deliberate on matters relating to the interests of the union, including foreign affairs, defense, economic affairs, and communications. The president, according to de Gaulle's scheme, was to be chosen by the metropolitan parliament in which overseas representatives would participate so that he would have authority over the entire French world. Only a powerful president, who would be both president of the republic and president of the French Union, could hope to defend the permanent interests of all parts of the union. He alone would be above partisan quarrels and in a position to assure the independence and security of France.

The MRP responded slowly to de Gaulle's prodding. During July and August its spokesmen in the Constitutional Committee objected to the concept of a union based on "free consent" arguing that such language implied that the ultimate goal of the overseas territories was separation from France. "It is better not to orient the imaginations of the natives toward certain hypotheses and there is a danger that they will misunderstand them when posed in the form of abstract general principles," Dr. Aujoulat insisted. Furthermore, he noted that in general the plan presented by the MRP followed that introduced by the RGR, and he defended the notion of a federal assembly for the union without an explicitly federal executive as a transitional arrangement.[102]

By the time the constitutional draft was ready for presentation to the Assembly on 20 August, it still reflected primarily the views of the native Intergroup rather than those of the MRP and the RGR, despite their repeated efforts to secure changes, and despite the fact that the rapporteur, Paul Coste-Floret, was a member of the MRP. Herriot's response has already been noted. Even more critical in shaping the future stance of the MRP was the reaction of de Gaulle. In a statement to the press on 27 August he declared:

> The constitutional draft that is now before the National Constituent Assembly for deliberation does not respond, as it stands, to the necessary conditions. . . . United to the overseas territories

> that she opened up to civilization, France is a great power. Without these territories, she risks being one no longer. Everything commands us to organize on a new, but precise, design the relations between the metropole and the peoples of all races who are tied to her destiny.
>
> The constitutional draft merely affirms the principle of "free disposition" which, in the present state of development of the overseas territories and given the rivalry of the other great powers, can only lead the population to agitation, dislocation, and finally to foreign domination.
>
> The constitution should, on the contrary, affirm and impose the solidarity of all the overseas territories with France. In particular it should place beyond question the preeminent responsibility, and consequently the rights, of France in matters concerning the foreign policy of the entire French Union, the defense of all its territories, common communications, and economic matters of interest to the whole.[103]

De Gaulle's comments appear to have had an immediate influence on the MRP. When the Constitutional Commission resumed deliberation on the constitutional draft the MRP representative Paul Coste-Floret indicated that his group was still prepared to compromise on the French Union and to leave its institutions to be determined later by the National Assembly.[104] On the other hand, the government's decision to intervene in the drafting process and to present its own version of the French Union articles was in direct response to de Gaulle's criticisms. In order to amend the constitutional draft, the government needed to win a majority both in the Constitutional Committee and in the Assembly. To do that the MRP had to persuade the Socialists to abandon the positions they had maintained during the First and Second constituent assemblies in support of the Communists and the native deputies. The Socialists had been gradually moving away from their alignment with the Communist party on other constitutional issues during the weeks that followed the June elections, but as one MRP deputy later wrote, "the evolution of the Socialists had not yet taken place"[105] on colonial questions.

In marked contrast to the MRP, the Socialists approached the problems of the French Union from a tradition highly critical of the colonial activities of the Third Republic. Except for the short period during the first months of the Popular Front, the SFIO had never been responsible for colonial policy, and that brief experience had only changed the style, not the substance, of the party's concern with colonialism. The basic theme of the Socialist position, as indicated earlier, was one of humanitarianism and political reform along democratic lines.

Thus, as Léon Blum had explained to the Chamber of Deputies in 1927 in regard to a proposed electoral reform for Algeria which would have brought more native representatives into the metropolitan Parliament:

> Insofar as we are concerned, we would not want this question to develop in the direction of a larger representation for natives in the French Parliament. I say this, if not as the opinion of my party, at least as an opinion shared by most of my comrades. We would like to see colonial legislation leading more and more clearly toward *self-government,* as in the case of the dominions.

Later, in the midst of a bloody uprising in Morocco in 1933 the SFIO had declared:

> The Socialist party, faithful to the great tradition of Jaurès, raises its indignant protest against these criminal and senseless military operations. . . . It asks . . . all its federations and sections to organize meetings and popular demonstrations against a policy of colonial conquests which socialism has always condemned and which is leading to a world war. . . . Down with capitalist imperialism![106]

The principal product of this tradition had been the stillborn Blum-Violette plan for reform in Algeria originated during the Popular Front.

The new constitution, in the Socialists' eyes, was to mark the beginning of a new era in relations with the colonies; and, as such, it symbolized a clear break with the past. Thus, the Socialists proposed to the First Constituent Assembly a plan to include in the constitution a Declaration of Rights, which would dramatize the new status of the colonial peoples and underscore the universal character of the freedoms it embraced. All the inhabitants of the union were to enjoy a common citizenship with a right to representation both in the National Assembly, which was to be the only legislative body, and in a consultative Council of the Union whose advice had to be sought on all colonial matters. In addition, the Socialists proposed to create popularly elected local assemblies in the overseas territories and to replace the local colonial officials (governors or governors-general) with "resident-ministers," who would be political figures responsible to the Assembly.

In these proposals, all but one of which were later abandoned or extensively altered, there is a note of fundamental optimism revealed by the implicit assumption of harmony underlying the entire scheme. In the new postcolonial era, when force would be removed from the relations between the metropole and the overseas territories, cooperation was expected to replace conflict. The "sovereign" Assembly was expected willingly to "consult" with the Council of the Union and presumably to act on its advice, while equal direct suffrage was believed to be the basis for choosing deputies who would represent all shades of opinion in the colonies—French settlers as well as natives. The basis of this optimism was to be found in the great humanitarian principles of internationalism and egalitarianism that formed the backbone of French Socialist thought.

All three of these fundamental themes: the rejection of past colonial policies "based on oppression," the recognition of legal equality with full social and political rights, and the coincidence of both the foregoing with universal humanitarian aims were clearly stated to the Constituent Assembly by Edouard Depreux.

> I am pleased to recognize that the constitution, in filling out the birth certificate of the Fourth Republic also fills out the death certificate of the last fleeting whims of French imperialism. . . .
>
> That means that it creates the French Union. It means that the French republic, in the clearest and most categorical manner refuses to recognize any differences among her children whether of religion, race, or color.
>
> She proclaims it proudly to the entire universe because she wants to be faithful to the engagements that she solemnly contracted at Brazzaville, but even more because she wants to be faithful to her own genius, to her universal aspirations.[107]

As had been the case with Jaurès in 1911, however, the commitment of the Socialists in 1946 was to the rights and liberties of man, not to the rights of states to self-determination. Thus, it followed easily enough, that for countries that were obviously still underdeveloped and in need of guidance, France had an obligation to provide help. The enfranchisement of the exploited colonial peoples could best be brought about from inside, rather than from outside, the French Union, especially when one of the leading parties was the SFIO, which was devoted to the interests of the colonial peoples and had made room for some of their leading figures, such as Blaise Diagne, Lamine-Guèye, and Léopold Senghor, within its ranks.

Particularly when seen in conjunction with the Socialists' devotion to highly centralized political and administrative institutions, these declarations reveal how deeply the Socialist plans for the French Union were imbedded in the republican colonial myth. Just as Jaurès could condemn the violence of colonialism in principle and still accept the continuation of colonial administration as a means for the fulfillment of humanitarian social and economic goals, the Socialists of 1946 believed that the French Union would replace colonial exploitation with a voluntary association that would keep the colonies closely linked to France.

In the First Constituent Assembly Socialist deputies played a major role in shaping the French Union articles. Léopold Senghor and Lamine-Guèye, both prominent party spokesmen on colonial issues, led the native deputies in the Committee on Overseas Territories and in the Constitutional Committee. Marius Moutet, the minister of overseas France throughout the period of tripartism, had devoted his entire parliamentary life to colonial problems and had been an advocate of reform ever since 1917. Other prominent Socialists occupied key positions in the government: Félix Gouin became the head of the Provisional Government after de Gaulle's resignation in January 1946, and André Le Troquer occupied the Ministry of Interior, which carried with it responsibility for Algeria. In the Assembly Vincent Auriol succeeded Gouin as president of the Constituent Assembly, and André Philip presided over the Constitutional Committee.

It is hardly surprising, therefore, that the April Draft reflected many of the Socialists' views of the union. The principles of a community based on free consent, equal rights for all, and a common citizenship were all consistent with their doctrines. The structure of the union also reflected the Socialist image which stressed the creation of local assemblies in the colonies and envisioned the union held together by overlapping layers of representative bodies instead of by an arbitrary executive. Although the April Draft seemed to imply that the overseas territories would eventually achieve the status of associated states, each of which would enjoy a large measure of autonomy, it left such changes under the control of the metropolitan legislature and hence did not imply any diminution of French sovereignty.

During the Second Constituent Assembly the Socialist outlook began to change when, in the face of increasing demands from the Algerian nationalists and other native autonomists, the pressure of their governmental responsibilities began to increase. Although technically responsible for all colonial territories apart from Algeria, Moutet was powerless to control events in Indochina because the French Expeditionary Force was under the direction of the head of the government, Georges Bidault, who acted on the advice of an interministerial committee on which the Socialists were greatly outnumbered. The balance of political power within the government sometimes prevented the Socialists from acting, as when Edouard Depreux, who replaced Le Troquer as interior minister in the Bidault government, sought to approve the electoral regulations drafted by the Socialist governor-general of Algeria, Yves Chataigneau, which would have assured the election of the Algerian nationalists. Bidault prevented issuance of the order after the Communist party agreed to support him; their principle concern, as Maurice Thorez explained, was to limit the gains of the Algerian nationalists.[108]

The Socialist position was thus particularly difficult. On one hand they were concerned not to alienate the native deputies whose support was crucial to the SFIO's future prospects as well as to its present desire to prevent the communists from taking the credit for the colonial reforms. (The votes of eleven black African deputies were to give Vincent Auriol an absolute majority on the first ballot and assure his election as first president of the Fourth Republic in January 1947.) On the other hand, the SFIO could not offend the MRP without risking a breakup of the Tripartite Government, which would leave them alone to face the Communists. As a result of their intermediate position the Socialists were cast in the role of mediators. On the issue of the French Union, for example, Socialist deputies intervened to suggest formulas that would conserve some of the language of the native Intergroup plan, but avoid the sharp criticisms of French policy that evoked strong resentment among the moderates.[109] On another occasion when the parties were in furious disagreement over the government's Algerian policy, Depreux sought to calm the passions and to reassure every faction in turn that its interests were being protected. In a speech that was a brilliant tour de force the minister of the interior—

1. reassured the moderates and MRP concerning the Algerian nationalist's intentions: "I note that from this podium M. Hadj Saïd categorically and formally rejected any idea of violent revolution. . . . I said to M. Ferhat Abbas, 'Some people claim that you want to throw the French into the sea and adopt a policy of autonomy!' He replied with the greatest energy that he considered that it would be a crime not only against the whole of France but against his Muslim friends to adopt such a policy and that he would condemn separatism to his dying breath."
2. disclaimed any special consideration was given to Messali Hadj: he insisted that the Algerian nationalist leader's sentence to twenty years in exile was set aside not because of pressure from the UDMA, but out of "respect for republican legality."
3. consoled the French settlers' deputies: "Those colons, those officials, those honest folks, those workers . . . those people have the right to know that they won't be abandoned."
4. warned the settlers: "There must be an end to exploitation of the natives. The time when certain methods could be used is over."
5. put the MRP and PCF on notice: "A government would be unworthy to hold office in France if it were not capable of saying to the Muslims and Europeans at the same time, 'No! You will not have the atrocious choice between the suitcase and the coffin!' "
6. admonished the radicals in his own party: "The French presence in Algeria, a presence which, of course, will be maintained, is all the more indispensable when France will carry over there social justice along with liberty. . . . The French presence having been maintained in Algeria, it will augment its economic development. . . . Let us say that we want to practice

a humane, comprehensive policy that conforms to the secular genius of the France of the Rights of Man."

At length, Depreux concluded with the observation:

> We owe it to ourselves to renounce, and we do so, the traditional colonial procedures which, alas, are too classic and not just in France. Divide and rule, fomenting quarrels in order to impose or maintain imperial domination, all that is outmoded. . . .
>
> But neither should it be anymore that imprudent nationalisms attempt to accumulate, to use the divisions among the different French political parties to achieve anti-French designs that are harmful to Muslim workers.
>
> The development of Algeria requires a fraternal, confident, affectionate understanding of one another without distinction as to origin, race or religion. . . . France still has a glorious role to play in Algeria. . . . France will remain in Algeria because she is France and because she is humane.[110]

Efforts such as these to find compromises acceptable to its partners in government and to the native deputies created discontent within the ranks of the SFIO that further undermined its effectiveness. At the same time when Herriot and de Gaulle were attacking the constitutional draft which they had supported, the leaders of the Socialist parliamentary group were being attacked by some of the local federations at the Thirty-eighth Party Congress in Paris. The insurgents, led by Guy Mollet, accused the party leadership of abandoning revolutionary principles and to the surprise of virtually everyone succeeded in ousting Daniel Mayer and installing Mollet as secretary-general. In keeping with its new, more radical approach the congress adopted a resolution asserting that "in the colonial area, the Socialist party will combat all forms of imperialist exploitation and aid the peoples of the overseas territories in their struggle for emancipation." [111] It also called for the Socialist ministers to quit the government, a step that the parliamentary group leaders were still not prepared to adopt.

In an effort to restore his own position within the SFIO, as well as to resolve the deepening constitutional deadlock, Vincent Auriol resolved to try once more to find a formula that would be acceptable to both the Communists and the MRP and that would allow the parties to put an end to the Provisional Government. To accomplish this it would be necessary to resolve the conflict over the French Union and, hence, to compromise the differences that separated the metropolitan parties without altogether alienating the native deputies.

The Colonial Myth and Party Rivalries

Why was it so difficult for the Constituent Assemblies to find an acceptable solution to the problem of the French Union? Part of the answer is given by the nature of the task; establishing a constitution posed problems that transcended those encountered in drafting ordinary legislation, especially when the parties involved were engaged in bitter rivalry. Moreover, to these factors one must add the fact that the contenders were Frenchmen who greatly admired rhetorical skill and shared a special propensity for verbal combat. An MRP leader, Henri Teitgen, sensed the significance of these factors.

> Any legislative endeavor provides an opportunity for bringing to bear a certain number of ideologies. When the question is one of drafting a constitution, the parties' underlying philosophies play a role of primary importance. And in a country like France where, even if one does not admit it, one likes to philosophize and one is a born metaphysician, projects of this sort arouse the deep, underlying aspirations of the parties, even when they deny it.
>
> That is where the secret of the difficulties we have encountered probably lies. If it were only a question of technique, of choosing ways and means; if we were in agreement on the ends, we would quickly have reached an agreement on the techniques as well and rapidly elaborated a constitution. If we encounter difficulties, it is because the elaboration of a constitution brings out all the differences in the profound conceptions we hold of the political and social order.[112]

In retrospect it was clear that the native and metropolitan deputies held quite different conceptions of what constituted a desirable political and social order, and these differences contributed significantly to the difficulty of reaching agreement on the French Union constitution. Even when they used similar language to state general principles, their underlying values were often in conflict. As the preceding analysis has shown, the Assembly adopted the principle of equality as the basis for the union but it could not agree on the meaning of citizenship. Similarly, there was universal support for reforms that would bring greater freedom to the colonial peoples but no agreement at all on the ultimate goal which such reforms should serve. Humanitarian values were also widely asserted but there was little agreement on social and economic implications that might derive from such values. There was even more disagreement about the meaning of organizational concepts such as autonomy or federalism which clearly meant different things to different groups both within the metropole and overseas. Consequently, it is not surprising that the Assembly found it difficult to agree on constitutional rules for the union.

Underlying the institutional controversies were deep and ultimately irreconcilable value conflicts. At one extreme some deputies sought freedom from French rule in order to assert the national identities of their own communities. At the other extreme many were striving to maintain French security and increase French national power, which required suppressing the separate political identities of the colonial peoples. This basic disagreement was largely obscured by two others. The metropolitan parties assessed French security needs very differently and disagreed among themselves on how to meet those needs. The native deputies also found that conditions in their respective territories were quite different, and hence they too formulated different strategies to achieve their ends and evolved different attitudes toward the French Union.

The election of the Algerian autonomist deputies and the arrival of the Vietminh delegation at the Fontainebleau Conference seem to have been the catalyst that moved the Second Constituent Assembly to confront the problem of the French Union. By asserting openly that the goal of the French colonial experience should be full independence from France, the UDMA deputies forced the other metropolitan and native representatives to choose how far they were willing to go in the direction of decentralizing real political power. The UDMA, like the Vietminh and other native deputies from those parts of the former empire that enjoyed both cultural unity and a modest level of economic development, boldly advocated the creation of a loosely structured, polyarchic community of states, each of which was to enjoy full internal autonomy.

At the opposite extreme, the UDSR and the Radical-Socialists, together with de Gaulle and other military and civilian officials, became convinced that both for domestic and international reasons no diminution of French sovereignty could be permitted, even if dissident nationalist movements had to be put down by force.

Between these two positions most of the metropolitan and native deputies took stands that reflected the relative importance they attached to the values of independence or French power and the preference they had for decentralized or hierarchic institutions. The Malagasy nationalists were close to the pole of independence, since they defended a position within the Assembly that was very similar to that advanced by the Vietminh in the negotiations at Fontainbleau. They recognized the French Union only as an association of states, not a single nation. The Algerian nationalists were more equivocal in their demands for total autonomy and indicated a willingness, for a time at least, to participate in a political union with France that would protect Algerian economic interests and safeguard French settlers in Algeria.

Both the metropolitan Marxist parties endorsed the basic principle of emancipation for the colonies, and the Communists occasionally pronounced the term *independence*. Neither group envisaged the French Union as a step toward independence, however. Instead, it was to be an alternative form of emancipation that, in the Communist view, would unite the peoples of the overseas areas with the people of France in order to give them the advantages of living under a socialist government. The French Socialists also were convinced that existing conditions were so threatening to France and the economic situation of the colonies so unfavorable that unity between France and the colonies was essential in order to ensure continued social and economic progress overseas. Both favored autonomy for the colonies, but they interpreted it to mean primarily a reduction in the role of the colonial administration and an increase in the power of local political or economic organizations which they expected to dominate.

The native deputies from the African colonies and from the Antilles, Guyane, and Réunion ranged widely across the middle of the constitutional spectrum. Some leaned toward greater local autonomy, but many favored closer association with France preferring to seek their fortunes within the political parties of the metropole.

Few of those deputies formulated demands for national recognition, but most were insistent that drastic changes be made in colonial administration and local government.

The MRP shared some of those views, though its paternalistic approach to colonial problems led to greater emphasis on defining central institutions for the union rather than local ones. The MRP also shared many of the fears of the PRL and the small factions on the far Right that tended to stress the importance of protecting French sovereignty and to treat colonial problems purely as an aspect of metropolitan politics.

None of the groups within the Assembly, with the possible exception of the Malagasy nationalists, conceived of decolonization as an immediate option. All the native deputies were willing to participate in the French Union on some terms, provided it was designed to promote their ultimate interests and so long as it held open the possibility for further changes in the future. All the metropolitan deputies wanted to see the union come into being as long as it did not actively promote separation of the colonies from France. The basis for an agreement, therefore, certainly did exist. Moreover, in spite of the differences in outlook discussed above, it might not have been too difficult to arrange a constitution to meet the minimum requirements of all parties, had the French Union been the only issue at stake in the Constituent Assembly. In reality, the future of the French Union depended on the disposition of a number of other issues on which the major metropolitan parties were deeply divided. Consequently, when faced with the failure of the Fontainebleau Conference to obtain concessions from the Vietminh and the denunciations of the constitutional draft by Herriot and de Gaulle, Georges Bidault decided that the time had come for the government to resolve the problem of the French Union. That decision resulted in an open confrontation between the partisans of autonomy and the defenders of French sovereignty that eventually destroyed the narrow range of consensus that had survived up to that point in the constitutional negotiations.

8. THE FORMULA FOR UNITY

The attacks on the constitutional draft by Herriot and de Gaulle aroused such concern within the Constituent Assembly that on 29 August it voted to refer the French Union articles back to the Constitutional Committee for further deliberation.[1] There the three major governmental parties negotiated a compromise text for the French Union. Their task was complicated by the opposition of the native deputies who also insisted that major alterations be made in the government's draft before they would consent to support it. The outcome of these negotiations was conditioned by three factors: (1) the internal politics of the MRP and the conceptions of its leader, Georges Bidault; (2) the price set by the Communists for their support; and (3) the threat of a boycott of the constitution by the native deputies. As it emerged from the Constituent Assembly the constitution contained many ambiguous or contradictory provisions and left some very essential matters unresolved. On the other hand, the process of arriving at a formula for unity left deep dissatisfactions on both sides and nearly destroyed whatever consensus had survived regarding the need for unity between France and the colonies. In the end, the colonial myth was enshrined in the new constitution, but in reality it had lost most of its compelling appeal. The concept of decolonization remained as remote as ever from the consciousness of most metropolitan deputies, but the reality of decolonization had advanced among the overseas deputies.

Revising the Constitutional Draft

The MRP had benefited from its close identification with de Gaulle in the elections of 2 June, and it went to considerable lengths to appear as the defender of his constitutional conceptions. Nevertheless, there was a wide gap between the party leaders and de Gaulle that reflected both differences in personality and conflicting roles. These differences were acute in the case of relations between Bidault and de Gaulle. As leader of the internal Resistance movement Bidault regarded himself as a major figure in French public life, yet during the Provisional Government he had lived under the shadow of de Gaulle and only emerged from that position after de Gaulle's resignation in January 1946. Elected to succeed Félix Gouin after the June elections, Bidault formed a new government balanced among MRP, Socialists, and Communists and promised to complete the new constitution by October.[2]

Determined to assert his own leadership at last, Bidault was enraged when Herriot and de Gaulle took it upon themselves to lecture the nation on the need to preserve the French Union. Although many considered him a man of the Left because he had opposed the Munich settlement in 1938, and had attacked the Action Française, Bidault had a traditional, conservative conception of government in which the state authorities were predominant. Moreover, as a professor of history and a man whose entire life had been built around the cultivation of intellect, Bidault was as conscious of France's historical role as was de Gaulle. He also tended to view other peoples from that perspective, hence, he never considered that any country that lacked a historic tradition could possibly be regarded as an independent state. Soon after his election as provisional president, Bidault was confronted with serious threats to the French position in Indochina and later encountered demands for autonomy from nationalists in Algeria. His reaction to both was equally negative.

Acting on the advice of Admiral d'Argenlieu and of General Leclerc, who had opposed the resort to force in Vietnam and supported the 6 March agreement but now denounced Ho Chi Minh as "a great enemy of France" and the man responsible for ordering the assassination of pro-French Vietnamese,[3] Bidault decided to make no concessions to the Vietminh. On 5 July he instructed the head of the French delegation to the Fontainebleau Conference, Max André, not to agree under any circumstances to a change in the international position of Vietnam, lest it desert the French orbit for that of the Soviet Union.[4]

Bidault's position on Algerian autonomy was just as uncompromising. On 23 August, at the conclusion of the lengthy debate on the government's Algerian policy, he reminded the Assembly that when his government was invested in June, it had announced its determination

> to maintain the French presence in all the territories which she unites in her fraternity. The government and the Assembly, I am sure, will remain faithful to the engagement they undertook in common. . . . I know, the government knows, that we are at a moment in the history of the world when the general upheaval translates itself into a great thrust toward emancipation. Here and there in the world, not without torment, not without difficulties, not without convulsions, . . . adaptations are occurring in the direction of that thrust.
>
> But is it imaginable that such changes should mean a cutting off, a renouncing, a secession? What an error it would be to look for greater liberty apart, in a solitude that is impossible because it would immediately be peopled by misery, quarrels, or new presences. Now, more than ever before, nature abhors a vacuum. The movement of the world demands adaptations, and the government is ready to present the plan for them to this Assembly.[5]

On the basis of such evidence it would appear that Bidault needed no prodding either from de Gaulle or from the Radicals to intervene in the drafting of the French Union articles. Indeed, the Interministerial Committee headed by Alexandre Varenne, the former governor-general of Indochina, had proposed a plan for the union on 26 July. The Constitutional Committee refused to consider it, despite the objections of the MRP spokesman, Paul Coste-Floret, on the ground that only the Assembly had constituent powers. On that occasion Varenne indicated that the government had not yet reached a decision on the French Union, but the plan he submitted indicated the direction of its thinking.[6]

Entitled a Charter of the French Union, it consisted of eight brief articles. The union was defined as being based on "free consent" and linking the republic, which included the overseas department and territories, with the associated states whose relationship to France depended on the treaties and agreements that established the French protectorates. The central organs of the union were to be the president, the High Council, and the Assembly. The president of the republic was also to be the president of the Union, and he was to function as the central executive power assisted by an advisory council of ministers and delegates from the associated states. The Assembly represented all the associated states, overseas territories, and departments, along with metropolitan France. The metropolitan parliament, in which the overseas departments and territories would also be represented, had full power to enact basic laws for those departments and territories.[7]

It became evident at the time of Herriot's speech on 27 August that the government would have to intervene in order to obtain fundamental changes in the constitutional draft that had been adopted by the Constitutional Committee. As Moutet warned the Assembly, if the committee did not revise the French Union articles to assure that "French sovereignty would be respected" then the government "would be obliged publicly to affirm its position." [8] Three distinct but interrelated conflicts followed. The first found the government opposing the Constitutional Committee; the second took place within the government between the Communists and the president; and the third found the native deputies opposing the government and the majority of the Constitutional Committee.

The Government versus the Constitutional Committee

Departing from the precedent followed during the First Constituent Assembly, the minister of overseas France, Moutet, appeared before the Constitutional Committee on 11 September to express the government's concern about the French Union articles and to offer suggestions for their revision. Carefully measuring his words, Moutet explained that the government did not question the Assembly's sole right to vote the constitution, however, on matters that affected vital international interests touching upon French sovereignty, it felt obliged to alert the Assembly to certain dangers and to offer information and advice.

The government, by which he meant primarily President Bidault, had a number of objections to the existing draft. It seemed to orient the overseas territories toward autonomy rather than toward a close union with France. It based the union on a free choice among alternatives that remain undefined. It provided no effective executive for the union, nor any other common organs of government.

It seemed to encourage a special form of nationalism instead of uniting the overseas territories closely with France. Most of all, it was explicit only about the obligations France owed to the colonies.

> It seems that France gives everything and receives nothing. One can gather from this text that the constitution, insofar as it concerns the French Union, has one essential vice and that is that it is not a constitution. It does not fix a single constitutional principle; it gives no body to the idea of the French Union. That is the only thing that has been omitted. Was that done voluntarily? It is possible.[9]

Moutet then offered the committee a new proposal which he described as not a formal draft, but "the synthesis of countless studies" undertaken by various committees over the years. He suggested that the committee adopt it as a basis for deliberations and later confer with the government to avoid any conflict between the two in public sessions. Moutet then outlined twenty-two articles that fell into four sections: a definition of the union, a description of its major organs, the special provisions for the overseas departments, and the personal rights of residents of the union. Among the most significant changes or additions since the previous Interministerial proposal were:

1. The definition of the union stressed that the overseas departments and territories formed part of the indivisible republic, and it made no mention of "free consent."
2. A new article stipulated that the members of the union combine all of their means for the defense of the whole union with the French government coordinating and directing that defense.
3. The High Council was clearly intended to be "an embryo of a government" for the union.
4. The Assembly of the Union included representatives of the republic (both metropolitan and overseas areas) and the associated states, with a special representation for French settlers overseas. The metropolitan members were to be designated by the Council of the Republic and the overseas members by the territorial assemblies. Its powers were advisory; it could also propose legislation to the French government and to the High

Council, but only the National Assembly could vote laws. Its advice was obligatory on all measures affecting the overseas areas, but was not binding.

5. Representation for the overseas territories was to be maintained in both houses of the metropolitan parliament.
6. A new "citizenship of the French Union" was to be established for all persons living in the union who did not possess French civil status.

These texts, according to Moutet, were being proposed by the government after three deliberations during which they received unanimous support. The objective, he asserted, was double: "to give life to the French Union and to go to the extreme limit of liberalism." [10]

The Constitutional Committee clearly resented this intrusion by the government into what all the members considered the committee's exclusive domain. The reasons for their anger were easy to understand. In part it was a simple question of institutional rivalry—the Assembly alone had been granted constituent powers under the terms of the referendum, and the Constitutional Committee was its designated agent; the government was enjoined by its own ministerial declaration from intervening in the drafting process. This formal arrangement did not correspond to the real division of power, however, because the party leaders held the power to instruct their spokesmen on the Constitutional Committee how to vote. Some of those leaders were themselves members of the committee, as for example was its president, André Philip; but in other cases decisions were taken by party leaders who occupied positions in the government or in the Assembly, but not in the committee. Since party discipline was often weak, especially among the Socialists and MRP, it was not unusual to find that party spokesmen accepted compromises that were later rejected by the leadership and attacked when the draft reached the Assembly.

In any situation where rival bills emanated from different committees, the Assembly was the final arbiter; but if one of the drafts was sponsored by the government, it would ultimately prevail since only the government could pose the question of confidence. The Constitutional Committee was aware of this inequality of power, and it too added to the sense of resentment.

Finally, the committee was clearly offended that the draft it had devised following weeks of discussion and sometimes difficult negotiation had been summarily cast aside in favor of a plan whose entire conception was totally different from its own. Even the MRP leader, Coste-Floret, who had presented the original MRP scheme to which the government plan bore some resemblance, was not prepared for the sudden change of policy. The Communist and Socialist spokesmen clearly had not been informed by their parties of what had been decided in the Council of Ministers, for they were extremely critical of the move. Etienne Fajon, the Communist party's principal spokesman on the committee, contested Moutet's assertion that the government had actually reached a decision at all and maintained that the Council of Ministers had never even seen the government's plan.[11] In the week that followed Moutet's appearance before it, the committee asserted its authority by extensively amending the government draft in an effort to salvage as much as possible of its own text. It was not an easy task, since the government scheme proposed to create the central institutions of the union, but to leave the local government questions to be settled later; while the committee draft concentrated on providing local political institutions for the overseas territories, but left the central institutions to be constructed later in conformity with general principles set forth in the constitution. The MRP perforce defended the government plan, while the Communists criticized it and the Socialists attempted to frame compromise formulas.

For example, Paul Ramadier, a leading Socialist, agreed with the MRP view that the constitution could properly introduce changes in methods of legislation or administration but that it was essential that the union not alter the boundaries of the republic or disturb its political composition. "The French republic has the contours that history has designed; we have no right to reduce them. . . . [Establishing a separate category of associated territories] will have as its consequence the reduction of the national territory, and I hope that this consideration will make those hesitate who are tempted to break the unity of the republic." [12]

On the other hand, Ramadier also suggested that the committee amend the government draft to require that the local assemblies in the overseas territories be consulted before the metropolitan Parliament established their local regime. The Socialists also sided with the Communists and native deputies in an unsuccessful effort to delete a provision in the government draft providing special representation in local assemblies for different segments of the overseas population.[13]

The committee presented its revised draft of the French Union articles (which had become identified as Title 8 of the proposed constitution) to the Assembly on 18 September 1946. Only one week remained before the date set by the government for a final vote on the constitutional draft, it having been decided that any further delay would make it impossible to complete the new elections before the second week in November when inclement weather might force a postponement until spring. Thus the pressure of time added to the existing frustrations but also provided an incentive to compromise differences. The colonial debate lasted forty-eight hours and demonstrated two things: the metropolitan parties were still undecided about the union, and the native deputies were distressed by the government's plan and critical of the new direction it implied for French policy in regard to the overseas areas.

The Price of Unanimity

The MRP was represented in the debate by Jean-Jacques Juglas, deputy from the Seine département and president of the Committee on Overseas Territories, and by Coste-Floret, who was also the rapporteur for the Constitutional Committee. Coste-Floret did his best to reconcile the new draft with the old, insisting that it had three purposes.

> The texts that are submitted to you today are the result of the collaboration of the government, whose text was taken into consideration, and the Constitutional Committee, which used every effort to improve it. We think that by extending the scope of the initial text and placing in the constitution of the republic the federal organs of the French Union, we are creating an instrument of a kind that will realize an idea that is rich with promises and surely fruitful for the future.[14]

Juglas announced the MRP's support for the text because it corresponded to the established doctrine of his party, because "it is supple and contains many nuances," because it defined the elements of the union, because it provided for extensive local autonomy but also recognized that "the republic is one and indivisible," and, above all, "because the fact that it has been approved by the parties represented within the government gives this project . . . a particular value." [15]

Léopold Senghor presented the Socialist position. He reviewed the evolution of the colonial constitution and stressed the unanimity that had been reached in the First Constituent Assembly on colonial questions. Unfortunately, those agreements were being questioned, he said, and many plans were being proposed that raised serious objections among the Socialists. Most of his speech concerned the misgivings that he and his colleagues felt about the new draft to which he referred only indirectly. "In a word," he concluded, "the French Union must not be built like a cage that no one will want to enter. For the French Union to be durable, it must . . . be founded on liberty and equality, the preconditions for human fraternity, for French fraternity." [16]

The Communist position was even more ambiguous than that of the Socialists. It was presented by Yves Angeletti, a deputy from the Marne département who was neither a prominent party official nor one of the party's specialists on colonial affairs. He began by calling on all the deputies to "remove ourselves as far as possible from any spirit of partisanship, and in any case to exclude any intention of underhanded maneuvers that would tend to influence other parts of the constitution. Our double concern will be, on one hand, to maintain the French presence everywhere and, on the other, to found the French Union on the free and voluntary adhesion of the populations that compose it." [17]

The union, he argued, can only be built by common consent, and that implied a federal organization. However, "the present situation does not lend itself to the immediate, definitive formation of a federal system." The PCF would have preferred, he explained, not to include in the constitution the central organs of the union; nor, for that matter, did it approve of other parts of the government proposals in which "we detected residues of the spirit of the *pacte colonial* which said, 'Everything for the metropole and by the metropole.'" Yet he urged the native deputies to have faith in France because "it is the future of the French Union and in a certain sense the future of France that is at stake at this moment" and because "the French people . . . were ready to take the lead in every struggle for social emancipation." [18] In short, while the Communists favored a plan for the union that was the opposite of the new draft, they planned to rise above partisanship and accept it, possibly with some amendments.

Why did the party that had supported the most extreme demands of the native deputies for local autonomy, had approved the principle of complete independence for Madagascar, Algeria, and Indochina, and had opposed any central institutions for the union now agree to adopt a constitution it had consistently rejected? Three possible reasons can be adduced despite the lack of documentary evidence. First, the PCF may have accepted the French Union on the same grounds that it accepted the rest of the constitutional draft: it was the only means of putting an end to the provisional regime. Moreover, since de Gaulle had vigorously denounced Title 8 along with the rest of the constitution, perhaps it was not as dangerous as the party leaders had feared.

Next, it is possible that the PCF endorsed the government's plan for the union in the expectation that it would soon fail and that another reform would permit the changes which in any case were thought to be unavoidable. The party had done the same thing in regard to economic policy, opposing drastic reforms that would have greatly strengthened the French economy and supporting Pleven's economic policy that promised several years of severe inflation. Its general aim, so long as the party was in the government but not yet able to control national policy, was to prevent any basic reforms that tended to strengthen the capitalist system. Moreover, the Communists could still hope that within the immediate future their position would improve and that they would then be in a position to claim the credit for colonial reforms. In the meantime they could at least be certain that whatever action the government took regarding the union would be the responsibility of the MRP and that it would embarrass the Socialists, who would have no alternative but to agree to it, even more than themselves.

Finally, the Communist leaders appear to have agreed to support Bidault on the issue of the French Union because they received in return some valuable support on an issue of much more direct interest to themselves. According to Elgey, "Bidault let Maurice Thorez understand that he would bring about the adoption of the civil service act, which was a principle objective of the Communists, if Thorez would promise to approve Title 8 in exchange." [19] This private deal between the leaders of the two largest parties was not widely known at the time, but its effect was to assure Bidault a free hand in dealing with the Constitutional Committee on the matter of the union, since the Socialists were no more willing than either of their partners in the government to provoke a new crisis with the elections at hand. Having gained unanimous consent for his draft of Title 8 in the government, Bidault was in a position to threaten a vote of confidence if the Constitutional Committee insisted on presenting a different plan to the Assembly.

During a recess in the Assembly debate on Title 8, Bidault appeared before the Constitutional Committee to review his objections to their draft and to insist that the government's proposals be restored to their original form. During his lengthy statement he warned the committee several times that if they did not comply with his request, a confidence motion would be introduced.

> On the question of the French Union, I have been authorized by the government to pose the question of confidence if it is necessary. But I prefer to avoid this extreme procedure; that is why I have desired that the committee hear the voice of a unanimous government. The entire government insists in the most forceful manner that the committee take its proposals into account.[20]

Bidault's decision to intervene in the constitutional process seems to have been the result of a number of factors, some of them political and others purely personal. In his political autobiography Bidault repeatedly accuses de Gaulle of having deliberately complicated the task of framing a new constitution by attacks that weakened the government, by proposing solutions he knew to be unacceptable, and by refusing to live up to his responsibilities. "What he [de Gaulle] wanted was not to succeed but to maneuver, not to reach his goal but to prevent others from reaching theirs." [21] This personal antagonism, which had its roots in the earlier rivalry between the two men during the Resistance, certainly influenced Bidault to act decisively on a question that de Gaulle had singled out for special criticism. Under no circumstances would Bidault accept the criticism that he had been responsible for any diminution in French sovereignty or any attempt to decolonize.[22]

But there were also several obvious political incentives that may have encouraged Bidault's move, even though he disavowed them. In his speech at Bayeux and in his press declarations de Gaulle was appealing to the French people over the heads of their elected representatives and was attacking the principle of tripartism. Those initiatives were beginning to have some effects, and on 18 September René Capitant announced the formation of a new political movement, the Rassemblement du Peuple Français (RPF), to support the views de Gaulle had elaborated. This move, coming on the heels of both Herriot's and de Gaulle's speeches on the French Union, suggested that the MRP was in danger of losing its supporters to a new Gaullist movement whose patriotic appeals were finding a growing audience. These developments placed the MRP in a dangerous position. If it wanted to retain its image as "the party of fidelity," it might be forced to oppose the constitutional draft and to quit the Tripartite Government. On the other hand, if it remained in the government, it risked losing its electors to the new Gaullist movement and incurring the blame for a constitution, many parts of which it found objectionable.

Bidault's strategy was to revise the constitution to meet de Gaulle's objections, as far as that was possible within the framework of the Tripartite Government, and to rely on the public's desire for an end to the provisional regime to carry the referendum and to hold the majority of conservative voters. Since no basic change in metropolitan institutions would be acceptable, apart from some further negotiation on representation in the upper house of the legislature, it was essential to secure a constitution for the French Union that did not jeopardize France's position overseas. His timing seems to have been dictated as much by de Gaulle's actions as by the legislative calendar, which was rapidly coming to an end. These factors may also have led him to pose the question of confidence, which was a particularly heavy-handed way of dealing with the Assembly. Bidault's lack of parliamentary experience—he had been a deputy for less than a year and, like most of the African deputies, was still unfamiliar with the finer points of parliamentary procedure—may have added to the haste with which the government issued its ultimatum to the Constitutional Committee. But it was de Gaulle's denunciation of the revised texts of Title 8 in his press conference of 19 September that was the final straw.

He termed the new texts, which were very similar to the ideas he had suggested in his 27 August statement, "a sham which does not 'hook-up' [*accroche*] the federal institutions to anything but fictions"[23] and called for the defeat of the constitution in the referendum. This uncompromising stance left the MRP no alternative but to support tripartism and hope for the best.

Bidault also had a number of other substantive objections to the Constitutional Committee's draft of Title 8. In his autobiography he explained, "I decided to intervene when the committee appointed to draw up the constitution approved a text 'denouncing colonial systems based on domination.'"[24] In fact, however, the record of the committee shows that his criticisms were more substantial than that comment suggests.

The government approved an article to be included in the Preamble that said, in part:

> The French Union is an association of nations and peoples combining their resources and their efforts to develop their civilization, perfect their institutions, ensure their security, and increase their well-being.
>
> Within this union, France intends to remain faithful to her traditional mission vis-à-vis the peoples called to participate in it.
>
> Setting aside any system of colonization founded on arbitrariness, she constitutes the best guide for them toward their own administration and the management by themselves of their interests and a guarantee of respect for the rights and liberties proclaimed or confirmed above.[25]

In the committee's version the text had been altered to read:

> The French Union is composed of nations and peoples *who agree* to combine or *to coordinate* their resources and in order to develop their *respective* civilizations, to perfect their *democratic* institutions, increase their well-being, and ensure their security.
>
> *France solemnly recalls that* her traditional mission is *to lead the peoples whom she has taken into her charge to the freedom to govern themselves* and to *democratically* manage their own affairs. *Refusing to accept* systems of colonization based on *oppression,* she guarantees *to all men and women living in the French Union,*

> *equal access to the public service* and *the individual or collective exercise* of the rights and liberties proclaimed or confined above.[26]

The committee text did not actually "denounce systems of colonization founded on oppression"; that formula was discarded in favor of the milder expression "refuses to accept" systems based on oppression. However, it conveyed an entirely different spirit than the government text and clearly implied a large measure of reciprocity between France and the states that composed the union. Words such as "govern themselves" replaced "administration," and "combine or coordinate" was used instead of merely "combine" to express a greater measure of shared authority. The repetition of "democratic" and the reference to "individual or collective exercise" of rights both reinforced the pluralistic approach taken by the committee from the beginning and contrasted sharply with the distinctly hierarchical implications of the government's text. Consequently, although he did not say so openly, Bidault's criticism of the committee's text implied a rejection of the pluralistic conception of the union and an insistence on a different type of organization in which France's role was predominant at every point.

The concern to assure metropolitan predominance in all the institutions of the union became clearer as the committee heard Bidault's other objections to their draft. These centered on two major questions: how were the inhabitants of the metropole and the overseas areas to be represented in the various assemblies, and what formal legal status were they to share? The government wanted to guarantee some representation for French settlers in the colonies at the local level and in the metropolitan and union assemblies. The committee, on the other hand, did not want to make any reference to separate representation in the constitution, and consequently had deleted a provision in the government proposal for "persons holding French civil status" to elect representatives to the Assembly of the Union. Where elections to the National Assembly were concerned, the government was willing to compromise and leave the matter to the electoral law to determine. In regard to the Assembly of the Union and the territorial assemblies in the overseas territories, however, Bidault made no concessions.

> The committee has not accepted this point of view. I hope that it will not force the government to undertake a test of force on this

point by posing the question of confidence. We consider this question to be essential: it is the matter of what is called "the single college." I do not believe that it would be impossible to find an acceptable formula, but if one is not found, the government will maintain its text.

With regard to the territorial assemblies . . . there too [the government] will hold to its text.[27]

Another minor difference concerned the selection of metropolitan members of the Assembly of the Union whom the government proposed to have the Council of the Republic designate, while the committee preferred that they be chosen by the National Assembly. A transactional formula was accepted allowing the former to select one-third and the latter two-thirds of the councilors.

More serious was the dispute over the powers of the assemblies both at the local and union levels. The committee had insisted that the local assemblies be consulted when the organic laws that determined the administrative system of the overseas territories were adopted. It had also provided for the appointment of a "delegate" to head the French administration in those territories. The government rejected both these changes, which clearly implied a large measure of autonomy for the former colonies. Instead of merely naming a "delegate," Bidault insisted that the constitution retain the traditional formula describing colonial governors: "The representative of the government in each territory or group of territories is the depository of the powers of the republic. He is the head of the local administration. He is responsible to the government for his acts." [28] Moreover, if there was to be consultation between the National Assembly and other legislative bodies, then it should be with the Assembly of the Union, he argued, "because it is necessary to maintain the hierarchy of the assemblies." [29]

Bidault proposed to resolve the question of citizenship by creating a new "citizenship of the union" that would apply to everyone in the entire union; French citizenship would be restricted to those persons who qualified for it under both civil law and public law. This position was totally opposed to the committee's previous text, but Bidault was adamant: "I demand that the committee limit itself to that principle and not exceed it." [30]

Finally, Bidault objected to a text which the committee had inserted at the urging of representatives of the French settlers in Morocco and Tunisia that enabled them to retain their representation in the new legislatures. He pointed out that, although he was sympathetic to their wishes, such an action could have dangerous international repercussions. In Morocco, for example, such a unilateral revision of the protectorate agreement might provoke an appeal by the sultan to the United Nations. "That would be madness on our part," Bidault commented. Equally dangerous would be the possibility that other countries would demand reciprocal privileges for their citizens who were resident in France. The disruptive consequences that could be envisioned as a result of any efforts to provide representation for French citizens residing outside the territories of the republic were potentially far more serious than the advantages to be gained.[31]

Given the scope and intensity of Bidault's criticisms, the Constitutional Committee had no alternative but to resume its deliberations on the government draft and to eliminate from Title 8 those parts that were inconsistent with the government's text. Some possibility for negotiation still remained, but Bidault's comments indicated that it was the committee that would have to make most of the sacrifices, and he urged its members to consider practical consequences rather than theoretical questions.

> Theoretical principles are less important than practical results. At a time when Algeria, Tunisia, and Morocco are going to enter an important stage in their development it is important to build a framework based on what is possible. France should remain the guide and guarantor of those peoples; she should give proof of generosity but also of wisdom. . . . The committee can delete what it does not like, but it may not add to the government text.[32]

Before the committee could complete a second revision of Title 8, however, a disagreement arose between metropolitan and native deputies that threatened to destroy the French Union before it was born.

The Native Deputies' Reaction

The most critical issue for the native deputies was whether or not they were to enjoy equal political status with other Frenchmen. Both the April Draft and the committee's revised draft clearly gave them assurances that all subjects would enjoy the right of citizens. The government text cast new doubt on their status, however, since it stipulated that there was to be special representation in the Assembly of the Union for "persons holding French civil status." When questioned about the intent of that text, Bidault's comments were not reassuring.

Senghor had asked the president of the Provisional Government directly what was meant by "persons of French civil status." Were they all those who do not have a personal status [that is, those not subject to traditional native justice in civil matters] or only those Frenchmen of European origin?" [33] Bidault replied that there was no question of taking back any rights that had been acquired, but then he added, "for the four communes of Senegal, for example." Thus, he implied that only those rights that antedated the Constituent Assembly might be regarded as having been "acquired." When pressed by Senghor, Abbas, and Houphouët to explain further the government's intentions, Bidault merely repeated that there was no plan to take back anything that had been granted and that the government would continue to move forward, *mais pas jusqu'à culbute.*[34]

The native deputies' misgivings crystallized into opposition to Article 7 of the government text because by giving separate representation in the Assembly of the Union to French settlers in the overseas areas of the republic it in effect gave a constitutional sanction to the principle of separate electoral colleges for French and native voters. Such a division smacked of racism, and, as Senghor insisted, "We cannot constitutionalize racism of any sort. We are unmovable on that point." [35]

The Constitutional Committee attempted to avoid the issue of the double college by substituting another formula that might not exclude it entirely but would at least avoid mentioning separate representation. Moutet had suggested one such formula; he proposed deleting any mention of special representation for French settlers in Article 7, which created the Assembly of the Union, and stipulating that some proportion of the metropolitan councilors must be chosen from among French settlers overseas. Another alternative was suggested by Paul Bastid, who offered an amendment that provided for "the possibility of special representation," but did not require it.

The RGR spokesman, René Malbrant, rejected Moutet's suggestion because it left the selection of councilors up to the National Assembly and the Council of the Republic, hence the larger parties would be in a position to determine which settlers would be designated to sit in the Assembly of the Union. That left only the alternatives of adopting the Bastid amendment or deleting any reference to separate representation. The Communist party moved to vote first on their motion to delete the offensive phase entirely. The committee divided along strict party lines, 21 (Communists, Socialists, and UDMA) in favor and 21 (MRP, RGR, PRL) opposed; hence, the amendment failed. Next the Bastid amendment was put to a vote and passed with 21 votes in favor and only 15 opposed, the Socialists having abstained.[36]

"Racism is not what you intend, but that will be the result," Senghor warned as he and the other native deputies, Abbas, Houphouët, and Lamine-Guèye left the room. Césaire remained behind only long enough to discuss the article concerning the overseas departments, and then he too withdrew. Pierre Cot despairingly observed, "Look where we are now just because some of our colleagues do not want to understand a moral problem. It is insane; it's enough to make one cry!" When Bidault was confronted by a delegation of native deputies the following day, he protested against their allegations, "You want to show by your resignation that France is a racist country, and you know that is false." "Monsieur le Président," they replied, "the question is whether we are Frenchmen like all the rest." [37] That question had gradually assumed primary importance for the native deputies during the preceding weeks as they watched the government override the desires of the Constitutional Committee and transform the constitutional drafts to which they had attributed great importance.

The native deputies had objected to the government proposal from the start. The original version of the Interministerial Committee's plan and all the subsequent enlargements on it were predicated on the assumption that a large measure of assimilation was essential to the protection of French sovereignty. Abbas maintained, however, that the real problem was to guarantee the rights of the native peoples. "It is not a matter of distilling liberty a drop at a time but one of setting an example and living up to our high responsibilities," he asserted. Such aims could only be fulfilled by recognizing the need for a federal system that would allow real political autonomy to the member states, and that the government's draft did not allow. Unless it was altered, both Abbas and Ravoahangy declared that they would vote against the constitution.[38]

Other native deputies were more discreet but no less disappointed with the government's actions. "The work presented by the government," said Aimé Césaire, "is a monument of prudence. But the dramatic thing, or if you like, the grandeur of the period through which we are passing, is that prudence is not the same thing as wisdom." [39] Lamine-Guèye criticized specifically the texts regarding citizenship and representation, which suggested to him that the government was planning to impose a double-college electoral system for the overseas territories.[40] In addition, Sourou Migan Apithy, a Socialist deputy from Dahomey, complained that the government draft failed to provide a new system capable of guaranteeing each part of the future union a share of the responsibility and the sovereignty.

> Where the overseas territories are concerned, the [government's] secret desire is to maintain the status quo. . . . Our ideal is not to be French citizens. We simply want to enjoy the same rights and liberties in our own countries as the Frenchmen who live there with us. . . . Our ideal is not to mix in what are essentially metropolitan affairs, but to control the affairs of our own countries . . . subject to discussing with the French people those affairs that concern the larger whole which we form together. . . . The government project . . . bears the marks of reactionary influences.[41]

Another Socialist, Yacine Diallo from Guinée, expressed his disillusionment at the treatment accorded some of the native deputies by some metropolitan spokesmen who seemed not to want the Africans in the National Assembly and were attempting to make them second-class citizens. The only thing his supporters in the Parti Progressiste Africain wanted was "integration into the French family. It would not be in very good taste to maintain in subjection men who have never traded upon their attachment [to France]. Indeed, the idea of bargaining with us over integration into the French family, which we seek, shocks and revolts us." [42] Fily Dabo Sissoko from Soudan-Niger expressed the additional fear that forced labor, together with the indigénat, might be revived if there were no constitutional guarantees to prevent it. He noted that only that March his own nephew had been killed while working on a forced-labor battalion.[43]

Houphouët had summed up the concerns of many native deputies when he stressed the government's apparent intention to violate prior commitments.

> The fact that in September the government has reneged on the promise it made to us on 8 May, the day after the referendum, is for us overseas people a subject of real alarm. . . . But our greatest apprehensions arise from the contradictions between the texts of the Preamble and the articles of the constitution that are submitted for our examination. On one side, there are the generous principles that unfortunately do not have the force of law. On the other, there is the crystallization in a constitutional text of a situation of fact. . . .
>
> Why this reticence about recognizing that the inhabitants of the overseas territories have the rights and liberties that are attached to the status of French citizen? Accomplishing the same duties, it seems to me that it is only justice not to haggle with them over these rights and liberties. There must no longer be cut-rate soldiers and miserable pensioners in the one, indivisible republic.[44]

The native deputies were determined to boycott the committee and the Assembly until the government relented on the question of separate representation for French settlers and until it agreed to include in the constitution a guarantee that future political changes would be possible. They were willing to compromise on many points, but not on the principle of equal citizenship. Finally, the government was obliged to yield because, as Fajon stressed, "if this departure signifies a definitive refusal to participate in the work of the Assembly, it will remove the entire significance from the adoption of the texts on the French Union." [45]

When the Assembly convened to debate the provisions of Title 8, the minister of overseas France, Moutet, introduced an amendment deleting the objectionable reference to separate representation for settlers. In its place he inserted a phrase that was the result of lengthy negotiations with the native deputies. "An organic law will determine under what conditions the various parts of the population may be represented." A similar understanding was reached with regard to representation in the territorial assemblies where, according to Article 71H of the draft, an ordinary law would determine the electoral system, legislative competence, and composition.[46]

The question of citizenship was also resolved to the satisfaction of the native deputies by including the text of the Lamine-Guèye Law in Article 71K of the draft. "By constitutionalizing this provision today," Coste-Floret noted, "France gives to our brothers overseas an added guarantee by assuring them that an ordinary law cannot in any case take away from them the advantages thus granted." [47] Lamine-Guèye responded to the gesture by reminding the Assembly of the immense outpouring of popular enthusiasm evoked by the adoption of the law of 7 May throughout black Africa. Hence, there had been great anxiety about the fate of that law, and Lamine-Guèye was glad to reassure his colleagues that it would be maintained. "We recognize that not only is it maintained, it is given a constitutional character which will have a profound reverberation in the overseas territories. . . . [It] will perhaps be the most solid cement in the work that we are building here." [48]

The Assembly also approved an amendment introduced by the Constitutional Committee that gave the National Assembly full legislative power in matters of criminal law and civil liberties and made such laws automatically applicable overseas. The executive's power to rule by decree in all other matters was limited by the requirement that the advice of the Assembly of the Union be sought before action was taken. It was not necessary, however, that the Assembly of the Union concur with the government before its decrees took effect.[49] Finally, the government also acknowledged that the constitution should provide for changes in the political status of the various parts of the union in the future. An article was introduced permitting such changes, subject to the control of the metropolitan Parliament in consultation with the territorial assemblies and the Assembly of the Union. Thus, the native deputies received satisfaction for their demand that "the existing condition of the overseas territories not be fixed for all eternity." [50]

At the conclusion of the first reading of the constitution Bidault expressed satisfaction with the unanimous vote in favor of the French Union articles, and he observed:

> Together we have established a foundation that, I believe, is unmatched anywhere in the world. A few more difficulties may still

> arise, but we have overcome many of them together—I emphasize, together. . . .
>
> We have begun to build a great community with a concern for liberty and a respect for history; a single community under a single flag.[51]

After a brief second reading that produced only minor revisions, the constitution was adopted on 28 September by 440 votes to 106. All three government parties supported the new draft, while the RGR and other conservative groups opposed it. Ferhat Abbas and his fellow Algerian UDMA deputies all abstained, as did the two native deputies from Madagascar. All the other native deputies from black Africa and the old colonies voted with their metropolitan party affiliates in favor of adoption.[52] The following day de Gaulle renewed his attack on the Assembly and the constitutional draft calling it simply a revised version of the defeated April Draft, since it still did not provide for a strong, independent executive power. Instead, he demanded a totally different system of government that, among other things, would establish "a French Union which would be a union and which would remain French."[53] On 9 October de Gaulle again urged all Frenchmen to vote against the constitution and warned them that if it were adopted, the party system would soon produce "first weakness, then anarchy, finally dictatorship; all three of which could be mortal risks in the situation in which we find ourselves."[54]

The effect of this unbending opposition was to transform the referendum into something of a vote of confidence for or against de Gaulle, much as the first referendum had been a test of the Communists' popularity. Once again it was doubtful that the constitutional texts had been studied by more than a tiny minority of voters. The result was a defeat for everyone. The government managed to rally a plurality of 35 percent in favor of the constitution; but 31 percent supported de Gaulle, and 34 percent abstained entirely. Most voters seemed primarily concerned to put an end to the provisional regime.

The results of the referendum of 13 October in the overseas areas are too fragmentary to permit detailed analysis. Remembering that only French citizens who held that status before 1945 were permitted to vote in the referendum, it would appear that the discontent voiced by the native deputies was reflected in the actions of their constituents. The shift from May to October was approximately 13 percent for all overseas areas taken together (see table 4). It was uniformly negative in all territories, but the most striking change occurred in Algeria, where both native deputies and French settlers' groups opposed the constitution for opposite reasons. In territories such as Senegal, Martinique, Guyane, and Réunion, where the electorate included large numbers of native voters, the results were less decisive, but a majority was opposed to the revised draft. These results indicate clearly that the division that had manifested itself within the Assembly was also beginning to develop among the general population in the overseas areas.

TABLE 4

Comparison of the Referendum Results in the Overseas areas, May–October 1946

	May	*October*
For	30%	20%
Against	26%	29%
Abstaining	44%	50 + %

SOURCE: Husson, *Elections et referendums.*

The Formal Institutions

In view of the deep divisions that had emerged within the Constituent Assembly over the French Union, it is not surprising that the formal framework that finally emerged was complex and contradictory. Title 8 was the longest of the twelve titles that comprised the Constitution of the Fourth Republic. It contained twenty-three articles which, together with parts of several other articles and a section of the Preamble, defined the French Union, indicated its goals, and specified its basic operating rules. Many aspects of its operation have been the subject of extensive controversy among French legal scholars and colonial writers, and it is impossible here to review that literature.[55] An overview of the formal institutions is essential, however, in order to appreciate the way conflicting ideas were built into the legal edifice.

The general form of the French Union has been described as "something approaching a confederation"[56]—that is, a union composed of states, each of which retains its individual identity as an international entity—rather than a federal system, in which the constituent units have only domestic identities. Such formal legal distinctions were misleading, however, for the French Union did not correspond to any existing type of constitution. Instead, it is probably more useful to view the work of the Constituent Assemblies from a political rather than a legal perspective and to recognize that the French Union was devised primarily as a means of tying together a revived, democratic, republican France and an assortment of overseas areas that previously had been united almost exclusively by military and administrative ties.[57] In this context citizenship became for some a political symbol marking the unity of the empire. To others it meant the application overseas of legal rights, obligations, and immunities associated with membership in a democratic republic as these had come to be understood in metropolitan France. Thus citizenship had both an authoritarian and a democratic aspect, and depending on which one was emphasized, the nature of the French Union appears quite different. The wording of the Preamble, which also set out the general form of the French Union, made explicit reference both to the symbols of unity and to those of autonomy and democracy.

> On the morrow of the victory gained by the free peoples over the regimes that attempted to enslave and degrade the human person, the French people proclaim anew that every human being, without distinction of race, religion, or creed, possesses inalienable and sacred rights. They solemnly reaffirm the rights and liberties of man and the citizen consecrated by the Declaration of Rights of 1789 and the fundamental principles recognized by the laws of the republic. . . .
>
> . . . France, together with the overseas peoples shall form a union founded upon equality of rights and duties, without distinction of race or religion. The French Union shall consist of nations and peoples who combine or coordinate their resources and their efforts in order to develop their respective civilizations, increase their well-being, and ensure their security. Faithful to her traditional mission, France proposes to guide the peoples for whom she has assumed responsibility into the freedom to administer themselves and to manage their own affairs democratically; rejecting any system of colonial rule based on arbitrary power,

she shall guarantee to all equal access to public service and the individual or collective exercise of the rights and liberties proclaimed or confirmed above.

Similarly, the general principles underlying the formation of the French Union, which were enunciated in Articles 60–62, contained references suggesting that some of the units comprising the union were to act autonomously. For example, the associated states were linked to France by an international agreement (Article 61) that preserved their international status. An effort to emphasize this autonomy by allowing members of the union "to agree to combine their resources in order to guarantee the defense of the whole union," was defeated during the second reading, hence, the final version merely asserted that "the members of the French Union shall combine their resources." The final phrase of Article 62 left no question but that "the government of the republic shall undertake the coordination . . . and direction of the policies appropriate to prepare and ensure this defense."

The extent of real autonomy was also limited by the definition of the republic contained in Article 60. In addition to metropolitan France it included the overseas departments and territories, which meant that nearly all of the former colonies apart from the mandated territories and the protectorates were considered parts of the "one and indivisible" republic.[58] This classification was partly obscured by Article 85, which asserted that "the French republic, one and indivisible, shall recognize the existence of territorial units. The units shall be the communes and départements and the overseas territories." This clearly implied that overseas territories were nothing more than subordinate units of local government, an impression that was reinforced by Article 86, which gave the metropolitan Parliament the right to modify "the extent, the possible regrouping, and the organization of the communes and départements and overseas territories" by ordinary law.

The final texts of Articles 80–82 also left considerable confusion about the meaning of citizenship, some of which, as explained earlier, was intentional; and magistrates and legal scholars who have tried to explicate them never resolved the ambiguities.[59] In view of the very deep and long-standing disputes over the meaning of citizenship, the constitution merely stated the principle of equal rights and left to Parliament the responsibility for applying it to the widely varying conditions in the overseas areas.

> 80. All subjects of the overseas territories shall have the status [*qualité*] of citizen, by the same right as French nationals of metropolitan France or of the overseas territories. Special laws will lay down the conditions under which they exercise their rights as citizens.
>
> 81. All French nationals and subjects of the French Union shall have the status of citizen of the French Union, which shall ensure to them the enjoyment of the rights and liberties guaranteed by the Preamble to the present constitution.
>
> 82. Citizens who are not subject to French civil law shall retain their personal status [i.e. subject to Koranic law] so long as they do not renounce it. This status may in no circumstance constitute a ground for refusing or restricting the rights and liberties pertaining to the status [*qualité*] of French citizen.

It was also generally recognized that to be a citizen in any sense meant to enjoy a right of representation; but how that right was to be exercised also gave rise to serious disagreements. The constitutional solution arrived at was, if anything, even more unsatisfactory than the definition of citizenship, for the provisions set forth in Articles 66–68 contain a flagrant contradiction.

> 66. (i) The Assembly of the French Union shall consist: half of members representing metropolitan France, and half of members representing the overseas departments and territories and associated states.
>
> (ii) An organic law will decide the conditions under which the different sections of the population may be represented.
>
> 67. The members of the Assembly of the French Union shall be elected, for the overseas departments and territories, by the territorial assemblies; they shall be elected, for metropolitan France, in the proportion of two-thirds by the members of the National Assembly representing metropolitan France and one-third by the members of the Council of the Republic representing metropolitan France.
>
> 68. The associated states may designate delegates to the Assembly

> of the Union within limits and conditions settled by a law and a domestic act of each state.

The contradiction in these few lines is striking. As Alfred Grosser later commented:

> The text is clear; the indivisible republic is very neatly divided into metropolitan France and into the overseas departments and territories, which found themselves placed on the same level as the "associated territories"; the metropole counting for one part and all the other territories together for one, regardless of the number of inhabitants or peoples. What is more, the last clause [of Article 66] indicates that individual equality within the population (that of the metropole, the associated states, or the overseas departments?) is not respected either.[60]

As part of the French republic, the overseas territories were granted a special status which, according to Article 74, "takes into account their particular interests within the framework of the general interests of the republic." The inhabitants of the overseas territories continued to enjoy the right to elect deputies to the National Assembly and the Council of the Republic, as well as to send delegates to the Assembly of the French Union. In addition, some were given the right to representation within a system of local government bodies that included both the territorial assemblies of the various territories and the "federal" assemblies in the large administrative federations of West and Equatorial Africa. The details of this arrangement were spelled out in Articles 77–79, which left the metropolitan Parliament in complete control of the enabling legislation.

What the constitution created, therefore, was a system of representation on three levels: local, metropolitan, and union. In each instance, however, the metropolitan Parliament held the authority to determine the composition, competence, and powers of the local assemblies and to regulate the conditions under which deputies would be elected.

Thus, the constitution embodied a dual inequality—an inequality of states and an inequality of individuals. Metropolitan France enjoyed effective superiority in relation to the overseas areas as a whole, and the electoral law assured that French colonists and assimilated natives would continue to be represented in spite of their numerical inferiority to the masses of nonassimilated indigenous peoples. At the local government level, too, the forms of democratic representation were adopted, but the separation of the electorate into two colleges deprived the most numerous groups of equality and guaranteed the resident French community a large voice in local affairs. Furthermore, these representative bodies were intended to be advisory rather than legislative. For the overseas territories, the metropolitan Parliament was the ultimate legislative authority, and while the Assembly of the French Union had the right to discuss or propose legislation relating to the overseas territories, its decisions were not binding on either the government or the National Assembly.[61] The powers of the local assemblies in the overseas territories were also restricted, in practice, to an advisory capacity even though the constitution left their precise limits to be set by the metropolitan Parliament.

Within the French Union, executive powers were vested in a committee, the High Council of the French Union, which was presided over by the president of the union. This central office was to be filled by the president of the French republic. The other members of the High Council were to be representatives of the various governments in the associated states together with "a delegation of the French government." Hence the High Council was to be a body made up principally of ministers and civil servants, whose function was not primarily to formulate policy but "to assist the [French] government in the general direction of the union." [62] Since the other members—the associated states—were considered to be sovereign states, the constitution could not require them to participate and merely asserted that "they shall be entitled to accredit" representatives to the president of the union. Thus, even if all the states that theoretically were eligible to participate had done so (in fact, only the associated states of Cambodia, Laos, and Vietnam ever did), it is evident that the French government played the central role in the "direction" of the union's executive.

At the local government level within the overseas territories there was also an effort made in the constitution to clarify the role of the colonial governors. According to Article 76: "The powers of the republic shall be vested in the representative of the government in each territory or group of territories. He shall be the head of the territorial administration. He shall be responsible to the government for his actions." Clearly, the executive was to be responsible only indirectly to Parliament and not at all to the local assemblies. Thus the control of the Ministry of Overseas France remained intact—at least in principle—under the terms of the constitution. The only route by which the peoples of the overseas areas could hope to exercise any formal control over the colonial administration, therefore, was through the metropolitan Parliament, which elected the government. The predominant position of metropolitan officialdom is still more evident in relation to the judiciary; for Chapter 9 of the constitution, which defines the structure of the judicial system, omitted any mention of the overseas areas. While representatives of those regions were not excluded from appointment to the fourteen-member High Council of the Judiciary or to judicial posts, the primary concern of the constitution was to assure the independence of the judiciary from political pressures rather than to achieve a balance between metropolitan and overseas members.

Therefore, if one simply looks at the way the constitution defined the structure of the French Union, it is apparent that alongside the democratic language of citizenship, representation, and the Rights of Man, there was a clear-cut determination to assure metropolitan preeminence in all the organs of government. That was exactly Bidault's intention, and he clearly took great satisfaction from it, as he later wrote, "If you read the articles concerning the French Union in the constitution of 28 September 1946, . . . you can see how falsely we were accused of trying to decolonize." [63] However, Bidault was able to force his will on the Constitutional Committee and the Assembly only at the price of undermining the consensus that had emerged between metropolitan and native deputies and of largely destroying the unifying force of the colonial myth.

9. DECLINE OF THE COLONIAL MYTH

A sense of shared values and an awareness of common expectations for the future are more important in determining the fate of a constitution than are formal institutions. The colonial myth, despite its internal contradictions and ambiguities, embodied many such values and expectations. It worked to promote consensus among groups with widely different interests by holding constantly before them an image of a democratically governed community in which each could find a legitimate role and from which each drew psychological satisfactions as well as practical advantages. One major consequence of the party conflicts described in the two previous chapters was that they led both metropolitan and native deputies to question each other's commitment to the common ideal of a democratic French Union. By the final hours of the Second Constituent Assembly the native deputies, in particular, felt that they had been deceived about the metropolitan commitment to democratic institutions for the overseas areas. On the other hand, many metropolitan deputies were convinced that the natives' professed devotion to unity with France was a sham. Such suspicions interacted to bring about a serious decline, if not the total destruction, of the colonial myth and to render the institutions of the French Union suspect in the eyes of its members.

The depth of the government's misgivings became evident in small ways as well as large. Between the first and second readings of the draft constitution Bidault insisted that the committee delete from the Preamble any reference to "self-government" and restore the term "self-administration," while Varenne requested that an allusion to improving "respective civilizations" as a goal of the union be amended to omit "respective."[1] Such seemingly petty objections were symptomatic of a deep malaise, which became evident in the closing hours of the Assembly in the vulgar attacks on Ferhat Abbas and other native spokesmen and, more importantly, in the treatment of two major bills; the electoral law and the Local Assemblies Bill. The discussion of the budget for the Ministry of Overseas France was also the occasion for some bitter criticism of the union.

Within the narrow limits of governmental unity, Moutet sought to preserve the advantages granted to the native deputies in earlier drafts. Yet even he, who clearly had little sympathy for Bidault's intervention on the French Union articles, entertained many reservations about the pace and scope of colonial reforms. He objected, for example, to altering the existing framework of colonial administration by giving real power over local affairs to local elected assemblies until those assemblies had proven themselves. Moreover, it is clear that disturbances in Indochina, Madagascar, and elsewhere only reinforced his reluctance to permit the adoption of laws that might weaken the French colonial administration.

> We do not refuse to envisage any sort of evolution, but we have just witnessed certain evolutions. In some countries that were handed over to banditry and anarchy, a French administrative armature has reestablished along with order, peace, that is to say, true civilization. [*Strong applause on the Left, the Center, and the Right*] When that armature has disappeared, when that administration has been absent, we know where that has led us.
>
> These examples are too recent and too painful for us to forget them at the moment when we are discussing the constitutional law of the French Union, or for us to leave to an indeterminate future the establishment of the uncertain powers of an administration which will thus take on a totally new character.[2]

The situation in Indochina aroused special resentment among other metropolitan deputies who, like André Mutter, received telegrams from French residents pleading for help and recounting stories of assassinations, rapes, thefts, and fire bombings by the Viet-minh. Mutter, whose son was serving in Indochina at the time, demanded help and insisted that the government also reassure the families whose sons were fighting that "their sacrifices were not in vain and that their children were fighting for something, that is, to maintain the prestige of France." He went on to attack the agreements of 6 March with Ho Chi Minh, whose government he claimed lacked any authority to rule in Vietnam, and to demand that the government "affirm here that on every occasion it intends to maintain the prestige of France and the magnificent work that we have achieved in Indochina, the pearl of the Orient." [3]

Some other spokesmen for French settlers also objected to the reforms already voted and cited other dangers. André Schock from the Ivory Coast, complained about the economic chaos there, which he attributed to the reforms in the labor law resulting from the suppression of forced labor.[4] François Quilici, a citizens' college deputy from Algeria, had deeper misgivings about the future of the union.

> What is grave about this text concerning the French Union, in my opinion, is that it envisages only one outcome to the evolution of the populations grouped under our flag: their emancipation—whose natural and in a sense fatal goal, and we must recognize it, is secession. For these peoples whom we are pushing along the way to emancipation not to emancipate themselves from us completely would be a unique and very French miracle. I want to believe in the French miracle.—M. Maurice Schumann: We do believe in it.—M. Quilici: But I really think we exaggerate.[5]

The electoral law drew special opposition from Quilici because, according to his view, the extension of citizenship to many Muslims who then voted in the citizen's college left only those who were opposed to France in the second college. "We create . . . all the conditions favorable to the separatist spirit. . . . But it doesn't stop there, and that is what has been overlooked in this Assembly. It leads to an invasion, to a submersion of the metropolitan assemblies —that is, the sovereignty of the nation." [6]

Feelings ran so high among the metropolitan deputies that on at least two occasions Jacques Duclos felt it necessary to remind his colleagues that, although the Communist party was sympathetic to the native deputies' demands, the PCF was no less determined than any other party to protect French sovereignty.

> The discussion . . . had given rise to interpretations that might permit some to think that [the PCF] is not concerned, as are all the other groups in this Assembly, to assure the permanence of

> the French presence in the various parts of the world where the flag of our country flies.
>
> If France were absent, her absence would signify the presence of others. We know that too well for our group not to have an exact sense of certain necessities.[7]

Later, in explaining the Communist vote in favor of the constitutional draft, Duclos reaffirmed the same position.

> We made concessions. . . . On the French Union one finds in the new text less vigorous thought than in the project of 5 May. We did not go as far in this domain as we would have wished. However, . . . we know that the presence of France in many points of the globe is a factor for progress and freedom. Its absence would be exploited against the associated peoples themselves whom we want to see forever more united within the French Union.[8]

This attitude on the part of the Communists was of critical importance in accounting for the government's subsequent action on the electoral law. In that case, the PCF and the MRP agreed on a text that differed on two vital points from the one adopted by the Interior Committee. That committee had decided to take no position on the principle of separate representation for French settlers and to examine one colony at a time to decide whether local conditions indicated that a double college was appropriate. A subcommittee was given the task of working out an agreement on the subject with the interested native deputies. Following those meetings the committee decided to suppress the double college in French West Africa but to maintain it in French Equatorial Africa, the Cameroons, and Madagascar. At that point, however, the government intervened to force the committee to revise its text by increasing the number of first-college seats from 1 to 2 and reducing the native college from 5 to 4 in Equatorial Africa.[9] The Socialist party strongly opposed this change and denounced the government's action claiming that "an electoral 'gang' has been established in the Palais Bourbon" that resulted in "an electoral black market" between the Communists and the MRP. As a result of their deal, Max Lejeune asserted, the number of metropolitan seats had been increased from 522 to 544 while the number of seats for Algeria and the overseas territories were reduced from what had been provided in the previous electoral law of 13 April. Furthermore, he maintained that the PCF expected to win 10 of the new seats, the MRP 7, and 5 would probably go to the RGR and the SFIO.[10]

The same alignment of Communist and MRP votes also allowed the government to prevent a final vote on the Local Assemblies Bill which was delayed until the final hour of the session to permit passage of the Civil Service Act that had been drafted largely by the Communist vice-president of the Council of Ministers, Thorez. Despite the fact that the Local Assemblies Bill had been adopted by a large majority in the First Constituent Assembly and had been revised after the government indicated some reservations about it in August, with the Ministry of Overseas France participating actively in the task, Bidault refused to permit it to come to a vote. As a last-minute compromise the government promised to create the assemblies by decree on an interim basis.[11] These actions clearly suggest that the MRP and the PCF were willing to sacrifice the interests of the overseas deputies not just to safeguard what they regarded as compelling national interests, but also to gain some very specific electoral advantages and fulfill less exalted interests of their respective parties.

The government-sponsored texts of the constitution and of the electoral law, and the government's action on the Territorial Assemblies Bill all reflected and reinforced the traditional metropolitan perspective on the colonies. The image of the French Union they conveyed was hierarchical, centralized, and arbitrary. France assumed the role of guide, tutor, director, and patron of the former colonial peoples whose inferiority was clearly implied in the explicit control over all matters of national political importance given to the metropolitan Parliament.

Within this hierarchical system of associated states, overseas territories, and departments there were numerous formal bodies with little real power whose primary aim was to provide a democratic shelter behind which the traditional administrative system could operate without restraint from local elected authorities. Decisions in the French Union were to be made at the center, in Paris, and change brought about from the top down by administrative regulations instead of being inspired and controlled from the overseas areas through the open confrontation of political forces. The resulting institutions permitted various forms of consultation between elected representatives in the local assemblies or the Assembly of the Union and those members of the government or officials of the Overseas Ministry who held the real power. But it clearly left all critical decisions regarding the French Union in the hands of the metropolitan government, which meant, in practice, the senior officials of the Overseas Ministry and the Ministry of Interior. Carefully isolated from direct political accountability to either the metropolitan or native electorate, those officials would carry on much as they had done for most of the preceding century.

The government seems, in fact, to have purposely structured the union in a way that would prevent most issues from assuming a political form at the local level and to have tied the colonies securely to metropolitan France because it was only in Paris that the power and authority to make major political decisions could ever be assembled.

The Native Deputies' Resentment

It was precisely the hierarchical, unitary character of the government's proposals, in addition to the arbitrariness of Bidault's actions, that most profoundly disturbed the native deputies. More than the occasional disparaging remarks from conservative colleagues, what most distressed them was the total disappearance from the final texts of any gesture of mutual responsibility or shared authority. Houphouët indicated the seriousness of the problem.

> The French Union, which is vital for the future of France and the overseas territories, should be based on reciprocal confidence and mutual comprehension. However, it appears, not only from some articles appearing in a certain press, but also from our discussion in committee and from the remarks of certain colleagues who have preceded me at this rostrum, that confidence does not reign within the great family. We are working under the sign of distrust; we must dissipate these more or less well-founded fears if we wish to build something durable.[12]

The Algerians, whose proposals for local autonomy had been rejected by the Assembly without even a serious discussion, were particularly bitter. The root of the problem, as Abbas explained, lay in the profound differences that characterized the most basic assumptions of the native and metropolitan deputies. Some colleagues continued to view

> French presence in the overseas territories as a symbol of prestige, of authority, and subordination. . . .
> —[*A voice from the Right:*] and of honor . . .
> —M. Jean Legendre [PRL]: and of civilization!
> [Abbas:] The government's intervention added to this difficulty. This intervention did not facilitate the task of the committee, on the contrary, it complicated it. The Assembly attempted to make some corrections in the initial text, but it did not introduce that breath of liberty that alone is able to arouse enthusiasm and win heartfelt support. . . .
>
> The government text . . . has codified a neo-colonialism that is as disastrous and as dangerous as its namesake: the colonial regime of yesterday. The government forced the suppression of the notion of a union based on free consent that had been adopted by the previous Assembly. . . . Do you think that the colonial peoples will not see that as an obvious regression? [13]

If France really intended to set an example for the rest of the world, Abbas argued, she would have renounced the policy of assimilation, abandoned the practice of direct administration, and ended the centralized, bureaucratic political system that "paralyzes initiative in the overseas countries." She would have chosen to settle the fate of the French Union by negotiation with all the peoples of the union, "in the reciprocal respect for the higher interests of France and the legitimate aspirations of those peoples." Only by such a mutual accord could the French Union ever become "a great federation of free peoples cemented by the common cult of liberty and human brotherhood." [14]

It was exactly that "common cult of liberty and human brotherhood" which was undermined by the government's determination to give increased representation to French settlers in parts of black Africa and Madagascar. Ravoahangy angrily denounced the electoral arrangements proposed for his island constituency.

> You cannot proclaim the abolition of distinctions between races and then maintain it in practice. You cannot grant citizenship to

> all the subjects of the overseas territories and then wipe out that provision by creating first- and second-class citizens. . . .
>
> The existence of a double-college system would constitute an injustice to the native population of the Grand Isle . . . —2 million native electors [out of a total population of over 4 million] would have only three deputies while 20,000 first-college electors would have two deputies.[15]

"The hierarchy you want to impose on us will provoke a total disapproval and disaffection in French Equatorial Africa," declared Félix Tchicaya.[16] Earlier he had warned the Assembly and the government that the long series of disappointments suffered by the native deputies was creating a critical spirit among the overseas peoples and making their confidence in France conditional; but the government had ignored him.

> It is a fact that this risk of serious disaffection is something that the French people are running if they do not have the courage to disavow the errors that were so often committed not by them but in their name. . . .
>
> Do not lead the peoples overseas to believe in a vast mystification, in the existence of principles for internal usage which, outside the metropolitan hexagon, will be nothing but advertising slogans whose augurs laugh among themselves.
>
> If you refuse to give independent peoples equal rights, you turn your back on all your political doctrine. And in addition, you create a deception whose consequences we will be unable to limit.[17]

The government's actions were especially painful to the black African Socialist deputies. Lamine-Guèye, in particular, had labored long and diligently in cooperation with Moutet to arrange compromise after compromise in an effort to bridge the gap between the government texts and those acceptable to the native deputies. Reluctantly the African deputies had voted the constitutional draft, but they refused to support the electoral law, as Lamine-Guèye explained: "We will not vote for it because we think this bill misrepresents a certain number of principles and necessities. . . . We will not vote for it because we are against the principle of the double college as it has been instituted." [18]

Looking ahead to the referendum, Lamine-Guèye recognized that it was important to maintain unity, and he observed that the native deputies agreed to proclaim that the Assembly, like its predecessor, had accomplished important reforms: the citizenship law, the elimination of forced labor, the restoration of political and civil rights for natives in the overseas territories. Nevertheless, he indicated that the native deputies did not intend to support the constitution without reservations. "We simply would have liked the Assembly to allow us to return to our respective territories with the moral possibility of defending with real conviction and ardor the entire statute as it was elaborated, as well as its complement, the electoral law." [19]

The native deputies' enthusiasm for the constitution was still further diminished by the government's action on the Local Assemblies Bill. That measure had been one of their primary objectives throughout both Constituent Assemblies. No other reform, with the exception of the suppression of forced labor and the extension of citizenship, had such direct relevance to the future political development of their countries. Moreover, the native deputies had waited patiently while the government brought to the floor and adopted all its priority legislation, including the War Damages Act and the Civil Service Act. Hence, they were stunned and outraged when the government's spokesman, Jean Letourneau, the minister of posts, telegraphs, and telephones, announced that the government would not support the Local Assemblies Bill.

Lamine-Guèye, the rapporteur for the bill, warned the government that

> the operation that is being imposed on us—whose spirit and tendencies I never suspected—is a very regrettable operation.
>
> At the moment when you are creating the French Union; when, within that French Union, assemblies are supposed to function which are going to send representatives to the Council of the Republic, to the Assembly of the Union, into all the consultative organisms that have been envisaged in the constitution, the effect would be disastrous from the viewpoint of the nation if tonight your gesture appeared to mean more or less: 'We tip our hats and leave to a decree the problem of settling such a serious question.' [20]

Other deputies were much more outspoken. Félix Tchicaya warned that the government's action in postponing debate on the Local Assemblies Bill "risked provoking feelings of reprobation, disgust and contempt" in his country.

> I do not want that. I do not want that for us or for France.
>
> Yesterday, I took the floor in this Assembly to signal a very grave danger which the government has not cared to take into account. . . . We did not come here just to ratify decisions taken without us, but to take part in the constitutional and legislative work. We cannot return home without bringing to those who elected us the proof that we have been working together with you. The government must understand the gravity of its action.[21]

Mme. Eboué protested in her late husband's name as well as in her own against the government's decision. "If Eboué were here . . . he would have affirmed that it is not possible that France would renege on the engagements it made." [22] The government had clearly decided to ignore the promise it had made following the defeat of the April Draft that none of the rights acquired by the natives of the overseas territories would be taken back, and the native deputies were bitterly resentful. Houphouët summarized their progressive disillusionment with the constitution, the electoral law, and now the Local Assemblies Bill.

> We have allowed the government to impose its viewpoint upon us both in the constitutional bill and in the electoral law. But now that it is simply a question of the local assemblies, we do not understand the reasons that oblige the government to postpone this vote. . . . What will we say tomorrow to those who await us? The government refused us everything. Thus we are not constituents, we are mere figureheads. . . . You must not destroy by yourselves the effect of the revolutionary act which you accomplished by calling us to sit in this Assembly.[23]

Under strong pressure from the native deputies, the government agreed to create the assemblies by decree during the next week so that native members of the Council of the Republic would be able to participate in the election of the first president of the republic, who would also be the first president of the French Union. It was an unhappy conclusion to the long constitutional debate because for the native deputies this action represented not only an added proof of their weakness vis-à-vis the metropolitan government; it also marked the continuation of a system of colonial government by administrative decrees that they had sought at all costs to eliminate. Hence, Lamine-Guèye was understating the feelings of his colleagues when he observed that although the goal of unity with France was still widely accepted, "a conviction that we do not hold ardently and completely will be very difficult to make others share." [24]

The Failure of Unity

The colonial myth embodied the ideal of a democratically organized community of nations and peoples. The native deputies had shared many of the values of liberty and political equality that were alleged by all the French political groups to be the basis of republican government in that country. For a time they were also confident that with the aid and support of metropolitan France, the benefits of modern political and economic life could be brought to their own peoples. Some, whose people had previously enjoyed large measures of real independence prior to the imposition of French rule in the nineteenth century, were also able to look to the creation of a French Union as a means of restoring more autonomy to their own institutions. Hence, the ideal of a large, multinational community of French peoples was one that large numbers of native political leaders could acknowledge and accept at least as an important step, toward full autonomy, if not as a sufficient goal in itself.

By the end of the Constituent Assembly, however, this consensus had been undermined to the point where the colonial myth no longer held any appeal for many of the native deputies. The constitution and the electoral law both contained all the generous principles of equality and liberty, but they were contradicted repeatedly by articles that minimized local autonomy and left the metropolitan administration in effective control of all the overseas areas. The electoral law introduced overt discrimination where the constitution proclaimed there was to be none. By preserving the symbols of French power and authority in the colonial world, the constitution may have satisfied the psychological needs of some metropolitan groups for a renewed sense of national grandeur, but it did so at the cost of alienating native support. In the end, the Constitution of the French Union contributed to the ultimate destruction of the Fourth Republic rather than to its grandeur.

First, by making changes in the French Union a matter of constitutional revision, it placed formidable political barriers in the way of any significant institutional reform. Not only was there a strong prejudice in France against constitutional revision, traditionally a tactic of the antidemocratic Right during the Third Republic, there was the more immediate likelihood that any gesture toward constitutional revision would reopen the bitter controversy about metropolitan institutions as well as those of the French Union.

Second, by making the day-to-day administration of the overseas areas subject to the general direction of the metropolitan government, the constitution forced that body to assume responsibility for policies that, under the very best circumstances, would be extremely difficult to manage, given the weakness of the political parties and the lack of unity in every metropolitan government.

Finally, by depicting the normal state of affairs between France and the overseas areas as one based on authoritative control by the metropolitan bureaucracy, the constitution encouraged the government's inclination to resort to force in order to compel acceptance of metropolitan directives. This situation had already arisen in Indochina, where an open battle raged between the nationalist Vietminh and the French army. It was a pattern soon to be repeated in Madagascar in 1947 and in Algeria on a much larger scale beginning in 1954.

Furthermore, throughout most of the Fourth Republic, external conditions were not favorable for France, whose principal security interests lay outside the French Union. Consequently, the constitution, by linking the overseas areas closely to metropolitan institutions, increased the probability that French internal and international commitments would conflict with the requirements of unity within the union. A looser structure would not have removed the possibility of such conflicts, but by legitimizing local autonomy in the overseas areas it might have spared France the traumatic shocks of two bloody colonial wars and would certainly have reduced the destructive effects of decolonization on the metropolitan body politic.

It is quite probable that in an era when nations around the globe were attaining formal independence from their colonial overlords no scheme for preserving unity between France and its colonies could have succeeded. The various plans for the French Union offered by the native deputies had the advantage, nevertheless, of offering a basis for a gradual transition toward full independence within a framework of shared interests that might have diminished tensions and tended to minimize violence. Why was such a plan not adopted? The evidence is clear that many metropolitan deputies would have accepted the scheme adopted by the Constitutional Committee and based on the native Intergroup proposals. It did not do so only because the Bidault government intervened to prevent it. That action seems to have been predicated not on economic interests or high-level strategic concerns but on a concatenation of factors including personalities, party rivalries, and international violence against French citizens in Indochina and elsewhere. Among those factors, the unrelenting opposition to the constitution voiced by General de Gaulle and his attacks on the French Union were a major incentive to block further reforms. Similarly, the French Communist party contributed directly to the defeat of a more flexible French Union both by its votes and by the threat that it posed to the future of French democracy. The most important single factor in accounting for the government's actions, however, was the image of colonial relationships held by an important segment of the French political elite for whom unity with the colonies was conceivable only if French authority and sovereignty were unchallenged and centralized control over the colonies undiminished. Because there were so many to whom autonomy meant secession, the government was able to act against the overwhelming opposition of the native deputies and many of their metropolitan supporters.

The Bidault government, by imposing its particular version of the French Union, hoped to preserve the image of France as a world power capable of asserting its influence against other states, international organizations, and local nationalist groups that challenged its authority. It also effectively safeguarded the interests of an important segment of the colonial, military, and foreign affairs bureaucracy, and it may have contributed to the sense of French prestige and grandeur at a time when the metropolitan public was undergoing deep distress and no doubt hungered for such rewards. This version of the colonial myth found its apotheosis and its disgrace in the struggle to preserve French Algeria. The most important cost of adopting such a policy, however, was the destruction of those humanitarian, egalitarian, and libertarian elements of the colonial myth that made it appealing to the new elite of native leaders. Once they discovered that the institutions of the French Union were to be forced upon them largely against their will and did not offer either freedom or equality within the framework of a generous republic, they gradually abandoned their faith in the institutions and in France. In place of the French colonial myth, they began to develop new myths, such as the myth of African socialism or the myth of Arab unity, which were consistent with their new roles as the rulers of independent states.

NOTES

Introduction

1 *La France d'outre-mer,* p. 274. Translation from the French is my own, here and throughout, unless otherwise noted.
2 Several general histories of decolonization give a general overview of the French experience. Among the most comprehensive are Rudolph von Albertini, *Decolonization,* and Henri Grimal, *La Décolonisation.*
3 See David Goldsworthy, *Colonial Issues in British Politics,* and Georges Fischer, *Le Parti travailliste et la décolonisation de l'Inde* (Paris, 1966).
4 The conflict over Indonesia has been recounted by Louis Fischer, *The Story of Indonesia* (New York, 1959), while the Dutch experience with decolonization is analyzed by Arendt Lijphart in his perceptive study *The Trauma of Decolonization.* It is also revealing to compare French attitudes with those of the Belgians, who were unwilling to prepare for decolonization and unable to control the process when it could no longer be avoided. On that experience see René Lemarchand, *Political Awakening in the Belgian Congo* (Berkeley and Los Angeles, 1964).
5 This use of the concept of a political myth is derived primarily from the works of Harold D. Lasswell; see especially Harold D. Lasswell and Abraham Kaplan, *Power and Society: A Framework for Political Inquiry* (New Haven, 1950), pp. 117–33. Other writers who have stressed the role of political myths include Karl W. Deutsch, *The Nerves of Government* (New York, 1963), and Kenneth Boulding, *The Image* (Ann Arbor, Mich., 1956). On the distinction between "myth" and "ideology" see Ben Halpern, "'Myth' and 'Ideology' in Modern Usage," *History and Theory* 1 (1961) : 129–49.
6 I regret that Raoul Girardet's book *L'Idée coloniale en France de 1871 à 1964* (Paris, forthcoming) was unavailable at the time this study was completed.
7 Charles de Gaulle, speech at Bordeaux, 15 May 1947, *Discours et messages,* 2 : 81.

Chapter 1

1 *Journal officiel, annales de l'Assemblée Nationale Constituante élue le 21 octobre 1945* (cited hereafter as *JO, ANC-1*), *Débats,* 11 April 1946, p. 1715.
2 The comprehensive bibliographical essay with which Stephen H. Roberts concludes his *History of French Colonial Policy* provides one of the best available introductions to the French literature on colonial problems and policies of the Third Republic prior to 1930. Among the more important general works are Georges Hardy, *Histoire de la colonisation française;* Charles-André Julien, *La Politique coloniale de la France sous la Révolution, le Premier Empire, et le Restauration;* Henri Brunschwig, *La Colonisation française;* Henri Blet, *France*

d'outre-mer, vol 3, *L'Oeuvre coloniale de la Troisième République* (Paris, 1950); Hubert J. Deschamps, *Les Méthodes et les doctrines coloniales de la France du XVIe siècle à nos jours.* Apart from Roberts's study, there are very few works in English that treat the colonial policies of the Third Republic. Among the most important of these are Herbert I. Priestley, *France Overseas;* Raymond Leslie Buell, *The Native Problem in Africa;* Agnes Murphy, *The Ideology of French Imperialism.*

3 For an interesting criticism of the more important English and European works, see John A. Scott, *Republican Ideas and the Liberal Tradition in France,* p. 12*n*3. The description of republicanism that follows owes much to the scheme presented by ibid., pp. 11–44. Daniel Mornet, *La Pensée française au XVIII*[e] *siècle,* 2d ed. (Paris, 1929), offers a critical analysis of the intellectual background.

4 On the question of centralization of power and its coherence with republican doctrines see Walter R. Sharp, *The Government of the French Republic,* pp. 23–33, 138–39, and the interesting series of essays collected by Robert Pelloux, *Libéralisme, traditionalisme, décentralisation.* Noteworthy among the latter is Georges Gojat's essay "Les Corps intermédiaires et la décentralisation dans l'oeuvre de Tocqueville." Tocqueville argued that the republic ultimately came to be as closely identified with the tradition of centralized political power as the ancien régime, largely because the bourgeois fear of the aristocracy remained strong throughout the first half of the nineteenth century. See his *L'Ancien régime et la Révolution* (Paris, 1856). The problem is evoked also by the liberal writer Lucien Anatole Prévost-Paradol in *La France nouvelle,* while the republican defense of centralized power was restated in the present century by Clemenceau in "Un Débat sur la décentralisation," in Pelloux, *Libéralisme, traditionalisme, décentralisation,* where he commented on arguments offered by Paul Boncour and Charles Maurras. "Seeing themselves dislodged from the central power by the voters in legislative elections," he wrote, "they [Maurras and the supporters of decentralization on the extreme Right] have a notion to take refuge, as in so many fortresses, in the last hiding places that have been kept for them by ignorance, the prejudices of the ancien régime, and the base superstitions of the Roman Church" (p. 159).

5 David Thomson's study *Democracy in France* offers a brief and rewarding analysis of this complex development. Many writers have shared his views, and while what follows is based primarily on Thomson's analysis, other works offer much the same conclusions. For example, Roger Soltau, *French Political Thought in the Nineteenth Century;* Sharp, *French Republic;* and Scott, *Republican Ideas.*

6 This period is given full analysis in Georges Weill, *Histoire du parti républicain en France.* Cf. René Rémond, *La Droite en France de 1815 à nos jours* (Paris, 1954).

7 Soltau, *French Political Thought,* p. 492.

8 "Adresse des deputés de la colonie de St. Domingue par laquelle ils demandent d'être admis aux Etats Généraux," 8 June 1789, reprinted in B. F. Hyslop, *A Guide to the General Cahiers of 1789* (New York, 1936), pp. 418–19. For a very brief analysis of the colonial policies of the revolutionary period, see Pierre François Gonidec, *Droit d'outre-mer,* 1 : 39–52. More complete treatment is given by Julien, *La Politique coloniale.* See also Paul L. J. Gaffarel, *La Politique coloniale de la France de 1789 à 1830,* and J. F. Saintoyant, *La Colonisation française pendant la révolution et l'empire,* 3 vols. (Paris, 1930–31).

9 Robespierre, speech to the Constituent Assembly, 13 May 1791, quoted in Marcel Merle, *L'Anticolonialisme européen de Las Casas à Karl Marx,* pp. 191–92.

10 Lainé, quoted in Marcel Dubois and Auguste Terrier, *Les Colonies françaises,* pp. 103–04.

11 Priestley observes that "the French people showed their disapproval [of the occupation of Algeria] when the minister of the navy, d'Haussez, and the admiral who had led the movement, Duperre, were defeated in their candidacies

for parlement. . . . The new government of Louis Philippe hardly knew what to do with its troublesome heritage" (*France Overseas,* p. 30). See also Brunschwig, *La Colonisation française,* pp. 19–28. The views of the colonial advocates are cited at length in Dubois and Terrier, *Les Colonies françaises,* pp. 117–26. See also Roberts, *History of French Colonial Policy,* p. 6. Among other supporters of the regime, General Foy termed the colonies "useless," while the financier and statesman Jacques Lafitte denounced them as "regrettable" (Deschamps, *Méthodes et doctrines,* p. 99).

12 Deschamps, *Méthodes et doctrines,* p. 105. See also Brunschwig, *La Colonisation française,* pp. 31, 33.

13 Priestley, *France Overseas,* p. 60.

14 Deschamps, *Méthodes et doctrines,* p. 109.

15 Prévost-Paradol, quoted in Dubois and Terrier, *Les Colonies francaises,* p. 268. On the colonial outlook of the Second Empire see especially Brunschwig, *La Colonisation française,* chap. 2. Thomson discusses the social and political structure of the regime in *Democracy in France,* pp. 30–35 and chap. 2; while Soltau offers a detailed analysis of the intellectual reaction under the Second Empire in *French Political Thought,* chaps. 7, 8, and 9.

16 In addition to those works cited in notes 2 and 15, the following offer especially interesting analyses of the policies of the Third Republic during the years before 1914: Arthur Girault, *Principes de colonisation et de législation coloniale,* which went through five editions, the latest in 1927; Joseph Chailley-Bert, *Dix années de politique coloniale;* Jules Harmand, *Domination et colonisation;* and Charles Regismanset, *Questions coloniales.*

17 Gabriel Charmes, *Politique extérieure et coloniale* (Paris, 1885), p. 159.

18 Weill, *Histoire du parti républicain,* pp. 199–200.

19 John F. Cady, *The Roots of French Imperialism in Eastern Asia,* esp. chaps. 2–5.

20 This report is reprinted together with other letters and documents on the antislavery efforts of the Second Republic in Maurice Satineau, *Schoelcher, héros de l'abolition de l'esclavage dans les possessions françaises,* pp. 46–47. An interesting evaluation of Schoelcher's position in the republican tradition of antislavery is offered by Aimé Césaire in his introduction to another collection of documents, Victor Schoelcher, *Esclavage et colonisation.* The policies of the Second Republic are given careful treatment in Roberts, *History of French Colonial Policy,* chaps. 1, 3, and 5.

21 The decree of 22 November 1849 established such a commission. On the role of Schoelcher, see, in addition to the works cited in note 20, Albert Duchêne, *La Politique coloniale de la France,* pp. 196–97. The precedent established by Schoelcher was followed under the Third Republic by the Conseil Supérieur des Colonies. Its success was extremely limited, however, and after only three years of operation it ceased to have any influence over governmental policy. Later it became, as Roberts remarks (*History of French Colonial Policy,* p. 137), "so moribund that it seemed fitting at one time to include dead men in its list of members!"

22 Louis Rolland and Pierre Lampué, *Droit d'outre-mer,* p. 133.

23 Deschamps, *Méthodes et doctrines,* p. 108.

24 Ibid., pp. 111–12. See also Jules Ferry, *Les Affaires de Tunisie,* p. 3.

25 Paul Leroy-Beaulieu, *De la colonisation chez les peuples modernes,* p. xiv. For a detailed description of the polemical and analytical contributions of Leroy-Beaulieu, see Murphy, *The Ideology of French Imperialism,* chaps. 3 and 4.

26 Murphy, *The Ideology of French Imperialism,* chaps. 1 and 2, offers an extensive discussion on the role of French geographical societies in shaping public opinion and stimulating interest in exploration. See also Henri Brunschwig, *Mythes et réalités de l'impérialisme colonial français,* pp. 23–29.

27 See Hubert Deschamps's Introduction to the selected colonial writings of Galliéni,

Galliéni pacificateur, comp. Hubert Deschamps and P. Chauvet (Paris, 1949), pp. 20–26. Writings of other colonial expansionists are collected in Captain Joseph Emile Froelicher, *Trois colonisateurs;* idem, *Une Ame de chef, le gouverneur général Van Vollenhoven* (Paris, 1920).

28 Frederick L. Schuman, *War and Diplomacy in the French Republic,* esp. part 2, pp. 57–128. See also Jacques Bardoux, *La Défaite de Bismarck, l'expansion coloniale française et l'alliance russe* (Paris, 1953).

29 Bardoux, *La Défaite de Bismarck,* p. 168. See also Fresnette Pisani-Ferry, *Jules Ferry et le partage du monde.*

30 *Journal officiel, debats à la Chambre des Députés* (cited hereafter as *JO, Chambre*), 28 July 1885, p. 1670. This speech was bitterly attacked by the radical republicans under the leadership of Clemenceau. For the latter's remarks see *JO, Chambre,* 31 July 1885, pp. 1677–86. It is interesting to compare Ferry's views with those of A. T. Mahan whose great work *The Influence of Seapower upon History* appeared only five years later. Mahan perceived the importance of colonies for the growth of sea power, but saw France as unsuccessful in its colonial quests because the French lacked "a strong natural impulse" to colonize. This argument was revived in a more refined form a decade later by Léopold de Saussure in his *La Psychologie de la colonisation française.* Saussure claimed that "assimilation" was a natural reflex for all Frenchmen whose orientation toward life was shaped by "an ancient faith in the original unity of the human species and in the inherent virtue of a universal formula" (p. 8).

31 *JO, Chambre,* 28 July 1885, p. 1668.

32 Léon Hugonnet, *Le Reveil national* (Paris, 1886), cited in Pisani-Ferry, *Jules Ferry,* p. 41.

33 Frédéric Passy, quoted in Pisani-Ferry, *Jules Ferry,* p. 40.

34 François Goguel, *La Politique des partis sous la IIIe République,* pp. 68–69.

35 Pisani-Ferry, *Jules Ferry,* p. 245.

36 *JO, Chambre,* 11 May 1890, p. 750. Roberts, *History of French Colonial Policy,* p. 21, refers to this speech and observes, "Obvious as it may seem now, it was a unique conception in the France of 1890 to visualize an Empire from the Chad to the sea and the Congo to the Mediterranean, and even to postulate any unified plan." The debate concerned an expedition to Dahomey, and its outcome turned primarily on the principle of protecting the "honor of the flag."

37 Cf. Paul L. T. Gaffarel, *Notre expansion coloniale en Afrique,* chap. 4., and Brunschwig, *Mythes et réalités,* pp. 111–37, on the role of the colonial press during this period.

38 Dubois and Terrier, *Les Colonies françaises,* p. 1031.

39 See, for example, the debate over the special budget for Algeria in 1904: *JO, Chambre,* 18 February 1904, pp. 397–436, 440–53, 460–78; the budget for Tunisia: *JO, Chambre,* 4 March 1905, pp. 755–73; and the general debate on the colonial budget for 1905: *JO, Chambre,* 2 February 1905, pp. 126–43, 148–71. See also Blet, *France d'outre-mer,* vol. 3; Jean Marie Antoine de Lanessan, *Principes de colonisation;* and idem, *Les Missions et leur protectorat* (Paris, 1907).

40 Harmand, *Domination et colonisation,* pp. 8–9. For a discussion of Harmand's contribution to colonial theory see Gonidec, *Droit d'outre-mer,* 1 : 95–96.

Chapter 2

1 Albert Sarraut, *La Mise en valeur des colonies françaises,* pp. 36–61.

2 H. W. V. Temperley, *History of the Peace Conference at Paris,* 6 vols. (London, 1924), 6 : 500–23. See also Quincy Wright, *Mandates under the League of Nations,* pp. 24–33.

3 Henri Simon, in *JO, Chambre,* 17 September 1919, p. 4393.

4 Ibid., p. 4395. See also Etienne Antonelli, *L'Afrique et la paix de Versailles.*

5 *Journal officiel, Débats au Sénat* (cited hereafter as *JO, Sénat*), 19 February 1920, p. 17.
6 Sarraut, *Mise en valeur,* p. 18.
7 Ibid., p. 17.
8 Ibid., p. 19. Morel's remarks are quoted on p. 29, and Sarraut's response appears on pp. 29–30.
9 Albert Sarraut, *Grandeur et servitude coloniales,* p. 20.
10 Sarraut, *Mise en valeur,* pp. 88–89.
11 Ibid., pp. 103, 114–27. See also Sarraut, *Grandeur et servitude,* pp. 166–71.
12 Sarraut, *Mise en valeur,* p. 116.
13 Prosper Enfantin, *Oeuvres de Saint-Simon et d'Enfantin,* 16 vols. (Paris, 1866). vol. 11, quoted in Merle, *L'Anti-colonialisme,* pp. 348–49.
14 Etienne Cabet, quoted in Merle, *L'Anti-colonialisme,* pp. 354–55.
15 Marcel Emerit, *Les Saint-Simoniens en Algérie.*
16 Jean Léon Jaurès, *Oeuvres de Jean Jaurès,* 5 : 90–92. See also Jean Bruhat, "Jaurès devant le problème colonial," *Cahiers Internationaux de Sociologie* 10 (March 1958) : 43–62. Jaurès's speeches on colonial problems of 1908 were later reprinted in Jean Léon Jaurès, *Contre la guerre au Maroc* (Paris, 1936).
17 Jean Léon Jaurès, *Dépêche de Toulouse,* 6 October 1912. See also Robert Thomas, "La Politique socialiste et le problème colonial de 1915 à 1920," *Revu Française d'Histoire d'Outre-Mer* 47 (1960) : 241–44; and Harvey Goldberg, *Jean Jaurès.*
18 Léon Blum, Speech at the SFIO Congress, 1945, quoted in Georges Lefranc, *Jaurès et le socialisme des intellectuels* (Paris, 1968), pp. 144–45. See also Manuela Semidi, "Les Socialistes français et le problème coloniale entre les deux guerres (1919–39)," *Revue Française de Science Politique* 18 (1968) : 1115–54.
19 The principal texts have been collected in Karl Marx and Friedrich Engels, *On Colonialism.*
20 Karl Marx, "British Rule in India," *New York Daily Tribune,* 25 June 1853, reprinted in Marx and Engels, *On Colonialism,* pp. 38–39.
21 Friedrich Engels, Letter to Bernstein, reprinted in Marx and Engels, *On Colonialism,* p. 338.
22 Demetrio Boersner, *The Bolsheviks and the National and Colonial Question,* pp. 23–27.
23 Karl Marx and Friedrich Engels, *Historisch-Kritische Gesamtausgabe,* edited for the Marx-Engels-Lenin Institute (Moscow) by N. Riazanov and V. Adoratsky, 7 vols. (Berlin, 1931), 3 : 336–37, 341–42, and Karl Marx, *Correspondence* (New York, 1934), pp. 207–08; quoted in Boersner, *Bolsheviks,* p. 22. See also Reinhold Niebuhr, *The Structure of Nations and Empires,* chap. 14.
24 From the documentary record of the Stuttgart Congress, *Internationaler Sozialisten-Kongress zu Stuttgart 18. bis 24. August 1907,* p. 24; quoted in Boersner, *Bolsheviks,* p. 30.
25 *The Communist International, 1919–1943,* documents selected and edited by Jane Degras, 3 vols. (London, 1965), 2 : 532.
26 Ibid., pp. 546, 547–48.
27 The major texts have been collected and briefly annotated in Jakob Moneta, *Die Kolonialpolitik der französischen KP* (Hanover, 1968); the official doctrine is outlined in Georges Polizer, *Principes fondamentaux de philosophie* (Paris, 1954), pp. 471–81, 503–18. Another selection of texts was published by the Communist party in 1963 under the title *La Lutte du parti communiste français contre le colonialisme.* See also Jacques Arnault, *Le Procès du colonialisme.*
28 "Résolution du VIIe Comité Executif (élargi) de l'Internationale Communiste," quoted in André Marty, "Notions d'histoire," Cours 17, Parti Communiste Français (7 January–10 May 1952), app. 3 (mimeo). See also "Extracts from a Manifesto of the Eastern Bureau of the ECCI against the War in Morocco," in *The Communist International, 1919–43,* 2 : 220–22.
29 Quoted in Angelo Tasca [Rossi], *A Communist Party in Action,* p. 75.
30 In the Treaty of London, Britain had agreed to grant Italy large slices of the

Austrian territory; an indemnity and a promise of compensation in case the other Allies made colonial gains at the expense of the Central Powers; plus a share in the eventual partition of Asia Minor in exchange for her participation on the Allied side. For a discussion of the London pact and the secret treaties see Temperley, *History of the Peace Conference,* 1 : 169–70, 4 : 287–95, 6 : 1–22.

31 Priestley, *France Overseas,* provides a description of the colonial conflicts in Tunisia, Morocco, Egypt, and the Levant. As he observes, "France was determined to hug the obligations of colonialism because she still wished to maintain the grandeur" (p. 408). See also Emanuel Moresco, *Colonial Questions and Peace.*

32 Colonial questions were treated in two works that grew out of the Tenth International Studies Conference in Paris in 1937: *Peaceful Change: Procedures, Population Pressure, the Colonial Question, Raw Materials, and Markets: Proceedings of the Tenth International Studies Conference* (Paris, 1938), and Moresco, *Colonial Questions and Peace.* On the role of the IIIC see Quincy Wright, *Mandates,* pp. 79–86.

33 Charles-André Julien, *L'Afrique du nord en marche,* pp. 63–65.

34 For brief accounts of early nationalist activity in French Africa see Lamine-Guèye, *Etapes et perspectives de l'union française,* pp. 37–44; Hubert J. Deschamps, *L'Union française,* chap. 4; François Joseph Amon d'Aby, *La Cote d'Ivoire dans la cité africaine,* pp. 33–38; Jean de La Roche and Jean Gottman, *La Fedération française,* pp. 457–532. On kakisme and other messianic movements see Georges Balandier, "Messianismes et nationalismes en Afrique Noire," *Cahiers Internationaux de Sociologie* 14 (1953) : 41–65. The development of the trade union movement in Africa is discussed in A. Hauser, "Quelques relations des travailleurs de l'industrie à leur travail en AOF," *Bulletin de l'IFAN,* series B, 16 (1954) : 129–41.

35 Sarraut, *Grandeur et servitude coloniales.*

36 Duchêne, *La Politique coloniale,* p. 314. Similarly, Regismanset, another colonial official, declared, "The so-called policy of association will make France lose her colonial empire unless it is replaced with something less destructive." Quoted in Deschamps, *Méthodes et doctrines,* p. 169.

37 A. R. Fontaine, *Essai d'une politique indigène en Indochine* (Paris, 1927); Henri Labouret, *À la recherche d'une politique indigène dans l'Ouest Africain* (Paris, 1931); Robert Delavignette, *Les Paysans noirs;* idem, *Soudan-Paris-Bourgogne* (Paris, 1935); idem, *Les Vrais Chefs de l'empire* (Paris, 1939); idem, *Service africain* (Paris, 1946). The last was published in a revised English translation under the title *Freedom and Authority in French West Africa;* cf. Governor-General Marcel Olivier's reflections, *Six Ans de politique sociale à Madagascar.* See also Raoul Girardet, "L'Apothéose de 'la plus grande France'; l'idée coloniale devant l'opinion française (1930–35)," *Revue Française de Science Politique* 18 (1968) : 1085–1114.

38 Hubert Deschamps recalls this judgment, which he made in 1938, in *Méthodes et doctrines,* p. 172.

39 Kenneth Robinson, "Political Developments in French West Africa," in *Africa in the Modern World,* ed. Calvin W. Stillman, pp. 140–51.

40 Maurice Violette presented his experience in Algeria in *L'Algérie vivra-t-elle?.* For an excellent analysis of the attitudes of the various parties in Parliament on the Blum Violette plan see Marie-Renée Mouton, "L'Algérie devant le parlement français de 1935 à 1938," *Revue Française de Science Politique* 12 (March 1962) : 93–128.

41 See Julien, *L'Afrique du nord,* pp. 126–36.

42 Mouton, "L'Algérie devant le parlement français," pp. 121–23.

43 These were, respectively, the decrees of 8 September 1936, 20 March 1937, and 11 March 1937. See Pierre François Gonidec and Jean Kirsch, *Droit du travail dans les territoires d'outre-mer,* p. 40, and Pierre François Gonidec, "Une Mystique de l'égalité: le code du travail des territoires d'outre-mer," *Revue*

Juridique et Politique de l'Union Française (cited hereafter as *RJPUF*) 7 (1953): 176–96.

44 On the problem of forced labor and the development of trade unions in the overseas territories see: Gonidec and Kirsch, *Droit du travail,* pp. 21–48. Governor-General Olivier's *Six Ans de politique sociale* contains a defense of the practice of forced labor that was fairly widely accepted in the 1930s.

45 *L'Afrique Française* 46 (May 1936): 250–51.

Chapter 3

1 The most evenhanded treatment of Vichy France is to be found in Robert Aron and Georgette Elgey, *Histoire de Vichy.* Paul Farmer, *Vichy,* is also valuable, particularly for its insight into foreign policy issues.

2 Maxime Weygand, *Mémoires,* 3 : 321–23.

3 The evolution of Nazi propaganda on colonial questions is surveyed by Fritz T. Epstein, "National Socialism and French Colonialism," *Journal of Central European Studies* 3 (April 1943) : 52–64. A characteristic example of that literature is Karl Hanel, *Das Französische Kolonialreich* (Leipzig, 1940).

4 Robert Aron, *De l'armistice à l'insurrection nationale,* pp. 272–84; Henri Michel, *Vichy, année 40,* pp. 188–94. The role of Weygand is examined in Guy Raissac, *Un Soldat dans la tempête* (Paris, 1963). An overview of the relations between Hitler and Vichy by a postwar German scholar, Eberhard Jäckel, *Frankreich in Hitler's Europa* (Stuttgart, 1966), confirms the marginal role of the colonies in the thinking of both governments.

5 Pierre Boisson, quoted in Maurice Martin du Gard, *La Carte impériale* (Paris, 1949), p. 136. See also ibid., pp. 76–80, and Jacques Soustelle, *Envers et contre tout,* 1 : 94–99.

6 Robert Aron and Elgey, *Histoire de Vichy,* pp. 172–75. The recruitment of Vichy elites reflected a variety of different pressures at various times, and generalizations about them have been shown to be often false. For a general overview see ibid., pp. 160–82, 371–89, 491–507, 654–60.

7 De Gaulle, *Discours et messages,* 1 : 3.

8 Among the most important of de Gaulle's writings, in addition to his *Mémoires de guerre,* are: *Le Fil de l'épée; Vers l'armée de métier;* and the collected speeches, *Discours et messages,* cited in note 7. In addition see *La Discorde chez l'ennemi* and *La France et son armée.*

9 Stanley Hoffman, "De Gaulle's Memoirs: The Hero as History," *World Politics* 13 (October 1960) : 140–60; David Thomson, *Two Frenchmen;* Robert Aron, *An Explanation of de Gaulle* (New York, 1966); Paul-Marie de La Gorce, *De Gaulle entre deux mondes.*

10 See de Gaulle's Preface to his *Le Fil de l'épée.*

11 De Gaulle, *Mémoires de guerre,* vol. 1, *L'appel, 1940–42* (cited hereafter as de Gaulle, 1), p. 1.

12 De Gaulle, *Mémoires de guerre,* vol. 2, *L'unité, 1942–44* (cited hereafter as de Gaulle, 2), p. 516.

13 Alfred Grosser, *French Foreign Policy under de Gaulle,* p. 23.

14 De Gaulle and General Spears give contradictory accounts of these critical events in their respective memoirs, which subsequent historians have been unable to resolve. See Robert Aron, *An Explanation of de Gaulle,* chap. 1, for a brief overview of the period.

15 La Gorce, *De Gaulle entre deux mondes,* pp. 206–07.

16 De Gaulle, speech of 18 June 1940, *Discours et messages,* 1 : 3–4.

17 De Gaulle, speech of 19 June 1940, ibid, pp. 4–5. See also de Gaulle, 1 : 111, 196–99, 309–10.

18 Martin du Gard, *La Carte impériale,* pp. 76–90.

19 Ibid., pp. 49–95; Soustelle, *Envers et contre tout,* 1 : 101–37.
20 De Gaulle, *Discours et messages,* 1 : 18–19. See also the speeches of 3 August, 27 August, and 11 November 1940, ibid., pp. 21–22, 30–31, 40–42; and Soustelle, *Envers et contre tout,* 1 : 104.
21 De Gaulle, 1 : 523–24.
22 Ibid., pp. 504, 515, 536–40.
23 De Gaulle, *Mémoires de guerre,* vol. 3, *Le Salut, 1944–46* (cited hereafter as de Gaulle, 3), p. 84.
24 De Gaulle, 2 : 237–38.
25 Ibid., p. 240; see also 1 : 478, 2 : 565, 3 : 179–232.
26 See Arthur L. Funk, *Charles de Gaulle,* esp. chap. 5.
27 De Gaulle, 1 : 565–71.
28 Ibid., 3 : 223.
29 Ibid., 1 : 119, 303–05, 314–17.
30 Ibid., 3 : 196. See also Thomson, *Two Frenchmen,* p. 239.
31 De Gaulle, *Discours et messages,* 253–56.
32 De Gaulle, 3 : 105, 2 : 86–87, 381–85, 631.
33 Ibid., 3 : 21.
34 See de Gaulle, *La Discorde chez l'ennemi.*
35 La Gorce offers an excellent analysis of this period in *De Gaulle entre deux mondes,* pp. 163–65.
36 Ibid., pp. 278–94.
37 Quoted in Tasca, *A Communist Party in Action,* p. 76.
38 *L'Humanité,* 1 July 1940.
39 *Journal officiel, Assemblée Consultative Provisoire* (cited hereafter as *JO, ACP*), 21 November 1944, p. 311. Speech of Florimonde Bonte, one of only four Communist party deputies who were named to the Consultative Assembly.
40 De Gaulle, 2 : 126.
41 Ibid., 3 : 90, 130.
42 *JO, ACP,* 21 November 1944, p. 331. See also de Gaulle, 1 : 69–74, 127–29; and de Gaulle's speech of 7 May 1944, *Discours et messages,* 1 : 401–05.
43 De Gaulle, 2 : 3.

Chapter 4

1 De Gaulle, 2 : 567–68.
2 The Ministry of the Colonies published a transcript of the Brazzaville Conference entitled *Conférence africaine française de Brazzaville, 30 janvier–8 fevrier 1944* (cited hereafter as *Conférence de Brazzaville*).
3 Ibid., p. 28.
4 Ibid., pp. 29–30.
5 Ibid., p. 30.
6 Michel Devèze, *La France d'outre-mer,* p. 216.
7 The report is reprinted as an appendix in La Roche and Gottman, *La Fédération française,* pp. 586–627.
8 The recommendations of the Brazzaville Conference are summarized in Henri Michel and Boris Mirkine-Guetzévitch, *Les Idées politiques et sociales de la Résistance,* p. 339, and are briefly reviewed in "L'Evolution recénte des institutions politiques dans les territoires d'outre-mer et territoires associés," La Documentation française, *Notes et Etudes Documentaires,* no. 1847 (11 March 1954).
9 For two contemporary critiques of the conference, see Henry Solus, "La conférence de Brazzaville," *Le Monde Français* 2 (October 1945) : 54–62; and Jean Dresch, "Des Recommendations de Brazzaville à la constitution de l'union française," *Politique Etrangère* 11 (1946) : 167–78.
10 Michel and Mirkine-Guetzévitch, *Idées politiques et sociales,* p. 340.

11 Ibid., p. 341.
12 See Gonidec, *Droit d'outre-mer,* 1 : 185–91.
13 Michel and Mirkine-Guetzévitch, *Idées politiques et sociales,* p. 349.
14 Ibid., p. 340.
15 Ibid., p. 349.
16 Ibid., pp. 349, 353. Italics added.
17 "L'Evolution recénte des institutions politiques," p. 4.
18 Ibid.
19 Dresch, "Des Recommendations de Brazzaville," pp. 174–77.
20 All quotations are from "L'Evolution récente des institutions politiques," pp. 4–5.
21 Devèze, *La France d'outre-mer,* p. 181; La Roche and Gottman, *La Féderation française,* p. 536.
22 *Conférence de Brazzaville,* p. 21. See also de Gaulle, 2 : 184–86.
23 On wartime effects of forced labor see Gonidec and Kirsch, *Droit du travail,* pp. 40–48, 472–79, 539–44, 691–96.
24 De Gaulle, 2 : 182.
25 De Gaulle, *Discours et messages,* 1 : 353–54.
26 Julien, *L'Afrique du nord,* pp. 281, 284, 290–94.
27 Ibid., pp. 295–96.
28 Ferhat Abbas, *La Nuit coloniale,* gives an account of these events and an evaluation of the French policy in Algeria.
29 On the Casablanca Conference and the Free French see Funk, *Charles de Gaulle,* chap. 2, esp. pp. 83–88. Roosevelt's remarks were reported by Elliott Roosevelt, *As He Saw It,* pp. 115–16. The rise of nationalism in Morocco is analyzed in Robert Rezette, *Les Partis politiques marocains,* pp. 140–62, 173–88; and Robert Montagne, *Révolution au Maroc.*
30 Julien, *L'Afrique du nord,* pp. 95–101, 175–77. See also Habib Bourguiba, *La Tunisie et la France,* pp. 184–87.
31 General Alphonse Juin, *Mémoires,* 2 : 189–90. Roger Le Tourneau, *Evolution politique de l'Afrique du nord musulmane,* p. 105.
32 Bourguiba, *La Tunisie et la France,* p. 186. The 1942 statement appears in a secret letter to Habib Thamer, chief of the clandestine political bureau of the Neo-Destour, dated 8 August and smuggled to him from prison (ibid., pp. 177–182; and Julien, *L'Afrique du nord,* pp. 92–97). The social composition of the Neo-Destour is examined in *Tunisia,* edited by Charles A. Micaud, pp. 79–88. See also Félix Garas, *Bourguiba et la naissance d'une nation.*
33 Bourguiba, *La Tunisie et la France,* pp. 188, 192.
34 Ibid., pp. 195–96. See also Le Tourneau, *Evolution de l'Afrique du nord,* pp. 105–16.
35 David Gordon, *The Passing of French Algeria,* pp. 31–33.
36 Le Tourneau, *Evolution de l'Afrique du nord,* p. 347.
37 The events summarized here have been documented by many writers, including Robert Aron et al., *Les Origines de la guerre d'Algerie;* Julien, *L'Afrique du nord* (who cites the casualty figures, p. 303); Thomas Oppermann, *Le Problème algérien;* Charles Gallagher, *The United States and North Africa* (Cambridge, Mass., 1963); Gordon, *The Passing of French Algeria;* and le Tournèau, *Evolution de l'Afrique du nord,* pp. 348–54.
38 Le Tourneau, *Evolution de l'Afrique du nord,* p. 353.
39 For a detailed discussion of prewar administrative arrangements in French West Africa, see Buell, *The Native Problem in Africa;* Lord Hailey, *An African Survey;* and Delavignette, *Freedom and Authority.* A useful summary is offered by Robinson, "Political Developments," pp. 142–51.
40 Thomas Hodgkin and Ruth Schachter, *French-speaking West Africa in Transition,* p. 386. In addition, other writers have pointed to the appearance of specific regional organizations with broad programs of social and political reform. See Amon d'Aby, *La Côte d'Ivoire,* pp. 36–37; also, Thomas Hodgkin,

Nationalism in Colonial Africa, pp. 142–46, and his "Political Parties in British and French West Africa," *Information Digest,* no. 10 (London, 1953).

41 Hodgkin and Schachter, *French-speaking West Africa,* p. 387.

42 Amon d'Aby, *La Côte d'Ivoire,* pp. 41–44. In the Ivory Coast, Prince Kouamé Adingra led about ten thousand of his followers, together with his aged father, Kouadio Adjoumani, king of Bondoukou, into exile in the Gold Coast.

43 Devèze, *La France d'outre-mer,* pp. 157–58. De Gaulle mentions this incident in his *Mémoires,* 2 : 31. See also La Roche and Gottman, *La Fédération française,* p. 533.

44 Priestley, *France Overseas,* pp. 369–93. On the origins of French concern with the Middle East, see Robert de Gontaut-Biron, *Comment la France s'est installée en Syrie* (Paris, 1923), and Etienne Lamy, *La France du Levant* (Paris, 1900).

45 De Gaulle, 2 : 158–80, esp. pp. 164–68, 171–75. The crisis is discussed from the point of view of Vichy in Martin du Gard, *La Carte impériale,* pp. 191–221.

46 De Gaulle, 2 : 202–03.

47 Ibid., pp. 194–99.

48 Cordell Hull mentions the president's irritation about this affair in his *Memoirs,* 2 : 1245. See also Funk, *Charles de Gaulle,* pp. 195–205.

49 Hull, *Memoirs,* 2 : 1544.

50 *Communiqué,* Roosevelt to Hull (27 November 1943), p. 1245.

51 De Gaulle, speech of 14 March 1945, *Discours et messages,* pp. 532–34.

52 A sensitive eyewitness report of conditions in Indochina during this tragic period is offered by Paul Mus, "L'Indochine en 1945," *Politique Etrangère* 11 (1946): 349–74, 432–64. See also his *Le Destin de l'union française,* and Ellen J. Hammer, *The Struggle for Indochina.*

53 De Gaulle, 3 : 227. On French plans for the reoccupation of Indochina and United States reactions see Marcel Vigneras, *Rearming the French,* chap. 24.

54 The origins of this text and the ambiguities surrounding the meaning of the term *French Union* are explained in Mus, *Le Destin de l'union française,* pp. 82–86.

55 De Gaulle, 3 : 226.

56 Albert Duchêne, "La notion française du protectorat," *Le Monde Français* 2 (1946) : 386.

57 De Gaulle, *Discours et messages,* 1 : 533–34.

58 Amon d'Aby, *La Côte d'Ivoire,* p. 54.

59 *Le Monde,* 14 July 1945; *Année Politique,* 1944–45, pp. 245–48.

60 The general features of the electoral procedure are discussed in Raoul Husson, ed., *Elections et réferendums,* which provides a complete summary of the results. In table 1, compiled from these data, the figures in the column "Voters" are those given for the number of registered voters (*inscrits*) in the election of 21 October 1945.

61 *Le Monde,* 11 July 1945.

Chapter 5

1 Léon Blum, *L'Oeuvre de Léon Blum,* vol. 6, *Naissance de la Quatrième République,* pp. 25–26.

2 The Communist claim to have lost 75,000 members during the occupation has frequently been disputed; but if it is considered to represent total losses from all causes, it is probably accurate. Not all of the 75,000 were executed by the Nazis, however, as the party slogan implied.

3 Georgette Elgey, *La République des illusions,* p. 16.

4 Etienne Fajon, quoted in *Année Politique,* 1944–45, p. 234.

5 Alfred J. Rieber, *Stalin and the French Communist Party, 1941–47* (New York and London, Columbia University Press, 1962), chaps. 9, 12, provides a detailed

analysis of the relationship between the French Communist party and the Soviet Union during this period.

6 De Gaulle, quoted in Elgey, *La République des illusions,* p. 80.

7 Ibid., pp. 192–93.

8 Ibid., p. 106.

9 See chapter 6 for a discussion of the Indochina problem.

10 Gordon Wright, *The Reshaping of French Democracy,* p. 179.

11 De Gaulle, speech at Bayeux, *Discours et messages,* 2 : 5–11.

12 De Gaulle, declaration of 27 August, statement of 19 September, and speech at Epinal, 29 September, ibid., pp. 18–33.

13 Elgey, *La République des illusions,* pp. 215–16.

14 De Gaulle, declaration of 9 October 1946, *Discours et messages,* 2 : 34.

15 According to one well-qualified commentator, "Most of the West African deputies owed their election in 1945 to some administrative support" (Ruth Schachter Morgenthau, *Political Parties in French-speaking West Africa,* p. 84).

16 See Amon d'Aby, *La Côte d'Ivoire,* chap. 2, and Edward Mortimer, *France and the Africans,* pp. 60–70, for a description of conditions surrounding the 1945 elections.

17 Ferhat Abbas, *Le Jeune algérien,* quoted in Jean Lacouture, *Cinq hommes et la France,* p. 272.

18 Ferhat Abbas, *Manifeste du peuple algérien,* quoted in Lacouture, *Cinq hommes et la France,* p. 285.

19 Abbas, *La Nuit coloniale,* pp. 160–61.

20 Oppermann, *Le Problème algérien,* p. 72.

21 Abbas, *La Nuit coloniale,* p. 164.

22 Ibid., p. 169. The indemnities were never paid because the governor-general's office insisted that the matter had been closed. Abbas denied that any settlement was reached and asserted, "No Algerian ever received what was due him. On the other side, all Frenchmen were indemnified. There was arbitrariness even in the face of death!"

23 "Proposition de loi tendant à établir la Constitution de la République Algérienne," *Journal officiel, Assemblée Nationale Constituante élue le 2 juin 1946* (cited hereafter as *JO, ANC-2*), *Documents Parlementaires,* no. 358, 2 August 1946, pp. 309–12.

24 Abbas, *La Nuit coloniale,* p. 168.

25 The eleven UDMA deputies were almost all members of the liberal professions: three were doctors (Ben Khelil, Francis, Saadane), one a pharmacist (Abbas), three lawyers (Hadj Saïd, Mostefai el-Hadi, Sator), two professors (Boutarene, Mehdad), one landowner (Bey Laggoun), and only one commercial employee (Ben Keddache) (ibid., pp. 162–63). The local administrator in Sétif characterized the UDMA as a moderate party and explained, "Even if their program is nationalist, they are men of Western culture, they look toward Paris rather than Cairo, and their avowed preference is for a policy of cooperation with France rather than for the violent methods of Messali" ("Rapport des authorités locales, Sétif," reprinted in Robert Aron et al., *Les Origines de la guerre d'Algérie,* p. 309).

26 Abbas, *La Nuit coloniale,* p. 169.

27 Lacouture, *Cinq hommes et la France,* p. 304.

28 *JO, ANC-2, Débats,* 28 September 1946, pp. 4230–32. Details of the incident were reported in *Le Monde,* 1 October 1946.

29 See Morgenthau, *Political Parties in West Africa,* pp. 74–90.

30 Ibid., p. 83.

31 Ibid., p. 133.

32 Lamine-Guèye, *Etapes et perspectives de l'union française,* p. 9.

33 In addition to matters of budget and personnel, the Committee on Overseas Territories played an important role in shaping administrative regulations and

legislation dealing with political freedoms, labor conditions, police powers, and citizenship for natives of the overseas territories. See ibid., p. 56.

34 Morgenthau, *Political Parties in West Africa,* pp. 137–38.

35 A summary transcript (*Comptes-rendus Analytiques*) of the discussions of the Constitutional Committee was published as *Séances de la Commission de la Constitution, Assemblée Nationale Constituante élue le 21 octobre 1945.* A second volume covered those of the Second Constituent Assembly elected 2 June 1946. They are cited hereafter in shortened form as *ANC-1, C/C* and *ANC-2, C/C.*

36 Devèze, *La France d'outre-mer,* pp. 222, 225, 268.

37 Latrille, quoted in Georges Chaffard, *Les Carnets secrets de la décolonisation,* 1 : 36.

38 Ibid., 1 : 102–03.

39 Morgenthau, *Political Parties in West Africa,* pp. 78–79.

40 *JO, ANC-2, Débats,* 19 September 1946, p. 3850.

41 A few French writers have maintained that the April Draft Constitution was rejected both overseas and in the metropole. Thus, Devèze discovered "a preponderant vote" against it, *La France d'outre-mer,* pp. 262–63, and Henri Culmann agreed, *L'Union française,* pp. 46–47. Compare, Dorothy Maud Pickles, *French Politics,* p. 155, and Morgenthau, *Political Parties in West Africa,* p. 43 and app. 6.

42 Devèze, *La France d'outre-mer,* p. 267.

43 Morgenthau, *Political Parties in West Africa,* p. 46.

44 Devèze, *La France d'outre-mer,* p. 267.

45 See for example the remarks of M. Castellani, *JO, ANC-2, Débats,* 19 September 1946, p. 3851.

46 Devèze, *La France d'outre-mer,* pp. 265–67, summarizes the proposals of the Etats Généraux and quotes portions of their resolutions. All quotations included here are taken from that account.

47 Ibid., pp. 254, 271; Amon d'Aby, *La Côte d'Ivoire,* p. 54.

48 *Témoignage Chrétien,* 7 September 1945. Col. F. Bernard, "L'Indochine restera française si," quoted in Jean-Pierre Gault, *Histoire d'une fidelité,* p. 221.

49 *Témoignage Chrétien,* 30 November 1945, quoted in ibid. At this time, the Vietnamese Catholics were participating in the government of Ho Chi Minh and agitating in favor of independence. The subsequent disruption of the nationalist coalition threw them over to the side of the French, and they then became bitterly anti-Communist. Metropolitan Catholic opinion followed the same general pattern.

50 Marcel Merle, "Les facteurs religieux de la politique extérieure française," *Forces religieuses et attitudes politiques dans la France contemporaine,* ed. René Rémond, chap. 6. See also, Gault, *Histoire d'une fidelité,* chap. 6, esp. pp. 217–28. For a different assessment of the Church's role, see François Méjan, *Le Vatican contre la France d'outre-mer.* At a later period many of the same problems were also discussed in Protestant journals such as *Le Semeur, Foi et Vie,* and *Christianisme Sociale.*

51 Peter Novick, *The Resistance versus Vichy* (New York, Columbia University Press, 1968), provides the most complete analysis of the post-liberation purges in English. According to his estimates, the number of cases heard by the French courts was 124,751. Of these, 2,853 were condemned to death but only 767 were executed. In addition, penalties involving hard labor or imprisonment were meted out to 38,266. In total, approximately one-half of 1 percent of the entire state bureaucracy was purged. (*Resistance versus Vichy,* pp. 184–88). The impact of the purges on the colonial service was significant, but the long-run effects were minor according to William B. Cohen, *Rulers of Empire,* pp. 169–70. Jean-Baptiste Duroselle examines their effect on the diplomatic service in "French Diplomacy in the Postwar World," in Stephen D. Kertesz and Matthew A. Fitzsimmons, *Diplomacy in a Changing World,* pp. 216–17.

52 Chaffard, *Carnets secrets,* 1 : 34.
53 Lacouture, *Cinq hommes et la France,* p. 199.
54 Devèze, *La France d'outre-mer,* p. 249.
55 Chaffard, *Carnets secrets,* 1 : 62–3.
56 The incidents in the Ivory Coast are described by Chaffard, *Carnets secrets,* 1 : 35–59. The situation in Morocco is reported by Lacouture, *Cinq hommes et la France,* pp. 200–02; Julien, *L'Afrique du nord,* p. 363.
57 Mus, *Le Destin de l'union française,* p. 227.

Chapter 6

1 U.S., Department of State, *The United Nations Conference on International Organization,* p. 235. The French delegate, M. Naggiar, exaggerated the lack of direction in the Dumbarton Oaks proposals but may have accurately captured the spirit of his own delegation when he observed, "We felt somewhat like Cinderella, inasmuch as we had no shoes with which to walk" (ibid., p. 682).
2 De Gaulle, 3 : 199.
3 Ibid., p. 201. See also his speech of 25 April 1945, *Discours et messages,* 1 : 544.
4 Paul Giacobbi, *Le Monde,* 22 March 1945.
5 U.S., Department of State, *The United Nations Conference on International Organization, Documents,* 10 : 622 (Doc. 115, II/4/44, 20 June 1945, Annex D). See also United Nations, General Assembly, *Report of the Fourth Committee on Trusteeship Agreements* (A/258), 1946, summarized in *International Organization* 1 (1947) : 208–16. See also Huntington Gilchrist, "Colonial Questions at the San Francisco Conference," *American Political Science Review* 39 (1945): 981–87.
6 United Nations, General Assembly, *Verbatim Records of the Plenary Meetings,* 18 January 1946, p. 251.
7 United Nations, General Assembly, *Summary Records of the Fourth Committee* (Part 1), 11 December 1946, p. 162.
8 Ibid., p. 163. The Indian representative, Mr. Menon, caustically observed that the French statements regarding administration "as an integral part" had little value. "The statements of the French representative affirming that this phrase did not imply French sovereignty over the territories covered by the French agreements were invalidated by the appearance before the committee of a member of the French parliament [Douala Manga Bell] who was a citizen of the Cameroons, a territory under French administration. It would have been impossible for him to be elected to the sovereign parliament of France unless the Cameroons were under French sovereignty" (ibid., p. 169).
9 *ANC-1, C/C,* 18 January 1946, p. 243.
10 Louis Aujoulat, Interpellation no. 43, *JO, ANC-1, Débats,* 21 February 1946, p. 422.
11 Statements of Aujoulat, *JO, ANC-1, Débats,* 20 March 1946, p. 902; see also statements of Jean Pierre-Bloch and Douala Manga Bell, ibid., pp. 907, 908.
12 Soustelle, ibid., p. 1033.
13 Aujoulat, ibid., p. 903.
14 Bidault, ibid., p. 1038.
15 François Borella, *L'Évolution politique et juridique de l'union française depuis 1946,* pp. 103–04.
16 Ibid.
17 A revealing discussion of the subsequent impact of the United Nations trusteeship system is offered by David E. Gardinier, *Cameroon, United Nations Challenge to French Policy.*
18 The Japanese had seized some offshore islands near Hainan in 1939. In August 1940 Vichy signed an agreement giving up control over the Yunnan railway,

which was being used to carry American military aid to China. A second agreement of 9 May 1941 conceded part of Cambodia to Siam, then an ally of Japan; and in July 1941 a third concession permitted Japanese troops to enter southern Indochina. The French garrison in Indochina at that time consisted of roughly 90,000 poorly armed troops. They were without any chance of resupply or reinforcement and had neither air nor naval support. Hence, Admiral Decoux had no possibility of resisting Japanese demands. See Admiral Jean Decoux, *A la barre de l'Indochine,* part 1.

19 Philippe Devillers, *Histoire du Viet-Nam de 1940–1952,* p. 142. This work is the most careful study of events in Indochina currently available. The summary of events given here is derived primarily from it and from a later book by Devillers and Jean Lacouture, *Vietnam.*

20 De Gaulle, press conference of 10 July 1944, *Discours et messages,* 1 : 418.

21 De Gaulle, message of 15 February 1945, ibid., pp. 520–21.

22 *Journal officiel, Assemblée Consultative Provisoire, Débats,* 12 March 1945, p. 437 (cited hereafter as *JO, ACP, Débats*).

23 De Gaulle, radio address of 14 March 1945, *Discours et messages,* 1 : 532–34.

24 *JO, ACP, Débats,* 20 March 1945, p. 596.

25 Ibid. p. 558.

26 Ibid., 1 August 1945, p. 1722.

27 Jean Sainteny, *Histoire d'une paix manquée,* p. 47. See also Mus, *Le Destin de l'union française,* p. 43.

28 *JO, ACP, Débats,* 19 March 1945; statement of Hettier de Boislambert, p. 556; statement of Gaston Monnerville, pp. 563–64.

29 De Gaulle's concluding phrase ("Nous sommes tous parfaitement rassemblés") was ambiguous; it seems to have been intended not simply as a statement of shared sentiments but as a recognition of the continuing necessity for his own leadership. This interpretation is supported by the comments of de Gaulle's secretary at the time, Claude Mauriac, in *Un Autre de Gaulle,* pp. 116–17.

30 According to a Reuters dispatch, there were 89,000 French troops in Indochina by December 1946. Reuters quoted military experts in Paris who predicted that if full-scale military operations became necessary, another 200,000 troops would be needed to "reconquer" Indochina. The full strength of the French army at that time was estimated at about 500,000 men. (*New York Times,* 21 December 1946).

31 Quoted in Sainteny, *Histoire d'une paix manquée,* pp. 183–84.

32 Devillers, *Histoire du Viet-Nam,* p. 337, see also Chaffard, *Carnets secrets,* 1 : 64–79.

33 Quoted, Devillers, *Histoire du Viet-Nam,* p. 296. See also remarks of Aujoulat, *ANC-2, C/C,* 24 July 1946, p. 187.

34 The Constituent Assembly did not participate directly in the Fontainbleau negotiations. The three major governmental parties were indirectly linked with its outcome, however, since each had one representative on the French delegation. The MRP member was M. Juglas, the newly designated chairman of the Committee on Overseas Territories; the Socialists were represented by M. Rivet and the Communists by M. Lozeray. Most of the actual policy formulation was done in the Interministerial Committee on Indochina, where the parties were represented much less equally. The Communist member, Minister of Armaments Charles Tillon, did not participate in the decisions, and the two Socialists, Jules Moch and Marius Moutet, were heavily outnumbered by MRP ministers and civil servants who made up the majority of the committee. Its president was Alexandre Varenne, a man who had displayed very liberal sentiments during the 1930s but who, as a former governor-general of Indochina, was closely identified with the outlook of the colonial service.

35 Devillers, *Histoire du Viet-Nam,* pp. 302–03.

36 Memorandum of 2 August 1946. See ibid., p. 301.

37 The Vietminh apparently miscalculated the strength of the Left and overestimated the willingness of the Socialists and Communists to risk a government crisis over Indochina. Their subsequent willingness to agree to a continuation of negotiations in January 1947 on the same issues that were not resolved at Fontainebleau suggests that they expected the elections to the first Legislative Assembly to result in the formation of a government with a Left majority that would be more sympathetic to their claims. If this was their calculation, then it would appear that they had misjudged the mood of the public as well as the temper of the Assembly, both of which were becoming more nationalistic.
38 Devillers, *Histoire du Viet-Nam,* p. 292.
39 *JO, ANC-2, Débats,* 27 August 1946, p. 3335. See also chap. 7.
40 Ibid., p. 3337.
41 *JO, ANC-1, Débats,* 20 March 1946, p. 1037.
42 Ibid.
43 De Gaulle, declaration of 27 August 1946, *Discours et messages,* 2 : 19; see also his press conference of 19 September 1946, ibid., p. 24.

Chapter 7

1 Claude Bée, "La Doctrine d'intégration," *Recueil Penant* 56 (June 1946), pp. 33–34.
2 Doudou Thiam, *La Portée de la citoyenneté dans les territoires d'outre-mer,* part 1.
3 Gilbert Zaksas, *ANC-1, C/C,* 22 February 1946, p. 442.
4 Gabriel d'Arboussier, rapporteur for the Territorial Assemblies Bill, *JO, ANC-1, Débats,* 25 April 1946, p. 2242.
5 Marius Moutet, *ANC-1, C/C,* 25 January 1946, pp. 258–59.
6 Gaston Monnerville, *JO, ANC-1, Débats,* 12 April 1946, p. 1756.
7 Tingitanus [pseud.], "Introduction," to Robert Lemaignen et al., *La Communauté impériale française,* p. 10. See also Pierre-Emmanuel Guillet, *JO, ANC-1, Documents,* no. 885, 5 April 1946, p. 856.
8 Lemaignen, *La Communauté impériale française,* pp. 45, 49.
9 Paul Viard, *JO, ANC-1, Débats,* 25 April 1946, p. 2242.
10 Léopold Senghor, ibid., 11 April 1946, pp. 1713–15. The quotation is from the printed text of his supplementary report, *JO, ANC-1, Documents,* no. 885, 5 April 1946, pp. 855–56.
11 Ibid., pp. 850–51.
12 Ibid., p. 851.
13 Ibid., pp. 855–56.
14 Ibid., p. 855.
15 Report of Joseph Raseta and Joseph Ravoahangy, ibid., no. 946, 9 April 1946, pp. 935–36.
16 All three deputies from Madagascar—Raseta, Ravoahangy, and Georges Boussenot, the citizens' college deputy—agreed that the Pierre-Bloch amendment was intended to divide the island. See their remarks, *JO, ANC-1, Débats,* 25 April 1946, pp. 2243–44. The amendment was adopted over their protest (ibid., p. 2264). The enabling act was passed amid accusations of trickery during the last day of the Assembly session (ibid., pp. 2382–83).
17 Report of Aimé Césaire, *JO, ANC-1, Documents,* no. 520, 26 February 1946, pp. 519–21.
18 Ibid.
19 See the supplementary report of Césaire, ibid., no. 624, 8 March 1946, pp. 593–94, and the remarks of Léon de Lépervanche, *ANC-1, C/C,* 18 January 1946, p. 240; and ibid., 28 February 1946, p. 493.
20 *JO, ANC-1, Documents,* no. 376, 7 February 1946, pp. 373–74. The Constitu-

tional Committee agreed without discussion to reserve the question of Algeria, *ANC-1, C/C,* 26 February 1946, p. 455.

21 Lamine-Guèye, *Etapes et perspectives,* p. 9.

22 D'Arboussier, *JO, ANC-1, Débats,* 25 April 1946, p. 2241 and his report, *JO, ANC-1, Documents,* no. 1081, 17 April 1946, pp. 1081–86.

23 Ibid., no. 1198, 25 April 1946, p. 1177.

24 Ibid., no. 1081, 17 April 1946, pp. 1085–86.

25 Saïd Mohamed Cheick, *JO, ANC-1, Débats,* 25 April 1946, p. 2250.

26 D'Arboussier, *JO, ANC-1, Documents,* no. 1081, pp. 1082–83.

27 Lamine-Guèye, *JO, ANC-1, Débats,* 5 April 1946, pp. 1536–38.

28 Gaston Monnerville, ibid., 12 April, pp. 1756–57.

29 Jacquest Soustelle, ibid., p. 1757.

30 Moutet, ibid., p. 1758.

31 Report of René Malbrant, *JO, ANC-1, Documents,* no. 1211, 25 April 1946, p. 1190.

32 See Pierre Sanner, "Budgets et fiscalité des territories d'outre-mer," in *L'Economie de l'union française d'outre-mer,* pp. 295–314.

33 *JO, ANC-1, Documents,* no. 1211, p. 1189.

34 Jacques Pellier, "L'Union française depuis la guerre," in *Annuaire de la vie économique française,* vol. 18, *La France économique de 1939 à 1946,* pp. 680–720; and Pierre Soudet, "Les Plans d'investissements d'outre-mer," *L'Economie de l'union française d'outre-mer,* pp. 188–214.

35 *ANC-1, C/C,* 24 April 1946, pp. 779–81, and plenary debate, *JO, ANC-1, Débats,* 25 April 1946, pp. 2254–56.

36 Lamine-Guèye, ibid., p. 2555, and ibid., 18 April 1946, pp. 2021–22.

37 Both the UDSR and MRP referred to the French Union articles as part of the basis for their opposition to the April Draft. See René Pleven, ibid., 19 April 1946, p. 2062, and François de Menthon, ibid., pp. 2063–64. The rapporteur for the draft constitution, Pierre Cot, accused the MRP of preventing a federal solution and forcing the Constitutional Committee to adopt ambiguous provisions for the union and then using those results to attack the April Draft; ibid., p. 2065. Socialist leader Guy Mollet echoed the charge, ibid., p. 2069; but Paul Viard denied it, ibid., pp. 2069–70.

38 De Gaulle, *Discours et messages,* 2 : 5–11, see chapter 8.

39 *ANC-2, C/C,* 26 June 1946, pp. 14–19, 22–42.

40 "Constitutional articles presented by M. Ferhat Abbas and the Intergroup of native representatives from the overseas territories," ibid., pp. 214–15.

41 Abbas, ibid., 26 July 1946, p. 228. See also Lamine-Guèye, ibid., p. 230; Senghor, ibid.; and Pierre Cot, ibid., p. 229.

42 Senghor, ibid., p. 245.

43 Senghor, ibid., p. 250.

44 Gabriel d'Arboussier reported in an interview with the writer that the African deputies appreciated these advantages at the time.

45 *JO, ANC-2, Documents,* no. 358, 2 August 1946, pp. 309–12.

46 Ibid., p. 311.

47 *JO, ANC-2, Débats,* 18 September 1946, p. 3804.

48 Ibid.

49 *JO, ANC-2, Documents,* no. 358, p. 310.

50 Ibid., p. 311.

51 For examples of Abbas's role as spokesman for other native nationalist groups outside Algeria see *ANC-2, C/C,* pp. 206, 227, 231, 242.

52 Daniel Boisdon, *JO, ANC-1, Débats,* 7 March 1946, p. 607.

53 Marius Moutet, *ANC-1, C/C,* 25 January 1946, p. 260.

54 Parti communiste français, *Histoire du parti communiste français* (Paris, 1964), pp. 491–92. See also Maurice Thorez, *Oeuvres complètes,* 5 : 5; and Parti communiste français, *Le Parti communiste français dans la lutte contre le colonialisme.*

55 Jacob Moneta, *Le PCF et la question coloniale,* pp. 144–50.
56 Joany Berlioz, "L'Afrique du Nord, foyer d'activité hitlérienne et anti-française," *Cahiers du Communisme* 22 (1945) : 47–53.
57 *L'Humanité,* 30 June 1945, quoted in Moneta, *Le PCF et la question coloniale,* pp. 154–55.
58 The Central Committee declaration appeared in *L'Humanité,* 12 May 1945, and the account of the delegation's intervention was reported in the weekly organ of the Algerian Communist party, *Liberté,* on the same day. Both are reprinted in Moneta, *Le PCF et la question coloniale,* p. 156.
59 Henri Lozeray, "La Question coloniale," *Cahiers du Communisme* 22 (1945) : 71–76; and "La Lutte du peuple français pour la démocratie et l'émancipation des peuples coloniaux," *Cahiers du Communisme* 23 (1946) : 368–78.
60 Rieber, *Stalin and the French Communist Party,* p. 320.
61 Communist spokesmen frequently referred to the Soviet Union as a model for French colonial reform along "federal" lines. For example, see André Marty, "La Question algérienne," *Cahiers du Communisme* 23 (1946) : 678–705; and Devèze, *La France d'outre-mer,* p. 224. Engels's letter to Kautsky was reprinted in Marx and Engels, *On Colonialism,* p. 340.
62 Raymond Barbé, "La Politique du parti et les thèses colonialistes," *Cahiers du Communisme* 23 (1946) : 566–77. See also Julien, *L'Afrique du Nord,* p. 298; and Devèze, *La France d'outre-mer,* p. 225.
63 Marty, "La Question algérienne," p. 686.
64 Lozeray, *JO, ANC-2, Débats,* 19 September 1946, p. 3845.
65 Edgar Morin, *Autocritique,* pp. 64, 68, 79.
66 Jacques Duclos, *JO, ANC-2, Débats,* 28 September 1946, pp. 4237–38.
67 Aimé Césaire, *JO, ANC-1, Débats,* 11 April 1946, pp. 1719–20.
68 Césaire, *JO, ANC-2, Débats,* 18 September 1946, pp. 3796–97.
69 Pierre Cot, ibid., pp. 3815–16.
70 Ibid., p. 3817.
71 Ibid., p. 3818.
72 Moneta, *Le PCF et la question coloniale,* pp. 149–50, 301–03. See also André Marty, *L'Affaire Marty* (Paris: Deux Rives, 1955), p. 37; and Raymond Barbé, "Les Problèmes de l'union française," *Cahiers du Communisme* 23 (1946) : 971–79.
73 Lozeray, "La Lutte du peuple français," p. 369.
74 Barbé, "La Politique du parti," p. 577.
75 Barbé, "Les Problèmes de l'union française," p. 973.
76 See Etienne Fajon, "Du dixième au onzième congrès du parti," *Cahiers du Communisme* 24 (1947) : 459–74; Jean Guillon, "Le Viet-Nam et la politique nationale et coloniale," *Cahiers du Communisme* 24 (1947) : 217–45; and Raymond Barbé, "Ou va l'union française?" *Cahiers du Communisme* 24 (1947) : 399–412.
77 Brunhes, *JO, ANC-2, Débats,* 18 September 1946, p. 3788.
78 Ibid., p. 3789.
79 Léon Noel, *Notre dernière chance,* pp. 73, 75.
80 Bardoux, *ANC-1, C/C,* 5 February 1946, p. 325. See also Cohen, *Rulers of Empire,* pp. 161–62.
81 "X", "L'Organisation monétaire des pays d'outre-mer de l'union française," *L'Economie de l'union française d'outre-mer,* pp. 265–79.
82 Pellier, "L'Union française depuis la guerre," pp. 716–19.
83 Sanner, "Budgets et fiscalité des territoires d'outre-mer," pp. 312–13.
84 Some French writers have argued that such attitudes were particularly characteristic of business circles in Indochina whom they branded *"piastriotes."* See Lucien Bodard, *La Guerre d'Indochine* (Paris, 1963), vol. 2, *L'Humiliation;* and André Teulieres, *L'Outre-mer français, hier-aujourd'hui-demain* (Paris, 1970).
85 Paul Bastid, "Declaration du Rassemblement des Gauches Républicaines à propos du projet de constitution," *ANC-2, C/C,* 26 June 1946, p. 25.
86 Ibid., pp. 26–27.
87 Herriot, *JO, ANC-2, Débats,* 27 August 1946, p. 3333.

88 Herriot, *JO, ANC-1, Débats,* 21 March 1946, p. 639.
89 Herriot, *JO, ANC-2, Débats,* 27 August 1946, p. 3334.
90 Ibid., p. 3337.
91 Vincent de Moro-Giafferri, *Information Républicains Sociaux,* February 1952, p. 5. The political role of the Radical party is analyzed by Francis De Tarr, *The French Radical Party.* Herriot's role in "saving the French Empire" was celebrated at several Radical congresses. See Gabriel Cudenet, *Remarks at the Radical Party Congress* (Paris, 1956); Luc Durand-Réville, *Report at the Party Congress* (Toulouse, 1949); and Paul Dévinat, *Report at the Party Congress* (Deauville, 1950), in the stenographic reports of the congresses.
92 Moutet, *JO, ANC-2, Débats,* 27 August 1946, pp. 336–37.
93 Alfred Grosser, *La IVe République et sa politique extérieure,* p. 124.
94 *Année Politique* (1944–45), pp. 485–86. The colonial outlook of the MRP is discussed by Robert F. Byrnes, "The Christian Democrats," in Edward Mead Earle, *Modern France,* pp. 153–78; Gabriel A. Almond, "The Political Ideas of Christian Democracy," *Review of Politics* 10 (1948) : 750–65; Russell B. Capelle, *The MRP and French Foreign Policy,* pp. 89–91; Michael P. Fogarty, *Christian Democracy in Western Europe,* pp. 329–39; Mario Einaudi and François Goguel, *Christian Democracy in Italy and France,* pp. 148–49.
95 Viard, *JO, ANC-1, Débats,* 12 April 1946, p. 1715.
96 Viard, *ANC-1, C/C,* 18 January 1946, p. 242.
97 Zaksas, Fajon, Valentino, Hervé, ibid., 7 February 1946, pp. 355–59.
98 Coste-Floret, ibid., 12 April 1946, p. 692, and ibid., 15 April 1946, p. 724.
99 *JO, ANC-1, Débats,* 15 April 1946, p. 1847.
100 Viard, ibid., 25 April 1946, p. 2242.
101 De Gaulle, *Discours et messages,* 2 : 8–9.
102 Aujoulat, *ANC-2, C/C,* 24 July 1946, p. 186. The MRP plan was explained by Aujoulat, ibid., pp. 182–85; and the full text of the proposals appears on pp. 196–97.
103 De Gaulle, *Discours et messages,* 2 : 18–19.
104 Coste-Floret, *ANC-2, C/C,* 4 September 1946, p. 411.
105 Devèze, *La France d'outre-mer,* p. 259.
106 Léon Blum, quoted in Grosser, *La IVe République,* p. 112.
107 Edouard Depreux, *JO, ANC-1, Débats,* 23 March 1946, p. 1614.
108 Elgey, *La République des illusions,* p. 212.
109 Jean Le Bail, *ANC-2, C/C,* 26 July 1946, p. 234.
110 Depreux, *JO, ANC-2, Débats,* 23 August 1946, pp. 3283–85.
111 Quoted in Grosser, *La IVe République,* p. 114. For a discussion of the internal politics of the SFIO and the Thirty-eighth Congress see Bruce Desmond Graham, *The French Socialists and Tripartisme,* pp. 197–203.
112 Henri Teitgen, *JO, ANC-2, Débats,* 22 August 1946, p. 3236.

Chapter 8

1 *JO, ANC-2, Débats,* 29 August 1946, p. 3433.
2 On the relations between de Gaulle and Bidault see Elgey, *La République des illusions,* pp. 41–42, 126–31. For Bidault's own reflections on this period see his *Resistance,* chaps. 3–5.
3 Leclerc, letter to Maurice Schumann reprinted in Elgey, *La République des illusions,* pp. 161–62.
4 Ibid., p. 163.
5 Bidault, *JO, ANC-2, Débats,* 23 August 1946, pp. 3288–89.
6 Varenne, letter to André Philip, *ANC-2, C/C,* 26 July 1946, p. 217. Remarks of Coste-Floret, ibid., p. 219.
7 "Charte de l'union française," reprinted, ibid., p. 218.

8 Moutet, *JO, ANC-2, Débats,* 27 August 1946, pp. 3336–37.
9 A complete stenographic report of Moutet's remarks is included in *ANC-2, C/C,* 11 September 1946, pp. 477–82.
10 Ibid., pp. 483–86.
11 Fajon, ibid., p. 540.
12 Paul Ramadier, ibid., p. 513. This observation applied with special force to Abbas and the Communist party, as they recognized immediately (ibid., p. 514).
13 The vote to delete failed with 21 in favor and 21 opposed. The parties divided between Left (PCF, SFIO, and UDMA) and Right (MRP, RGR, and PRL).
14 Coste-Floret, *JO, ANC-2, Débats,* 18 September 1946, p. 3786–87.
15 Jean-Jacques Juglas, ibid., pp. 3804–05.
16 Senghor, ibid., p. 3792.
17 Yves Angeletti, ibid., p. 3787.
18 Angeletti, ibid., p. 3788.
19 Elgey, *La République des illusions,* p. 225. See also the statements of Bidault and Jacques Duclos, *JO, ANC-2, Débats,* 20 September 1946, pp. 3882–84.
20 Bidault, *ANC-2, C/C,* 19 September 1946, p. 586.
21 Bidault, *Resistance,* p. 119. On the constitutional experience see pp. 112–23.
22 Ibid., p. 121.
23 De Gaulle, *Discours et messages,* 2 : 24; see also La Gorce, *De Gaulle entre deux mondes,* pp. 161–68.
24 Bidault, *Resistance,* p. 120.
25 *ANC-2, C/C,* 19 September 1946, p. 580.
26 Ibid., p. 556; italics added.
27 Bidault, ibid., p. 586.
28 Bidault, ibid., p. 544.
29 Bidault, ibid., p. 587.
30 Bidault, ibid.
31 Bidault, ibid.
32 Bidault, ibid., pp. 588, 591.
33 Senghor, ibid., p. 589.
34 Bidault, ibid., p. 591. The concluding phrase translates literally: "but we will not turn somersaults." The implication seemed to be that Bidault refused to make what he considered to be undignified concessions.
35 Senghor, ibid., p. 599.
36 Ibid., pp. 559–600.
37 Quoted in Elgey, *La République des illusions,* p. 222. Bidault minimizes the entire affair (*Resistance,* p. 121), but its seriousness is evident in Lamine-Guèye's account as reported by Franz Ansprenger, *Politik im schwarzen Afrika,* pp. 72–73.
38 Abbas, *JO, ANC-2, Débats,* 18 September 1946, p. 3804.
39 Césaire, ibid., p. 3797.
40 Lamine-Guèye, ibid., pp. 3798–3801.
41 Sourou Migan Apithy, ibid., pp. 3802–03.
42 Yacine Diallo, ibid., pp. 3813–14.
43 Fily Dabo Sissoko, ibid., p. 3820.
44 Houphouët, ibid., 3849–50.
45 Fajon, *ANC-2, C/C,* 20 September 1946, pp. 609–10; see also the statements of Coste-Floret, Ramadier, and Bardoux, ibid., pp. 610–11.
46 *JO, ANC-2, Débats,* 20 September 1946, pp. 3897, 3906.
47 Coste-Floret, ibid., p. 3908.
48 Lamine-Guèye, ibid., p. 3909.
49 Ibid., pp. 3924–25, and *ANC-2, C/C,* 21 September 1946, pp. 620–22.
50 Articles 75 and 75 *bis, ANC-2, C/C,* p. 721.
51 Bidault, *JO, ANC-2, Débat,* 21 September 1946, p. 3928.
52 *Scutin* no. 72, ibid., 28 September 1946, pp. 4259–60.
53 De Gaulle, speech of 29 September 1946, *Discours et messages,* 2 : 30.

54 Idem., statement of 9 October 1946, ibid., p. 34.
55 See Borella, *Evolution politique et juridique;* Julien Laferrière, *Manuel de droit constitutionnel;* François Luchaire, *Manuel de droit d'outre-mer;* Rolland and Lampué, *Droit d'outre-mer;* Georges Vedel, *Manuel élémentaire de droit constitutionnel.*
56 Pierre Lampué, *Droit d'outre-mer,* p. 63.
57 Gonidec, *Droit d'outre-mer,* 1 : 376.
58 Although the term *overseas territories* was sometimes used loosely during the constitutional debates to refer to all the colonial territories, the constitution defined it more narrowly to include only those former colonies subject to direct French administration. They were the responsibility of the Ministry of Overseas France and included the large administrative federations of West and Central Africa, French Somalia, the Indian settlements, Cochin China, the Pacific dependencies, Madagascar and the Comoro Islands, and Saint Pierre and Miquelon. The United Nations trust territories of Togo and the Cameroons were called "associated territories" but were administered in the same way as the rest. Morocco, Tunisia, and the states of Vietnam, Laos, and Cambodia were potentially "associated states" whose relations were supervised by the Foreign Ministry. The "overseas départements" in Algeria, Guyane, Guadeloupe, Martinque, and Réunion were administered through the Ministry of the Interior.
59 The legal meaning of "citizen of the French Union" is explained by Pierre Lampué, "La Citoyenneté de l'union française," *RJPUF* 4 (1950) : 305–15. See also Daniel Boisdon, "Du sort des articles 81 et 82 de notre constitution de 1946," *RJPUF* 10 (1956) : 233–56; and Laferrière, *Manuel de droit constitutionnel,* p. 962. The Conseil d'Etat finally took the view that the Preamble, to which Articles 81 and 82 referred, had no legal force; see Conseil d'Etat, *Etudes et Documents* 2 (1948) : 46. Subsequent jurisprudence on this question was contradictory as shown by J. Foyer, "Mme. Cabet de Chambine v. Bessis, Cour d'Appel de Paris, 22 February 1951," *RJPUF* 5 (1951) : 132. The legal force of Articles 80 and 82 that proclaimed former native subjects to be citizens remained unclear; see Thiam, *La Portée de la citoyenneté.* The enabling legislation regarding nationality is summarized in Henri-Louis Brin, *La Nationalité française dans les territoires d'outre-mer.*
60 Grosser, *La IVe République,* p. 249.
61 Articles 71 and 72.
62 Articles 64 and 65.
63 Bidault, *Resistance,* p. 121.

Chapter 9

1 *ANC-2, C/C,* 21 September 1946, p. 618.
2 Moutet, *JO, ANC-2, Débats,* 20 September 1946, pp. 3903–04.
3 André Mutter, ibid., 3 October 1946, p. 4478.
4 André Schock, ibid., 3 October 1946, pp. 4478–79.
5 François Quilici, ibid., 28 September 1946, p. 4236.
6 Quilici, ibid., 4 October 1946, p. 4547.
7 Jacques Duclos, ibid., 20 September 1946, p. 3905.
8 Duclos, ibid., 28 September 1946, p. 4237.
9 See the remarks of François-Xavier Reille-Soult de Dalmatie, rapporteur for the electoral law, and those of Emmanuel d'Astier de la Vigerie, chairman of the Interior Committee, ibid., 4 October 1946, p. 4556.
10 Max Lejeune, ibid., 4 October 1946, p. 4560.
11 Jean Letourneau, minister of posts, telegraphs, and telephones, ibid., 5 October 1946, pp. 4714–15.
12 Houphouët, ibid., 19 Setpember 1946, p. 3849.

13 Abbas, ibid., 28 September 1946, pp. 4230–31.
14 Ibid.; see also statements of Ahmed Francis, ibid., p. 3894, and Mohamed Sator, ibid., p. 4550.
15 Ravoahangy, ibid., 4 October 1946, p. 4555.
16 Félix Tchicaya, ibid., 4 October 1946, pp. 4554, 4556.
17 Tchicaya, ibid., 19 September 1946, p. 3846.
18 Lamine-Guèye, ibid., 4 October 1946, p. 4559.
19 Lamine-Guèye, ibid., p. 4560.
20 Lamine-Guèye, ibid., 5 October 1946, pp. 4712–13.
21 Tchicaya, ibid., 5 October 1946, p. 4713.
22 Mme. Eboué, ibid., p. 4714.
23 Houphouët, ibid., p. 4713.
24 Lamine-Guèye, ibid., p. 4715.

BIBLIOGRAPHY

Books

Abbas, Ferhat. *Guerre et révolution d'Algérie.* Paris: Julliard, 1962. Vol. 1, *La Nuit coloniale.*

Aghion, Raoul. *The Fighting French.* New York: Henry Holt & Co., 1948.

Albertini, Rudolph von. *Decolonization.* Garden City, N.Y.: Doubleday, 1971.

Alduy, Paul. *L'Union française, mission de la France.* Paris: Fasquelle, 1948.

Amelot, Pierre. *Structures françaises.* Paris: Société d'Études et de Diffusion de l'Idée Française, 1946.

Amon d'Aby, François Joseph. *La Côte d'Ivoire dans la cité africaine.* Paris: Larose, 1951.

André, Col. C. R. *Le Reveil des nationalismes.* Paris: Berger-Levrault, 1958.

Annet, Armand. *Aux heures troublés de l'Afrique française, 1939–1943.* Paris: Editions du Conquistador, 1952.

———. *Je suis gouverneur d'outre-mer.* Paris: Editions du Conquistador, 1957.

Annuaire de la vie économique française. Paris: Recueil Sirey, 1948. Vol. 18, *La France économique de 1939 à 1946.*

Ansprenger, Franz. *Politik im Schwarzen Afrika.* Cologne: West-deutscher Verlag, 1961.

Antonelli, Etienne. *L'Afrique et la paix de Versailles.* Paris: B. Grasset, 1921.

Armstrong, Hamilton Fish. *Chronology of Failure: The Last Days of the French Republic.* New York: Macmillan Co., 1941.

Arnault, Jacques. *Du colonialisme au socialisme.* Paris: Editions Sociales, 1966.

———. *Le Procès du colonialisme.* Paris: Editions Sociales, 1958.

Aron, Raymond. *L'Algérie et la république.* Paris: Plon, 1958.

———. *Le Grand Schisme.* Paris: Gallimard, 1948.

———. *Immuable et changeante, de la IVe à la Ve République.* Paris: Calmann-Lévy, 1959.

———, and Blanchet, André. *Encyclopédie politique de la France et du monde.* Paris: Editions de l'Encyclopédie Coloniale et Maritime, 1946–48. Vol. 2, *La France et l'Union française.*

Aron, Robert. *Charles de Gaulle.* Paris: Perrin, 1964.

———. *De l'armistice à l'insurrection nationale.* Paris: Nouvelle Revue Française, 1945.

———. *The Liberation of France.* Translated by Humphrey Hare. 2 vols. London: Putnam & Co., 1963–64.

———, and Elgey, Georgette. *Histoire de Vichy, 1940–1944.* Paris: Fayard, 1954.

———; Lavagne, François de; Feller, Janine; and Garnier-Rivet, Yvette. *Les Origines de la guerre d'Algérie.* Paris: Fayard, 1962.

———, and Marc, Alex. *Principes du fédéralisme: le véritable fédéralisme français.* Paris: Le Portulan, 1948.

Ashcroft, Edward. *De Gaulle.* London: Odhams Press, 1962.

Aujoulat, Louis-Paul. *Aujourd'hui l'Afrique.* Tournai, Belgium: Casterman, 1958.

———. *La Vie et l'avenir de l'union française.* Paris: S.E.R.P., 1947.

Aurillac, J. *Le Régime politique et administratif de l'A.O.F.* Dakar, Senegal: Service d'Information du Haut Commissariat, 1949.

Bainville, Jacques. *La Défaite de Bismarck: l'expansion coloniale française et l'alliance russe.* Paris: Hachette, 1953.

Barron, Richard William. *Parties and Politics in Modern France.* Washington, D. C.: Public Affairs Press, 1959.

Bastid, Paul. *Les Grands Procès politiques de l'histoire.* Paris: Fayard, 1962.

Baumont, Maurice. *Gloires et tragédies de la IIIe République.* Paris: Hachette, 1956.

Bayet, Albert, and Albert François. *Les Ecrivains politiques au XIXe siècle.* Paris: Colin, 1907.

Behr, Edward. *The Algerian Problem.* New York: Norton, 1962.

Benoist-Méchin, Jacques Gabriel Paul Michel. *Sixty Days That Shook the West, the Fall of France, 1940.* New York: G. P. Putnam's Sons, 1963.

Berl, Emmanuel. *La France irréelle.* Paris: Grasset, 1957.

———. *Mort de la morale bourgeoise.* Paris: Hachette, 1965.

———. *La Politique et les partis.* Paris: Rieder, 1936.

Betts, Raymond. *Assimilation and Association in French Colonial Theory.* New York: Columbia University Press, 1961.

Bidault, Georges. *Resistance.* Translated by Marianne Sinclair. New York: Frederick A. Praeger, 1965.

Billotte, General Pierre. *Du pain sur la planche.* Paris: Plon, 1965.

Binet, Jacques. *Afrique en question, de la tribu à la nation.* Paris: Mame, 1966.

Blanchet, André. *L'Itinéraire des partis africains depuis Bamako.* Paris: Plon, 1958.

Blet, Henri. *Histoire de la colonisation française.* 3 vols. Paris: Arthaud, 1949–50.
Bloch-Morhange, Jacques. *Le Gaullisme.* Paris: Plon, 1963.
———. *Les Politiciens.* Paris: Fayard, 1961.
Blum, Léon. *L'Oeuvre de Léon Blum.* Paris: Albin Michel, 1958. Vol. 6, *Naissance de la IVe République 1945–1947.*
Bodin, Louis, and Touchard, Jean. *Front populaire, 1936.* Paris: Colin, 1961.
Boersner, Demetrio. *The Bolsheviks and the National and Colonial Question, 1917–1928.* Geneva: Librairie Droz, 1957.
Boisdon, Daniel. *Les Institutions de l'union française.* Paris: Berger-Levrault, 1949–50.
Bonnefous, Edouard. *Histoire politique de la Troisième République.* 6 vols. Paris: Presses Universitaires de France, 1956–65.
Bonnet, Col. Gabriel. *Les Guerres insurrectionnelles et révolutionnaires, de l'antiquité à nos jours.* Paris: Payot, 1958.
Bonte, Florimond. *À l'echelle de la nation; réponse à l'auteur de "À l'echelle humaine."* Paris: Editions du Parti Communiste Français, 1945.
Borella, François. *L'Évolution politique et juridique de l'union française depuis 1946.* Paris: Librairie Générale de Droit et de Jurisprudence, 1958.
Bosworth, William Arthur. *Catholicism and Crisis in Modern France: French Catholic Groups at the Threshold of the Fifth Republic.* Princeton, N.J.: Princeton University Press, 1962.
Bouchaud, R. P. Joseph. *L'Église en Afrique noire.* Paris: La Palatine, 1958.
Bourguiba, Habib. *La Tunisie et la France.* Paris: Julliard, 1954.
Bournot, Gilbert. *Synthèse et reformes coloniales.* Paris: Larose, 1945.
Boyer de Latour, Gen. Pierre. *Vérités sur l'Afrique du nord.* Paris: Plon, 1956.
Brin, Henri-Louis. *La Nationalité française dans les territoires d'outre-mer.* Paris: Recueil Sirey, 1954.
Brogan, Denis. *Citizenship Today: England, France, the United States.* The Weil Lectures. Chapel Hill, N.C.: University of North Carolina Press, 1960.
———. *France under the Republic: The Development of Modern France, 1870–1939.* New York: Harper & Row, 1940.
———. *The French Nation from Napoleon to Pétain, 1814–1940.* New York: Harper & Row, 1957.
———. *French Personalities and Problems.* London: Hamish Hamilton, 1946.
Bromberger, Merry and Serge. *Les 13 complots du 13 mai.* Paris: Fayard, 1959.
Bromberger, Serge. *Les Rebelles algériens.* Paris: Plon, 1958.
Brunet, Auguste. *Jules Simon et le problème de la constitution coloniale.* Paris: Charles-Lavauzelle, 1945.

Brunschwig, Henri. *La Colonisation française, du pacte colonial à l'union française.* Paris: Calmann-Lévy, 1949–50.

———. *Mythes et réalités de l'impérialisme colonial français, 1871–1914.* Paris: Colin, 1960.

Buell, Raymond Leslie. *The Native Problem in Africa.* New York: Macmillan Co., 1928.

Burdeau, Georges. *Droit constitutionnel et institutions politiques.* 8th ed. Paris: Librairie Générale de Droit et de Jurisprudence, 1959.

Bury, John Patrick T. *France 1814–1940.* London: Methuen & Co., 1956.

Buthman, William Cort. *The Rise of Integral Nationalism in France.* New York: Columbia University Press, 1939.

Cady, John F. *The Roots of French Imperialism in Eastern Asia.* Ithaca, N.Y.: Cornell University Press, 1954.

Cameron, Elizabeth Ripley. *French Reconstruction.* New Haven: Yale Institute of International Studies, 1948.

Camus, Albert. *Actuelles. III: Chronique algérienne. 1939–1958.* Paris: Gallimard, 1958.

Cantril, Hadley, and Rodnick, David. *On Understanding the French Left.* Princeton, N.J.: Princeton University Press, 1956.

Capelle, Russell B. *The MRP and French Foreign Policy.* New York: Frederick A. Praeger, 1963.

Castellan, Georges. *Histoire de l'armée.* Paris: Presses Universitaires de France, 1948.

Cayla, Léon. *Terres d'outre-mer.* Paris: Editions du Triolet, 1948.

Césaire, Aimé. *Discours sur le colonialisme.* Paris: Présence Africaine, 1963.

———. *Lettre à Maurice Thorez.* Paris: Présence Africaine, 1956.

———. *Toussaint L'Ouverture. Lā Révolution française et le problème colonial.* Paris: Présence Africaine, 1962.

Chaffard, Georges. *Les Carnets secrets de la décolonisation.* 2 vols. Paris: Calmann-Lévy, 1965–67.

———. *Indochine: dix ans d'indépendence.* Paris: Calmann-Lévy, 1964.

Chailley-Bert, Joseph. *La Colonisation française au XIXe siècle.* Paris: Dupont, 1900.

———. *Dix années de politique coloniale.* Paris: Colin, 1902.

———. *La France et la plus grande France.* Paris: Imprimerie Davy, 1902.

Chapman, Guy. *The Third Republic of France: First Phase 1871–1894.* New York: St. Martin's Press, 1962.

Charvet, Patrick Edward. *France.* New York: Frederick A. Praeger, 1955.

Chatelain, Jean. *La Nouvelle Constitution et le régime politique de la France,* 2d ed. Paris: Berger-Levrault, 1959.

Cheverny, Julien. *Éloge du colonialisme.* Paris: Julliard, 1961.

Cobban, Alfred. *A History of Modern France.* London: Jonathan Cape, 1962. Vol. 2.

Cohen, William B. *Rulers of Empire: The French Colonial Service in Africa*. Stanford, Calif.: Hoover Institution Press, 1971.
Coste-Floret, Paul, and Le Guenedal, André. *Construire l'union française*. Paris: Société d'Editions Républicains Populaires, 1948.
Cot, Pierre. *Le Procès de la république*. 2 vols. New York: Editions de la Maison Française, 1949–50.
———. *The Triumph of Treason*. Chicago and New York: Ziff-Davis Publishing Co., 1944.
Crawley, Aidan. *De Gaulle*. Indianapolis and New York: Bobbs-Merrill Co., 1969.
Crevaux, Paul Dominique. *Yves Chataigneau, fossoyeur général de l'Algérie*. Algiers: Les Editions Nationales, 1949–50.
Crozier, Michel. *The Bureaucratic Phenomenon*. Translated by the author. Chicago: Chicago University Press, 1964.
Culmann, Henri. *L'Union française*. Paris: Presses Universitaires de France, 1950.
Curtis, Michael: *Three against the Third Republic*. Princeton, N.J.: Princeton University Press, 1959.
Dansette, Adrien. *Histoire des Présidents de la République*. Paris: Le Livre Contemporain, 1960.
Dauphin-Meunier, Achille. *Histoire du Cambodge*. Paris: Presses Universitaires de France, 1961.
Davet, Michel Christian. *La Double Affaire de Syrie*. Paris: Fayard, 1967.
Debré, Michel. *La Mort de l'état républicain*. Paris: Gallimard, 1947.
———. *Le République et ses problèmes*. Paris: Nagel, 1953.
———. *Le République et son pouvoir*. Paris: Nagel, 1949–50.
Decoux, Admiral Jean. *A la barre de l'Indochine, 1940–1945*. Paris: Plon, 1950.
De Gaulle, General Charles. *La Discorde chez l'ennemi*. Paris: Berger-Levrault, 1924.
———. *Discours et messages*. 5 vols. Paris: Plon, 1970.
———. *Le Fil de l'épée*. Paris: Berger-Levrault, 1932.
———. *La France et son armée*. Paris: Plon, 1938.
———. *Mémoires de guerre*. Paris: Plon, 1955–60.
———. *Vers l'armée de métier*. Paris: Berger-Levrault, 1934.
Dehon, Emile. *La Nouvelle Politique coloniale de la France*. Paris: Flammarion, 1945.
De la Résistance à la Révolution. Paris: La Baconnière, 1946–48.
Delavignette, Robert. *Christianisme et colonialisme*. Paris: Fayard, 1960.
———. *Freedom and Authority in French West Africa*. London: Oxford University Press, 1950.
———. *Les Paysans noirs*. Paris: Stock, 1946.
———, and Julien, Charles-André. *Les Constructeurs de la France d'outre-mer*. Paris: Corrêa, 1946.

Deniau, Roger, *Avec tes défenseurs!* Paris: Editions de la Liberté, 1947.
Deschamps, Hubert J. *L'Éveil politique africain.* Paris: Presses Universitaires de France, 1952.
———. *Histoire de Madagascar.* Paris: Berger-Levrault, 1960.
———. *Les Méthodes et les doctrines coloniales de la France du XVI*[e] *siècle à nos jours.* Paris: Colin, 1953.
———. *L'Union française: histoire, institutions, réalités.* Paris: Berger-Levrault, 1952.
Despois, Jean. *L'Afrique blanche.* Paris: Presses Universitaires de France, 1958. Vol. 1, *L'Afrique du Nord.*
De Tarr, Francis. *The French Radical Party, from Herriot to Mendes-France.* London and New York: Oxford University Press, 1961.
Devèze, Michel. *La France d'outre-mere: de l'Empire colonial à l'Union française, 1938–47.* Paris: Hachette, 1948.
Devillers, Philippe. *Histoire du Viet-Nam de 1940 à 1952.* Paris: Editions du Seuil, 1952.
———. et Lacouture, Jean. *Vietnam: de la guerre française à la guerre américaine.* Paris: Editions du Seuil, 1969.
Dia, Mamadou. *Réflexions sur l'économie de l'Afrique noire.* Paris: Presence Africaine, 1961.
Dubois, Marcel, and Terrier, Auguste. *Les Colonies françaises, un siècle d'expansion coloniale.* Paris: Challamel, 1902.
Duchêne, Albert. *Histoire des finances coloniales de la France.* Paris: Payot et Cie., 1938.
———. *La Politique coloniale de la France.* Paris: Payot et Cie., 1928.
Duclos, Jacques. *Batailles pour la république.* Paris: Editions Sociales, 1947.
Dupeux, Georges. *Le Front populaire et les élections de 1936.* Paris: Colin, 1959.
Duquesne, Jacques. *L'Algérie ou la guerre des mythes.* Paris: Desclée de Brouwer, 1958.
Duroselle, Jean-Baptiste. *Histoire diplomatique de 1919 à nos jours.* Paris: Dalloz, 1953.
Earle, Edward Mead. *Modern France: Problems of the Third and Fourth Republics.* Princeton, N.J.: Princeton University Press, 1951.
Easton, Stewart C. *The Twilight of European Colonialism: A Political Analysis.* New York: Holt, Rinehart, and Winston, 1960.
L'Economie de l'union française d'outre-mer. Paris: Recueil Sirey, 1952.
Edelmann, Maurice. *France: The Birth of the Fourth Republic.* London: Penguin, 1944.
Ehrhard, Jean. *Communauté ou sécession.* Paris: Calmann-Levy, 1959.
———. *Le Destin du colonialisme.* Paris: Eyrolles, 1957.
Ehrmann, Henry W. *French Labor from Popular Front to Liberation.* New York: Oxford University Press, 1947.
———. *Organized Business in France.* Princeton, N.J.: Princeton University Press, 1957.

Einaudi, Mario. *Nationalization in France and Italy.* Ithaca, N.Y.: Cornell University Press, 1955.

———, and Goguel, François. *Christian Democracy in Italy and France.* Notre Dame, Ind.: University of Notre Dame Press, 1952.

Elgey, Georgette. *La République des illusions, 1945–1951: la vie secrète de la IVe République.* Paris: Fayard, 1965.

Emerit, Marcel. *La Révolution de 1848 en Algérie.* Paris: Larose, 1950.

———. *Les Saint-Simoniens en Algérie.* Paris: Société d'Edition "Les Belles Lettres," 1941.

Esquer, Gabriel. *Histoire de l'Algérie.* Paris: Presses Universitaires de France, 1960.

Fabre-Luce, Alfred. *Deuil au Levant.* Paris: Fayard, 1950.

———. *Journal de la France 1939–1944.* Paris: Amiot-Dumont, 1952.

Fall, Bernard B. *Street without Joy: Indochina at War 1946–1954.* Harrisburg, Pa.: Stackpole Books, 1960.

———. *Le Viet Minh, 1945–1960.* Paris: Colin, 1960.

Farmer, Paul. *Vichy: Political Dilemma.* New York: Columbia University Press, 1955.

Fassi, Alal el. *The Independence Movements in Arab North Africa.* Washington, D.C.: American Council of Learned Societies, 1954.

Fauchon-Villeplée, A. *Constitution et union française.* Paris: Berger-Levrault, 1953.

Fauvet, Jacques. *De Thorez à de Gaulle: les forces politiques en France.* Paris: Editions Le Monde, 1951.

———. *Histoire du parti communiste français, 1917–1965.* 2 vols. Paris: Fayard, 1964–65.

———. *La IVe République.* Paris: Fayard, 1959.

Favrod, Charles-Henri. *Le Poids de l'Afrique.* Paris: Editions du Seuil, 1958.

———. *La Révolution algérienne.* Paris: Plon, 1959.

Ferry, Jules. *Les Affaires de Tunisie.* 2d ed. Paris: Hetzel, 1882.

———. *Le Tonkin et la mère-patrie.* Paris: Havard, 1890.

Fischer, Georges. *Syndicats et décolonisation.* Paris: La Fondation Nationale des Sciences Politiques, 1961.

Fogarty, Michael P. *Christian Democracy in Western Europe, 1820–1953.* Notre Dame, Ind.: University of Notre Dame Press, 1957.

France during the German Occupation. 4 vols. Hoover Institute Studies. Stanford, Calif.: Stanford University Press, 1947.

François-Poncet, André. *Au fil des jours, propos d'un libéral, 1942–1962.* Paris: Flammarion, 1963.

Froelicher, Capt. Joseph Emile. *Trois Colonisateurs: Bugeaud, Faidherbe, Galliéni.* Paris: Charles-Lavauzelle, 1903.

Funk, Arthur L. *Charles de Gaulle: The Crucial Years, 1943–44.* Norman, Okla.: University of Oklahoma Press, 1959.

Furniss, Edgar Stephenson. *France: Troubled Ally.* New York: Harper & Row, 1960.

Gaffarel, Paul L. J. *Notre expansion coloniale en Afrique de 1870 à nos jours.* Paris: Alcan, 1918.

———. *La Politique coloniale en France de 1789 à 1830.* Paris: Alcan, 1908.

Ganiage, Jean. *Les Origines du protectorat français en Tunisie (1861–1881).* Paris: Presses Universitaires de France, 1959.

Gann, Lewis H., and Duignan, Peter. *Colonialism in Africa 1810 to 1960.* 2 vols. Cambridge: At the University Press, 1968–70.

Garas, Félix. *Bourguiba et la naissance d'une nation.* Paris: Julliard, 1956.

Gardinier, David E. *Cameroon, United Nations Challenge to French Policy.* London and New York: Oxford University Press, 1963.

Gault, Jean-Pierre. *Histoire d'une fidélité, "Témoignage Chrétien," 1944–56.* Paris: Témoignage Chrétien, 1963.

Gavin, Catherine. *Liberated France.* New York: St. Martin's Press, 1955.

Gay, Francisque. *Les Démocrates d'inspiration chrétienne à l'épreuve du pouvoir.* Paris: Bloud et Gay, 1952.

Genton, Jacques. *L'Afrique et l'union française.* Marseille: Imprimerie Moullot Fils Aîné, 1953.

Gillespie, Joan. *Algeria.* London: Ernest Benn, 1960.

Girardet, Raoul. *La Crise militaire française, 1949–1963.* Paris: Colin, 1964.

———. *La Société militaire dans la France contemporaine.* Paris: Plon, 1953.

Girault, Arthur. *Principes de colonisation et de législation coloniale.* Paris: Larose, 1895.

Godfrey, E. E. *The Fate of the French Non-Communist Left.* Garden City, N.Y.: Doubleday, 1955.

Goeau-Brissonniere, Yves. *Par delà de l'union française.* Paris: Société des Editions du Pas-de-Calais, 1958.

Goguel, François. *France under the Fourth Republic.* Ithaca, N.Y.: Cornell University Press, 1952.

———. *La Politique des partis sous la IIIe République.* 2d ed. 2 vols. Paris: Editions du Seuil, 1946.

Goldberg, Harvey. *Jean Jaurès.* Madison, Wis.: University of Wisconsin Press, 1962.

Goldsworthy, David. *Colonial Issues in British Politics, 1945–1961.* Oxford: Oxford University Press, 1971.

Gonidec, Pierre François. *Droit d'outre-mer.* 2 vols. Paris: Editions Montchrestien, 1959.

———. *L'Évolution des territoires d'outre-mer depuis 1946.* Paris: Librairie Générale de Droit et de Jurisprudence, 1958.

———, and Kirsch, Martin. *Droit du travail des territoires d'outre-mer.* Paris: Librairie Générale de Droit et de Jurisprudence, 1954.

Gooch, Robert Kent. *The French Parliamentary Committee System.* New York and London: D. Appleton-Century Co., 1935.

Gordon, David. *The Passing of French Algeria.* London: Oxford University Press, 1966.

Graham, Bruce Desmond. *The French Socialists and Tripartisme.* Toronto: Toronto University Press, 1965.

Grimal, Henri. *La Décolonisation, 1919–1963.* Paris: Colin, 1965.

Grosser, Alfred. *French Foreign Policy under de Gaulle.* Translated by Lois A. Patterson. Boston: Little, Brown & Co., 1967.

———. *La IVe République et sa politique extérieure.* Paris: Colin, 1961.

Guiot, Commandant. *En Syrie, combat sans histoire.* Paris: Editions La Couronne Litéraire, 1950.

Hailey, Lord. *An African Survey.* London: Oxford University Press, 1937.

Halévy, Daniel. *Décadence de la liberté.* Paris: Grasset, 1931.

Hammer, Ellen J. *The Emergence of Viet Nam.* New York: International Secretariat, Institute of Pacific Affairs, 1947.

———. *The Struggle for Indochina.* Stanford, Calif.: Stanford University Press, 1954.

Hardy, Georges. *Histoire de la colonisation française.* Paris: Larose, 1947.

Harmand, Jules. *Domination et colonisation.* Paris: Flammarion, 1910.

Hauriou, André. *Vers une doctrine de la Résistance, le socialisme humaniste.* Paris: Fontaine, 1944.

Hayes, Carleton J. H. *France: A Nation of Patriots.* New York: Columbia University Press, 1930.

Herriot, Edouard. *In Those Days.* New York: Old and New World Publishers, 1952.

Hervé, Pierre. *La Révolution et les fétiches.* Paris: La Table Ronde, 1956.

Hodgkin, Thomas. *Nationalism in Colonial Africa.* New York: New York University Press, 1957.

———, and Schachter, Ruth. *French-speaking West Africa in Transition.* New York: International Conciliation, Carnegie Endowment for World Peace, 1961.

Hoffman, Stanley, ed. *In Search of France.* Cambridge: Harvard University Press, 1963.

Homet, Marcel. *Afrique noire, terre inquiète. Garderons-nous nos colonies d'Afrique?* Paris: Peyronnet, 1938.

Huddleston, Sisley. *France: the Tragic Years, 1939–1947.* New York: Devin-Adair Co., 1955.

Hull, Cordell. *Memoirs.* 2 vols. New York: Macmillan Co., 1948.

Husson, Raoul, ed. *Elections et réferendums: 21 octobre 1945, 5 mai, 2 juin 1946.* Paris: Le Monde, 1946.

Isnard, Hildebert. *Madagascar.* Paris: Colin, 1955.

Isorni, Jacques. *Ainsi passent les républiques.* Paris: Flammarion, 1959.

Jaurès, Jean Léon. *Oeuvres de Jean Jaurès.* Compiled and annotated by Max Bonnafous. 8 vols. Paris: Rieder, 1931–37.

Jeanneney, Jean Marcel. *Forces et faiblesses de l'économie française, 1945–1959.* 2d. ed. Paris: Colin, 1959.

Juin, General Alphonse. *Mémoires.* 2 vols. Paris: Plon, 1959–60.
Julien, Charles-André. *L'Afrique du nord en marche.* Paris: Julliard, 1952.
———. *La Politique coloniale de la France sous la Révolution, le Premier Empire, et la Restauration, 1789–1815.* Paris: Centre de Documentation Universitaire, 1953.
Kertesz, Stephen D., and Fitzsimmons, Matthew A., eds. *Diplomacy in a Changing World.* Notre Dame, Ind.: Notre Dame University Press, 1959.
Kessel, Patrick. *Moi, Maréchal Bugeaud.* Paris: Editeurs Français Réunis, 1958.
Kircheimer, Otto. *A Constitution for the Fourth Republic.* Washington, D.C.: Foundation for Foreign Affairs, 1947.
Labouret, Henri. *Colonisation, colonialisme, décolonisation.* Paris: Larose, 1952.
La Coste, Yves; Nouschi, André; and Prenant, André. *L'Algérie, passé et present: le cadre et les étapes de la constitution de l'Algérie actuelle.* Paris: Editions Sociales, 1960.
Lacouture, Jean. *Cinq hommes et la France.* Paris: Editions du Seuil, 1961.
———. *De Gaulle.* Paris: Editions du Seuil, 1965.
——— and Simone. *Le Maroc à l'épreuve.* Paris: Editions du Seuil, 1958.
Laferrière, Julien. *Manuel de droit constitutionnel.* 2d ed. Paris: Domat-Montchrestien, 1947.
La Gorce, Paul-Marie de. *De Gaulle entre deux mondes.* Paris: Fayard, 1964.
———. *La République et son armée.* Paris: Fayard, 1963.
Lamine-Guèye, Amadou. *Étapes et perspectives de l'union française.* Paris: Editions de l'Union Française, 1955.
Lampué, Pierre. *Droit d'outre-mer.* Paris: Dalloz, 1958.
———. *L'Union française d'après la constitution.* Paris: Librairie Générale de Droit et de Jurisprudence, 1947.
Lancaster, Donald. *The Emancipation of French Indo-China.* London: Oxford University Press, 1961.
Lanesson, Jean Marie Antoine de. *Principes de colonisation.* Paris: Alcan, 1897.
Langer, William L. *The Diplomacy of Imperialism, 1890–1902.* New York: Alfred A. Knopf, 1935.
———. *Our Vichy Gamble.* New York: Alfred A. Knopf, 1947.
Lapie, Pierre-Olivier. *Mes tournées au Tchad.* London: John Murray, 1941.
———. *Le Tchad fait la guerre.* London: Hachette, 1943.
La Roche, Jean de, and Gottman, Jean. *La Fédération française.* Montreal: Editions d l'Arbre, 1945.
Lassaigne, Jean. *Constitution de la république française: 27 October 1946.* Paris: Recueil Sirey, 1947.

Laval, Pierre. *The Diary of Pierre Laval.* New York: Charles Scribner's Sons, 1948.

Lavergne, Bernard. *Une Révolution dans la politique coloniale de la France.* Paris: Mercure, 1948.

Lebel, Roland. *Etudes de littérature coloniale.* Paris: Peyronnet & Cie., 1928.

———. *Histoire de la littérature coloniale en France.* Paris: Larose, 1931.

Le Blond, Marius-Ary. *Après l'exotisme de Loti, le roman colonial.* 4th ed. Paris: Rasmussen, 1926.

Le Bon, Gustave. *Les Lois psychologiques de l'évolution des peuples.* Paris: Alcan, 1913.

Lebrun-Keris, Georges. *Mort de colonies.* Paris: Le Centurion, 1953.

Lemaignen, Robert; Senghor, Léopold Sédar; and Youtévong, Prince Sisowath. *La Communauté impériale française.* Paris: Editions Alsatia, 1945.

Leroy-Beaulieu, Paul. *De la colonisation chez les peuples modernes.* 4th ed. Paris: Guillaumin, 1898.

Le Tourneau, Roger. *Evolution politique de l'Afrique du nord musulmane: 1920–1961.* Paris: Colin, 1962.

LeVine, Victor T. *The Cameroons from Mandate to Independence*, Berkeley and Los Angeles: University of California Press, 1964.

Levy-Brühl, Lucien. *Les Fonctions mentales dans les sociétés inférieures.* Paris: Alcan, 1912.

Lidderdale, D. W. S. *The Parliament of France.* London: Hansard Society, 1951.

Ligou, Daniel. *Histoire du socialisme en France (1871–1961).* Paris: Presses Universitaires de France, 1962.

Lijphart, Arendt. *The Trauma of Decolonization, the Dutch and West New Guinea.* New Haven: Yale University Press, 1966.

Longrigg, Stephen Hemsley. *Syria and Lebanon under French Mandate.* New York: Oxford University Press, 1958.

Louis, Paul. *Le Colonialisme.* Paris: Société Nouvelle de Librairie, 1905.

———. *Histoire de socialisme en France, 1789–1945.* Paris: Rivière, 1946.

Luchaire, François. *Manuel de droit d'outre-mer.* Paris: Recueil Sirey, 1951.

Lüthy, Herbert. *France against Herself.* New York: Frederick A. Praeger, 1955.

Ly, Abdoulaye. *Les Masses africaines et l'actuelle condition humaine.* Paris: Présence Africaine, 1956.

McKay, Donald C. *The United States and France.* Cambridge: Harvard University Press, 1951.

Manevy, Raymond. *De la constituante à la constitution.* Paris: Editions du Chêne, 1945.

Mannoni, Dominque O. *Prospero and Caliban: The Psychology of Colonization.* London: Methuen & Co., 1956.

Marcus, John T. *French Socialism in the Crisis Years, 1933–36*. London: Stevens & Sons, 1958.
———. *Neutralism and Nationalism in France*. New York: Bookman Associates, 1958.
Martin, Kingsley. *French Liberal Thought in the 18th Century*. London: Ernest Benn, 1929.
Martin du Gard, Maurice. *La Carte impérial, histoire de la France d'outre-mer: 1940–45* Paris: Editions André Bonne, 1949–50.
———. *Courrier d'Afrique: Senegal-Soudan-Guinée*. Paris: Editions André Bonne, 1931.
Marx, Karl, and Engels, Friedrich. *On Colonialism*. Moscow: Foreign Language Publishing House, n.d.
Maunier, René. *Les Lois de l'empire: 1940–1942*. Paris: Domat-Montchrestien, 1942.
Mauriac, Claude. *Un Autre de Gaulle: journal 1944–54*. Paris: Hachette, 1970.
Maze, Jean. *Le Système: 1943–51*. Paris: Ségur, 1951.
Meisel, James H. *The Fall of the Republic*. Ann Arbor, Mich.: University of Michigan Press, 1962.
Méjan, François. *Le Vatican est-il contre la France d'outre-mer?* Paris: Fischbacher, 1958.
Mendès-France, Pierre, *Gouverner, c'est choisir*. Paris: Julliard, 1958.
Merle, Marcel. *Les Eglises chrétiennes et la décolonisation*. Paris: Colin, 1967.
———, comp. *L'Anticolonialisme européen de Las Casas à Karl Marx*. Paris: Colin, 1969.
Meynaud, Jean. *Les Groupes de pression en France*. Paris: Colin, 1958.
Micaud, Charles A. *Communism and the French Left*. New York: Frederick A. Praeger, 1963.
———. "French Political Parties: Ideological Myths and Social Realities," in *Modern Political Parties, Approaches to Comparative Politics*. Edited by Sigmund Neumann. Chicago: Chicago University Press, 1956.
———, ed. *Tunisia, the Politics of Modernization*. New York: Frederick A. Praeger, 1964.
Michel, Henri. *Les Courants de pensée de la Résistance*. Paris: Presses Universitaires de France, 1963.
———. *Vichy, année 40*. Paris: Laffont, 1966.
———, and Mirkine-Guetzévitch, Boris. *Les Idées politiques et sociales de la Résistance*. Paris: Presses Universitaires de France, 1954.
Mirkine-Guetzévitch, Boris. *L'Oeuvre de la Troisième République*. Montreal: Editions de l'Arbre, 1945.
Mitterrand, François. *Aux frontières de l'union française*. Paris: Julliard, 1953.
———. *Présence français et abandon*. Paris: Plon, 1957.
Moneta, Jacob. *Le PCF et la question coloniale, 1920–1965*. Paris: François Maspero, 1971.

Montagne, Robert. *Révolution au Maroc.* Paris: France-Empire, 1955.

Montvalon, Robert de. *Ces pays qu'on n'appellera plus colonies.* Paris: Bibliothèque de l'Homme d'Action, 1957.

Moon, Parker T. *Imperialism and World Politics.* New York: Macmillan Co., 1926.

Moore, J. M. *The Roots of French Republicanism.* New York: American Press, 1962.

Morazé, Charles. *Les Français et la république.* Paris: Colin, 1957.

Moresco, Emanuel. *Colonial Questions and Peace.* Paris: League of Nations, International Institute of Intellectual Cooperation, 1939.

Morgenthau, Ruth Schachter. *Political Parties in French-speaking West Africa.* London: Oxford University Press, 1964.

Morin, Edgar. *Autocritique.* Paris: Julliard, 1959.

Mortimer, Edward. *France and the Africans 1944–1960.* New York: Walker and Co., 1969.

Mounier, Emmanuel. *L'Eveil de l'Afrique noire.* Paris: Editions du Seuil, 1948.

Moussa, Pierre. *Les Chances économiques de la communauté franco-africaine.* Paris: Colin, 1957.

Murphy, Agnes. *The Ideology of French Imperialism, 1871–1881.* Washington, D.C.: Catholic University of America Press, 1948.

Mus, Paul. *Le Destin de l'union française de l'Indochine à l'Afrique.* Paris: Editions du Seuil, 1954.

Muselier, Vice-Admiral Emile. *De Gaulle contre le gaullisme.* Paris: Editions du Chêne, 1946.

Mveng, R. P. Engleberg, s.j. *Histoire du Cameroun.* Paris: Présence Africaine, 1964.

Naegelen, Marcel-Edmond. *Grandeur et solitude de la France.* Paris: Flammarion, 1956.

Naroun, Amar. *Ferhat Abbas ou les chemins de la souveraineté.* Paris: Denoel, 1961.

Navarre, Gen. Henri. *L'Agonie de l'Indochine.* Paris: Plon, 1956.

Niebuhr, Reinhold. *The Structure of Nations and Empires.* New York: Charles Scribner's Sons, 1959.

Noel, Léon. *Notre dernière chance.* Paris: Librairie Gedalge, 1956.

November, Andras. *L'Evolution du mouvement syndical en Afrique occidentale.* The Hague and Paris: Mouton, 1965.

Olivier, Marcel. *Six ans de politique sociale à Madagascar.* Paris: Grasset, 1931.

Oppermann, Thomas. *Le Problème algérien.* Paris: François Maspero, 1961.

Padover, Saul K. *France, Setting or Rising Star?* New York: Foreign Policy Association, 1950.

———. *French Institutions: Values and Politics.* Stanford, Calif.: Stanford University Press, 1954.

Paillat, Claude. *Vingt Ans qui déchirent la France.* 2 vols. Paris: Laffont, 1969.
Parti Communiste Français. *Le Parti communiste français dans la lutte contre le colonialisme.* Compiled by Monique Lafon. Paris: Editions Sociales, 1962.
Parti Socialiste. Groupe parlementaire. *L'Action socialiste à la seconde Constituante.* Paris: Editions de la Liberté, 1946.
———. *Les Socialistes, animateurs de la constituante.* Paris: Editions de la Liberté, 1946.
Pelloux, Robert. *Libéralisme, traditionalisme, décentralisation.* Paris: Colin, 1952.
Pickles, Dorothy Maud. *Algeria and France: From Colonialism to Cooperation.* New York: Frederick A. Praeger, 1963.
———. *France between the Republics.* London: Contract Publications, 1946.
———. *French Politics: The First Years of the Fourth Republic.* London and New York: Royal Institute of International Affairs, 1953.
Pierce, Roy. *Contemporary French Political Thought.* Oxford: Oxford University Press, 1966.
Pisani-Ferry, Fresnette. *Jules Ferry et le partage du monde.* Paris: Grasset, 1962.
Planchais, Jean. *Une Histoire politique de l'armée.* Vol. 2, *De de Gaulle à de Gaulle, 1940–67.* Paris: Editions du Seuil, 1967.
———. *Le Malaise de l'armée.* Paris: Plon, 1958.
La Politique étrangère et ses fondaments. Paris: Colin, 1954.
Pouquet, Jean. *L'Afrique occidentale française.* Paris: Presses Universitaires de France, 1954.
Poutier, Claude. *La Réforme de la constitution.* Paris: Recueil Sirey, 1955.
Power, Thomas F. *Jules Ferry and the Renaissance of French Imperialism.* New York: Kings Crown Press, 1944.
Prélot, Marcel. *Histoire des idées politiques.* Paris: Dalloz, 1961.
———. *Institutions politiques et droit constitutionnel.* Paris: Dalloz, 1957.
Prévost-Parodol, Lucien Anatole. *La France nouvelle.* Paris: Michel-Lévy Frères, 1868.
Priestley, Herbert I. *France Overseas: A Study of Modern Imperialism.* New York: D. Appleton-Century Co., 1938.
Ramadier, Paul. *Les Socialistes et l'exercice du pouvoir.* Paris: Laffont, 1961.
Reclus, Maurice. *Grandeur de "La Troisième" de Gambetta à Poincaré.* Paris: Hachette, 1948.
Regismanset, Charles. *Questions coloniales.* 2 vols. Paris: Larose, 1923.
Rémond, René. *La Droite en France de la restauration à nos jours.* Paris: Editions Aubier Montaigne, 1963.

———, ed. *Forces réligieuses et attitudes politiques dans la France contemporaine.* Paris: Colin, 1965.

Renouvin, Pierre. *Histoire des relations internationales.* Paris: Hachette, 1957–58. Vol. 7, *Les Crises du XXe siècle: de 1914 à 1945.*

Reynaud, Paul. *In the Thick of the Fight, 1930–45.* New York: Simon & Schuster, 1955.

Rezette, Robert. *Les Partis politiques marocains.* Paris: Colin, 1955.

Richard-Molard, Jacques. *Afrique occidentale française.* Paris: Berger-Levrault, 1949–50.

Roberts, Stephen H. *History of French Colonial Policy 1870–1925.* London: P. S. King & Son, 1929.

Robinson, Kenneth. *The Public Law of Overseas France since the War.* London: Colonial Studies Institute of Oxford, 1954.

Rolland, Louis, and Lampué, Pierre. *Droit d'outre-mer.* 3d ed. Paris: Dalloz, 1959.

Roosevelt, Elliot. *As He Saw It.* New York: Duell, Sloan & Pearce, 1946.

Rossillion, Claude. *Le Régime législatif de la France d'outre-mer.* Paris: Editions de l'Union Française, 1955.

Roure, André Maurice Rémy. *La IVe République.* Paris: Le Monde, 1948–50.

Royal Institute of International Affairs. *The French Colonial Empire.* London: Royal Institute of International Affairs, 1940.

Rudin, Harry R. *Germans in the Cameroons 1884–1914.* New Haven: Yale University Press, 1938.

Sainteny, Jean. *Histoire d'une paix manquée, Indochine, 1945–1947.* Paris: Amiot-Dumont, 1953.

Sarraut, Albert. *Grandeur et servitude coloniales.* Paris: Editions Sagittaire, 1931.

———. *La Mise en valeur des colonies françaises.* Paris: Editions Payot, 1923.

Sartre, Jean Paul. *Situations.* Paris: Gallimard, 1964. Vol. 5, *Colonialisme et néo-colonialisme.*

Satineau, Maurice. *Schoelcher, héros de l'abolition de l'esclavage dans les possessions françaises.* Paris: Mellottée, 1949–50.

Saussure, Léopold de. *La Psychologie de la colonisation française dans ses rapports avec les sociétés indigènes.* Paris: Alcan, 1899.

Savary, Alain. *Nationalisme algérienne et grandeur française.* Paris: Plon, 1960.

Schoelcher, Victor. *Esclavage et colonisation.* Paris: Presses Universitaires de France, 1948.

Schramm, Percy Ernst. *Deutschland und Ubersee.* Braunschweig, West Germany: Georg Westermann Verlag, 1950.

Schuman, Frederick L. *War and Diplomacy in the French Republic.* New York: McGraw-Hill Book Co., 1931.

Schwartz, Bernard. *French Administrative Law and the Common Law World.* New York: New York University Press, 1954.

Scott, John A. *Republican Ideas and the Liberal Tradition in France, 1870–1914*. New York: Columbia University Press, 1951.
Sharp, Walter R. *The French Civil Service: Bureaucracy in Transition*. New York: Macmillan Co., 1931.
———. *The Government of the French Republic*. New York: D. Van Nostrand Co., 1938.
Sherwood, Robert. *Roosevelt and Hopkins*. New York: Harper, 1948.
Siegfried, André. *De la IIIe à la IVe république*. Paris: Grasset, 1956.
Simon, Yves. *La Grande crise de la république française: observations sur la vie politique des français de 1918–38*. Montreal: Editions de l'Arbre, 1941.
———. *The Road to Vichy, 1918–1938*. New York: Sheed & Ward, 1942.
Soltau, Roger. *French Political Thought in the Nineteenth Century*. New Haven: Yale University Press, 1959.
Sophie, Ulrich. *Le Gouverneur-général Félix Eboué*. 2d ed. Paris: Larose, 1949–50.
Soulier, August. *L'Instabilité ministérielle sous la Troisième République (1871–1938)*. Paris: Recueil Sirey, 1939.
Soustelle, Jacques. *Le Drame algérien et la décadence française: réponse à Raymond Aron*. Paris: Plon, 1957.
———. *Envers et contre tout*. 2 vols. Paris: Laffont, 1947–50.
Stern, Jacques. *The French Colonies, Past and Future*. New York: Dedier, 1944.
Stillman, Calvin W. *Africa in the Modern World*. Chicago: Chicago University Press, 1955.
Strachey, John. *The End of Empire*. New York: Random House, 1960.
Tasca [Rossi], Angelo. *A Communist Party in Action: An Account of the Organization and Operations in France*. Translated and edited by Willmoore Kendall. New Haven: Yale University Press, 1949.
Taylor, Owen R. *The Fourth Republic of France*. London and New York: Royal Institute of International Affairs, 1951.
Tchernoff, J. *Le Parti républicain sous la monarchie de juillet*. Paris: Editions Pedone, 1906.
Tesson, Phillippe. *De Gaulle Ier, la révolution manquée: histoire du premier gouvernement de Gaulle, août 1944-janvier 1946*. Paris: Albin Michel, 1965.
Thiam, Doudou. *La Portée de la citoyenneté française dans les territoires d'outre-mer*. Poitiers: Société d'éditions africaines, 1953.
Thompson, Virginia. *French Indo-China*. London: George Allen & Unwin, 1937.
———, and Adloff, Richard. *The Malagasy Republic*. Stanford, Calif.: Stanford University Press, 1965.
Thomson, David. *Democracy in France*. 2d ed. London and New York: Oxford University Press, 1958.
———. *The Democratic Ideal in France and England*. Cambridge: Cambridge University Press, 1940.

———. *Two Frenchmen: Pierre Laval and Charles de Gaulle*. London: Cresset Press, 1951.
Thorez, Maurice. *Oeuvres complètes*. 18 vols. Paris: Editions Sociales, 1950–63.
Vedel, Georges. *Manuel élémentaire de droit constitutionnel*. Paris: Recueil Sirey, 1949–50.
Viard, René. *La Fin de l'empire colonial français*. Paris: G.-P. Maisonneuve et Larose, 1963.
Vigneras, Marcel. *Rearming the French*. Washington, D.C.: Office of the Chief Military History, Department of the Army, 1957.
Violette, Maurice. *L'Algérie vivra-t-elle?* Paris: Alcan, 1931.
Wahl, Nicholas. *Fifth Republic*. New York: Random House, 1959.
Wainhouse, David. *Remnants of Empire: the United Nations and the End of Colonialism*. New York: Harper & Row, for the Council on Foreign Relations, 1965.
Walker, Erie A. *Colonies*. Cambridge: Cambridge University Press, 1944.
Weber, Eugen. *The Nationalist Revival in France, 1905–1914*. Berkeley and Los Angeles: University of California Press, 1959.
Weill, Georges. *Histoire du parti républicain en France, de 1814 à 1870*. Paris: Alcan, 1900.
Weinstein, Brian. *Eboué*. New York: Oxford University Press, 1972.
Werth, Alexander. *The Destiny of France (1918–1937)*. London: Robert Hale, 1937.
———. *France in Ferment*. New York and London: Harper and Bros., 1934.
———. *France, 1940–56*. New York: Holt, Rhinehart and Winston, 1956.
———. *The Twilight of France, 1933–1940*. New York and London: Harper and Bros., 1942.
Weygand, Gen. Maxime. *Mémoires*. 3 vols. Paris: Flammarion, 1950–57.
White, Dorothy S. *Seeds of Discord*. Syracuse, N.Y.: Syracuse University Press, 1965.
Williams, Philip M. *Crisis and Compromise*. Hamden, Conn.: Archon Books, 1964.
———. *Politics in Postwar France*, 2d ed. London: Longmans Green and Co., 1958.
———, and Harrison, Martin. *De Gaulle's Republic*. London: Longmans Green and Co., 1960.
Wolf, John B. *France, 1814–1919: The Rise of a Liberal-Democratic Society*. Englewood Cliffs, N.J.: Prentice-Hall, 1940.
Wright, Gordon. *The Reshaping of French Democracy*. New York: Reynal and Hitchcock, 1948.
Wright, Quincy. *Mandates under the League of Nations*. Chicago: University of Chicago Press, 1939.
Wylie, Laurence W. *Village in the Vaucluse*. Cambridge: Harvard University Press, 1957.

Zeldin, Theodore. *Emile Olivier and the Liberal Empire of Napoleon III.* Oxford: Clarendon Press, 1963.
Zévaès, Alexandre. *Histoire de socialisme et du communisme en France de 1871 à 1947.* Paris: Editions France Empire, 1948.
———. *Histoire de la Troisième République.* Paris: 1946.
Zieglé, Henri. *L'Afrique équatoriale française.* Paris: Berger-Levrault, 1952.

Public Documents

Communist International, 1919–43. Documents selected and edited by Jane Degras. 3 vols. London: Oxford University Press, 1956–65.
La Documentation Française. "Aspects financiers et budgetaires du développement économique de l'union française," *Notes et Etudes Documentaires,* no. 1568. Paris, 1952.
———. "L'Évolution récente des institutions politiques dans les territoires d'outre-mer et territoires associés." *Notes et Etudes Documentaires,* no. 1847. Paris, 1954.
———. "L'Organisation générale de l'état civil en France (metropolitaine et d'outre-mer) et dans les territoires sous tutelle du Togo et Cameroun." *Notes et Etudes Documentaires,* no. 2010. Paris, 1955.
France. Assemblée Nationale Constituante. *Annales de l'Assemblée Nationale Constituante élue le 2 juin 1946.*
———. *Annales de L'Assemblée Nationale Constituante élue le 21 octobre 1945.*
———. Assemblée Nationale Consultative. *Débats.* Algiers, 1943–44.
———. *Bulletin officiel de la France d'outre-mer,* 1946.
———. Chambre des Deputés. *Débats parlementaires.*
———. *Chroniques d'outre-mer.*
———. Commission de la Constitution. *Séances de la Commission de la Constitution. Comptes-rendus analytiques.* 2 vols. Paris, 1946.
———. *Documents de l'Assemblée Nationale Constituante élue le 21 octobre 1945.*
———. *Documents de l'Assemblée Nationale Constituante élue le 2 juin 1946.*
———. *Documents parlementaires.*
———. *Journal officiel de l'état français.* Vichy, 1940–44.
———. *Journal officiel de la France libre.* London, 1940–43.
———. *Journal officiel de la république française.* Assemblée Nationale. *Débats parlementaires.*
———. *Lois et decrets.*
———. Ministère des colonies. *Conférence africaine française—Brazzaville.* Paris, 1945.
———. Ministère de la France d'outre-mer. *Bulletin d'information.*

United Nations. General Assembly, *Verbatim Records of the Plenary Meetings.*

———. *Summary Records of the Fourth Committee.*

United States. Department of State. *The United Nations Conference on International Organization.* Conference Series no. 83, 10 vols. Washington, 1946.

Unpublished Materials

Archives of André Marty. Microfilm. Cambridge. Harvard University Library, 1961.

INDEX

Abbas, Ferhat, 123–24, 228, 267, 289–90, 303; critique of French Union texts, 307–08; drafts "Manifesto," 117–19; forms Amis du Manifeste et de la Liberté, 122–23, 157; in Constitutional Committee, 156, 166; incident, 160–61; political views of, 156, 160, 230–34, 294; rejects constitutional draft, 291, 294

Abdullah, Ibn Husain, 132

Académie des Sciences Coloniales, 248

Agreement of 6 March 1946 (Indochina). *See* Treaties and diplomatic agreements

Algeria, 25; autonomy for, 231–33; constitution of, 220, 232; nationalist movement in, 65, 122–25

Amis du Manifeste et de la Liberté: Abbas forms, 122–23, 157; in elections of 1945, 123; leaders arrested and released, 125, 142, 158. *See also* Union Démocratique du Manifeste Algérien

André, Max, 203, 258, 274

Angeletti, Yves, 281

Anticolonialism, 19, 29, 49

Apithy, Sourou Migan, 291

April Draft Constitution, 149, 171–72, 203, 266, 289; adopted by Constituent Assembly, 228–29; Council of the Union to coordinate, 217; Declaration of Rights, 215; effect of rejection, 223–24; electoral law, 224; French Union institutions, 215; legislative system of, 217; Monnerville on, 213; on citizenship, 227; rejected (5 May 1946), 150, 228, 235

Arab League, 123

Arboussier, Gabriel d', 167, 220, 223; portrait of, 168–69; report on Local Assemblies Bill, 221–23

Argenlieu, Admiral Thierry d', 197, 201, 204, 274

Ashedi, Ora, 127

Assembly of the Union, 173, 275–77, 310; and local government, 293; constitutional provisions, 298–300; representation in, 286–89. *See also* Council of the Union

Assimilation, 13

Associated States: legal status of, 297

Association France-Vietnam, 175

Atlantic Charter, 181

Aujoulat, Dr. Louis, 166, 185, 186, 259, 261

Auphan, Admiral Paul, 79

Auriol, Vincent, 150, 265, 266, 268

Bainville, Jacques, 83

Balafrej, Ahmed, 120

Bao Dai, 133, 190–91

Barbé, Raymond, 244

Bardoux, Jacques, 248

Barnave, Antoine Pierre Joseph, 19

Barthes, René, 176

Bastid, Paul, 251, 289

Bell, Douala Manga, 185, 186, 259

Berlin Conference (1885), 35

Berlioz, Joany, 236

Bernstein, Eduard, 56

Bertho, Father, 259

Bevin, Ernest, 184

Bidault, Georges, 187, 266, 272–73, 289–90, 301, 302; action on Territorial Assemblies Bill, 306–07; conception of French Union, 274–77, 286–87; deal with Thorez, 282–83; formed government, 274; in Constituent Assembly, 283–87, 293; on Algeria, 274–75; portrait of, 274; relations with de Gaulle, 274, 283; speech to United Nations General Assembly (1946), 184

Bismarck, Prince Otto von, 34, 37, 56

Blum, Léon, 53, 144, 151, 202, 263

Blum-Violette plan (Algeria), 6, 71–72, 117, 122, 263

Boganda, Bartelemy, 259

Boisdon, Daniel, 234
Boislambert, Hettier de, 193, 195
Boisson, Pierre, 78, 176
Bonaparte, Charles Louis Napoleon. *See* Napoleon III
Borella, François, 188
Borgeaud, Henri, 155
Boulangist crisis, 38
Bourbon Restoration (1815–30), 16, 24
Bourguiba, Habib, 121; letter to Ferhat Abbas, 122
Bracke, Alexandre Marie [Desrousseaux], 57
Brazza, Savorgnan de, 36
Brazzaville Conference (1944), 102–15, 134, 152, 176; and suppression of forced labor, 112, 115; de Gaulle's views on, 115; proposed electoral reforms, 138; recommendations of, 107–13. *See also* Laws and decrees
Bretton Woods Agreement, 249
Brissot, Jacques Pierre, 19
Brunhes, Julien, 246
Bugeaud de la Piconnerie, General Thomas Robert, 25, 33

Caballero, secretary of Algerian Communist party, 237
Cabet, Etienne, 51
Caffery, Jefferson, 91
Caisse Centrale de la France d'Outre-mer (CCFOM), 225. *See also* Investment Fund for Economic and Social Development
Cambodia: in French Union, 197
Casablanca Conference (January 1943), 119
Casey, Richard G.: agreement with Catroux, 131
Castellani, Jules, 172
Catroux, General Georges, 118, 130, 175; proclaimed independence of Syria and Lebanon, 130–31
Césaire, Aimé, 219, 241, 290, 291
Charmes, Gabriel, 30
Charter of the French Union, 215. *See also* French Union, constitution of
Chasseloup-Laubat, François, Marquis de, 28
Chataigneau, Yves, 124, 158, 176, 177, 266
Cheick, Said Mohamed, 223
Chevance, General Paul, 155
Churchill, Winston, 87; and de Gaulle, 92; and Roosevelt, 132
Church of France, 15
Citizenship: "citizenship of the French Union," 252, 278, 287; conservative view of, 246; Constituent Assembly debates, 210, 270, 297–98; dual character of, 106, 211–12; in "four communes" of Senegal, 125; Lamine-Guèye law regarding, 293; MRP plan for, 259; native deputies' view of, 292–93; Preamble and, 296
Civil Service Act: adopted, 306; Bidault and Thorez agree on, 282–83
Clemenceau, Georges, 16, 34, 43, 102
Club de Massac, 19
Cochin China, Republic of, 201
Colbert, Jean Baptiste, 19
Colonial Exposition of 1931, 67, 68
Colonialism: in Second Empire, 28–29; Jules Ferry and, 37; nineteenth-century practice of, 33–40; principles of, 12–13, 37, 43, 46; Sarraut's view of, 46; twentieth-century developments, 46, 55; Universal Exposition of 1900 promoted, 39
Colonial myth, 2, 4, 18, 40, 208–09; and Indochina, 189; Césaire's criticism of, 241; communist version of, 61; definition of, 4–5; liberal version of, 23, 40; MRP view of, 257; origins and principal themes, 11–14; Radical party view of, 255; radical republican version of, 41–47; Socialist version of, 265; UDMA challenge to, 161
Colonna, Antoine, 155
Combes, Emile, 16
Comité de L'Afrique Français, 39, 73
Comité Franco-Malgache, 175
Committee on Overseas Territories, 221, 223; d'Arboussier on, 168–69; endorsed Intergroup Plan, 229; Houphouet on, 168; Lamine-Guèye on, 164–65, 265, 280; and Madagascar, 219
Communist International (Comintern): and PCF, 59; on colonialism, 58; Sixth Congress (1928), 59
Condorcet, Marie Jean de Caritat, Marquis de, 19
Confédération Générale du Travail Tunisien, 122
Conseil d'Etat, 223
Constituent Assembly (1791), 19–21
Constituent Assembly (October 1945–May 1946), 4, 8–9, 125, 137, 144, 189, 205–06, 208–09, 258, 306; colonial deputies in, 139, 153–71; de Gaulle, 147–52; elections of 1945, 138–43; metropolitan parties in, 145–52; Moutet speech, 206; referendum of 21 October 1945, 147. *See also* French Union; Laws and decrees; Local assemblies
Constituent Assembly (June–October

1946), 125, 137, 207, 260, 272, 273, 302; Abbas incident, 161–62; and Indochina crisis, 202–07; Herriot speech, 253–54; role of UDMA, 125, 158–60. *See also* French Union; Laws and decrees; Local assemblies
Constitutional Committee, 148–50, 229, 254, 290, 293; Abbas's role, 156; Algerian constitution, 220, 232–33; Bastid speech, 251–52; Bidault plan, 278–80; electoral system, 289; French Union articles, 203, 273–80, 285–87; Intergroup plan, 230; Madagascar, 218; Moutet, 276; native deputies boycott, 292
Consultative Assembly (1944–45), 99, 103, 104; de Gaulle speech, 193
Convention of 1792, 16
Coste-Floret, Paul, 259, 261, 262, 275, 279, 280, 293
Cot, Pierre, 230, 241–42, 289
Council of the Union, 252, 257, 261, 264; MRP proposals, 259. *See also* Assembly of the Union
Cournarie, Pierre, 176
Currency: revaluation of 1945, 249
Cuttoli, Paul, 155

Daladier, Edouard, 161
Dalat Conference, 200, 201
Dalloni, Marius, 166
Darlan, Admiral Jean François, 79; Darlan-Hitler agreement (1941), 130
Darnal, Albert, 193
Dèbes, Colonel, 202
De Broglie, Victor, duc de, 11
Decolonization, 1–2, 4, 8, 152, 301; effects of, 313
Decoux, Admiral Jean, 79, 190
Decrees. *See* Laws and decrees
De Gaulle, General Charles, 7, 124, 135–37, 144, 207, 244; attitudes toward United States, 90, 91–92; Brazzaville Conference, 102–04, 115; colonial doctrines, 82, 90, 102–04, 182; Constituent Assembly, 144, 149; constitutional views, 94–100, 146–47, 150–51, 228, 260–61, 268, 271–73, 284–85, 291, 314; foreign policy goals, 91–94, 99–102, 133, 143, 182; Free French movement, 76, 86–89; French politics, 93–99, 284; policy in Indochina, 134, 142, 191–93, 196, 201, 206; policy in Levant, 128, 130–31; policy in North Africa, 116–21; president of Provisional Government (1944–46), 81, 146–49; relations with Bidault, 274–75, 283; relations with Churchill, 87, 92–93; relations with Roosevelt, 90–92, 132; World War II, 86–90, 98, 143
Delavignette, Robert, 66, 169
Delcassé, Théophile, 38
De Lepervanche, PCF deputy (Réunion), 166
Dentz, General, 130
Depreux, Edouard, 264, 266, 267, 268
Destour party, 65
Devillers, Phillipe, 191, 205
Deyron, Léon, 155
Diagne Blaise, 265
Diallo, Yacine, 291
Diouf, Galandou, 139, 164
Duchêne, Albert, 68
Duclos, Jacques, 304

Eboué, Félix, 106
Eboué, Mme. Félix, 311
Edde, Emile, 131
Elections and referenda: election and referendum of 21 October 1945, 145–47, 154, 163, 294; election of 2 June 1946, 150, 154, 156, 166, 204; election of November 1946, 154; Popular Front, 1936, 153; referendum of 21 October 1945, 147–48; referendum of 5 May 1946, 150, 171; referendum of 13 October 1946, 151
Electoral law, 248, 304–05, 308–09
Elite, colonial: changes in, 153–79; defined, 152
Enfantin, Prosper, 50
Engels, Friedrich, 55; letter to Bernstein, 56; letter to Kautsky, 238
Estates General (1789), 19
Esteva, Admiral, 79
Etats Généraux de la Colonisation Française, 172–73, 228
Etats Généraux de la Renaissance Française, 140
Etienne, Eugéne, 38
Etoile Nord-Africaine, 65

Faidherbe, General Louis Léon César, 28, 33
Faisal, Emir, 129
Fajon, Etienne, 145, 279, 292
Ferry, Jules, 16, 30, 34–38, 43
FIDES. *See* Investment Fund for Economic and Social Development
Fonds de Solidarité Coloniale. *See* Investment Fund for Economic and Social Development
Fountainebleau Conference (Indochina), 200–02, 204, 270, 272, 274

Forced labor, 112, 115; suppression of, 304
Fourier, Charles, 51, 55, 57
Fourth Republic: adopted, 151; constitution, 295; reform of, 144. *See also* April Draft Constitution; French Union, constitution of
Free French movement, 76, 80–81, 89, 130–32, 136, 142–43, 175; colonial reforms, 102. *See also* Brazzaville Conference; Laws and decrees; Provisional Government
Free trade, 23
French Communist Party (PCF), 15, 220, 262, 266, 267, 273, 290, 304–05, 314; and Soviet Union, 97–98, 144–46; colonial policies of, 54–61, 97–98; in First Constituent Assembly, 144–50; in Provisional Government, 145–46; in Second Constituent Assembly, 279, 281–83, 305; in West Africa, 126–27, 168. *See also* Communist International
French Expeditionary Corps (Indochina), 200, 266
French National Liberation Committee (CFLN). *See* Free French movement
French Union, 1, 9, 144, 174, 187, 203, 226–28, 295. *See also* Citizenship; Local assemblies; Representation
— constitution of, 1, 4, 7–8, 11, 134, 151, 180, 202–09, 226, 235, 272, 279–88, 297–313; adopted, 294; Bidault government position, 277–93; Etats Généraux plan, 173–74; MRP plan, 255–62; Socialist approach, 262–64; UDMA plan, 159
— Indochina conflict and, 189–99; Madagascar in, 218; native deputies' role, 289–92
Freycinet, Charles, 30

Galliéni, General Joseph Simon, 33
Gambetta, Léon, 30, 38
Garibaldi, Giuseppe, 57
Gay, Francisque, 256
Giacobbi, Paul, 134, 177, 183, 192
Giap, Vo Nguyen, 190–91, 202
Giraud, General Henri, 97, 120
Gouin, Félix, 114, 265, 274
Grégoire, Abbé Henri, 19
Grosser, Alfred, 84, 299

Hadj, Messali, 158, 160, 267
Hardy, Georges, 68
Harmand, Jules, 40
Helleu, Jean, 131
Herriot, Edouard, 205–06, 274; attacks French Union draft constitution, 253–54, 268, 272–73
High Council of French Union, 275, 277–78
Hitler, Adolf, 62, 130
Ho Chi Minh, 65, 175, 190, 198, 201–02, 205, 228, 274, 304
Hopkins, Harry, 91
Houphouët-Boigny, Félix, 220–21, 289, 290, 292; on French Union, 307; on role of native deputies, 169–70, 311; portrait of, 167–68
Hugonnet, Léon, 36
Hull, Cordell, 132

Imperialism (Lenin), 58
"Imperial spirit," 28
Indochina, 8, 199, 201; declaration of 24 March 1945, 7, 135–37
Intergroup of Native Deputies, 228, 252, 261; and SFIO, 266–67; plan for union, 229–31
Interministerial Committee on Indochina, 204; Charter of French Union, 275
International Conference of Geographers (1876), 33
International Institute of Intellectual Cooperation (IIIC), 63
International Labor Office, Committee on Native Labor, 63
Investment Fund for Economic and Social Development (FIDES), 224–26, 249
Istiqlal party, 65, 120
Ivory Coast: Association des Colons de la Côte d'Ivoire, 172; forced labor in, 176, 304; resistance groups in, 127

Jaurès, Jean, 17, 51–52, 57–58, 264, 265
Juglas, Jean-Jacques, 280
Juin, General Alphonse, 120, 177
July Monarchy (1831–48), 16, 24–26

Kautsky, Karl, 57; letter from Engels, 238
Khmer Issarak (Free Cambodia) movement, 196–97
Khoury, Bechara, 131
Khrushchev, Nikita, 146

Labonne, Erik, 176–77
Labor law, 112–13, 115; effects in Ivory Coast, 304. *See also* Forced labor
Labouret, Henri, 69
Lacouture, Jean, 160
Lafargue, Paul, 57
Lainé, Pierre, 24
Lambert, colonial administrator, 176

Lameth, Alexandre Théodore Victor, 19
Lamine-Guèye, Amadou, 163, 170, 220–21, 227, 265, 290–93, 309–12; criticizes draft constitution, 291–93; law of 7 May 1946, 222; portrait of, 164–65; secession disavowed, 230–33. *See also* Citizenship; Forced labor; Local assemblies
La nouvelle politique indigène pour l'Afrique Equatoriale Française (Félix Eboué), 106
LaPorte, Jean, 57
Lassalle, Ferdinand, 55
Latrille, André, 167, 168, 176, 177
Laurentie, Governor Henri, 142, 165, 177
Laval, Pierre, 17
Laws and decrees: April Draft Constitution rejected, 223; Constitutional Law (10 July 1940), 76; Constitution of 4 November 1848, 31; decree abolishing forced labor (11 April 1946), 222; decree of 11 March 1937 (labor reform), 115; decree of 7 March 1944 (Algerian representation), 116; electoral law, 303; Lamine-Guèye law (citizenship) (7 May 1946), 222; law abolishing slavery (27 April 1848), 32; law establishing local assemblies (9 May 1946), 222; law of 30 Floreal, Year X (20 May 1802), 21; Local Assemblies Bill, 303; senatus-consulte (1854), 27
League for Independence of Vietnam. *See* Vietminh
League of Nations, 43, 61, 63, 129, 181, 184, 187; League Health Organization, 63
Le Brun Keris, George, 258
Leclerc, General Philippe, 177, 196, 197, 205, 274
Legendre, Jean, 308
Lejeune, Max, 305
Lemaignen, Robert, 214
Lenin: *Imperialism*, 58
Leroy-Beaulieu, Paul, 33
Letourneau, Jean, 310
Le Troquer, André, 265, 266
Ligue des Droits de l'Homme, 253
Local administration, 287. *See also* Assembly of the Union; French Union, constitution of
Local assemblies, 219, 227; law of 9 May 1946, 222–23; Local Assemblies Bill blocked, 306; native deputies' view of, 310–11; powers of, 287
Longuet, Charles Félix César, 57
Louis Philippe, King of France, 16, 25
Lozeray, Henri, 237, 239, 244
Lu Han, 196, 198
Lyautey, Hubert, 33, 68, 107

Malbrant, René, 166, 226, 247, 290
Marcoin, Auguste, 176, 177
Martel, French governor of Syria, 129
Martinaud-Déplat, Léon, 155
Marty, André, 239
Marx, Karl, 81; and socialism, 50; on colonial rule and nationalism, 54–56
Marxism and the National and Colonial Questions (Stalin), 58
Massu, Colonel Jacques, 196, 198
Mast, General Emmanuel, 178
Maunier, René, 70
Maurras, Charles, 83
Mayer, Daniel, 151, 268
Mayer, René, 155, 254
Mendès-France, Pierre, 87, 155
Mirabeau, Victor, Marquis de, 19
Mise en valeur, policy of, 44–49
Molé, Count Louis, 24
Mollet, Guy, 151, 268
Moncef Bey, 120
Monnerville, Gaston, 139, 195, 213, 224
Monnet, Georges, 167
Montalembert, Charles Forbes René de, 11
Montesquieu, Charles Louis de Secondat, Baron de, 19
Morel, Jean, 45
Morgenthau, Ruth Schachter, 163
Morlière, Louis, 177
Morocco, 153, 263, 288; nationalist movement in, 64–65, 119–20, 176–77
Moro-Giafferri, Vincent de, 254
Moutet, Marius, 115, 163, 164, 168, 177, 185, 206, 225, 235, 254, 265–66, 276, 303, 309; French Union constitution, 276–78, 289, 292; Local Assemblies Bill, 219, 289
Mouvement Republicain Populaire (MRP), 147, 201, 205, 227, 228, 261, 266, 267, 272, 273, 278, 279, 305; constitutional plan, 255–62; opposes April Draft Constitution, 150
Murphy, Robert, 117, 132
Mus, Paul, 179
Muselier, Admiral Emile, 87
Mussolini, Benito, 62
Mutter, André, 303

Naba, Mogho, 127
Naggiar, Paul Emile, 185
Napoleonic Empire: colonial policies of, 21–22; special laws of, 21
Napoleon III, Emperor of France, 20, 22, 26, 27, 32, 105

Nazi occupation, 77, 147
Nazi-Soviet Pact, 60; and PCF, 97–98
Neo-Destour party, 65, 120–21, 178
Nguyen-Ai-Quoc. *See* Ho Chi Minh
Noel, Léon, 247
NSDAP Kolonialpolitisches Amt, 77

Omar, El Hadj, 169
Ottoman Empire, 27, 40, 43

Parti du Peuple Algérien (PPA), 65, 123, 124, 158, 160
Parti Jeune Algérien, 65
Parti Republicain de la Liberté (PRL), 154, 272
Pasha, Nahas, 132
Pasquier, Pierre, 66
Passy, Frédéric, 37
Patch, General Alexander, 91
Pétain, Henri Philippe, 7, 17, 76, 79, 80, 87, 94, 127
Peyrouton, Marcel, 79, 175
Philip, André, 87, 265, 278
Pierre-Bloch, Jean, 219
Platon, Admiral, 79
Pleven, René, 177
Popular Front, 42, 50, 60, 62, 67, 71, 73, 115, 126, 129, 263
Prévost-Paradol, Lucien Anatole, 28
Proudhon, Pierre Joseph, 56, 81; foresees decolonization, 51
Provisional Government (1944–46), 2, 3, 104, 140, 142, 152–53, 192, 194, 269
Puaux, Gabriel, 176

Quilici, François, 155, 304
Quinzaine, La (journal), 175

Radical party, 254; French settlers in, 154
Radical Socialists, 147, 245, 271
Ramadier, Paul, 279
Raseta, Joseph, 218, 219
Rassemblement Démocratique Africain (RDA), 166, 168, 169, 170
Rassemblement des Gauches Republicains (RGR), 205, 255, 261, 290; elections of 2 June 1946, 150; opposes French Union constitution, 294; plan for French Union, 251–52; UDSR and Radicals join to form, 245
Rassemblement du Peuple Francais (RPF), 284
Ravoahangy, Joseph, 218, 219, 308; rejects constitutional draft, 291
Raynal, Guillaume Thomas, 19
Referenda. *See* Elections and referenda
Reichscolonialbund, 77
Religion, 64; Association of the Reformist Ulema of Algeria, 123; messianic movements in Africa, 66
Rencurel, Auguste, 155, 166
Representation: constitutional provisions, 298–301; French settlers, Morocco, Tunisia, 288; in Assembly of the Union, 286; inequalities in, 299–300; in National Assembly, 286; in territorial assemblies, 292–98; Moutet amendment, 292
Republicanism: definition of, 14–17; doctrine of political assimilation, 31; liberal, 22; radical views of, 29
Resistance, French: political ideas, 81
Revolution: of 1789, 5, 12, 15, 18, 22; Bolshevik, 17, 66
Rey, governor of Ivory Coast, 176
Rieber, Alfred, 238
Robert, Admiral Georges Joseph, 79
Robespierre, Maximilien de, 19, 20
Roch, Emile, 155
Roman law: and citizenship, 210
Roosevelt, Franklin D., 90, 91, 117, 119, 191; in Levant crisis, 132; relations with de Gaulle, 90–92
Rose, Jean, 172
Rousseau, Jean Jacques, 94, 95

Said, Noury, 132
Sainteny, Jean, 194, 198, 205
Saint-Simon, Louis de Rouvroy, Count de, 81
San Francisco Conference on International Organizations, 183, 189
Sangnier, Marc, 256
Sarraut, Albert, 1, 68; policy of mise en valeur, 44–49
Saurin, Paul, 73
Schock, André, 172, 304
Schoelcher, Victor, 11, 31
Schumann, Maurice, 162, 304
Second Empire (1852–70), 16, 23, 24, 27–28, 32
Section Français de l'International Ouvriére. *See* Socialist party (SFIO)
Senatus-consulte (1854). *See* Laws and decrees
Senghor, Léopold, 11, 163, 170, 221, 265, 289, 290; and April Draft Constitution, 216, 218; attacks Bidault plan, 281; portrait of, 165–66; secession disavowed, 230–33
Sieyès, Emmanuel Joseph, 19
Sihanouk, Norodom, 196, 197

Simon, Henri, 43
Sismondi, Jean Charles Leonard de, 25
Sissoko, Fily Dabo, 291
Smith, Adam, 54
Socialist party (SFIO), 53, 57, 278; election of November 1946, 154; French Union Constitution, 262–66; in Constituent Assembly, 148, 150; in Second Constituent Assembly, 266–69, 279–81; in Senegal, 163–64; in Thirty-eighth Congress, 151, 268
Société des Amis des Noires, 20
Solh, Riad, 131
Soltau, Roger, 17
Soustelle, Jacques, 177, 186, 224
Soviet Union, 3, 60
Spanish Civil War, 62
Spears, Major-General Sir Edward, 131
Sportisse, Alice, 166, 241
Stalin, Joseph, 60, 132; *Marxism and the National and Colonial Question,* 58
Syndicat Agricole Africain, 167, 176

Tall, El Hadj Seydou Nourou, 169
Tchicaya, Félix, 309, 311
Teitgen, Henri, 269
Témoignage Chrétien (Catholic weekly), 175
Thanh, Son Ngoc, 196, 197
Thiers, Louis Adolphe, 16, 104
Third Republic (1875–1940), 6, 12, 16, 23, 24, 29, 94, 105; colonial policy, 30; constitutional reform, 108, 144
Thorez, Maurice, 266, 306; and Bidault, 282–83; portrait of, 145–46
Trade unions: in Africa, 115
Tran Trong Kim, 190
Treaties and diplomatic agreements: Act of Vienna (1815), 21; agreements of 6 March 1946 (Indochina), 198, 200–01; Franco-Chinese agreement (28 February 1946), 198; Molotov-Ribbentrop Pact, 97; of Amiens (1802), 21; of Bordeaux (1881), 30; of London (1915), 62; of Paris (1814), 21, 24; of San Ildefonso (1 October 1800), 21; of Tientsin (9 June 1885), 38; Treaty of Lausanne (1924), 129; Treaty of San Remo (25 April 1920), 129; Treaty of 12 May 1881, 120
Tripartite Government (1946), 8, 149, 266
Tu Duc, 26
Tunisia: nationalist movement in, 65, 178
Turgot, Robert Jacques, 19

Union Démocratique du Manifeste Algérien (UDMA), 156, 159, 161, 231, 267, 270; and French Union Constitution, 294; plan for Algerian autonomy, 158–59, 232
Union Démocratique et Socialiste de la Resistance (UDSR), 154, 271; formed RGR (1946), 155. *See also* Rassemblement des Gauches Republicains (RGR)
Union des Républicains et Résistants (URR): allied with Communists, 167–68
United Nations, 3, 8, 188; Committee on Non-self-governing Territories, 188; French reactions to trusteeship system, 182, 186–87, 213; General Assembly, 183; Security Council, 188; Trusteeship Committee, 184, 188; trusteeship system, 181–82, 207

Valluy, General Etienne, 177, 198, 202
Varenne, Alexandre, 275, 302
Viard, Paul Emile, 166, 257, 258
Vichy regime, 2, 17, 76–78, 144, 147, 190; in West Africa, 125–27
Vietminh (League for the Independence of Vietnam), 190, 198, 228, 313; assaults on French garrisons, 200, 202, 205; Fountainebleau Conference on Indochina, 270–71; influence on Constituent Assembly, 201–04, 274; view of French Union, 200
Vietnam, 198–99
Viet-Nam Quoc Dan Dang (Vietnam Nationalist party), 66, 198, 202
Vignes, Alfred, 258
Violette, Maurice, 71
Von Epp, General, 77

Weygand, General Maxime, 76
Wilson, Woodrow, 43, 52
Wiltord, governor of Senegal, 176
World War I, 6, 64, 67; and French colonialism, 40–41
World War II, 3, 4, 7, 18, 208

Yalta Conference, 91
Youssef, Sidi Ben: cooperates with Istiqlal, 120; discusses future of Morocco with Roosevelt, 119